NEW JERSEY

NEW J

Illustrations by Ellie Wyeth
Maps by Liz Waite

RUTGERS UNIVERSITY PRESS　　New Brunswick and London

ERSEY

A Guide to the State

Barbara Westergaard

Library of Congress Cataloging-in-Publication Data
Westergaard, Barbara, 1930–
    New Jersey, a guide to the state.

    Includes indexes.
    1. New Jersey—Description and travel—
1981–   —Guide-books. 2. Automobiles—Road
guides—New Jersey.   I. Title.
F132.3.W47   1986   917.49′0443   86-31347
ISBN 0-8135-1242-5

Second printing, 1988

ACKNOWLEDGMENTS

Publication of this book has been aided by the generous support of the following New Jersey banks:

Commercial Trust Company of New Jersey
Horizon Bancorp
First Fidelity Bank, N.A. County
First Fidelity Bank, N.A. North Jersey
First Fidelity Bank, N.A. South Jersey
First Fidelity Bank, N.A. West Jersey
First Jersey National Corporation
Franklin State Bank
National Community Bank of New Jersey
Summit Bancorporation

E. WYETH

CONTENTS

Hoboken

INTRODUCTION

You will find in this guide information on several hundred of New Jersey's towns and parks. The guide is meant to serve both those who are contemplating a trip to New Jersey and are wondering what they can expect to find there, and those who are already in New Jersey and are wondering what there is to look at. It's meant, in other words, to serve not just tourists but those who live in or commute to or through the state, and it's meant to serve the many newcomers—victims of corporate relocation, New York City rents, or economic or political hardship in other parts of the world. The word "guide" is chosen advisedly: this book is meant to get you started on your explorations, not to describe everything you will discover.

New Jersey is a state of unusual diversity, particularly in relation to its size (with c. 7,500 square miles, it's the fourth smallest state in the nation). Consider for a moment some of the contrasts it presents. New Jersey is one of the nation's leading industrial states. Its chemical industry, the state's largest, is second only to that of Texas (and actually employs more people), and New Jersey is the country's leading producer of pharmaceuticals, detergents, and toiletries. Yet almost two-thirds of the state's land is in farms and woodlands, and the gross average income per farm is the highest in the nation. It is one of the country's leading producers of blueberries, cranberries, peaches, eggplant, and nursery stock. It is the country's most densely populated state, yet within it is the largest wilderness area east of the Mississippi. It has more helipads than any other state, yet it also has the third largest state-park system. A leader in the high-tech industries (10 percent of the nation's revenue from programming goes to New Jersey; 11 percent of its research budget is spent in the state), New Jersey is one of only four states where you can see 200 species of birds in one day, and it is the site of the largest annual gathering of migratory shorebirds. It has the third highest number of corporate headquarters, but is also the ninth state in wine production.

The contrasts extend to the landscape as well. The southern tip of Cape May (which is below the Mason-Dixon line) is only 144 miles from the Appalachian mountain ridges of the northwestern corner of the state. The flat and sandy lands of the southern portion of the state (actually, the coastal plain occupies over half the state's area) give way to the rolling hills of the central section, which in turn give way to the mountains of the north (the Kittatinny to the west, the Highlands to the east). In terms of feet above sea level, the mountains may not be high, but for a variety of reasons, including the lack of east-west passes in the Highlands, when you are in them, they look and feel high. This variety in terrain has produced a similar variety in ecosystems, and for that reason you can see an unusual diversity of plants and animals in New Jersey, with many species reaching their southern or northern limit in the state.

The natural contrast between north and south has been reinforced by the state's history. Early in its development (in 1676) the colony was divided in two, and East Jersey (roughly the same as today's northern New Jersey) and West Jersey (today's southern New Jersey) were owned by separate groups. The settlers in the two areas were different as well: largely Quakers in the south, a mixture of New Englanders, Scots, Dutch, and others in the north. Southern New Jersey was oriented toward Philadelphia, northern New Jersey toward New York. The appearance of many communities still reflects the differences in the way these groups built. The Dutch stone houses of northern New Jersey are perhaps the best known example, but you will also find in central and northern New Jersey many villages that are similar to New England villages, with white frame houses clustered fairly close together. In the southern Quaker towns, on the other hand, the streets are wider, and the color and texture of red brick often dominate your first impression of a town.

And consider the contrast between the past and the future: a state rich in 18th-century historical associations is the site of the laboratory that is developing what may become the world's principal source of energy in the 21st century. New Jersey was not just one of the 13 original colonies, but an important battleground in the Revolution, and on two occasions the capital of the country was here. The United States's first national historical park is in New Jersey. But New Jersey's leadership in the high-tech world is not new: you can visit sites and museums associated with the inventors of the telephone, the telegraph, motion pictures, the electric light, patent leather, submarines, revolvers, streptomycin, commercial blueberries.

Yet, in part because of its long-term division between the Philadelphia- and New York-oriented areas (Benjamin Franklin spoke of New Jersey as a barrel tapped at both ends), the state has had difficulty establishing an identity, and its negative image as an amalgam of oil refineries and toxic waste dumps has been tenacious. It's not as if no one has discovered New Jersey: tourism is in fact the state's second largest industry, generating some $11 billion a year in revenues, three-quarters of it from the shore. In terms of drawing tourists it is the fifth most popular state. Nevertheless, the New Jersey jokes continue, and the state's poor reputation—derived, many believe, from the fact that much of the world forms its impression of the state from driving through it on the turnpike—is becoming increasingly annoying to many New Jersey residents. At its northern end the turnpike goes right through one of the world's largest oil refineries, but to judge the rest of the state from this portion is clearly unfair. It's also unfair to the turnpike, which as eastern interstate highways go, is a pleasure to ride on: it's one of the safest, and even when the road is crowded, the traffic usually moves. And it's even unfair to the oil refineries, which can be breathtaking to look at, particularly at night. Since presumably every user of this book will have occasion to use the turnpike, the book closes with a tour of the turnpike.

Now, a few words on how to use the guide: except for the turnpike tour, the entries are arranged alphabetically by town. This means that if you are interested in a particular park, say, but don't know which town it's in, you should look in the index under parks and find the town you need. Similarly, if you don't find an entry for a town you're interested in, check the index under towns to see if the town you're looking for is part of a larger entry. If you're thinking of planning a trip around a visit to a museum, check the index for museums.

Each entry begins with the name of the town, followed by the county it's in and the major roads that lead to or go through the town. *I* followed by a number is an interstate, *US* a federal highway, *NJ* a state road, and *C* a county road. The dot on the state map at the beginning of each entry is meant to help you find that town on a larger map. The numbers in the entry headings are the population figures from the 1980 census. When no census figures are available for the community in question, the township it is part of appears in brackets. To avoid confusion I have sometimes indicated whether the figures refer to the borough, the township, or what the census calls a census-designated place (CDP). For the fast-growing areas—and there are many in the state—the 1980 census figures may be far too low. An asterisk tells you that a building or district is listed in the national register of historic places.

When a building or other place open to the public is listed, it is generally followed by its actual (not mailing) address and telephone number in parentheses. Times of opening come at the end of the description. (The months or days on either side of a dash are inclusive, that is October–March means October through March.) Admission charges are noted; exact amounts are not.

Although every attempt has been made to secure accurate and up-to-date information, it is always advisable to call ahead, particularly for smaller museums and historic houses. Hours change, and in many cases the curators have no substitutes to take over when they cannot be on the job. Do not be surprised if you reach the past president of the local historical society, who is no longer involved in the museum you want to visit. He or she will be glad to help you find the current curator. Even the state parks can change their hours as their budgets change. Definitions of summer and winter also vary. For the state parks and many seaside resorts summer usually means Memorial Day to Labor Day, but it is always best to call ahead. Since some admission charges can be high while others are nominal, you might want to check on those, too.

Parking fees are usually in effect in the state parks during the summer. For both state and county parks, it's a good idea to call about regulations if you want to camp, boat, fish, horseback ride, or hold group picnics. Also, when an entry says that an area is open to hunting or fishing, please remember that this means open to hunting or fishing with the proper license. For information about hunting and fishing regulations call 609-292-2965 or the number listed for the particular area.

Each entry should contain enough information to allow you to find your way to the place you're looking for, but you may want to call ahead for more detailed directions. The state gives away an excellent road map (available at state tourist centers and some state parks, by calling 609-292-2470, or by writing NJ Department of Commerce and Economic Development, Division of Travel and Tourism, CN 826, Trenton, NJ 08625). If, however, you're going to do any real exploring, you should arm yourself with a county map. These are particularly helpful now that most counties are posting numbered signs for most of their routes. (But be warned: some counties mark their roads with an abundance of signs; others may leave you feeling neglected.)

The state's Division of Travel and Tourism also publishes booklets and brochures useful to those who want to explore the state. There are many specialized guides available, including ones for antiques lovers, bird watchers, canoists, history buffs, naturalists, and shopping enthusiasts. Tourist centers and chambers of commerce at the major tourist areas have literature you may find useful. There are also wonderful books not specifically intended for the tourist on various parts of the state—John McPhee's *The Pine Barrens* and Charles Funnell's *By the Beautiful Sea* simply being among the best known—and most public libraries have large New Jersey collections. Many bookstores have New Jersey material, and the book sections in the larger state park visitor centers, in the Audubon sanctuaries, and in many historical museums are often good sources of local literature.

The preparation of this book has converted me and my husband into fervent, even proselytizing, patriots. I hope some of this fervor, much of which rubbed off on many who worked with me, will spread to those who use this guide.

I would have liked to thank here by name all the people all over the state who helped me with this guide, but as they number in the hundreds, I am afraid this is not possible. Some of my friends will recognize my unabashed exploitation of their ideas, which I trust they will take as an expression of gratitude. I would also like to single out the authorities at the New Jersey Turnpike, particularly Gordon Hector and Jack Seymour, for their unfailing cooperation and to thank Susan B. Scheuermann for letting me look at the turnpike material put together by the State Council of the Junior Leagues of New Jersey. And to all those who helped me, to those who accompanied me on my trips around New Jersey, to the members of historical societies, the curators of museums, the park superintendents and rangers, the officials of federal, state, county, and municipal agencies, the librarians, I offer my heartfelt thanks.

NEW JERSEY

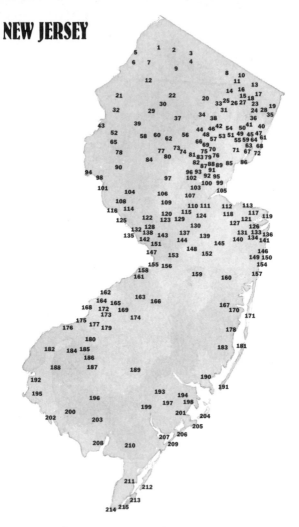

NEW JERSEY

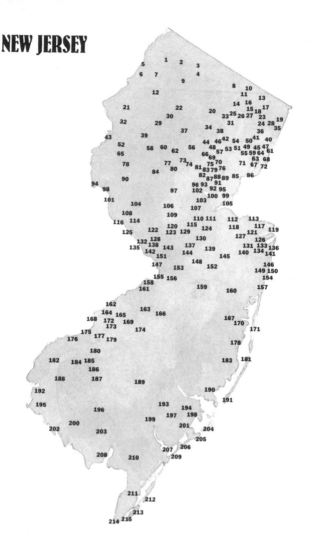

Absecon ATLANTIC (US 9, 30, NJ 157, C 585) 6,859

Although many visitors to the shore may think of Absecon as simply the entrance to Atlantic City, Absecon long predates Atlantic City (it was a stagecoach stop before the Revolution) and in a sense was essential to its development. In 1820, Dr. Jonathan Pitney, the man who more or less invented Atlantic City (see Atlantic City), moved to Absecon. His house still stands (N. Shore Rd.), as do other older houses on quiet streets away from the busy commercial highways. Known as the Reed house, it was built in 1799; Pitney's additions date from 1848.

Pitney was also involved in both the Methodist and Presbyterian congregations. Near his home is the brick United Methodist Church (50 W. Church St.), first built in 1823 and rebuilt in 1856. (Methodism had taken hold in Absecon when Francis Asbury visited in 1796–97.) The Presbyterian Church building (New Jersey Ave.) dates from 1867. (The first Presbyterian churchmen to preach in Absecon were also distinguished: John Brainerd in the 1750s, Philip Vickers Fithian in the 1770s.)

Absecon Wildlife Management Area contains over 3,500 acres of salt marsh in Reeds and Absecon bays. This is an excellent area for bird watching, fishing, boating, and waterfowl hunting. The town has a public boat ramp (Faunce Landing Rd., off US 9), and you can fish from the northern part of the old Brigantine Bridge.

About two miles south of Absecon in Pleasantville is the Firefighters Museum of Southern New Jersey (8 Ryon Ave.; 609-641-9300). The collection includes 11 fire engines, from hand drawn and horse drawn to motorized, as well as old equipment and other items related to fire fighting. Open by appointment.

Allentown MONMOUTH (C 524, 526, 539) 1,962

First settled by Quakers, Scots, and Dutch (and known as Allen's Town from the gristmill Nathan Allan built in 1706 near the site of the present mill), Allentown was an active mill-town by the mid-18th century. The village today retains many attractive 18th- and 19th-century buildings, both in its historic district* (approximately 24 blocks

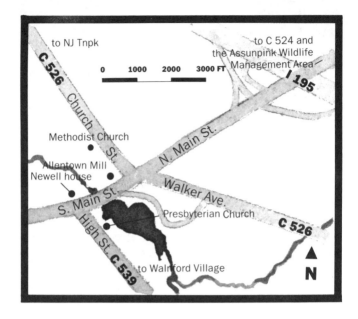

centered around the mill and N. and S. Main sts.) and along the county roads that radiate out from the center.

Small as it is, Allentown can claim two prominent citizens: Molly Pitcher, the Revolutionary War heroine who carried water to the soldiers during the Battle of Monmouth (see Freehold), and Dr. William A. Newell, founder of the United States Lifesaving Service. Newell worked out the principle of throwing a line in 1848 (Joseph Francis of Toms River improved the system by developing a closed lifeboat). Newell became a congressman in 1848 and again in 1865; he was governor of the state in 1856 and 1858. After serving as governor of the Washington Territory (1880–84), he returned to Allentown and once more took up his practice, living until 1901. His house is at the corner of Main and High sts. Allentown can also claim one of the first temperance organizations in the United States: the Allentown Sober Society, started in 1805.

The Allentown Mill★ (42 S. Main St.), built in the mid-19th century on the site of earlier mills, now houses several shops and artists' studios. The John Imlay house (28 S. Main St.) was built c. 1790. Some of its imported French wallpaper is in the Metropolitan Museum of Art and at Winterthur. The Allentown Presbyterian Church (20 High St.) was founded in the 18th century; this lovely building dates from the early 19th century. The Methodist Church (23 Church St.) dates from 1810 (enlarged 1830, rebuilt 1936), and the former Baptist Church (1879) serves as the town library (14–16 S. Main). The early 20th-century Farmers National Bank building (9 N. Main St.), listed in the state register of historic places, has become an art gallery.

One of the nation's largest wholesalers of seedlings, Kube Pak, Inc., is located just south of Allentown on C 526. In 12 acres of greenhouses, some 10 million seedlings (this comes to 100,000 flats) are raised each spring.

Two miles east of Allentown, also on 526, is Riding High Farm (609-259-3884), devoted exclusively to handicapped riders. Group and individual lessons are offered year round to riders of varying ages and disabilities. If you are interested in watching a lesson, call for an appointment. Stone Tavern horse park, the new state equestrian facility, is five miles east of Allentown, off 524, in the Assunpink Wildlife Management Area (see Roosevelt). Except in summer, the Monmouth County hunt (609-259-2364, 609-259-9728, 201-222-3712) rides out of the Allentown area three times a week (at 7:30 A.M.); call for information.

Three miles south of Allentown on Crosswicks Creek (C 539 east to Walns Mill Rd., right, or south, on Walns Mill) is Walnford Village* (Walnford Rd.; 201-842-4000). Established in 1734 by an Allentown merchant, it was purchased in 1771 by Richard Waln and once included a gristmill, sawmill, dye house, cooper's shop, blacksmith shop, and family mansion. Now a 36-acre county park, Walnford Village consists of a homestead surrounded by a gristmill (built in 1872 and operated until 1915), carriage shed, icehouse, and other outbuildings. The county hopes eventually to make it into a living museum.

Alpine BERGEN (US 9W, C 502) 1,549

The small, wealthy community of Alpine (in 1983 the average property value per resident was $250,000 and the average annual income per household was $187,000) is perched on top of the Palisades, which at this point rise abruptly 530 feet above the Hudson River. Volcanically formed, the Palisades, which were discovered by Verrazano in 1524, are a national natural landmark. Threatened with destruction by quarrying in the late 19th century, they were saved by a federation of women's clubs, and the Palisades Interstate Park was established in 1900.

The park headquarters are at exit 2 of the Palisades Interstate Parkway in an interesting stone building with wonderful views of the river. The Blackledge-Kearney House★ (Closter Dock Rd.; 201-768-1360), a fieldstone and frame mid-18th-century building known as Cornwallis's Head-quarters, was used by British Major General Cornwallis during the retreat of the American forces in November 1776, after Cornwallis's surprise attack at Fort Lee. Tours of the interior by appointment only. You can hike along the river and on the cliffs, and crabbing and fishing are allowed. In the northern section of the park, at State Line Lookout, you will find some 7½ miles of ski trails (for information on skiing call 201-768-1360). The park commission has planted wildflowers along the parkway. Intended as a way of decreasing maintenance costs, the plantings have drawn considerable comment because they look so attractive.

At various times such celebrities as Joe Piscopo, Eddie Murphy, and Stevie Wonder have lived in Alpine, a town without house numbers or mail delivery. After the Civil War millionaires built lavish estates along the Palisades,

The Palisades

most of which were destroyed with the establishment of the park and the building of the parkway. Edwin Armstrong, the developer of FM radio, lived in one of these mansions, and sent from his radio tower (still visible from exit 2 of the Palisades Parkway) the first static-free FM broadcasts. (In 1954 Armstrong killed himself by jumping from the tower.) The tower is now used for a microwave dish that relays cable TV.

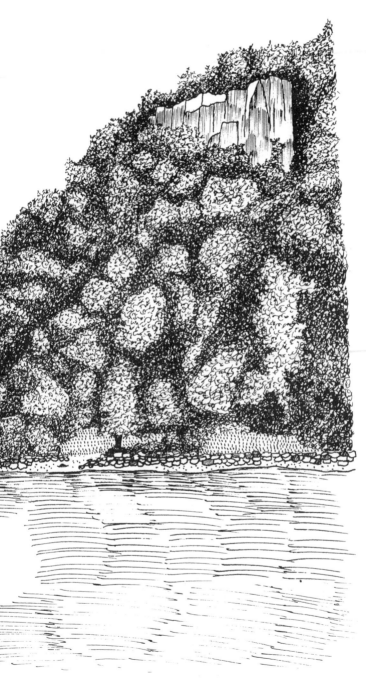

Asbury Park **MONMOUTH** (NJ 33, 66, 71) 17,015

The seaside resort of Asbury Park, named after the Methodist bishop Francis Asbury, was developed in 1870 by James A. Bradley, a New York brush manufacturer who had been visiting the camp meeting of Ocean Grove. Like Ocean Grove, Asbury Park was intended as a temperance resort, but in other respects it catered to more worldly tastes. ("Stimulated by the fiery influence of ice-cream and ginger-pop, its permanent and floating population may plunge into the vortex of social dissipation afforded by pool, billiards, bowling, smoking, and dancing" was Gustav Kobbé's description in 1889.) The first trolleys in New Jersey ran in Asbury Park in 1877, and Bud Abbott of Abbott and Costello was born here. Stephen Crane, author of *The Red Badge of Courage*, born in Newark to an old New Jersey family, was raised here and as a young man worked as a journalist out of Asbury Park. One of the country's worst marine disasters occurred off the Asbury Park beach when the *Morro Castle*, a cruise ship, burned under mysterious circumstances in 1934. Each February Asbury Park is host to the oldest family-run boat show in the United States, and its Labor Day parade, started in the early 1980s, is rapidly becoming a popular event.

Asbury Park suffered a decline in the 1970s and early 1980s, but is now undertaking a $500 million development project, which is expected to change its appearance considerably. Much of its early splendor remains, though, including the wide streets, the Convention Hall* (Ocean Ave.), a spectacular merry-go-round, and the Berkeley-Carteret Hotel (1925; Ocean Ave.). The boardwalk is still full of amusements, and the beach is still the beach (for information on beach fees, call 201-775-2100). Many rock-and-roll musicians developed their reputations in Asbury Park, including, of course, Bruce Springsteen; in 1986 the Asbury Park Rock 'n Roll Museum (Palace Amusements, Cookman and Kingsley aves.; 201-774-4491), one of the few in the country devoted to the history of rock and roll, opened. Open May–August, Sunday–Thursday, noon–11; Friday and Saturday, noon–midnight; September–April, weekends, noon–midnight.

Atlantic City

ATLANTIC (US 30, 40, 322, Atlantic City Expressway) 40,199

Because of the board game Monopoly, the names of Atlantic City's streets—Boardwalk, Park Place, Indiana Avenue—are as familiar to most Americans as those in their own town.

That the game depends on buying and selling and developing real estate is peculiarly appropriate, for Atlantic City itself was the creation of a speculative real estate venture. In 1850 today's resort was simply Absecon Island, an eight-mile stretch of sand with but a handful of inhabitants. For many years Dr. Jonathan Pitney, a doctor and congressman who lived nearby on the mainland, had mulled over the possibilities of building a railroad to the shore and developing the island. Atlantic City does have certain natural advantages as a resort: its sheltered location moderates the waves and the position of the Gulf Stream moderates the climate; nearby Philadelphia supplied a ready clientele. The rest was the work of the developers: the railroad was built in

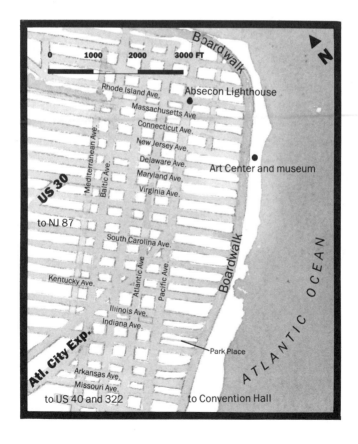

1852, and an engineer named Richard B. Osborne formulated a plan for the new city as grandiose as its name: streets parallel to the ocean were named after oceans (Baltic, Mediterranean, etc.), and streets at right angles were named for the states.

In 1870 Atlantic City built its first boardwalk, probably the first boardwalk anywhere. It was the joint idea of a hotel man and a railroad conductor who, in one version of the tale, didn't like sand in their hallways and corridors, or, in another, saw in the walkway the potential for increasing business. The original boardwalk was eight feet wide, made of wood laid directly on the sand. Today pine planking is laid on a steel and concrete foundation. Hotels, stores that catered to a wide variety of tastes, restaurants, and the kinds of attractions one finds at carnivals were built along the boardwalk, and several entrepreneurs built piers that jutted out into the ocean and featured similar attractions. For those tired of walking there were tram cars and push chairs, and these remain today in a modified form.

Another of Atlantic City's trademarks—salt water taffy—was also invented in the 1870s. And yet another— the Miss America pageant—resulted, like the city itself, from a deliberate promotion. Begun in 1921, the pageant has been held each fall since 1935. (The first Miss America, Annie Laurie, died in 1985.)

The word "airport" was apparently coined in Atlantic City, when the editor of the *Atlantic City Press* used it in referring to Bader Field. Opened c. 1918 (and sold to the city in 1922), it may have been the country's, perhaps the world's, first official airport. Ironically, airplanes were one of the major factors in Atlantic City's later decline, as lower air fares made it possible for people to vacation farther afield. And the country's first ferris wheel was built in Atlantic City in 1891, the brainchild of William Somers, not George Ferris.

To a large extent the resort flourished because of day trippers, but gradually as more and larger hotels were built, it became known as a center for conventions. After World War II, Atlantic City entered a long period of decline, broken only (and only partially) in the 1970s with the advent of state-authorized casino gambling. Since 1978, when the first casino opened, there has been an upsurge of speculative activity reminiscent of the 1890–1912 boom. Unfortunately, it has not solved the city's problems. Casino operations have become a $2 billion a year business; the casinos employ some 40,000 people and pay 62 percent of the municipal budget; over 30 million people visit Atlantic City each year (compared to 2 million before the casinos), which makes Atlantic City the top tourist destination in the United States. But the homeless rate is triple that of the country's ten largest cities, the unemployment rate is high (10.5%), and visitors approach the glitter of the casinos across what looks like a bombed-out wasteland—the city has been likened to "11 Taj Mahals in the midst of a war zone."

The casinos have, however, changed the appearance of the boardwalk. The trams and wicker push chairs (motorized now) are still there, as are the benches (a few facing the ocean, most facing the crowd) and the candy stores selling fudge and salt water taffy. Many of the piers are gone; the Million Dollar Pier, now called Ocean One, has been converted to a ship-shaped shopping mall. Most of the elegant hotels (including those listed in the national register of historic places) and the seedier of the shops are gone. The beautiful beach is still there, but even in its heyday Atlantic City was rather urban for a seaside resort. Unlike Las Vegas, Atlantic City allows no slot machines in public places other than the casinos (this still allows you over 16,000 opportunities to use a slot machine), and only hotels with 500 rooms can apply for casino status. The idea was to raise the tone of the resort and encourage people to stay longer, but neither goal has been achieved entirely.

Most visitors to Atlantic City are still day trippers, despite the efforts of the casinos to encourage longer stays (one-quarter of the country's population lives within a few hours' drive of the casinos). Most of them arrive on one of the 1,200 buses that enter the city each day. If you do come by car, be prepared to spend some time and energy, or perhaps just money, finding a place to park. You can use the jitney buses to get from casino to casino. There hasn't been rail service to Atlantic City in a long time, of course, but there is some expectation that it will be restored by 1989.

To protect their customers, the casinos may not use cards and dice more than 24 hours, after which they must be destroyed or have holes drilled in them. Over 2,450,860 decks of cards and 424,850 pairs of dice are destroyed each year; their mutilated remains are much in demand as souvenirs.

For those who like gambling or glitz or observing either of them, Atlantic City is an exciting place. Other options include strolling on the boardwalk and watching the people or shopping. The beach is patrolled by lifeguards in the summer months, and you can visit the Absecon Lighthouse★ (Pacific and Rhode Island aves.; 609-345-6328), another project inspired by Dr. Pitney. Built in the 1850s, the lighthouse, like the Barnegat Lighthouse, was designed by George Gordon Meade, later the Union commander at Gettysburg. Convention Hall (Boardwalk between Mississippi and Florida aves.; 609-348-7000), reputed to have the world's largest unobstructed room and the world's largest pipe organ, has recently been restored to all its 1928 glory. The Atlantic City Art Center on the Garden Pier (Boardwalk and New Jersey Ave.; 609-347-5844) has art exhibits that change monthly and a small historical museum featuring photographs and memorabilia from the city's past. Open daily except Christmas, 9–4.

There are abundant opportunities to fish and boat in the area. In 1986 the state leased its large Atlantic City marina to one of the casino operators, who plans to convert it to a major tourist attraction. Many other future projects are being talked about—from a convention center at a new railroad terminal to an aquarium to having cruise ships call at Atlantic City—so it is likely the city will continue to change.

Annual events, in addition to the Miss America contest, include an antique cars show in February and an arts festival in April.

Atlantic Highlands

MONMOUTH **(NJ 36)** 4,950

Formerly known as Portland Poynt, Atlantic Highlands was first settled in 1671. Developed as a Methodist camp meeting in 1881, it was incorporated as a borough six years later and today is more of a residential and less of a tourist community than some of its neighbors along Sandy Hook and Raritan bays. The Mt. Mitchell Scenic Overlook (Ocean Blvd.; 201-842-2000) is part of the Monmouth County park system; the mountain itself, at 250 feet, is the highest point along the mid-Atlantic seacoast and the first spot seen by ships coming in from the east. (If, however, the Fresh Kills landfill on Staten Island continues to grow at its present rate, it will become the highest spot by the end of the century.) There are coin-operated telescopes and picnic facilities at the park. Many fine views can also be had on the drive along Ocean Blvd. from the center of town to the overlook (sometimes called the Scenic Drive). Closer to the bay, on Bayside Dr., is Henry Hudson's Spout, a spring frequented by the Indians, by 19th-century packet steamers, and, according to tradition, by Hudson's crews as well.

The Adolph Strauss House (27 Prospect Circle; 201-291-1861, 201-291-4133, 201-291-2718) is a 20-room Victorian mansion built in the 1890s, operated as a house museum by the Atlantic Highlands Historical Society. In addition to its period furnishings, the museum features special exhibits, which change periodically. Open June–September, Sunday, 1–4.

Barnegat OCEAN (US 9, C 554) 8,702

 Located on an inlet of Barnegat Bay, Barnegat (from the Dutch Berende-gat, meaning an inlet with breakers) was regularly visited by the Indians during the summer months. It was first settled around 1720, and during the Revolution was the site of an important salt works. The community has always lived from the water, from the whalers and pirates of colonial days to the shipbuilders and fishermen, both commercial and sport, of more recent times. Although the village of Barnegat has preserved some of its past, the surrounding township is multiplying rapidly, and some of the waterfront growth is causing concern about pollution of the bay. (The township's population more than quadrupled between 1960 and 1970.)

The Barnegat Historical Society Heritage Center (E. Bay Ave.) so far consists of six historic buildings moved to the site to save them from destruction. Among them are the Lippincott-Falkenburg house, a typical bay house, probably from the 18th century, with hand-made nails and squared-off tree trunks used for structural members; the Edwards house, traced to 1813 but probably older; a barber shop; corn crib; necessary; and butcher shop. Open mid-June–mid-September, Friday and Saturday, 2–4. Also on E. Bay is the Barnegat Friends Meeting House, built in 1767; the cemetery has some gravestones that predate the meetinghouse. In town note the Wright Memorial Presbyterian Church (S. Main St.), acquired by the congregation in 1876, but before that used as an opera house (a later opera house was converted to a movie theater); the United Methodist Church, built in the 1880s (its early 20th-century steeple replaces an earlier one blown off in a gale); the former Tuckerton railroad station (Memorial Dr.), now a private house.

If you continue on E. Bay Ave. past the Heritage Center you will come to the bay and the town's public docks and beach.

Barnegat Light OCEAN (C 607)
619

This tiny seaside community at the northern tip of Long Beach Island can be reached only by crossing from the mainland on the Manahawkin Bay Bridge (NJ 72) or by boat. At the very tip of the island is Barnegat Lighthouse State Park (609-494-2016), 31 acres whose main attraction is the lighthouse★ (often referred to as Old Barney), built in the late 1850s after the earlier one (1834) fell into the sea in 1857. Designed by George Gordon Meade, the Union army commander at Gettysburg, and first lit in 1859, the lighthouse was decommissioned in 1927 when a lightship took over its duties. The lighthouse, 27 feet in diameter at the base and 15 feet above the walkway, is built of two concentric cones, which makes it flexible and permits it to sway in the wind. The hollow pipe in the center supports the cast-iron circular stairs and was designed to enclose the pendulum mechanism that used to turn the five-ton lens and lamp. There are splendid views for those willing to climb the 217 steps (but watch out for the sand falling from those climbing above you). A protective wall has been built to keep this lighthouse from following its predecessor into the ocean. The park also contains facilities for fishing, swimming, and picnicking.

The lens itself contained over 1,000 prisms, each of which could be individually adjusted, and the lamp was visible more than 30 miles out at sea. It can be seen today at the Barnegat Light Museum★ (5th St. and Central Ave.; 609-494-2096, 609-494-3407), housed in a 1904 one-room schoolhouse. In addition to the lamp, the museum contains memorabilia from the school and the area, including old fishing equipment, school desks and diaries, and old photographs. Around the museum are the Edith Duff Gwinn Gardens, a seashore garden of plants, trees, and herbs that are able to grow on a barrier island. Open June and September, weekends, 2–5; July and August, daily, 2–5. Groups by appointment.

Newark Bay. Best approached from the plaza at the Ave. C entrance, its 97 acres provide an interesting combination of formal landscaping, natural and open areas, and athletic facilities. You can ice-skate on the pond, and there are picnic grounds, playgrounds, and athletic fields. Much of the park's three-quarters of a mile of bay frontage is reclaimed land.

At 10 W. 47th St. is the Bergen Fire Department Museum★ (201-858-6199). It contains old equipment, including one of the oldest hose units in the state, photographs, and other paraphernalia. The building itself dates from 1875. Open weekdays 8–3:30. Groups by appointment. The urban park next door is locked on weekends.

Other buildings worth noting are the elegant public library, with its neoclassic wing design (Ave. C and 31st St.); the somewhat Spanish Romanesque Masonic temple (Ave. C at the entrance to Bayonne Park); the First Federated Church (Ave. C between 33d and 34th), built in 1866; Saints Peter and Paul (28th St. between Kennedy Blvd. and Ave. C), a Russian Orthodox church with bronze minarets; the red brick mid-19th-century mills now used by Maidenform (17th St. and Ave. E). The library (201- 858-6972) has in its gallery an exhibit of wall murals derived from postcards of 19th-century Bayonne. The scenes are occasionally displaced by temporary exhibits of other artworks. Open Monday and Thursday evening, 6–8; Saturday, 1–3.

Beach Haven OCEAN (C 607) 1,714

Beach Haven is located on Long Beach Island south of the Manahawkin Bay Bridge (NJ 72), the only land route to the island. The town has many Victorian seaside houses (Beach Haven's multiple resource area★ includes Atlantic, S. Atlantic, Beach, N. Beach, and Engleside aves. and Amber, Centre, Coral, Pearl, 2d, and 3d sts.). In the historic district, in the former Holy Innocents' Church (1881), is the Long Beach Historical Society museum (Engleside and Beach aves.; 609-492-0070). Its exhibits, which change periodically, focus on the history of the area. You might see a display of Victorian furniture or clothing or an exhibit showing the type of fishing once practiced in the area. The museum also offers a wide variety of special programs. Open June–August, daily, 2–4, 7–9. Groups by appointment.

For information on beach fees call 609-492-0111.

Beemerville SUSSEX (C 519, 629, 649) [Wantage Township]

A tiny crossroads community in rural Sussex County, Beemerville has long been the home of the Space family. Their farm today occupies over 425 acres, 100 of which are devoted to the Space Farms Zoo and Museum (C 519; 201-875-5800). The zoo, which now has over 500 animals, opened in 1927. At that time the family also ran a general store that served the local farm community. During the Depression many of the customers brought in family mementos in lieu of cash, which Mr. and Mrs. Space hung on the wall until they were redeemed. Out of these items grew the museum, which in the late 1970s moved into buildings that used to house the Rutgers University cattle research facilities. (At those facilities Sir Mutual Ormsby Jewel Alice in 1938 contributed semen for the country's first cooperative artificial breeding association.) The nine museum buildings contain a collection of old cars, tools, toys, firearms, sleighs, and the like. Open May–October, daily, 9–5. Admission charge (group rates by appointment).

While in Beemerville, note the windows of the First Presbyterian Church (c. 1840).

Belvidere WARREN (C 620, 624) 2,475

Located at the confluence of the Delaware and Pequest rivers, Belvidere was known as Greenwich on the Delaware until 1775. Now the county seat, Belvidere has grown very little over the last 50 years, one of the factors contributing to its special quality.

In the mid-18th century, there had been hopes that the power of the Pequest River could be harnessed and that Belvidere would become a flourishing industrial area. Robert Hoops, whose slaughterhouse supplied Washington's army when it was quartered in Morristown, had conceived the plan but was forced to sell his holdings along the river. The purchaser, Robert Morris (a signer of the Declaration of Independence and financier important to the revolutionary cause), tied up the lands with a restrictive deed that took an act of the legislature to set aside; many believe that deed permanently hobbled Belvidere's development. (The town is not without industry today; Hoffmann-La Roche employs 1,000 people at its vitamin-production plant.)

Belvidere's 19th-century historic district* encompasses Market, Race, Greenwich, and Mansfield sts. and the Pequest River, but it is worth exploring outside this area as well. Included in the historic district is Belvidere's large green, another factor contributing to the town's appeal. On one side of the green is the red brick county courthouse (Second St. between Mansfield and Hardwick sts.), built in 1827 shortly after Warren County became independent of Sussex County; it has been modified, and the roof line was extended forward some 25 years ago. In the middle of each of the other three sides of the square is a church: the Presbyterian on Mansfield, the Methodist (1826, 1849) on Hardwick, and the Episcopal on Third St. Many of the county's offices are located in Belvidere's old houses; particularly beautiful is the stone Cummins house (1834; Second and Mansfield sts.), now being used by the departments of education and mental health. Among many other attractive and

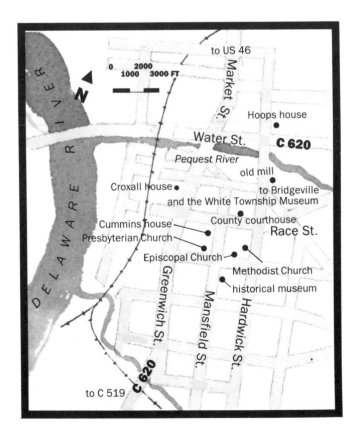

interesting buildings note the county library and courthouse annex (Hardwick St.); the old mill (Hardwick St.); the Croxall house (1780; Greenwich St.), built by Robert Morris for his daughter; the tiny Robert Hoops stone house (c. 1700; Prospect St.), probably servants' quarters; the Queen Anne house at Second and Greenwich sts.; the mid-19th-century brick house that serves as the municipal building (Second and Greenwich sts.); and the West Jersey Telephone Company building (Market and Paul sts.).

In an elegant 1850s house built of local brick the Warren County Historical and Genealogical Society runs a museum (313 Mansfield St.; 201-475-4298, 201-475-2512) specializing in the history of Warren County. The collection includes a wide variety of artifacts, ranging from the 1600s (a wooden plow brought over from the Netherlands) to the present. In the Victorian parlor is Eastlake furniture that belonged to the family who lived in the house. Special exhibits change about once a month. Open Sunday, 2–4, and by appointment.

Public access to the Delaware River for bank fishing is available just south of Water St.

About four miles east of Belvidere, in Bridgeville, is the White Township museum, located on Titman Rd. behind the White Township School at the intersection of NJ 46 and C 519 (201-475-2265). The first story dates to the 1770s, the second to the 1830s, when the building was converted from a house to a store. It has been restored as a store with an apartment upstairs and one room devoted to artifacts relating particularly to local history. Open June–September, 2d Sunday of the month, 2–4. Open other times between June and November by appointment.

Berkeley Heights UNION
(C 512, 527, 531)   12,549

Located in the Watchung Mountains and possibly named for Lord John Berkeley, who with Sir George Carteret, once owned all of New Jersey, Berkeley Heights was settled by the 18th century (but not so named until 1952). After a railroad spur reached it in the 1870s, Berkeley Heights became popular as a resort and vacation area. Now a residential suburb, the township experienced a dramatic increase in population after World War II.

In 1910 the community of Free Acres, one of the few attempts in the United States to put into practice the single-tax ideas of Henry George, was founded in Berkeley Heights. (Nineteenth-century philosophical anarchism was also an element in the thinking of Bolton Hall, Free Acres's founder, who saw in the colony a chance to support his principles and perhaps realize something on his investment in land at the same time.) The community, which lies in the southwestern corner of Berkeley Heights (along Emerson La., between Apple Tree Rd. and Beachwood La.), began as a summer retreat for poor New York City intellectuals and artists and gradually evolved into a year-round community. Although it has had to bend some of its original principles to accommodate the demands of the township of Berkeley Heights, within the 80-acre colony itself land is still held not by individuals but by the association, and problems involved in maintaining the roads, water system, public grounds, swimming pool, and the like are still resolved in open meetings at the 18th-century community farmhouse. James Cagney and MacKinlay Kantor are among the many well-known former residents of Free Acres.

Centered around Cataract Hollow Rd. within the Watchung Reservation (see Mountainside) is Feltville,* an 1840s mill village, known as the Deserted Village, and presently being restored. The Littell-Lord Farmhouse Museum* (31 Horseshoe Rd.; 201-464-0747), run by the Historical Society of Berkeley Heights, is housed in a mid-18th-century farmhouse and furnished primarily with 18th- and 19th-century objects. The farm occupies 18 acres, and on the property are several outbuildings, including a mid-19th-century spring house and a Carpenter Gothic house that served for a time as a school. Open Sunday, 2–4, and by appointment. Note also the Erie Lackawanna Railroad station (Plainfield and Springfield aves.), c. 1888, an outstanding example of stick style. Off Springfield Ave. is the Passaic River County Park, where you can fish, picnic, and walk on the nature trail.

At the AT&T Bell Laboratories (South St. and Mountain Ave.; 201-582-3275 [the entrance is actually in New Providence]) the transistor was developed, and Telstar, launched in 1962, was built. The first building here dates from the 1940s and marks the first move of a research laboratory to the suburbs. Close to 4,000 people work in this facility. In the lobby is a somewhat self-serving but interesting exhibit dealing with telecommunications; in one wing the exhibit deals with history, in the other with recent developments. Open weekdays, 8:15–5; weekends, 1–5. Sometimes closed Mondays for maintenance.

Bernardsville SOMERSET (US 202, C 525) 6,715

 Although Bernardsville's population has doubled over the last 50 years, it has not experienced the recent explosive growth of some of its neighbors in the Somerset hills. Not only has it not allowed corporations to build on its borders, it has also decided to build low-cost housing itself rather than let a developer build a large project that would also include some low-cost housing. Meryl Streep comes from Bernardsville, and it is the home of the well-known Gill-St. Bernard's independent school.

Not all its old estates remain in private hands. The Scherman-Hoffman Sanctuaries (Hardscrabble Rd.; 201-766-5787), for example, a New Jersey Audubon facility, occupies 250 acres of streams, lush floodplains, hardwood and second-growth forests, and open meadows that were once private. In the imposing 1930s Hoffman house is a museum with a collection of New Jersey birds, changing exhibits of bird paintings or photographs, and a special section for children. The sanctuaries are a haven for diverse plants and wildlife, and material for self-guided walks is available at the house. (When the house is closed, consult the map at the Scherman parking lot.) On Fridays and Saturdays in April and May, there are usually bird walks; call the office for information. The office is open Tuesday–Saturday, 9–5; Sunday 12–5; the trails are open daily, 9–5. Groups by appointment (fee charged for guided tours). The Hoffman house can be difficult to get to when there is snow on the ground.

In the northwest corner of the township is Little Brook Sanctuary (take C 659, Claremont Rd., north out of town to Post La.; left on Post La.; left on Mountain Top Rd.; right on Clark Rd.; right on Stevens La.), a 117-acre natural area of woods and rolling meadows belonging to the county park system.

Bevans [Sandyston Township]

A rural crossroads village in the Kittatinny Mountains, Bevans is within the Delaware Water Gap National Recreation Area, and the home of the Peters Valley Crafts Center (take C 521 west off US 206 toward Layton and Dingmans Ferry; turn left, or south, on the first road, C 615; 201-948-5200), a crafts community founded in 1970 as an unintended result of the Tocks Island project. The federal government, proposing a massive dam at Tocks Island in the Delaware River, had already bought the houses and evicted the tenants of several communities along the river before the project was stopped. Bevans was one of those communities. At Peters Valley artists in several crafts—among them pottery, woodworking, metalworking and smithing, weaving, and photography—live and work in the community year round and (except in winter) teach classes open to the public. Among the facilities at Peters Valley is a traditional Japanese wood-fired Anagama kiln, which is fired twice a year. (To watch a firing, call the office for the schedule.) The 19th-century Peters Valley historic district* includes an old cemetery, a Dutch Reformed Church, a Greek Revival house, farmhouses, and slate-roofed barns; several of the buildings are open to the public. A large, juried outdoor crafts show is held the last weekend in July. Gallery and store open daily, 10–5.

Also in Bevans is the popular Flatbrook-Roy Wildlife Management Area, over 2,000 acres of field and upland. The area attracts a wide variety of songbirds and migrating waterfowl and is an excellent place for hiking. Big and Little Flat Brook, both noted trout streams, run through the area, and at the office (on C 521 between Layton and Flatbrook-ville) you can see the Flatbrook Valley Club clubhouse. This fisherman's club, one of the many that used to line the streams, was formed in 1893; by 1911 it owned 12 miles of stream, which it stocked from its own pond. The club was sold to the state in 1943, and the only private club now remaining on Flatbrook is the Overlook, founded in 1937 and said to be a somewhat embattled hanger-on in the middle of the Delaware Water Gap recreation area.

Blackwood CAMDEN (NJ 42, 168, C 534) | 5,219

Settled in the early 18th century, Blackwood is the site of Camden County College (Little Gloucester Rd.), founded in 1967. Exhibits in the art gallery (room 105 in the College Community Center; 609-227-7200, ext. 289) change roughly once a month during the academic year. Open Monday–Thursday, 10–3:30; groups by appointment. For information on the public theater and music programs, call 609-227-7200, ext. 364.

East of the college (take C 534), in Pine Hill, is Ski Mountain, one of southern New Jersey's few ski slopes (Branch Ave.; 609-783-8564, 609-783-8484). The highest ridge in the southern part of the state provides a drop of about 200 feet. Open December–March, daily, 10–10. Admission charged.

East of Pine Hill in Clementon is the Clementon Amusement Park (144 Berlin Rd.; 609-783-0263), a 50-year-old amusement park with rides and a showboat on the lake. Open c. mid-April–mid-June and Labor Day–September, weekends, 12–8; mid-June–Labor Day, daily, 12–10. Admission charged.

Blairstown WARREN (NJ 94, C 521) 4,360

Situated on the Paulins Kill, Blairstown is the site of Blair Academy, founded in 1848 by John I. Blair, who made a fortune from the Lackawanna Railroad and other ventures. It opened as a coeducational independent school, but became all male in 1915 and in the 1970s reverted to being coeducational. Its 315-acre campus, atop a hill, is impressive, and the school now owns Blair's former estate. The downtown, traditionally characterized as stage-set western, is being spruced up.

West of the center of Blairstown is Raccoon Ridge, known as a spot for seeing hawks, and, on clear days, the Poconos, Catskills, and Shawangunks. Access is possible through the Yards' Creek Pumped Storage Station (south from Blairstown on NJ 94 c. 4 miles; right on Walnut Valley Rd. to the gates of the station; register here), where there is also a picnic area. You can hike from here into Worthington State Forest.

Worthington State Forest (Old Mine Rd. just off the last New Jersey exit from I 80; 201-841-9575) is a 5,800-acre tract that was once part of the Worthington estate. In 1912 the Worthington family built a terra-cotta pipeline down Mount Kittatinny to tap water from Sunfish Pond, a glacial pond (and a national natural landmark) that sits at 1,380 feet on the top of the mountain, surrounded by hardwood forest. The Douglas trail to the pond honors Justice William O. Douglas, who helped in the campaign to save Sunfish Pond from being converted into a reservoir. A popular section of the Appalachian Trail goes through the forest, and there are facilities for picnicking, swimming, fishing, skiing, hunting, and (from April through December) camping. Dunnfield Creek, which descends 1,000 feet from Mount Tammany to the Delaware, is one of the few streams in New Jersey to support native brook trout. The 100 acres surrounding it are particularly lovely in mid-June when the mountain laurel are blooming. Trail maps are available at the ranger's station, itself an old house belonging to the Van Campen family, early settlers in this area.

Farther north on the Old Mine Rd. (c. 7 miles north of I 80) are the Pahaquarry copper mines. Thought by some to have first been worked in the mid-17th century, these mines were worked for a brief time in the mid-19th century, and for the last time in the early 20th. The single bar of ingot produced in the last attempt is on display at the New Jersey State Museum in Trenton. During the summer the National Park Service offers guided interpretive walks (call 717-588-6637), and you are free to explore throughout the year. The trails can be rugged here. Groups by appointment. The Old Mine Road extended 140 miles from the mines to what is today Kingston, New York (it used to be known as Esopus). Some controversy now surrounds the dating of the Old Mine Road, long believed to be the first commercial road of any extent in the colonies. (Parts of the road are no longer maintained and can be rough on a car.)

Bloomfield ESSEX (Garden State Pkwy

Bloomfield in the 18th century was a suburb of Newark. In 1794 some of its residents decided to form their own church and two years later named the church in honor of Joseph Bloomfield, a revolutionary war general who was later (1801–12) to become governor of the state. The town, established in 1812, took its name from the church.

The sandstone church, finished in 1797 but altered several times in the 19th century, is known as the First Presbyterian Church on the Green (Broad St. opposite Park Ave.). According to legend, the deacon moved the surveyor's stakes in the middle of the night to make the church larger. The green itself, thought to be New Jersey's largest, was a revolutionary war parade ground, purchased by the town and converted to a park. The Bloomfield Green historic district* encompasses Montgomery, Spruce, State, Liberty, and Franklin sts. and Belleville Ave. and includes buildings from the 18th to the 20th century. On the green, note the parish house (at Church St.), a brick and sandstone Greek Revival building (1840) of considerable charm; the manse (Park Place south of Monroe Place), a clapboard building dating from 1800; Bloomfield College, another Presbyterian institution; and the yellow brick Seibert building (1807), once part of Bloomfield Academy.

On the second floor of the library (90 Broad St.; 201-429-9292) is the museum of the Bloomfield Historical Society. This small museum contains memorabilia from Bloomfield's earlier years, including some examples of items manufactured in town. (The Peloubet-Pelton Organ Company and the Thomas Oakes Woolen Mills were both located in Bloomfield.) Open Wednesdays 2–4; other times by appointment. The Oakes estate,* a 31-room Colonial Revival mansion built in 1895, one of the two Oakes houses still standing (the other, c. 1875, is at Belleville and Williamson aves. and is occupied by a funeral home), is now the home of the Oakeside-Bloomfield Cultural Center (240 Belleville Ave.; 201-429-0960). The center presents a fall (October–December) and spring (March–May) program of lectures, exhibitions, and concerts. During those months the building is open Sunday 1–4.

There are two county parks in Bloomfield, both designed by the noted Olmsted firm. To the north is Brookdale Park (Bellevue Ave.; 201-482-6400; go north on Broad St.,

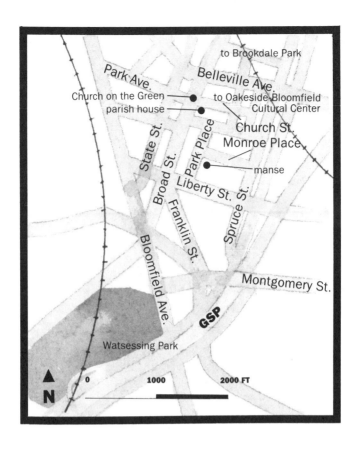

C 509, to the intersection with Watchung; part of this park is located in Montclair), 121 acres with playgrounds, picnic grounds, playing fields, tennis courts (some with lights), places to fish, and fitness and interpretive trails. To the south is Watsessing Park (Glenwood Ave.; 201-482-6400; take Broad St. south to the intersection with Bloomfield Ave., when Broad St. becomes Glenwood; this park is shared with East Orange). The 70-acre park includes playgrounds and playing fields, a network of paths, and a natural ice-skating area.

Boonton MORRIS (I 287, US 202, C 511)
8,620

Situated on a ledge overlooking the Rockaway River, Boonton was a prosperous iron town during much of the 19th century. What may have been the first rolling and slitting mill in the country operated in the 18th century at

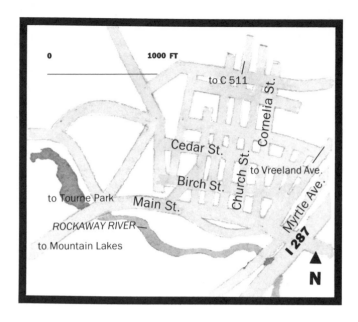

nearby Old Boonton (since the early 20th century at the bottom of the Jersey City reservoir), but Boonton's real prosperity developed after the building of the Morris Canal in the 1830s. Because Boonton is built on a steep hill, was once one of the most important iron centers in the country, and did not decline completely after the iron industry went elsewhere (the first plant to manufacture Bakelite was in Boonton), its downtown has a distinctive character. The 19th-century historic district★ encompasses Main, Church, Birch, Cornelia, and Cedar sts. Note particularly the public library★ (1849; 619 Main St.), the Miller-Kingsland house★ (c. 1740, 1808; 445 Vreeland Ave.), and the railroad station★ (1904; Myrtle Ave.), now converted to a restaurant. Note also the pre–World War I brick factories along Myrtle Ave. east of the station. Boonton has also preserved attractive older residential districts.

A mile or two southwest of Boonton on C 618 is Mountain Lakes (population 4,153). The railroad station (1919; Midvale Rd.) in this wealthy suburb of small homes built on many lakes is on land once owned by Hero Bull, a former slave, and the cornerstone was laid by Belle de Rivera, a well-known suffragette. The station has been converted to a restaurant.

Just west of Mountain Lakes and Boonton is Tourne Park (Powerville and Old Denville rds.; 201-829-0474), 463 acres of county land with facilities for softball, picnics, hiking (there is even a wildflower trail), cross-country skiing, and sledding.

Bordentown BURLINGTON (US 130, 206, C 528, 545) 4,441

 Situated on a bluff overlooking the Delaware River at the confluence of Crosswicks Creek and the Delaware, Bordentown was settled in 1682 by an English Quaker, Thomas Farnsworth, and was originally known as Farnsworth's Landing. It takes its name from Joseph Borden, who arrived 35 years later, organized travel by stage and boat between New York and Philadelphia, and ended up owning most of the land in present-day Bordentown. A transportation center, Bordentown was for many years an important town, and the list of famous people connected with it is out of all proportion to its size. The historic district* (Farnsworth, Second and Third aves., Crosswicks, Prince, Walnut, Burlington, Park, and Spring sts.) takes up a large portion of the town, and despite the heavy loss of notable buildings through fires of suspicious origin, an extraordinary amount of the past remains to be explored.

The first American to sculpt in wax, Patience Lovell Wright, grew up in Bordentown in the mid-1700s. After her husband's death she supported herself doing what had begun as a hobby. In England during the Revolution, she served as a spy for the colonies. Her son Joseph, born in Bordentown, designed the first American coin. The Wright house is at 100 Farnsworth Ave.

Francis Hopkinson, lawyer, poet, musician, political satirist, designer (he helped design the great seal of New Jersey and the American flag), composer (his "Ode to Music" is the first piece written by someone born in America), member of the Continental Congress, and signer of the Declaration of Independence, married Ann Borden, the daughter of Joseph Borden, and lived at 101 Farnsworth Ave. The mid-18th-century Farnsworth house is a national historic landmark. Hopkinson's son Joseph wrote the words to "Hail Columbia" and is buried in the Old Burial Ground (Church St. toward the river).

Thomas Paine, best known perhaps for the stirring pamphlets he wrote supporting the revolutionary cause, lived at 2 W. Church St., and Clara Barton, who was to found the Red Cross in 1881, opened one of the state's first free public schools in 1852. The schoolhouse stands at 142 Crosswicks St. The 18th-century Gilder house (Crosswicks St. opposite

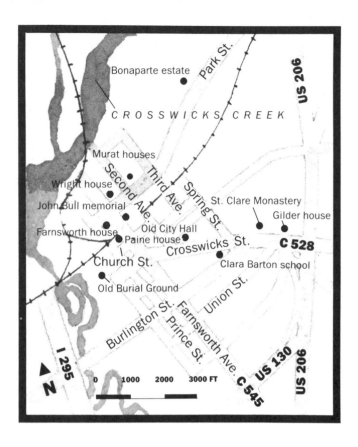

Union St.) was the birthplace of Richard Watson Gilder, editor of *Century Magazine*, and home to many of the other distinguished members of his family. The ground-floor rooms have been furnished by the Bordentown Historical Society. Gilder Field, behind the house, is a 15-acre municipal park with picnic facilities, which was built in the mid-1930s by the WPA (Works Progress Administration).

The John Bull, the country's first railroad engine, was shipped in parts from England and assembled in Bordentown, without instructions, by a man who had never seen one. A memorial to him is in the center of town (Farnsworth Ave. by the railroad tracks).

For some 18 years in the early part of the 19th century, Bordentown was the home of Joseph Bonaparte, former king of Naples and Spain and older brother of Napoleon. The only building from his day that remains on his estate at Point Breeze★ (US 206 and Park St.), now occupied by a Catholic order, is the garden house, although some of the furnishings are preserved in the Gilder house and a Bonaparte chalice is in the St. Clare Monastery (1885; Crosswicks St. near Union St.). The row houses at 47–53 Park

St. were, however, once part of a girls' boarding school run by Bonaparte's nephew Prince Lucien Murat and Murat's wife, the former Caroline Frazer of Bordentown.

Since the buildings mentioned here represent only a fraction of what Bordentown has to offer, you would be well advised to pick up a brochure that outlines a self-guided walking tour. These are available at the Historical Society headquarters at the Old City Hall (11 Crosswicks St.; 609-298-1740), an 1888 building that once housed the police and fire departments and the courtroom. In the tower is a Seth Thomas clock dedicated to William F. Allen (1846–1915), the designer of standard time, who was born in Bordentown. Exhibits in the Old City Hall include a display of early lighting devices and Bordentown memorabilia, and you can also see the former jail cells. Open Tuesday–Thursday, 10–4 (with a one-hour lunch break); Friday, 12:30–3; Saturday, 10–3; Sunday, 1–3. Guided tours by appointment.

At the end of Farnsworth Ave. you can walk along the bluff; at the end of Prince St. you can go down to the river, where there is another small municipal park with picnic facilities. Some days you may notice the smell of cranberries from the large Ocean Spray processing plant, warehouse, and distribution center at the edge of town.

Three miles south of Bordentown is a branch of the Bucks County Vineyard (US 130). For tours of the winery call 800-362-0309.

Branchville SUSSEX (US 206, C 519)   870

Unlike some other Sussex County communities, the tiny borough of Branchville, situated near some of the state's most beautiful scenery, has only grown some 25 percent over the last 50 years. At the Garris Center (Broad St.; 201-729-6662, 201-875-4393) the Culver Brook Restoration Foundation runs a small museum focusing on local artifacts. Open by appointment.

About three miles west of Branchville is Stokes State Forest (US 206, C 519; 201-948-3820), one of the six nearly contiguous undeveloped public areas in the western part of Sussex County.

The state began purchasing land for this reserve in 1907, buying over 5,000 acres, some of it at $1.00 an acre. The forest is named in honor of Governor Edward Stokes, who donated the first 500 acres. Much of the original hardwood forest was burned to feed the iron industry and to clear land for farming, but between 1919 and 1942 the state and the CCC (Civilian Conservation Corps) planted over 650,000 trees.

The state's largest year-round resident environmental center, the School of Conservation at Stokes, is located at the site of one of the largest CCC camps in the country. The CCC built barracks, developed the forest's trail network, and created a lake by damming a stream. Montclair State College took over the abandoned buildings in 1949 as a field campus, and although the state now has financial responsibility for the school, Montclair State's teachers and graduate students still supervise instruction for the 10,000–12,000 students and teachers who spend from two to five days here each year.

Within Stokes State Forest is a large variety of forest types, of other plant and animal life, and of recreational possibilities. The extensive trail network allows many types of hiking, from a stroll to something more strenuous. Tillman's Ravine is a particularly picturesque 500-acre natural area with interesting rock formations and a hemlock forest that has not been cut in over 100 years. Some of its hemlocks are 150 years old, and the density of the woods so cools the ravine that warblers nest here, unusual this far south. The Tinsley Trail has a geological area, where the record of the last glacier can be read in the rock formations. From Sunrise Mountain there is a spectacular view out over the New Jersey Highlands and the Poconos, and hawks often appear at eye level. (This is a prime site for viewing hawks during the fall migration.) There are bubbling springs and beavers are active in the streams. The Appalachian Trail goes through Stokes, and dog-sled racing began here in the winter of 1985–86. Camping and picnic facilities are available.

Adjacent to Stokes are two wildlife management areas, Hainesville and Flatbrook-Roy (see Bevans). The Hainesville area consists mostly of fields, hedgerows, and woodlands, with one 30-acre pond.

About a mile east of Branchville on US 206 (turn left at Plains Rd. in Augusta) is the fairground for the 50-year-old Sussex County Farm and Horse Show, a nine-day event that in 1985 drew 175,000 visitors. Although there is a midway, the fair concentrates on agricultural exhibits and contests.

If you continue east to NJ 94 (when 206 turns right, stay straight on NJ 15), and turn left (north) on 94, in about three miles you will come to the Old Monroe Schoolhouse★ (201-827-4459), which dates back to at least 1819. This restored one-room building is a rare example of a hand-hewn stone schoolhouse. The museum's educational program includes holding classes for visiting school groups in the schoolroom, using McGuffey readers, slates, slate pencils, and the like. There are picnic facilities on the ground. Open May–October, 1st Sunday of the month, 1–4. Groups by appointment.

About a mile and a half south of Branchville (take 519 to C 655 and turn left or west) is the Homestead Complex, a group of county buildings (library, rest home, juvenile detention home), built on the site of an old farm. In the 1830s the farmhouse, with a stone addition, became the county almshouse, and another addition was made when the building was converted to a convalescent home in the 1950s.

Bridgeton CUMBERLAND (NJ 49, 77, C 552) 18,795

Bridgeton, which celebrated its 300th birthday in 1986, was first settled in 1686 when Richard Hancock built a sawmill at the head of the Cohansey River. The community grew considerably when the river was bridged in 1716 (at which point its name changed to Cohansey Bridge), becoming the county seat in 1749. In the mid-1760s it became known as Bridge Town and finally (because a bank printed the wrong name on its letterhead), in 1816, as Bridgeton. A raceway was dug in 1814, and the Cumberland Nail and Iron Company became Bridgeton's largest industry until it closed in the 1890s. More recently, Bridgeton was a center for food processing and glass manufacturing. Although these industries are no longer active in Bridgeton, other industries have moved in, and there are plans to revitalize the Cohansey as a low-cost shipping lane. Bridgeton is also faring well as a tourist center.

When the Cumberland Nail Company folded, the city bought its property, an unusual move for 1903, and

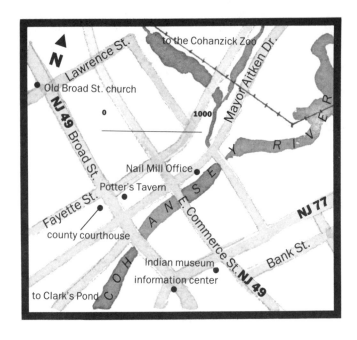

created the City of Bridgeton Park (609-455-3230). The park's 1,200 wooded acres (one-sixth of Bridgeton's area) contain a lake; an amphitheater; picnic, swimming, and boating areas (the raceway is used by canoists); sports facilities; nature trails; the Nanticoke Lenape Village (built as part of the 300th-birthday celebrations); and the Cohanzick Zoo, said to be the largest municipal zoo in New Jersey. A Memorial Day run is held each year to benefit the zoo. The Indian village (609-455-6910), with its wigwams (one left unfinished to show the structure) and ceremonial long house, illustrates life in the 17th century. Eventually special programs will be offered at the village. Open by appointment. Also in the park is the Nail Mill Office Museum (1 Mayor Aitken Dr.; 609-455-4100). This small museum features memorabilia from the nail industry, pottery, glasswork, and lanterns; there are special exhibits each month. Open Tuesday–Sunday, 11–4. Groups by appointment. Next to the museum is Dame Howell's School (c. 1830), an example of an early dame's school, which was moved to the park in the 1970s.

Bridgeton's historic district★ is New Jersey's largest: its 2,200 colonial, federal, and Victorian buildings make up one-third of the town's structures. Particularly noteworthy is Potter's Tavern★ (51 W. Broad St.; 609-455-4100), a small clapboard tavern dating from 1773, which has been restored and furnished as an 18th-century tavern. Here New Jersey's first newspaper, the *Plain Dealer*, a wall sheet, was published weekly between Christmas Day 1775 and March 1776. Open Friday–Sunday and legal-holiday Mondays, 11–3.

The Old Broad Street Presbyterian Church* (W. Broad and Lawrence sts.; 609-455-0809), built in the meeting-house style out of bricks burned on the site on land donated by a Quaker, was begun in 1792. When the builders ran out of money, the state legislature authorized a lottery to provide the necessary funds. The church still uses two Atsion stoves with their original cast-iron flue pipes in place, made in New Jersey c. 1815, the original collection poles, and the whale-oil lamps added as an amenity in the early 19th century.

The George Woodruff Indian Museum (150 E. Commerce St.; 609-451-2620), in the Bridgeton Free Public Library, features artifacts collected within a 30-mile radius of the library. Open Monday–Saturday, 1–4; closed Saturdays in July and August. The library's 1816 building originally housed the bank whose mistake led to Bridge Town becoming Bridgeton.

In the county courthouse (Broad and Fayette sts.) is Cumberland County's own liberty bell, cast in 1763 and rung to announce the Declaration of Independence. The town is also proud of its Hall of Fame, located in the 55-acre Bridgeton Recreation Area across from Alden Field. The museum features local (and other) sports heroes. Open weekdays, 10–12, 1–3. Other noteworthy buildings include St. Andrew's Church (1864; 186 E. Commerce St.); the Buck house (297 E. Commerce St.), built for Jeremiah Buck, a mill owner, in 1808; and the Giles house (143 W. Broad St.), built in 1791 by one of George Washington's generals, perhaps visited by Lafayette, and now offering bed and breakfast accommodations. The administration building for the school system (Bank St.) was the city's first public school (1847).

Perhaps the best way to see Bridgeton is to start at the information center, housed in the former railroad station (early 1900s) at the junction of NJ 49 and 77 (609-451-4802, 609-455-3230, ext. 262). You can pick up a free walking-tour map and rent an audio cassette for your walk. Walking, trolley, and escorted motorcoach tours can also be arranged. Open weekdays, 8:30–4:30; weekends, 9–4. Closed major holidays. Many special events take place along the riverfront promenade, particularly in summer.

Some three miles south of Bridgeton (take 553 or Clarks Pond Rd.) is Clarks Pond Wildlife Management Area, 78 acres with three ponds where you can fish. About four miles northwest of Clarks Pond is Dix Wildlife Management Area, with about 2,500 acres. Some three-quarters is marshland, but the rest is divided between hardwood forests and farmland. Here you can fish, hike, hunt, and trap.

Brigantine ATLANTIC (NJ 87) 8,318

Built on a barrier beach reachable by car only from Atlantic City, Brigantine started as a real estate speculation in the 1920s. A hotel and some 100 houses were built before the crash put an end to the development. Population growth took off after World War II; the opening of the Atlantic City casinos intensified that growth, and the population, half of which lives on the island year round, has doubled since the 1960s. You can see some of the 1920s flavor in the Brigantine Inn (1400 Ocean Ave.) or in the Byzantine-looking church (1927) on 8th St. S. At 3625 Brigantine Ave. is the Marine Mammal Stranding Center (609-266-0538), a rehabilitation center devoted to rescuing stranded or injured whales, dolphins, porpoises, and turtles, and making it possible for them to return to the sea. Founded roughly a decade ago and operated by the only person in New Jersey (and one of only six in the Northeast) licensed to work on marine animals, the center in 1986 added to its holding pool and administration building a small marine-life museum. The exhibits include products of economic value derived from marine life, fiberglass casts of various species, and a tank containing local marine life. Museum open daily in the summer (Memorial Day to Labor Day), 12–8; in the winter, 12–4 on weekdays, 12–6 on weekends. Groups by appointment.

For beach information call 609-266-7600.

Burlington BURLINGTON (US 130, C 541, 543) 10,246

"The identifying mark of BURLINGTON (20 alt., 10,844 pop.) is the single track of the Pennsylvania Railroad that runs through the center of the main street without benefit of curb or fence. In many other respects Burlington seems to have changed little from its eighteenth century character as capital of the Province of West New Jersey."

These sentences were written 50 years ago when the great WPA guide to New Jersey was published. Amazingly, both are still accurate. It is indeed startling to see the tracks in the middle of the city (and trains do tie up traffic, even if they no longer belong to the Pennsylvania Railroad), yet much of Burlington, with its wide streets and heavy use of red brick, has the particular aura of an 18th-century southern New Jersey town.

Settled in 1677 by Quakers from Yorkshire and London (who divided the area so that the Yorkshiremen lived east of High St. and the Londoners west of it), Burlington became the capital of the Province of West New Jersey in 1681, and when West and East Jersey were joined in 1702, shared the honor of being capital with Perth Amboy. A pottery joined the sawmill and gristmill in the 1680s, other industries followed, and by the 1740s Burlington's port ranked with those of New York, Philadelphia, and Boston. Although the port is no longer active and Burlington went through a period of stagnation common to many eastern cities, it now shows the positive effects of an active redevelopment program.

On W. Broad St. in the small brick Proprietors Office many old documents relating to early transactions in West Jersey are stored, including the original Concessions and Agreements, signed by the Proprietors in England in 1676. The Council of Proprietors has met in Burlington in mid-April each year since 1688, usually on the sidewalk. A plaque on the side of the bank marks the spot.

Burlington can claim a large number of firsts, among them the oldest educational trust in the country. Burlington Island (Matinicunck Island when the Swedes established a trading post on it in 1624) was given to the town in 1682 with the stipulation that the revenue be used for the schools. The country's first regular public transportation began here, when regular stagecoach service between Burlington and Perth Amboy was initiated in 1733 (there had, of course, been irregular stages between the two cities long before). Although its current sandstone building dates from 1864, the Library Company of Burlington (23 W. Union St.), founded in 1757, is the oldest continuously operating library company in New Jersey (Trenton's was founded in 1750, but discontinued operation for many years).

Burlington can also claim many famous citizens. Captain James Lawrence of "Don't give up the ship" fame (his words as he was dying in a battle in the War of 1812; his men were unable to carry out his command) was born in 1781 at 459 High St.★ (c. 1696; front portion added c. 1750). James Fenimore Cooper, the novelist, was born next door★ (c. 1780; 457 High St.) in 1789. Although Cooper did not spend much time in Burlington (the family left for upstate New York shortly after his first birthday but did return occasionally when the father was serving in Congress in Philadelphia), his house has become a historic house museum, run by the Burlington County Historical Society (609-386-4773). The society also operates as a museum the Pearson How House★ (453 High St.) and the Aline Woolcut House. All are open Monday–Thursday, 1–4; Sunday, 2–4.

The cast-iron plow was developed (in 1797) by a Burlington resident, Charles Newbold. In the 1830s, during the silkworm mania that afflicted much of New Jersey and other eastern states, Burlington planted what was probably more mulberry trees (over 300,000 of them) than any other city and in 1838 built a cocoonery. (A cold spring the next year killed thousands of trees, and the mania.) James H. Birch,

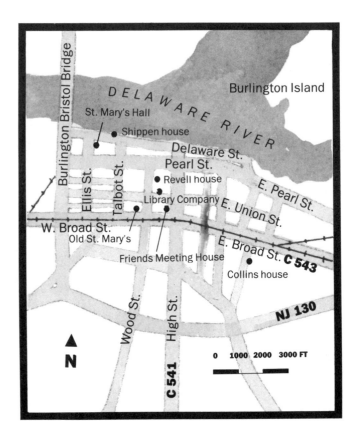

known as the wagonmaker to the world, began business in Burlington in 1862 on Broad and Liberty sts. His 15-acre plant closed after World War I, but while he was in business, he manufactured some 200 models, shipping out 10,000 carriages in a good year, and even exporting jinrikishas to the Orient.

Ulysses S. Grant had a house here (c. 1813; 309 Wood St.) and may have been on his way to Burlington when he learned the news of Lincoln's assassination. His daughter went to St. Mary's Hall-Doane Academy (south side of Delaware St. at Ellis), an Episcopal girls' school founded in 1837. (Its Gothic Revival Chapel of the Holy Innocents, 1845–47, was designed by John Notman.) The Edward Shippen family of Philadelphia had a summer home along the Delaware (c. 1756; Talbot St. at the river). Peggy Shippen, who spent summers here and also visited her uncles in Oxford but apparently didn't like New Jersey (see Oxford), married Benedict Arnold and seems to have had a good deal to do with his eventual betrayal of his country.

Burlington can also claim some interesting churches. Old St. Mary's Episcopal Church* (southwest corner of Wood and W. Broad sts.), a brick church dating to 1703, is one of the oldest church structures in the state; it still uses a silver communion service presented to the congregation by Queen Anne. The new St. Mary's (1854) was built from a design of Richard Upjohn, the architect of Trinity Church in New York City. The two churches and the cemetery between them form a national historic landmark. The Friends Meeting House (west side of High St. near Broad) was built in 1783 to replace one built a century earlier, which the congregation had outgrown. It still retains much of its original hardware and many of the original windowpanes. The Indian king Ockanickon was buried behind the meetinghouse in 1681; a plaque commemorating him is under an ancient sycamore tree.

On Wood St. is the Revell house (1685), probably the oldest house in the county. Benjamin Franklin told the story of a kindly woman in the Revell house who gave him gingerbread one day when he missed his ferry back to Philadelphia and of how he wandered about Burlington with the piece of gingerbread in his hand. At the annual Wood St. fair each fall, gingerbread is sold to commemorate the event. On the northeast corner of Broad and York sts. is another house with a connection to Franklin—the Collins

Burlington

house (c. 1750). Isaac Collins produced the state's first modern newspaper, the *New Jersey Gazette* (1777–86), printing it at the same shop Ben Franklin had earlier used to print the country's first currency.

The city's revitalization plan affects the area along the Delaware, too, where a linear park is being developed. Another waterfront site to note (in addition to St. Mary's Hall and the Shippen house) is the Grubb estate (Grubb was a Civil War general and ambassador to Spain; the house dates to 1850).

Burlington's 18th- and 19th-century historic district★ includes W. Delaware, Wood, and Broad sts., and there are many other buildings of interest not mentioned here. (Elias Boudinot, for example, lived on Broad St. when he was superintendent of the Mint in Philadelphia; in a 1730s building is a drugstore that's been there over 100 years; at York and Penn sts. is the Quaker School, which dates from 1792.) A walking-tour pamphlet is available at the city hall, and

there are walking and bus tours year round. Call Dr. Kamaras at 609-386-3993 for information.

For group tours of the Public Service Electricity and Gas generating plant, call 201-430-5862 (8:30–4).

West of Burlington in Edgewater Park (take 130 west and turn right, or north, on C 630, or Cooper St.) is the White-briar farmhouse (1029 Cooper St.; 609-871-3859), part of which dates from 1739, the rest from 1886. Tours (for groups, by appointment only) vary with the season but can include demonstrations of colonial crafts. Admission charge.

If you take 130 west and turn left, or south, on Cooper Rd. you reach the township of Willingboro. For five years (1958–63) Willingboro was known as Levittown, after the post–World War II builder who achieved international fame by building large subdivisions of similar, reasonably priced houses.

Caldwell ESSEX (C 508, 527) 7,624

Situated along the Watchung Mountains, Caldwell was named for the Reverend James Caldwell of "Give 'em Watts, boys" fame (see Springfield), who was involved in organizing the Presbyterian congregation in 1779 (the settlement had been known as Horse Neck). Grover Cleveland, the only president of the United States to be born in New Jersey and the only one to serve two nonconsecutive terms, is probably Caldwell's most famous native son. His birthplace* (207 Bloomfield Ave.; 201-226-1810), a clapboard house dating from 1832 that once served as the Presbyterian manse, has been operated as a memorial since 1913 (Cleveland died in 1908 and is buried in Princeton). Many of Cleveland's personal belongings, including his wooden cradle, the desk he used when he was mayor of Buffalo, a chair he used in the White House, and a piece of his wedding cake, are on exhibit. Open Wednesday–Friday, 9–12, 1–6; Saturday, 9-12, 1–5; Sunday, 1–6. Group tours by appointment.

Caldwell College (Ryerson Ave.; 201-228-4424), founded in 1939, became coeducational in 1986. Exhibits in its Visceglia Art Gallery are open to the public weekdays, 8:30–4:30.

Camden CAMDEN (I 76, 295, 676, US 30, 130, C 537, 543, 551) 84,910

Camden began as a satellite of Philadelphia and remained dominated by it until the coming of the Camden and Amboy Railroad in 1834. The city was settled by Quakers, the first of whom was probably William Cooper, who in 1681 built a house on Pyne Poynt. Cooper ran the ferry to Philadelphia, and as late as the mid-19th century, ferrying goods and people to Philadelphia was still the town's primary industry. The settlement was long known as Cooper's Ferry despite the fact that it had been renamed to honor the earl of Camden, friend of the colonies. (The name Camden was first used unofficially in 1773 as part of a real estate venture; it became official in 1828.) A few of the houses of William Cooper's descendants remain standing: Pomona Hall, for example (discussed below); the Benjamin Cooper house (1734; Erie St., east of Point St.), which served as headquarters for the commander of the British and Hessian outpost during the occupation of Philadelphia and now houses the offices of a ship repair company; the shell of the Joseph Cooper, Jr., house* (c. 1695; Erie and 7th St. in Pyne Poynt Park); the Samuel Cooper house (1790; 1104 N. 22d St.).

Camden has been the seat of Camden County since the 1840s, although there was a long gap between the formation of the county in 1844 and the building of the first court-house in 1853, caused by irregularities in the voting on where to place the county seat. Its courthouse (Market and 6th sts.), which houses both city and county offices, dates from 1931 and is one of the tallest in the state. The Benjamin Franklin Bridge, painted a medium shade of blue, was the longest suspension bridge in the world when it was opened by President Coolidge in 1926. In 1933, the country's first drive-in movie theater was built in Camden.

Camden became a large industrial city toward the end of the 19th century and reached its peak in the 1950s. Considered the state's most economically distressed big city (the population has been falling, unemployment has been a problem, and boarded-up buildings are not uncommon), it has recently been making a comeback. During Camden's industrial heyday, a wide range of products was manufactured, the best known being pens, canned foods, phonograph records, and ships. The earliest of these was pens: the Esterbrook company began manufacturing steel pens in 1858; it later switched to fountain pens. Its successor company is still active.

The Campbell Soup Company was set up in 1869 when Joseph Campbell and Abram A. Anderson began packing fancy peas and tomatoes, but the company's growth exploded when John T. Dorrance, who developed the idea of condensing soup, was hired as a chemist in 1897. Dorrance eventually became head of the company and died in the 1930s a very wealthy man. (One story has it that the inheritance tax on his estate was so large that even though it was the Great Depression, for a time the state did not need to worry about funds for relief.) At the company's waterfront plant (Market and Front sts.) note the water towers, four soup cans with hats on. At its headquarters building the company sponsors a museum (Campbell Place; 609-964-4000) devoted to tureens and other objects connected with

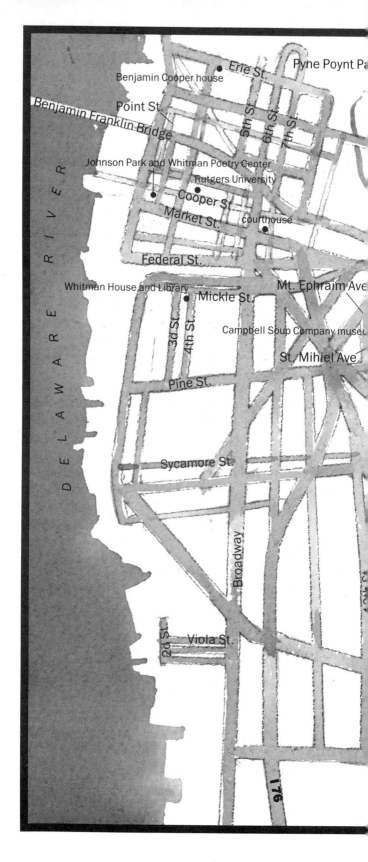

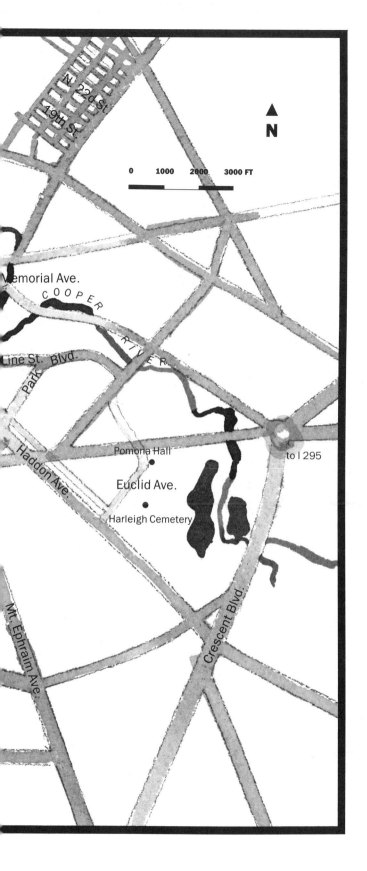

N 22d St

19th St.

N

0   1000   2000   3000 FT

Memorial Ave.

C O O P E R

Line St.   Blvd.

R I V E R

Park

Haddon Ave.

Pomona Hall

Euclid Ave.

Harleigh Cemetery

to I 295

Mt. Ephraim Ave.

Crescent Blvd.

serving and eating soup; the pieces in the collection date from 500 B.C. to the present. Tureen makers seem to exhibit an unusual degree of fantasy in their work, and even if you know nothing about porcelain, you will probably find these pieces accessible and fun to look at. Open weekdays, 9–4:30. Groups by appointment. An appointment is also necessary to see the museum's 20-minute film on making tureens (call 609-342-6440).

Eldridge R. Johnson was running a repair shop in Camden when, in 1894, a customer brought in a broken phonograph. Whether Johnson repaired the machine is not clear, but he did develop a way to improve it, moving from Thomas Alva Edison's cylinder to a plate. In 1901 Johnson formed the Victor Talking Machine Company, and in the early years of the 20th century, all the major performers traveled to Camden to record for Victor. In the 1920s he sold the company to what is now part of RCA, and he too died a wealthy man. Johnson Park, the site of Cooper Library* (1916–18; Cooper and 2d sts.), now the Walt Whitman Poetry Center (609-757-7276), was his personal gift to the city. His legacy to Camden includes the RCA plant, which today employs over 4,000 people. At the old waterfront plant (Market and Front sts.) note the His Master's Voice dog, in its round record-label format, in the tower and the word "Victor" chiseled over one of the doors. The poetry center features art exhibits, theater programs (including a year-round children's theater series), poetry readings, and concerts. Gallery open weekdays, 9:30–4:30.

The last of the major industries was shipbuilding; at their peak the Camden yards had a tremendous capacity and built or refitted many of the warships used in both world wars. The industry's final moment of glory came with the launching of the nuclear-powered steamship *Savannah* in the late 1950s. Although ships are no longer built in Camden, the port, which occupies over 250 acres at the most navigable part of the Delaware River, is experiencing a revival, and in 1985 over 2 million tons moved through it. Among the goods coming into Camden by sea are lumber from British Columbia, bulk salt for road salting from Chile, and iron ore from Norway.

As part of an ambitious plan to revitalize the waterfront further, a 90-acre tract from the port north to the Walt Whitman Bridge will be developed: the Campbell Soup Company is remodeling its plant and building a new headquarters, RCA is remodeling its plant, and the New Jersey

Sports and Exposition Authority is building a regional aquarium, scheduled to open in 1989. The final project is expected to include a park, a marina, offices, a hotel and conference center, housing, shops, and a promenade suitable for outdoor events.

Camden's most famous resident was undoubtedly Walt Whitman, who came here to live with his brother, an inspector of pipes at a local foundry. By the time his brother moved to Burlington, Whitman had made enough money from *Leaves of Grass* to buy his own house at 330 Mickle St. The house and the building next door are operated by the state as the Whitman House and Library (609-964-5383). (The Walt Whitman Neighborhood* is bounded by Mickle, 3d, and 4th sts.; if you continue on Mickle St. toward the river, you will come to the Dr. Ulysses S. Wiggins Waterfront Park, where you can get a wonderful view of the river and both the Camden and Philadelphia waterfronts.) Whitman lived in the house, which dates from the 1840s and is now a national historic landmark, from 1884 until his death in 1892, and many of the items he lived with are there to see. The library, established in 1984, contains the Colonel Richard Gimbel collection of rare and out-of-print editions of Whitman's works, as well as writings on Whitman. Open Wednesday–Friday, 9–12, 1–6; Saturday, 10–12, 1–6; Sunday, 1–6. Whitman is buried at Harleigh Cemetery (Haddon Ave.), where you can read on his headstone the epitaph he wrote for himself.

Another famous Camden resident was Peter McGuire, commonly credited with having thought up the idea of Labor Day. He moved to Camden in 1884, two years after he first suggested the holiday and two years before he became the first secretary of the American Federation of Labor. Labor Day was first celebrated in New Jersey in 1887.

Rutgers University, Camden (Cooper and 3d sts.) grew out of a small two-year college that was incorporated into Rutgers in 1950. The campus is a blend of converted Victorian and modern buildings.

Pomona Hall* (Park Blvd. and Euclid Ave.; 609-964-3333), built in 1726 by Joseph Cooper, Jr., with an addition by Marmaduke Cooper in 1788, is run as a house museum by the Camden County Historical Society. This lovely Georgian brick building is furnished primarily with objects from the 18th and 19th centuries. At the same site the historical society also operates another museum and a library. The museum's collections include early craft tools, American glass, fire-fighting equipment, and toys; there are also changing exhibits. Pomona Hall and the museum are open Monday–Thursday, 12:30–4:30; Sunday, 2–4:30. Groups by appointment.

One of Camden's most successful revitalization projects has been encouraging children, with the aid of professional artists, to paint murals on buildings, thereby reducing the amount of graffiti. Among the buildings with murals are PATCO and the Garden State Wholesale Building Supply Co. on Pine St. and the Goodwill Industries (25th and Federal sts.). There are also murals on Haddon St. heading toward the hospital and on the back wall of the historical society's complex facing the athletic field.

The Fairview district* (Hull and Olympia rds., Mt. Ephraim Ave., Crescent Blvd.) is a neighborhood of brick houses built in 1917 by the planner and architect Electus Litchfield.

Cape May CAPE MAY (Garden State Pkwy exit 0, US 9) 4,853

Calling itself the oldest seaside resort in the United States, Cape May City* is one of a handful of cities to be designated a national historic landmark. Situated at the southern tip of the state (below the Mason-Dixon line), the city is a living museum of Victorian architecture. Over 600 Victorian buildings, most dating from the 1880s to c. 1910, are preserved in an area of less than two square miles.

Named for (and by) the Dutch explorer Captain Cornelius Mey, who pronounced the area as pleasant as his homeland and claimed it for the Netherlands in the 1620s, the peninsula was first settled early in the 1600s by whalers. Cape May began to become well known as a resort shortly before the Revolution—an advertisement for a house appearing in the *Pennsylvania Gazette* in 1766 mentioned that the property would be "very convenient for taking in" tourists—but it was not until the early 19th century, with the introduction first of regular steamship connections between Philadelphia and Cape May (1819) and later of train service (1830s) that Cape May achieved its reputation as a fashionable and special place. It was so popular in the 1840s and 1850s that ships from Philadelphia to Cape May ran daily and so fashionable that it liked to be known as the "playground of presidents." Abraham Lincoln stayed at the Mansion House in 1849 when he was still a congressman; Franklin Pierce visited in 1855, James Buchanan in 1858, Ulysses S. Grant in 1873, and Chester A. Arthur in 1893. In the summers of 1890 and 1891 President Benjamin Harrison's summer White House was at the Congress Hall Hotel, although he himself stayed in Cape May Point. Other noteworthy visitors included the bandmaster and composer John Philip Sousa, who wrote a "Congress Hall March," Senator Henry Clay who came in 1847, and Henry Ford, who in the early 1900s staged an automobile race on the beach against Louis Chevrolet (driving a Fiat) and Alexander Christy (driving a Winton). Ford in his Ford was ahead, but a wave broke over the car and the motor stalled. To pay his hotel bill he offered stock in his company, which was refused, and he finally sold his car to Dan Focer, who opened an agency in Cape May three years later, becoming the country's first Ford dealer.

Tourists at first stayed in private homes, but soon seaside hotels were built. For two seasons Cape May boasted the world's largest hotel—the Mount Vernon, with over 3,000 rooms. It burned in 1856, as did many of Cape May's buildings over the years. In fact, the city's present appearance is largely a result of the rebuilding that took place after a fire in 1878 destroyed most of the city's tourist accommodations. (Cape May's charm also reflects its decline in popularity: after Atlantic City's rise in the early 1900s, new building virtually ceased in Cape May.)

Although the beaches, despite serious problems with erosion, are an obvious attraction (for many beaches it is best to check on tides to make sure you can enjoy both sand and water), and fishing and boating are also popular, most people come to Cape May to spend time in the town. The best way to see the town is on foot or bicycle. Maps are available for self-guided walking tours, and the Mid-Atlantic Center for the Arts (609-884-5404) sponsors walking tours and trolley tours (daily in July and August, weekends only the rest of the year; in the summer there are special tours for children aged 6–12; groups of over 20 can arrange in advance for individualized tours). There are also many special events: Victorian week, spanning two weekends, and featuring tours of many private homes, in October; a quilt and decoy show in May; a Christmas candlelight tour; and Victorian dinners at various times throughout the year. Call for specific schedules.

To tour on your own stop in at the Welcome Center (407 Lafayette St.; 609-884-3323) or the information booth at the head of the Washington St. pedestrian mall (Ocean St.). Built as a Presbyterian church in 1853, the Welcome Center became an Episcopal church in 1903 and now serves as a community center. The information booth was formerly a guardhouse in Philadelphia's Fairmount Park. At both places you can pick up brochures, information, and beach passes. (For information on beaches, you can also call 609-884-8411, ext. 28.)

Not to be missed is the Emlen Physick House (1048 Washington St.), a 16-room stick-style house designed by Frank Furness, which sits on over eight acres in the center of town. It was built in 1881 for Physick, a member of a prominent Philadelphia medical family (his grandfather is often referred to as the father of surgery). Now open as a house museum, the building contains furniture, toys, clothes, and other Victorian artifacts. Of particular note are the Eastlake-style furniture, much of it designed by Furness, and the papier-mâché (lincrusta) wall coverings. Also on the property is the Carriage House, now the home of the Cape May County Art League (1050 Washington St.; 609-884-8628), founded in 1929 and said to be the oldest continuously operating county art league in the country. The league offers classes and lectures and sponsors a variety of special events. Exhibits in the galleries change roughly

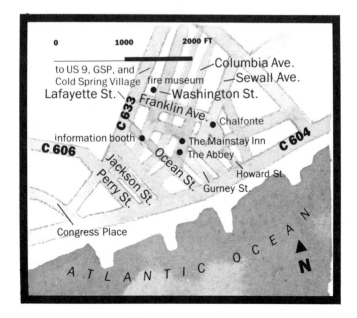

once a month. Gallery open Tuesday–Saturday, 10–4; Sunday, 11–4. A collection of 19th-century tools is exhibited in a barn behind the Carriage House.

Almost any street has its rewards. Compared to some other Victorian seaside resorts, Cape May has an unusual variety of buildings. It also sports an unusual abundance of gingerbread and other decorative exuberance. Some of the most interesting private houses have been converted to bed-and-breakfast inns or hotels. The Abbey (Columbia Ave. and Gurney St.), for example, an 1869 Gothic Revival estate built by a Pennsylvania coal baron, has a 60-foot tower and elaborate stained-glass windows. The Mainstay Inn (635 Columbia Ave.) was a gentlemen's gambling club. The Wilbraham Mansion (133 Myrtle Ave.) was an 1840s farmhouse expanded in 1900 by Philadelphia industrialists. Windward House (24 Jackson St.), an Edwardian shingle-style house, has unusual stained and beveled glass. The oldest hotel, the Chalfonte (Sewell and Howard sts.), was built in 1876 as a private home by Colonel Henry Sawyer, who was taken prisoner in the Civil War by the Confederates and exchanged for a son of Robert E. Lee. Volunteers help maintain and restore the Chalfonte on working weekends in fall and spring. Space prohibits listing all the enjoyable buildings here, but the brochures available from the information centers will help identify them.

The Cape May Fire Museum (Franklin Ave. and Washington St.; 609-884-7547), constructed on the site of the town's original firehouse, features a 1928 LaFrance pumper and other memorabilia. Open daily, 8–8, May–October; 8–5, November–April.

The United States Coast Guard's only station for training recruits is located on 500 acres northeast of the center of town (609-884-6900). During the summer season graduation is held outside Friday at 11 (weather permitting). At 10 a film, *Life at Boot Camp*, is shown in the auditorium. Both events are open to the public. The Coast Guard also schedules several sunset parades each summer.

Northwest of town (take US 9 to Lincoln Blvd.) is the terminal for the Cape May–Lewes, Delaware ferry (609-886-2718). The trip takes just over an hour, and the ferries run all winter.

North of town is Historic Cold Spring Village (Seashore Rd.; 609-884-1810), intended as a reconstruction of a 19th-century southern New Jersey village. Buildings from other sites in the county have been set up here, among them what may be the oldest house in the county, the Spicer Leaming house (c. 1740); the Cape May Point jailhouse

(c. 1880); the Dennisville Inn (18th century); a blacksmith's shop; and two railroad stations. Crafts workers, including a blacksmith, weaver, tinsmith, and potter, demonstrate their crafts and sell their products in the shops. The visitor center has a permanent exhibit of 19th-century life, and a nautical museum is scheduled to open in 1987. Special programs—antiques shows, decoy shows, banjo concerts, colonial encampments—take place on weekends. Open Memorial Day–September, 10–5. Admission charge.

Cape May Court House CAPE MAY (US 9) 3,597

 The seat of Cape May County, Cape May Court House, though still small, has seen its population double over the last 25 years. Known as Middletown when the first courthouse was built in 1745, the city now uses its mid-19th-century white frame courthouse* for meetings, conducting county business elsewhere.

The Cape May County Historical and Genealogical Society Museum occupies the John Holmes House (US 9; 609-465-3535). The house dates to the 18th century, the earliest part to 1755. It contains 18th- and 19th-century period rooms and a wide variety of artifacts, from medical aids to children's toys. In the barn are whaling implements, Indian artifacts, the lens from the Cape May Point lighthouse, and other maritime-related exhibits. Open mid-June–mid-September, Monday–Saturday, 10–4; mid-September–December and April–mid-June, Tuesday–Saturday, 10–4. The last tour begins at 3. Closed Sundays and holidays. Groups by appointment. Admission charged.

Roughly two miles north of town on US 9 is the Cape May County Park (609-465-5271). Its 120 acres include a natural area with jogging, nature, and bicycle trails and a wide variety of facilities for active sports. There is also a small zoo with domestic and exotic animals. Open daily, 9–dark.

About four miles north of town on US 9 is Leaming's Run Gardens and Colonial Farm (near the Avalon Blvd. intersection; 609-465-5871). There are 25 gardens on 20 acres, each garden constructed with a different theme; paths lead you from one calculated effect to another. This is an unusually peaceful spot in the midst of a busy resort world.

Also on the property is a small reproduction of a colonial farm. Open 15 May–20 October, 9:30–5. Admission charged.

Just beyond Leaming's Run is Beaver Swamp Wildlife Management Area, 1,700 acres of swamp, dense forest, creeks, and small ponds. Here you can hike, bird watch, and hunt; this is also a good spot to see muskrats, beavers, and river otters.

Cape May Point Cape May (C 606, 629) 255

Cape May Point was founded as Sea Grove in 1875 by a group of wealthy Philadelphia Presbyterians, including John Wanamaker, of the department store family, later postmaster general under Benjamin Harrison (Harrison spent his summers at the point in the 1890s). Apparently their aim was to establish a beach community like the successful Methodist ones at Ocean Grove and Ocean City. (Visitors journeying to Cape May by boat used to dock here and travel overland the three miles to Cape May City.) Still primarily a summer community, Cape May Point has some typical seaside resort architecture. Saint Peter's-by-the-Sea, a gray wooden church with white gingerbread trim, was taken from the Philadelphia centennial exhibition in 1880 and moved to Cape May Point by train. The erosion problem at the point is extreme: this is the church's fourth location; the last one, two blocks away, is now in the ocean.

Even before the community was founded, there was a lighthouse at the point. The current one,* built in 1859, is the third, the land the previous two stood on now being underwater. It is still being used, and on a clear night you can see its light for 19 miles. The Mid-Atlantic Center for the Arts (609-884-5404) plans to restore the lighthouse and operate a museum in it, which is scheduled to open in 1987. The museum will be devoted to the history of the lighthouse service, the evolution of lighthouse design, and the community of New Jersey shore and Delaware Bay lighthouses. In the meantime, climb to the top and see the spectacular view.

This is prime territory for bird watchers, one of the best spots in the country for observing migratory birds, particularly raptors (birds of prey). On the Atlantic Flyway, it is the last stop on the southern journey before the 18-mile flight over the open water of Delaware Bay. Birds congregate here, resting, eating, and waiting for good weather.

The New Jersey Audubon Society (707 E. Lake Ave.; 609-884-2736) has been studying migration at the point since 1975. The observatory and research center are open weekdays 8:30–4:30; weekends as well in spring and fall. (Hotline 609-884-2626.)

The Cape May Migratory Bird Refuge (Sunset Blvd. opposite S. Bay Shore Rd.; 215-925-1065) is a 188-acre reserve between Cape May and Cape May Point, owned by the Nature Conservancy. A well-marked trail goes through the meadow to the beach and back by another route. Open daily dawn to dusk.

Cape May Point State Park (Lighthouse Ave.; 609-884-2159) consists of some 190 acres of sand dune and freshwater marsh used during World War II as a coastal defense base. In 1942 bunkers were built here (and across the bay at Lewes, Delaware) 900 feet from the sea. Today you can see them at low tide. The dunes were blown away by Hurricane Gloria in 1985 and have been replaced by a smaller system, but the park is losing land to erosion at the rate of 30 feet a year. At the visitor center (once a military building) you can pick up trail guides and brochures describing the flora and fauna. There is an aquarium containing local marine life and there are a few other exhibits of local wildlife. The park has facilities for picnicking and fishing, observation decks for watching the birds, and over three miles of trails, including several stretches of boardwalk; there is also a ½-mile trail for the handicapped. Guided tours in summer.

At the end of Sunset Blvd. (C 606) is Sunset Beach, a good spot to find Cap May diamonds. These are pebbles of clear quartz smoothed and rounded by weathering, which, when polished, take the light like a precious stone. At Sunset Beach you can also see the remains of an experimental concrete ship, used in World War I. It was apparently being towed to be used as part of a wharf but broke loose in a storm and sank.

North of Sunset Beach is Higbee Beach, part of the Higbee Beach Wildlife Management Area, 616 acres of beach, dune, woodlands, fields, and ponds. Higbee Beach is another good place to look for Cape May diamonds (in fact, it used to be called Diamond Beach) and for birds. The area is important as a nesting and resting station since Pond Creek Meadow is the last freshwater area before the flight across Delaware Bay. Seventeen endangered species of birds frequent the area. It is also very popular with people, some

10,000 of them from 49 countries visiting each year. Some of them swim, sunbathe, picnic, hike the trails, watch the spectacular sunsets, and, in season, hunt, but the main attraction is the birds.

Cassville OCEAN (C 528, 571) [Jackson Township]

The crossroads community of Cassville* was important to the development of cranberry cultivation in the Pine Barrens. John Webb began growing cultivated berries in the 1840s and also developed the idea for the mechanical berry sorter; his success encouraged others to follow his example. Today, what is most noticeable about Cassville is its Russian settlement. If you drive into the village on C 571 from the north, you cannot miss the gilt onion domes of two Russian Orthodox churches. St. Vladimir, the one to the south, is modeled on a 16th-century Russian chapel. The trees that 30 years ago surrounded all the houses (and made them look like Russian dachas) have been giving way over the years to American lawns, and you are less likely to see women in babushkas than you once were. Rova Farms, founded in 1934 under the auspices of a Russian mutual aid society, was a cooperative community on 1,400 acres with 3,000 shareholders (the Rova Farms district is listed in the state register of

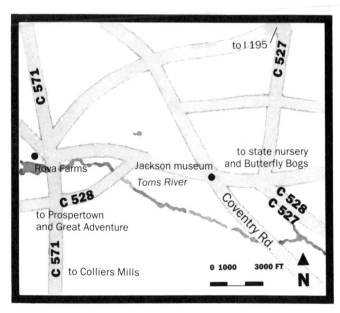

Cassville

historic places). The children of the original members are evidently losing interest in the venture, but Rova Farms is still open for old-style Russian meals and a flea market Tuesday, 6 A.M.–4 P.M. and weekends, 10–6.

Jackson Township (population 25,644) is an extensive township that has seen its population more than quadruple over the last 25 years. Ocean County as a whole is one of the fastest growing counties in the state, and because of the number of retirement colonies has been dubbed the St. Petersburg of the North. Jackson Township has its share of retirement colonies, but it also has large tracts that remain undeveloped. One of these is the 450-acre state seedling nursery, moved here from Washington Crossing State Park in 1982 and located on the site of the state's former quail farm (C 527, 528, between the Meadowbrook and South Wind retirement communities c. 4 miles south of I 195 exit 17; 201-928-0029). Ten of the acres are devoted to the seed orchards, and long-range plans call for eventually turning some of the woodlands into demonstration areas and developing nature trails. You can hike here and fish in the Tom's River, which flows through the tract and is stocked with trout. The nursery is open to the public, weekdays, 8–4. Groups by appointment. Across 527, 528 from the nursery is the Butterfly Bogs Wildlife Management Area (Bennetts Mill Rd.), 103 acres of pitch pine and scrub oak.

Farther west is Colliers Mills Wildlife Management Area (accessible from 528 and 571), over 12,000 acres of both pitch-pine and scrub-oak uplands and white-cedar swamp lowlands, with fields, wetlands, and six major impoundments. One of the most heavily hunted areas in the state, Colliers Mills offers opportunities for hikers and bird watchers on its sandy roads. The Pine Barrens tree frog and bluebirds are some of the unusual animals to be seen here.

Prospertown Lake Wildlife Management Area (access road off C 537 just north of Prospertown) consists of 125 acres with facilities for fishing, swimming, and boating; the beach (201-462-9616) is run by the state's parks department.

Behind the Jackson municipal building (C 528 and Coventry Rd.) is a restored (and expanded) one-room schoolhouse now functioning as a museum (201-928-1200). A classroom atmosphere has been re-created, and the collection features local artifacts, including memorabilia related to cranberry and blueberry cultivation and to the Lakehurst Naval Air Engineering Station, site of the explosion of the dirigible *Hindenburg* in 1937. Open weekdays by appointment (the museum hopes to establish regular hours soon).

Just north of Prospertown Lake is Six Flags Great Adventure (C 537; 201-928-3500), an amusement park and safari. Open daily, June–August; more limited schedule March–May and September; hours vary. Call for the exact schedule.

Chatham MORRIS (NJ 24) 8,537

A colonial town that in the mid-19th century attracted commuters and in the late 19th century became, with Madison, a center for rose growing, Chatham has converted many of its older buildings to modern uses. This is particularly apparent on Main St., but you will find attractive older buildings throughout the Chatham historic district (listed in the state register of historic places), which also includes Parrot Mill and Tallmadge rds. and Summit, Hedges, Hillside, and University aves.

South of the center of town (take Fairmount Ave., C 638, to Southern Blvd., C 647, and turn left) is the Great Swamp Outdoor Education Center (247 Southern Blvd.; 201-635-6629). Located at the eastern border of the Great Swamp National Wildlife Refuge, the center is part of the Morris County Park Commission's Loantaka Brook Reservation. (Somerset County's Lord Stirling Environmental Education Center is located at the western edge of the refuge; see Basking Ridge.) At the education center is a one-mile path of trail and boardwalk. The center has an active educational program for children and adults, including weekend nature walks.

Cherry Hill CAMDEN (I 295, NJ 70)
68,785

 The township of Cherry Hill, a rural township until the 1950s (and known as Delaware Township until 1961), has seen its population increase tenfold since the 1940s. Best known then as the site of the Garden State Park race track (NJ 70; 609-488-8400), built in 1942, Cherry Hill is basically a commuter town with many big hotels, housing developments, and shopping malls. The Cherry Hill Mall (NJ 38 at Haddonfield and Church rds.), in fact, was one of the first enclosed malls, and its skylit corridors, fountains, courts, plantings, and sculpture were frequently published as examples of good design. The Garden State Park burned in 1977. When it reopened in 1985 as a state-of-the-art facility, its glassed-in paddock and mahogany sculpture of a horse's head caused considerable comment. In 1985, after almost 100 years in the outskirts of Trenton (at the site of the Johnson sculpture atelier; see Hamilton Township), the New Jersey State Fair moved to the Garden State Park. Boasting the biggest midway in North America, the fair, which predates statehood—it was first held in Burlington County in 1745—lasts ten days.

Barclay Farmstead★ (Barclay Lane, off NJ 70 east between the Kings Highway, NJ 41, and I 295; 609-795-6225) is a living-history museum showing Quaker farm life in the first half of the 19th century. The land was first settled in 1684, but the present house probably dates to the mid-

1820s; the property was bought by a member of the Cooper family, a descendant of the founder of Camden, as a summer retreat. (The Barclay Farm housing development is on land that belonged to the original Barclay farmstead.) The house is decorated in 1840s style, there are changing exhibits, and special events focus on activities that could have taken place at the farm, like quilting and weaving. A program that celebrates both Hanukkah and Christmas takes place the second weekend in December, but most programs do not occur at set times; call for information. Also on the property are an herb garden, a forge barn with an 1830s blacksmith's shop, a corn crib, and a Victorian spring house. Some of the land is rented to members of the community who farm it. A foot bridge leads over the pond and connects with a nature trail along the north branch of the Cooper River. Open Tuesday–Thursday, 1:30–3:30. Closed mid-December–mid-January. Tours by appointment.

On Old Cuthbert Rd. is the Samuel Coles house* (1743), and at the intersection of Kings Highway and Church Rd., note the gatehouse at the Colestown Cemetery* (1858).

Chester MORRIS (US 206, NJ 24, C 510, 513) 1,433 (borough) 5,198 (township)

Chester, originally Black River, is a popular tourist town, which was settled early in the 18th century, primarily by immigrants from Long Island. By 1740 the community was known as an iron village, its mills supplying munitions to the revolutionary army. The iron industry flourished in the second half of the 19th century, and many of the town's handsome buildings date from that prosperous period. By the 1890s the discovery of the Mesabi range in Pennsylvania had ended local iron mining.

A walk along Main St., Hillside Rd., Budd Ave., and Grove St. will reveal many restored and converted buildings often with plaques giving their builders' names and the dates they were built. (The Historical Society publishes a walking tour, available at local stores.) At the northwest corner of Main St. and Hillside Rd. stands the Brick Hotel (now the Black River and Raritan Publick House), whose brick portion dates from c. 1810. A stagecoach stop for many years, it was used for a while in the mid-19th century

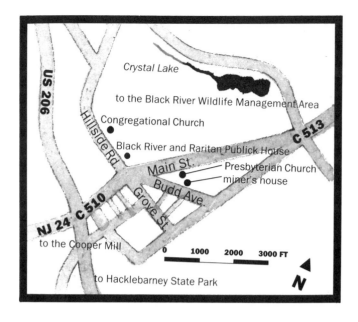

Crystal Lake

to the Black River Wildlife Management Area

Congregational Church

Black River and Raritan Publick House

Main St.

Presbyterian Church

miner's house

Budd Ave.

Grove St.

Hillside Rd

US 206

C 513

NJ 24 C 510

to the Cooper Mill

0   1000   2000   3000 FT

to Hacklebarney State Park

N

as a school. The Congregational Church (Hillside Rd.)
dates from 1856, the Presbyterian (Main St.) from 1852. An
example of a two-family miner's house can be found at
60 Budd, an 18th-century house at 50 Budd. Many of the
roads leading into the center of town are lined with
attractive houses, and at the intersection of US 206 and
NJ 24 is Larison's turkey farm, housed in an early 19th-
century building.

Two miles west of Chester on NJ 24 (formerly the Washington Turnpike, opened early in the 19th century) stands
the Cooper Mill (201-644-0342), the last surviving building
from a community known as Milltown or Milldale. It is a
working mill with two sets of grinding stones, which is run
by the Morris County Park Commission. The current mill
was built in 1826 by Nathan Cooper, but a flour mill had
been on the site in the 1760s and a sawmill and gristmill in
the 1780s. The wooden water wheels were replaced by metal
ones in the 1850s, and the mill incorporated the latest in
19th-century technological improvements. It is set up now
to represent a typical gristmill of the 1880s. Open 10–5,
weekends and holidays, May–October; Friday–Tuesday,
July and August. Guided tours run every half-hour until 4,
and visitors can purchase stone-ground whole-wheat and
corn flour made at the mill. Group tours by appointment.
At any time of year you can hike on the undeveloped trails
that start from the mill's parking area and go along the
Black River.

About three miles southwest of Chester is Hacklebarney
State Park (take Hacklebarney State Park Rd. off 24 or

Pottersville Rd. off 206; 201-879-5677). Established in 1924, when Adolphe E. Borie donated 32 acres to the state in memory of his mother and granddaughter, the park now contains 890 acres. Much of the park lies in a beautiful gorge along the Black River, and the footing is rugged on some of the trails. The streams are stocked with trout, there are beautiful picnic sites, and in winter you can sled and cross-country ski. Open daily, 8 A.M.–7 P.M.

Also along the Black River, about two miles north of Chester, is the Black River Wildlife Management Area (North Rd., C 513), some 3,000 acres open to hikers, bird watchers, and hunters.

Clark UNION (Garden State Pkwy exits 135, 136, C 509) 16,699

Named for Abraham Clark, a signer of the Declaration of Independence, what is now the township of Clark was settled late in the 17th century. The first mill was built on the Rahway River in the late 1700s, and for a time in the 19th century the American Felt Company was active in Clark. One of the first to buy land in the area was Dr. William Robinson, who arrived in 1686. His small red farmhouse, c. 1690, called Dr. Robinson's plantation* (593 Madison Hill Rd.; 201-388-8910), has been restored. In addition to showing what a 17th-century farmhouse would look like, the house has exhibits of artifacts and period craft demonstrations. Open April–December, 1st Sunday in the month, 1–4. Groups by appointment other times.

The Oak Ridge Golf Course (Oak Ridge Rd.; 201-574-0139) is a county facility located on land that belonged to a later Robinson, and the clubhouse uses the former Robinson homestead. Its kitchen wing is prerevolutionary; the central section dates to the early 19th century, the library wing to the Civil War. Directly adjacent, and also part of the county system, is the Ash Brook Reservation, 650 acres that have been described as a haven for golfers and bird watchers. (The Ash Brook golf course is off Raritan Rd. in Scotch Plains: 201-756-0414; pitch and putt: 201-756-0550.)

Clayton GLOUCESTER (NJ 47) 6,013

During the Depression the Clevenger brothers set up a glassworks in the family stables (E. Linden and Vine sts.). Over the years they acquired many of the old South Jersey molds and began reproducing old South Jersey bottles (see Millville). Open weekdays, 9–3 (public tours are not given because of insurance costs).

Northeast of the town is Scotland Run Park and Wilson Lake (Clayton-Williamstown Rd.), a county facility of over 940 acres. You can boat, fish, and swim on the lake, and trails are being developed. The county is also establishing a nature center for schoolchildren. Before you get to the park you will skirt the Glassboro Wildlife Management Area (see Glassboro).

Clinton HUNTERDON (I 78, US 22, NJ 31, C 173, 513)

Clinton, situated at the confluence of Spruce Run and the Raritan River, is remarkable for the beauty of its site. The entire town, which lies on the migratory route of many bird species, is a bird and wildlife sanctuary.

At the junction of the two rivers are two mills separated by a 200-foot waterfall. The red mill, now the Clinton Historical Museum Village* (56 Main St.; 201-735-4101), was built c. 1763 by David McKinney to grind flax seeds for linseed oil. Later owners used it to grind grain, as a gristmill, and, from 1903 to 1920, to grind talc and graphite. The museum, opened in 1963, displays a wide variety of artifacts dealing with daily life from the colonial to the Victorian period—farm tools, clothing, machinery, china, spinning wheels and looms, and furnishings. On the grounds (known as the James R. Marsh Park) can be seen the limestone cliffs, kilns, crushers, and tenant house involved in the 19th-century production of lime for fertilizer. The tenant house now contains a turn-of-the-century general store, a barbershop, and the interior of the old Lebanon post office. Also in the park are a schoolhouse dating from 1860, church sheds (used by parishioners to park their wagons during services) from two of Clinton's churches, and a log cabin built as a bicentennial project. Many special events take place in the park, and the gift shop and office are open year round. Museum open April–October, weekdays, 1–5; weekends, 1–6. Guided tours for groups by appointment. Admission charged.

Across an 1870 iron bridge is the old stone mill*, an early 19th-century stone gristmill in use until the 1950s. Now the home of the Hunterdon Arts Center (7 Center St.; 201-735-8415), it has been converted into a beautiful building containing galleries, a theater, and a sales room. A recent renovation has restored the building to its 1836 appearance—the stucco applied in the late 19th century has been removed, revealing the original gray fieldstone with red brick arches over the doors and windows. The renovation will also increase gallery space and help prevent the flooding that has plagued the building. The galleries feature changing exhibits, and the center is also used for concerts, educational programs, a children's summer theater program, and such special events as an antiques show and the annual crafts show. Galleries and sales room open Tuesday–Friday, 12–4:30; weekends, 1–5.

It is worth walking along Main, Center, and Water sts. The Clinton House dates from c. 1736, and there are many buildings from the Civil War period. (See, for example, the Municipal Building, c. 1865, on Leigh St. off Main.)

Three miles north of Clinton, on Van Syckles Rd. off NJ

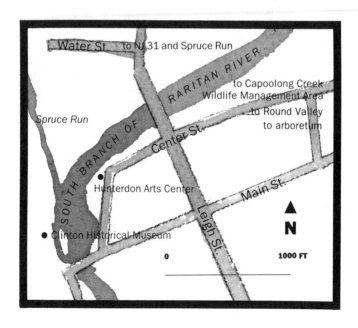

31, is the entrance to Spruce Run Recreation Area (201-638-8572). This park, which includes New Jersey's third largest reservoir (1,290 acres of surface and 15 miles of shoreline), offers abundant opportunities for swimming (between Memorial Day and Labor Day; on nice weekends it is

Hunterdon Arts Center, 1986

advisable to get to the swimming area early), boating, fishing, and, in winter, ice boating, ice-skating, and ice fishing. The camping and picnicking areas are in particularly lovely spots. Call for details on facilities and regulations. Adjacent to the western end of the park is the Clinton Wildlife Management Area, a heavily used area of fields and woodland, which is open for fishing, hunting, and hiking. Camping area open April–October. Office open summer (Memorial Day–Labor Day), daily, 8–8; winter, weekdays, 9–4:30. Parking fee in summer.

About eight miles east of Clinton (off US 22) is another, larger (4,000 acres) state park, Round Valley Recreation Area (Stanton-Lebanon Rd., C 629; 201-236-6355), with a large (1 mile by 3 miles) reservoir surrounded by hilly, wooded land. This park, too, has abundant opportunities for swimming, boating, and fishing (particularly trout), and there is a special area for scuba diving. There are wilderness campsites accessible only by foot or boat. In winter you can ice boat, skate, ice fish, and cross-country ski. The hiking and bridle trails can be rugged, but they offer beautiful views, and there are gentler paths as well. Open year round, but hours vary with the season. Parking fee for day-use area Memorial Day–Labor Day.

Some six miles south of Clinton on NJ 31 is the Hunterdon County Arboretum, a 63-acre special-purpose park, and the headquarters of the Hunterdon County park system (201-782-1158). Conceived as an educational and experimental resource, the facility contains a greenhouse, composting toilets, a gray water filtration system, and a passive solar heating unit. The display gardens concentrate on evaluating trial varieties of plants. There is an 1890 gazebo in the garden, and there are two miles of nature trails, including a boardwalk trail through a wetland study area.

Another three miles south on 31, turn left (east) on W. Woodchurch Rd. for Deer Path Park. There are woods, meadows, a pond, and playing fields, with places to fish, picnic, and skate. Eventually the park will include trails for bicycling, jogging, and cross-country skiing.

One of the few streams in New Jersey that can support trout naturally can be found about three miles south of Clinton. Take 513 to 617 and continue to the Capoolong Creek Wildlife Management Area, which runs along an old railroad right-of-way.

Colts Neck MONMOUTH (NJ 34,
C 537) 7,888

One of Monmouth County's fastest-growing townships (the population has increased more than 2½ times in the last 25 years), and one of the most expensive (one national survey in 1985 found Colts Neck the second most expensive housing market in the United States), Colts Neck has long been known as a township of horse farms. The horse industry brings in to the state as much as $3 billion a year in revenues. Standardbreds are the leading breed, followed by quarter horses, but there is an active thoroughbred breeding and training business as well. Although some of Colts Neck's farms have been sold to developers, there are still enough left to make a drive along C 537 and the smaller roads off it a treat to horse lovers, especially in the spring. There are some older houses to be seen (try Bucks Mills Rd.) as well as the Colts Neck Inn, built in the early 18th century by a member of the Laird family (see below).

Dorbrook Park (on both sides of C 537 between Laird and Hockhockson rds.; 201-842-4000) is a recently opened 380-acre county park. A farmhouse has been converted into an activity center, at which a wide variety of programs and events takes place. The land remains undeveloped, but you are welcome to walk on the grounds (one path takes you along the reservoir).

Also in this Scobeyville section of Colts Neck is the Laird distillery, established in 1780, where each year several million bushels of apples are converted into applejack. Before Prohibition there were over 350 cider distilleries in the country; Laird's, run by a family that has been making apple brandy in Monmouth County since the 17th century, is the last remaining one.

Cranbury MIDDLESEX (C 535,
539) 1,255

First settled in the late 17th century, the village of Cranbury* today presents a striking concentration of 19th-century architecture with a few 18th-century buildings as well. David Brainerd preached to the Indians here in the 1740s; Brainerd Lake and the Brainerd Institute (an 1860s school at 96 N. Main St.) are named for him. Cranbury's first inn was built in 1686, and the current one (S. Main St., north of Station Rd.) dates from 1780; Aaron Burr changed horses here in 1804 after his duel with Alexander Hamilton. (Another inn, this one c. 1850, used to be on Main St. but was moved to Maplewood and Scott aves. and has been converted to apartments.) Farther south on Main St. is the site of the Dr. Hezekiah Stites house, where George Washington, the marquis de Lafayette, and Hamilton were entertained en route to the Battle of Monmouth (see Freehold).

Both the United Methodist Church (1848; N. Main St.) and the First Presbyterian Church (1839, 1859; S. Main St.) look like picture-book examples of early-American church architecture. Note also the old schoolhouse★ (1896; 23 N. Main St.; 609-395-0544). It houses the township offices and municipal court and serves as a community center where art exhibits are held and a variety of programs presented.

The Cranbury Museum (4 Park Place; 609-655-3736, 609-395-0430) is in a 19th-century house (c. 1834), which retains an original window and an early stairway. The museum is furnished to give a sense of what a 19th-century small-town home would be like; there are also special exhibits (past ones included cut glass, quilts, and Victorian clothing) that change every few months. Open weekends, 1–4, and by appointment.

A walking-tour brochure, which will explain the history of the buildings in the historic district and make your visit much more interesting, has been prepared by the Cranbury Historical and Preservation Society (which runs the Cranbury Museum) and the Middlesex County Cultural and Heritage Commission and Coalition of Historic Organizations and Site Owners (for information call 201-745- 4489). The Historical Society also sponsors a biennial house tour.

Although there is some industry in the township outside the village—General Foods, for example, and Carter Wallace—and Cranbury is facing development pressures, the land surrounding the village is still largely agricultural—potatoes, grain, and soybeans are major crops—and half the township has been designated an agricultural preservation area.

Cranford UNION (Garden State Pkwy exit
137, C 509)   24,573

The Minnisink Trail once went across the area now occupied by this attractive town, which takes its name from Stephen Crane, one of the original associates who laid the town out in 1699 (and a forebear of the novelist). At one time there were 11 mills on the Rahway River, and during the Revolution, grain for George Washington's army was ground here and woolen blankets for the soldiers manufactured in what is now called Droescher's Mill★ or The Mill (347 Lincoln Ave. E.); the 18th-century structure, the only one of the original 11 to survive, has been converted to an office building. It is worth taking a look at this lovely corner. It is also worth looking at the brown shingle First Presbyterian Church (Springfield and N. Union aves.) and driving out N. Union to see some of the large houses.

The Josiah Crane, Jr., House (124 N. Union Ave.; 201-276-2713) is maintained by the Cranford Historical Society as a museum and library. The earliest records of the house are from the 1840s, but parts may be older, and other parts were added in the 1860s and 1960s. The museum concentrates on Cranford history and has many early photographs, but it also has an extensive collection of Indian artifacts. Open September–June, Thursday and Sunday, 2–4. Groups by appointment.

At Nomahegan Park (Springfield Ave.) you can fish, skate, bicycle, and picnic. The park also has athletic fields, a playground, and a two-mile fitness course. Other points along the river where you can fish include McConnell Park (Eastman St.) and Sperry Park (Riverside Dr.).

Crosswicks BURLINGTON (C 660, 672,
677)   Chesterfield Township

Crosswicks, settled in the late 1670s by English Quakers, is said to be the only community in the United States to bear that name. Although the land around Crosswicks is being developed, the village center, which makes up the Crosswicks historic district★ and includes 18th- and 19th-century buildings on the Chesterfield-Crosswicks Rd. (C 677) and Front St., preserves a strong flavor of the past.

David Brainerd first preached to the Indians here in 1745; his attempts to teach the Indians trades that would enable them to fare better in the colonial world were thwarted by his failing health. Traditionally, Crosswicks claims to be the home of Taylor's Pork Roll, named for John Taylor, a descendant of one of Crosswick's earliest settlers, who ground ham for the market in 1856. Today it is the home of one of the few horseradish farms in New Jersey.

The Chesterfield Friends' Meetinghouse (just northeast of the intersection of Front and Church sts.), a large two-story brick building, dates from 1773. Built partly with bricks from an older structure, the building still has its original flooring and one of the few Atsion stoves (purchased in 1772 and made in Atsion of New Jersey bog iron) to be found in New Jersey. In the revolutionary battle of 23 June 1778 Hessian troops used the meetinghouse as a barracks and hospital, and one of the cannonballs fired during that battle (by Continentals) is still to be seen in the north wall (secured with cement). After the Battle of Trenton, Continental troops occupied the building.

Dover MORRIS (US 46, NJ 15) 14,681

Dover was formerly an iron town and for a time the shipping center for New Jersey's iron industry. The iron industry was active in this area more or less steadily from the 18th century, and the Dover mines continued in operation until the late 1950s. Dover's Blackwell St. historic district* (including portions of Blackwell, Dickerson, Sussex, Bergen, Essex, Morris, Warren, Prospect, and Dewey sts.), a mixture of 19th- and 20th-century buildings, is of interest: note, in particular, the Baker building* (16 W. Blackwell St.), dating from 1884, and the former Delaware, Lackawanna and Western Railroad station* (N. Dickerson St.), dating from 1901. The Old Stone Academy (25–27 E. Dickerson St.), c. 1827, once housed the state's first coeducational boarding school.

Dover has a large and relatively prosperous Hispanic population, which makes up roughly one-quarter of the town's population. Almost half come from, or are descendants of people coming from, one town in Puerto Rico. The original Hispanic settlers were recruited as farmers by the federal government in the 1940s. A special Hispanic festival is held every Labor Day.

One mile north of town on NJ 15 (in part occupying the former village of Spicertown) is the U.S. Army Armament Research, Development and Engineering Center (ARDEC), also known as the Picatinny Arsenal. This is a large operation (6,000 civilian and 250 military employees) where much of the army's research and development of nuclear weapons takes place. In Building 2 is the ARDEC Museum, with displays of weapons, munitions, and other military items from the revolutionary war to the present. There are also displays relating to this post in particular and to the surrounding communities, as well as films, an outdoor display, and a videotape theater. Open weekdays, 9–3. Groups by appointment (201-724-3222). You can also take a walking tour of parts of the arsenal, which dates from the 19th century, but includes a revolutionary graveyard and an 18th-century forge. The post was struck by lightning in 1926, which resulted in a spectacular series of explosions. The flames could be seen from New York City, and evidence of the explosion can still be found today. A self-guided-tour brochure is available at the museum.

In the southwestern corner of the town is Hedden County Park (Concord Rd., Reservoir Ave., and Ford St.; 201-829-0474), 245 acres with facilities for hiking, bicycling, boating, fishing, picnicking, and, in winter, cross-country skiing and ice-skating.

East Brunswick MIDDLESEX
(NJ Tnpk exit 9, NJ 18, C 527)   37,711

In the southeastern corner of the rapidly growing East Brunswick Township (25 years ago the population was less than 20,000), along the South River, is the historic district of Old Bridge★ (Emerson, Squire, Oak, Maple, Kossman, Pine, Chestnut, and Main sts., Rutgers and River rds.). The district encompasses some 42 acres with about 80 structures, roughly one-fifth of them shops. The soil here led to the early development of the pottery and ceramics industry; potters are known to have worked in this area by the mid-18th century (the first settlers came toward the end of the 17th century). In what was formerly the Simpson Methodist Church (c. 1860) is the East Brunswick

Museum (16 Maple St.; 201-257-1508). The museum's permanent collection includes household objects, Indian artifacts, and photographs, and the rotating exhibits focus on both fine arts and historical subjects. Open weekends, 1:30–4; group tours other times by appointment. A self-guided walking-tour brochure of the district is available from the Middlesex County Cultural and Heritage Commission (201-745-4489).

At Dunhams Corner Rd. is the East Brunswick Park (201-398-6886), 97 acres with facilities for swimming and ice-skating. Just west of East Brunswick Park (off Church La.) are the Tamarack Golf Course (201-821-8881) and Ireland Brook Park, both county facilities. Ireland Brook Park, which will eventually be linked to the golf course and Davidson's Mill Pond (see South Brunswick), is as yet undeveloped; some of its 385 acres will be designated conservation areas, and some hiking trails will be developed. East of East Brunswick Park are the Middlesex County fairgrounds (Cranbury Rd.); among the regular events taking place at the fairgrounds is the historic car festival, held in the fall. The township plans by the late 1980s to convert some of its land along the Raritan River into a conservation area and to restore the marina.

East Hanover MORRIS (NJ 10)
9,319

 The rapidly growing township of East Hanover has seen its population more than double in the last 25 years. Within the village of Hanover (part of East Hanover, not Hanover, Township) note the First Presbyterian Church★ (Mt. Pleasant Ave. opposite Hanover Ave.), from the 1830s, and the mid-18th-century Halfway House★ (174 Mt. Pleasant Ave.). In the Nabisco Company headquarters (De Forest Ave. and River Rd.; 201-884-4000), built on the site of a golf course, is an art gallery. The shows held in this large space have varying themes, but try to emphasize New Jersey artists. Shows change every 6–8 weeks. Open Sunday–Friday, 12–4.

West of the Nabisco gallery (take De Forest back to Ridgedale Ave.; turn right or north and continue to Klinger Rd.) is Troy Meadows, 300 acres of marshy land created by the last glacier. This national natural area is the largest remaining cattail marsh in New Jersey, one of the few places in the state where you can see bog turtles, and an excellent spot for bird watchers (there is a boardwalk).

East Rutherford BERGEN
(NJ Tnpk exit 16W, NJ 3, 20)   7,849

Much of East Rutherford's land is taken up by the Meadowlands Sports Complex (201-935-8500), a project begun by the New Jersey Sports and Exposition Authority in the 1970s. The concrete complex, which was erected on the marshlands of the Hackensack Meadowlands (see Lyndhurst), contains a race track, stadium, and indoor arena, all protected against flooding by a system of dikes, lagoons, and pumps. Some 10 million visitors a year come to watch thoroughbred and harness racing; professional football, soccer, basketball, and hockey; college sports; the circus; ice shows; auto racing; and concerts. The race track used to make a little extra money by selling manure to Pennsylvania mushroom growers, but the current popularity of foreign mushrooms has spoiled that market, and the Sports Authority is looking into other ways, such as preparing and marketing ready-to-use fertilizer and soil conditioner, to profit from this unavoidable byproduct. It is also studying ways to help compulsive gamblers. Admission charges.

Edgewater BERGEN (NJ 5,
C 505)   4,628

A long, narrow borough situated on the Hudson River, Edgewater was a popular resort for Manhattanites in the late 19th century, and has been a center of shad fishing since colonial times. Although commercial shad fishing has declined over the last 50 years (from some 300 fishermen in the thirties to about 100 in the eighties, and very few of those operate off the New Jersey side), you can still see the fishermen at work in the Hudson in the spring. A famous Ford Motor Company assembly plant★ (309 River Rd.), built in 1929–31 to the design of Albert Kahn Associates, is being converted into housing for over 700 families.

Docked near the Alcoa Edgewater works★ (700 River St.) is the *Binghampton*★ (725 River Rd.), a ferryboat built in 1904–5 in Newport News. The only double-ender ferryboat still floating in the Hudson, the *Binghampton* was in continuous service between Hoboken and New York City from 1905 to 1967 and carried some 125 million passengers. She is now used as a restaurant.

Edison Township
(I 95, US 1, NJ 27, C 501, 514, 529, 531) 70,193

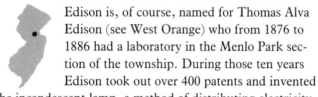

Edison is, of course, named for Thomas Alva Edison (see West Orange) who from 1876 to 1886 had a laboratory in the Menlo Park section of the township. During those ten years Edison took out over 400 patents and invented the incandescent lamp, a method of distributing electricity, the phonograph, the carbon telephone transmitter, the dynamo, the magnetic separator, and the electric traction railway. The laboratory and its contents (not to mention a considerable quantity of Middlesex County soil) were transported by Henry Ford to his Greenfield Village in Michigan, and on the exact spot of the laboratory was erected in 1937 the Art Deco Thomas A. Edison Memorial Tower★ (Christie St. off NJ 27; 201-549-3299, 201-287-0900, ext. 265), a cement tower 131 feet high with an amber glass replica of an incandescent light at the top. Within the tower and the outlying buildings are some of the machines Edison invented, memorabilia, and an eternal light that commemorates the first practical incandescent bulb. Open Wednesday–Friday, 12:30–4; weekends, 12:30–4:30. Also Tuesday, 12:30–4, June–August. Groups by appointment.

Like many New Jersey townships, Edison is made up of several older communities. In Piscatawaytown (in the western section of the township) the Episcopal congregation was established in the late 17th century. The present St. James Episcopal Church (2136 Woodbridge Ave., C 514), a white frame building with a Doric portico, dates from the 1830s. Its 1724 building was occupied by British troops during the American Revolution (British soldiers are buried in the churchyard; there are also some 17th-century headstones). A late 18th-century replacement was destroyed by a tornado in the 1830s, and the pulpit is supposed to have washed up on Staten Island. Many of the materials from the old church were used in constructing the church you see today. If you turn off onto Park Way (south off Woodbridge Ave.) you will see some older houses and the Edison Commons with the Old Town Hall.

At the eastern edge of the township, in Bonhampton, note the late 18th-century Grace Reformed Church (Woodbridge Ave. and Grace St.) and the Bonhampton School (2825 Woodbridge Ave.), built in 1908 and recently converted to a professional building.

The township is home to many corporate headquarters, research facilities, and factories. The Mobil Company laboratory was the first laboratory in the nation to win a safety award from OSHA (Occupational Safety and Health Administration); the Ford Motor Company plant (US 1; 201-632-5940) offers tours for groups of 15–30 by appointment only; the four-square-mile Raritan Center (NJ Tnpk exit 10), carved out of the old Raritan Arsenal, is the largest business park in the state—when complete it will have some 11 million square feet of office space, distribution centers, a hotel, a conference center, a health club, and retail outlets.

On the northwest side of US 1 is the 241-acre Roosevelt Park (201-548-2648), the county's oldest park. Plays and concerts are given in the summer, and there are nature and hiking trails, tennis courts, playing fields, a cross-country running course, fishing ponds, a model-boat area, and places to ice-skate in the winter.

Also on the site of the Raritan Arsenal are Middlesex

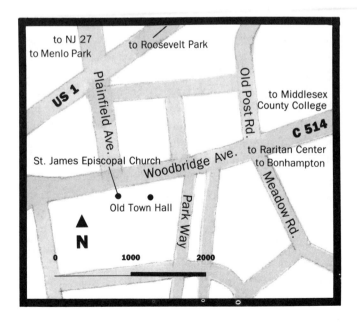

County College (Woodbridge Ave.; 201-548-6000) and Thomas A. Edison Park (Mill Rd.; 201-225-1523), formerly Raritan Arsenal Park. The college, founded in the 1960s, is still using some of the army's old buildings. When there are exhibits, Edison Hall Gallery (201-548-6000, ext. 380) is open to the public weekdays, 9–5; Saturday, 9–3; the performing arts center (201-548-6000, ext. 367) is also open to the public. (For the daily schedule of activities open to the public, call ext. 327 or 420.) The park consists of 161 acres on the flatlands to the north of the Raritan River estuary; it has a hiking trail and a fitness trail, tennis courts, playing fields, and a track.

A self-guided-tour brochure for Edison Township is available from the Middlesex County Cultural and Heritage Commission (201-745-4489.)

Egg Harbor City ATLANTIC
(C 561 Alt., 563) 4,618

Settled by Germans in the 1850s, Egg Harbor City (which is part of Galloway Township, not Egg Harbor Township, and is not on Egg Harbor) derives its name from a never-realized scheme to connect it by canal to the Mullica River. After the discovery in 1858 that the land was extremely well suited for growing grapes, more Germans emigrated to Egg Harbor City. (Note the street names in the area: Bremen, Frankfurt, Darmstadt, Heidelberg, Hamburg, among others.) Yet it was a Frenchman from Rheims, Louis Nicholas Renault, who established the best-known venture, the Renault Winery (72 N. Bremen Ave., 2¼ miles northeast of the intersection of Bremen and Moss Mill Rd., C 561 Alt.; 609-965-2111), listed on the state register of historic places. The oldest continuously operating winery in the United States (during Prohibition the winery produced its "medicinal" Renault tonic with an alcohol content of 22%), it was at one time the country's largest producer of champagne. Occasionally on a back road in South Jersey, you will come across one of the company's 20-foot promotional champagne bottles, now a little dingy, standing in front of a liquor store. At the winery there is a small collection of wine and champagne glasses, including some medieval ones, and you can tour the facilities. Special events are scheduled, including a grape stomping in the fall. Tours

Monday–Saturday, 10–5; Sundays and holidays, 12–5 (last tour, 4:15). Admission charge for tour. Closed New Year's Day, Easter, Thanksgiving, and Christmas.

Elizabeth UNION (NJ Tnpk exit 13, US 1, 9, NJ 27, C 514) 106,201

Elizabeth is Union County's oldest and largest community. Elizabeth, in fact, is the state's first permanent European settlement (going back to 1664), its oldest English-speaking settlement, and its first colonial capital (from the mid-1660s to 1686). Today primarily an industrial and commercial town (the world's largest producer of liquid and frozen egg products is located here), Elizabeth is also the seat of New Jersey's youngest county (Union County was founded in 1857).

As in other industrial cities, the population has been declining, although the loss has not been as extreme as elsewhere, and various revitalization plans are underway. For over 100 years (1873–1982) Elizabeth was the home of the Singer Sewing Machine Company's oldest plant, which at its peak employed 10,000 people. The site (Trumbull and First sts.) is now being converted into an industrial park. (The Port Authority of New York and New Jersey is developing a nearby Elizabethport site as another industrial park.) The Jersey Central Railroad station★ (Julian Place), built in the 1890s and closed in 1976, is being converted into a restaurant.

The city's role as a transportation center goes back to the 18th century, when it was an important ferry link to New York City; regular steam service began in 1808. The railroad lines running right along the water were important to its industrial development. In the late 1950s, the Port Authority of New York and New Jersey developed a new terminal at Port Elizabeth (not the same as Elizabethport), which has since become a major container-ship port (almost 10 million long tons were handled there in 1984; see New Jersey Turnpike tour, 103). The Goethals Bridge, which crosses Arthur Kill to reach Staten Island, was opened in 1928. This cantilevered structure carries close to 10 million vehicles each way annually.

The list of Elizabeth's famous residents is long. James Caldwell, known as the fighting parson (see Springfield), became minister of one of the oldest English-speaking congregations in New Jersey, the First Presbyterian, in 1761. During the Revolution he often preached with loaded pistols on either side of the Bible and with armed sentries guarding the church, and he preached the Sunday after the British burned the parsonage. The church itself was burned in 1780, and the present building* (Broad St. and Caldwell Place) dates from 1784. Caldwell, killed by an American sentry in 1781 (see Westfield), is buried in the graveyard. In 1946 another fire destroyed most of the interior, so that today's church has been rebuilt inside the 18th-century walls. (The restoration took the church back to its colonial interior, rather than reconstructing its 19th-century Gothic one.) Upstairs is a small museum of colonial artifacts. Tours can be arranged on request; call 201-353-1518.

Among Caldwell's famous parishioners at First Presbyterian were William Livingston, the state's popular first governor (he was reelected until his death in 1790; his house, Liberty Hall, at Morris and North aves., is a national historic landmark; see Union); Elias Boudinot, a lawyer and president of the Continental Congress (and as such the

Port Elizabeth

signer of the peace treaty with Britain), member of the U.S. Congress, initiator in Congress of the resolution leading to the establishment of Thanksgiving Day, and superintendent of the Mint at Philadelphia; Jonathan Dayton, Continental army general, congressman, and developer of Dayton, Ohio; and Abraham Clark, one of New Jersey's five signers of the Declaration of Independence. Princeton University was founded in Elizabeth, in 1746 (it was known then as the College of New Jersey), by one of Caldwell's successors at First Presbyterian, Jonathan Dickinson.

Other prominent residents of Elizabeth include Lorenzo Da Ponte, librettist for Mozart's *The Marriage of Figaro*, *Don Giovanni*, and *Così fan tutte*, and Admiral William F. Halsey (his birthplace at 134 W. Jersey St. is now an inn).

Boudinot's house, Boxwood Hall★ (1073 E. Jersey St.; 201-648-4540), built c. 1750 by Samuel Woodruff, the mayor of Elizabeth, and purchased by Boudinot in 1772, is a state historic house museum. Boudinot gave a funeral oration over Caldwell's body from its steps; George Washington visited the house en route to his inauguration as the country's first president; Alexander Hamilton lived with the

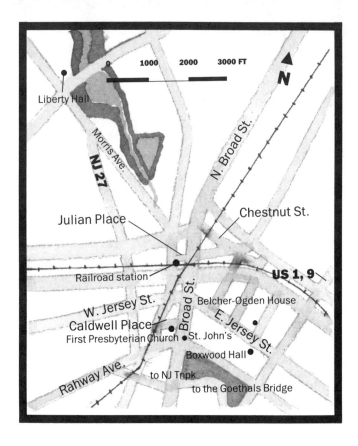

Boudinots while attending school in town. When Boudinot
became superintendent of the Mint, he sold the house to
Jonathan Dayton; during the time Dayton lived there the
marquis de Lafayette was a guest (early in the 20th century,
Lafayette's great-grandson visited Boxwood). Open
Wednesday–Friday, 9–12, 1–6; Saturday, 10–12, 1–6;
Sunday, 1–6.

In the same block is the Belcher-Ogden House★ (1046 E.
Jersey St.; 201-634-4112). This historic house museum is
run by the Elizabethtown Historical Foundation. Dating
from c. 1742, the house was owned for a time by Jonathan
Belcher, royal governor first of Massachusetts and New
Hampshire and then of New Jersey (from 1747 until his
death in 1757), who was also active in promoting the College
of New Jersey. The house was later occupied by Colonel
Aaron Ogden, a senator from New Jersey and governor in
1812. Open by appointment.

Across the street is the Nathaniel Bonnell house (1045 E.
Jersey St.; 201-355-1776), which until recently served
as the state headquarters for the New Jersey Society of the

S.A.R. It dates from c. 1682, and is probably now the town's oldest house.

St. John's Episcopal Church (Broad St.; 201-351-1218), founded in 1705, was once the largest Episcopal congregation in the state, but like many other inner-city churches, has a much smaller congregation today. Elizabeth Seton's parents were married in St. John's (the church keeps its old register on display), Winfield Scott was a member, the Kean family vault is in the churchyard, and Jonathan Dayton is buried under the church. The splendid Gothic building, dating from 1859, has five Tiffany windows; an Italian font is the church's only colonial possession. A large population from the French Caribbean migrated to Elizabeth after the French Revolution (Elizabeth today has the state's largest concentration of Haitians); note the fleurs de lis on the gravestone of a lady from Martinique (1799). Tours by appointment.

Englewood BERGEN (NJ 4, C 501, 505) 23,701

Once known as a bedroom community for wealthy commuters, Englewood now has a large number of multifamily houses and low-income housing projects, as well as a large commercial center. John Travolta was born here, and since the late 1960s the painter Richard Anuskiewicz has lived here. In 1951 Englewood was the site of the first customer-dialed long-distance telephone call in the United States, when Englewood's mayor called the mayor of Alameda, California. (Through the Bergen St. windows of the telephone building at Bergen and Engle sts., you can even see the circuitry, not possible in later windowless telephone buildings.) Vince Lombardi coached at St. Cecilia's High School (Demarest St.; the school is part of a large stone complex with some interesting buildings) before moving on to college and professional teams. Englewood was also the site of Helicon Hall, Upton Sinclair's ill-fated experiment in communal living. Built with the royalties from Sinclair's exposé of the meat-packing industry, *The Jungle* (1906), Helicon Hall burned after six months. The 20-room house built on its site was occupied for many years by Victor

Wallace Farris, inventor of the paper milk carton and the paper clip.

Gloria Swanson was another Englewood resident. She lived in the 32-room Italian villa of the Gloria Crest estate (N. Woodlawn Ave.), built in 1926 by a member of the Polish royal family (and named for his wife, not Swanson). To see some of the houses that gave Englewood its reputation, drive up the hill on N. Woodlawn Ave. (east off Palisade Ave.). On your left will be the Dwight-Englewood preparatory school (northeast corner of N. Woodlawn and Palisade; among its graduates are George Schultz and Brooke Shields). Gloria Crest is farther up the hill on your right.

The John Harms Center (20 N. Van Brunt St.; 201-567-5797) in downtown Englewood occupies a 1926 building, unprepossessing on the outside, but reflecting on the inside its origin as a "movie vaudeville emporium." It houses a nonprofit regional theater whose season runs from September to March or April. Other groups, such as the New Jersey Symphony Orchestra, also appear at other times, and art exhibits are often hung in the upstairs lobby. Box office open year round, weekdays, 9–5; Saturday, 10–1.

Many of Englewood's older downtown buildings have been converted to new uses. The Renaissance Office Court (northeast corner of Bergen and Engle), for example, built in 1917, was once the well-known Englewood High School. It was next a junior high and then a grade school before being converted to its present use. Note also the Intarome building (71 E. Palisade), the former Citizen's National Bank building, and the railroad station (now a restaurant).

Even in this built-up area you can still see some early Dutch stone houses. Many are on Grand Ave.; the Red Cross, for example, is in the early 18th-century John G. Benson house★ (60 Grand Ave.), and others are farther south on Grand (at 228,★ 285,★ 370,★ and 488).

In the midst of this densely populated area are the Flat Rock Brook Center (443 Van Nostrand Ave., the eastern end of Van Nostrand; 201-567-1265) and Allison Woods Park (Jones Rd.), 150 acres of woodland, with wetlands, two ponds, a stream, meadows, and a stone quarry with 180-million-year-old volcanic formations. There is a nature center here with an award-winning commercial solar design. The center coordinates educational programs with the local schools, but you are also free to wander on the trails. Grounds open dawn to dusk; office weekdays, 9–5. Groups by appointment.

Englishtown MONMOUTH (C 522, 527) 976

Englishtown is known today primarily because of its huge weekend flea market, but it also has historical interest because of its connections with the Battle of Monmouth. Washington and his men spent the night here before the battle, eating at the Village Inn★ (Main and Water sts.). After the battle Washington and Lord Stirling used the dining room of the inn to draw up the charges that were used in General Charles Lee's court martial. Lee also used the dining room to write some of the letters that sealed his guilt. Built in 1732, the inn was for a long time one of the oldest continuously operating taverns in the state. It is now being restored and will reopen as a museum. Note also the municipal building (13 Main St.), probably early 19th century, which served as a tavern for many years.

Ewing Township MERCER (I 95, NJ 29, 31) 34,842

A rapidly growing township that developed primarily as a suburb of Trenton, Ewing Township is the home of Trenton State College. The college moved to its 225-acre Hillwood Lake campus over 50 years ago, when many of its red brick buildings were built. The William Green house,★ however, dates from the 18th century and is being restored by the college and the township. Trenton State began as a normal school in the 1850s (it was then located in Trenton); it now has five undergraduate schools, 5,000 students, and a reputation for quality. Tours of the campus start from Green Hall, room 105, Friday at 10. The Holman Hall Art Gallery (609-771-1855) presents six exhibits a year; these are open to the public September–June, weekdays, 12–3; Thursday evening, 7–9; Sunday, 1–3. The music department (609-771-2551) puts on concerts of classical music almost every week; call for the schedule. In Ewing the state also raises useful bugs (in the Beneficial Insect Rearing Laboratory) and makes all the signs used on state-maintained roads (in the Department of Transportation Fernwood complex).

The Benjamin Temple house★ (27 Federal City Rd.; 609-737-8887) is a mid-18th-century house with a mid-19th-century addition, which was moved to its present location in the 1970s. The 27-acre park in which it sits formed part of the tract that James Monroe suggested would be suitable for the country's capital (which, of course, is how Federal City Rd. got its name). The house is being restored, and it is hoped that the 18th-century portion and the kitchen will be open to the public on a regular basis in 1990. Tours by appointment.

Fairfield ESSEX (US 46) 7,987

Abutting the Great Piece Meadows, Fairfield is a town without an obvious center. It boasts an attractive red sandstone early 19th-century Dutch Reformed Church★ (Fairfield and New Dutch rds.), but the 18th-century Van Ness homestead★ (236 Little Falls Rd.) stands neglected and deteriorating. At the A. Horowitz and Sons bookbindery (300 Fairfield Rd.; 201-575-7070) is the Horowitz Museum of Bookbinding and Graphic Arts, a fascinating collection of old machines and hand tools used in printing and binding. The company also possesses a large technical library on binding. Open weekdays, 10–4, by appointment only.

Overlooking the Caldwell-Wright Airport is a restaurant decorated to look like the English farmhouse that served as the 94th Bomb Group's headquarters during World War II, with sandbags protecting the walls, and uniforms, photographs, posters, and other memorabilia on display.

Fair Lawn BERGEN (NJ 4, 208, C 507) 32,229

Fair Lawn, an old Dutch settlement, gained attention as the site of Radburn,★ a world-famous experiment in postautomobile city planning. The concepts behind Radburn, which was built in 1929 by Clarence Stein and Henry Wright, have been widely influential in continental and British town planning. Organized in superblocks, Radburn segregated cars from people and had the fronts of the houses face common greens. Parking was close enough to a house to enable a shopper to carry groceries easily, but children could walk to school without ever crossing a street. The Depression interfered with completion of the original plan, and many post–World War II houses coexist with the 1929 buildings. To get a better sense of the original flavor, look at the photographs in the lobby of the commercial building at Plaza Rd. and High St. The Radburn historic district* includes Fair Lawn, Berdan, and Prospect aves. and Plaza and Radburn rds. (For information write or call the Radburn Association, 29–20 Fair Lawn Ave., 07410; 201-796-1300.)

Just west of Plaza Rd. on Pollitt Dr. is the Cadmus House,* an 1800 Dutch stone house, which was recently moved (it weighed 50 tons) to its present site. Once part of a farm that covered half of present-day Fair Lawn, the house is being converted to a museum. Other early stone houses can be seen on River and Dunkerhook rds.

West of Radburn near the Passaic River is the Garretson Forge and Farm Restoration* (4–02 River Rd.; 201-797-1775, 201-796-2387). The Garretson family left the Netherlands in 1660 and bought this land in 1668. Six generations lived on the farm until Mary Garretson died in 1950. The property was rescued from a developer and is gradually being restored. The main section of the 18th-century house was made of dressed stone; the sandstone blocks were held together with mortar made of river mud

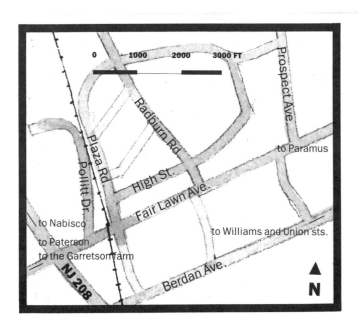

mixed with straw and hogs' hair (the kitchen wing used un-dressed stone). The carriage shed and the kitchen wing with its beehive oven have also been restored. There are periodic displays here of 19th- and 20th-century artifacts, early iron work, antique farming tools, and the findings from the ar-chaeological dig being undertaken by Ramapo College. Open Sunday, 1–4; weekdays by appointment.

One of the county's bicycle-pedestrian paths starts from Williams and Union sts.

Tours of the Nabisco Fair Lawn Bakery (2211 Route 208 at McBride Ave.; 201-797-6800, ext. 5208) are possible on Tuesday mornings and Thursday afternoons, October– May (Oreos, the world's most popular cookie, are made here). Reservations accepted in August.

Far Hills SOMERSET (US 202, C 512, 523) 677

Situated on the east bank of the North Branch of the Raritan River, Far Hills is part of Som-erset County's estate and hunt country. The Somerset Art Association (Prospect St. and Peapack Ave.; 201-234-2345), primarily an art school, has exhibits, lectures, and other programs open to the public. The association sponsors a large outdoor show the end of September. Open weekdays, 9:30–2; Saturday, 9:30–12.

South off US 202 on Far Hills Rd. (C 512) is the Leonard J. Buck Garden (Layton Rd.; 201-234-2677). Now part of the county park system, the garden was once the private rock garden of a wealthy mining engineer. The rock formations on its 33 acres are covered with rare plants from Europe, Asia, and North America. In 1986 an extensive col-lection of ferns was added to the garden. Open Monday– Saturday, 10–4; Sunday, 1–6. Groups by appointment (fee charged for guided group tours). Just north of the garden is Moggy Hollow, a national natural landmark. This is a nar-row ravine walled off at one end by a ledge of basaltic rock that was once the spillway of the Glacial Lake Passaic. From the ledge, you can see terraces of glacial debris.

If you continue south on 512, crossing I 287 and Douglas Rd., you will come to the headquarters, museum, and library of the United States Golf Association, located on the grounds of a 62-acre 1919 estate, whose main house was designed by John Russell Pope. Recently renovated, the museum displays its permanent collection chronologically. Included are artifacts from ancient Scottish, Flemish, and Dutch games that were the ancestors of today's golf. There is also a gallery with changing exhibitions. Open weekdays, 9–5; weekends, 10–4. Closed holidays.

On the west bank of the North Branch directly across from the center of Far Hills is Bedminster (population 2,469), another hunt-country village that attracted some attention as the site of the state's first Mount Laurel housing. The Hills housing development (US 202) is noticeable in a town that used to have five-acre zoning for single-family houses.

The Somerset Hills Handicapped Riders Club at Crossroads Farm (take Lamington Rd., C 523; c. 2½ miles southwest of 202 turn left onto Larger Cross Rd.; 201-234-1907) welcomes visitors during lessons. Call for information.

Farmingdale MONMOUTH (C 524, 527) 1,348

 A village with interesting 18th- and 19th-century buildings, Farmingdale was once known as Marsh's Bog and then as Upper Squankum. The historic district runs along Main St. from Asbury Ave. to the W. Main St.– N. Main St. fork.

About three miles south of Farmingdale (take Main St.) is Allaire State Park (C 524, 2 miles west of Garden State Pkwy exit 98, 1 mile east of I 195 exit 31; 201-938-2371). The park itself is lovely—with hiking, cross-country skiing, and nature trails (the red nature trail crosses an excellent example of a swamp forest); bridle paths; a nature center; and facilities for picnicking, canoeing, and camping—but what sets it off from other parks is Allaire Village.

Allaire Village was once a flourishing part of New Jersey's bog-iron industry. A sawmill operated on this site in 1750, and an ironworks was here in 1813. In 1822 James Allaire, who operated a foundry in New York City and had cast the brass air chamber for Robert Fulton's steamboat, the *Clermont*, and the iron cylinder of the *Savannah*, the first steamship to cross the Atlantic, bought the property (then

Allaire Village

known as Howell Furnace or Howell Works). Presumably he saw it as a source of iron for his New York foundry. The community he built at Allaire (it took this name after his death in 1858) was not just self-sufficient, common enough in the 1830s, but contained a church and school as well. Stoves, pots, screws, some pipe, and hand irons were cast here before the works stopped operating in 1846. Allaire's son lived on in the village until 1901, apparently resisting any offers to make use of its facilities. Arthur Brisbane, a noted editor with the Hearst newspapers, bought the property in 1907, building himself a home across from the village. Starting in 1927 he leased the village to the Monmouth Council Boy Scouts for $1 a year, and they began the work of restoring the village. In 1941 Brisbane's widow deeded the village to the state.

Because so much of the village was left, restoration was relatively easy. Of particular note is the furnace stack, but all the buildings—the general store, the farmhouse, the blacksmith shop, the tenant's house, the enameling shop, and more—are of interest. The church (c. 1831), with its unusually placed steeple (at the rear, not the front), is still used for services in the summer. The village sponsors many special events: there are craft demonstrations in the afternoon on summer weekends, an annual crafts fair in the summer, a re-creation of St. Nicholas Day as it would have been in 1823, a farmers' market, theater on the green, and the like (for information about special programs, call 201-938-2253). Children (and only children) may fish in the millpond, there are horse-drawn wagon rides and pony rides, and the Pine Creek Railroad runs a steam train on a short loop through the park (there are plans to enlarge the trip).

Finesville

Village open May–Labor Day, Monday–Saturday, 10–5, Sunday, 12–5; September and October, Saturday, 10–4, Sunday, 12–4. The railroad operates daily July and August, weekends April–June and September and October, 12–5. Admission charged for village and railroad. Brochures are available in the visitor center.

Two miles south of Farmingdale on Preventorium Rd. is the Howell Park and Golf Course (201-938-4771), a county facility consisting of 300 acres of gently rolling land bordering the Manasquan River. You can also hike here and canoe and fish in the river.

Finesville WARREN (C 627) [Pohatcong Township]

Situated on the Musconetcong River, considered one of the state's finest trout streams, the attractive village of Finesville has many lovely 18th- and 19th-century stone buildings. The Riegel Paper Corporation, now part of the James River Corporation and one of the country's largest manufacturers of printing papers, began operations in a converted gristmill in Finesville in 1862.

The Alba Vineyard (C 627, slightly over 2 miles south of Warren Glen and north of the bridge at Riegelsville; 201-995-7800) operating out of a 100-year-old cut-lime-stone dairy barn and outbuildings, grows grapes on the slopes of the Musconetcong Valley. Roses are planted at the ends of the vine rows, and there are lovely views from the top of the vineyard. Picnic facilities have been set up in a grape arbor. Open for tours Tuesday–Friday, 1–5, Saturday, 11–5, Sunday, 12–5. Closed Tuesdays, January–April. Large groups by appointment.

About two miles north of Finesville (take 627 north to Warren Glen and turn south on 519 to the intersection with Dennis Rd.) is the Musconetcong Gorge Nature Preserve, part of the Hunterdon County park system, which is developing trails in the preserve. This is a rugged area of over 350 acres, with steeply wooded terrain overlooking the Musconetcong River. There are many small streams and a variety of plant and wildlife.

Flemington HUNTERDON (NJ 12, 31, C 523) 4,132

Since 1785 the seat of Hunterdon County, Flemington takes its name from Samuel Fleming, who bought land from William Penn and Daniel Coxe and in 1756 built the house now known as Fleming Castle. Flemington's first industries depended on agricultural products, but gradually poultry and cattle became more important than crops. The Flemington Auction Market, in fact, was considered the first successful cooperative egg and livestock market. (Its building has been converted to office space.) Known as an important center for flour milling, Flemington also had iron foundries, and the first of its well-known potteries dates to the early 19th century. The Flemington Cut Glass Co. (156 Main St.; 201-782-3017) opened in 1908 (in 1920 it began selling seconds from the front of its factory, thus presaging today's factory outlets; see below). You can watch the glass cutters at work, weekdays, 10–4:30. The Stangl company's old kilns can still be seen at the Pfaltzgraff outlet (Mine St.), but except for the cut glass, all these earlier industries are gone.

Some 65 percent of Flemington's structures are listed in the state and national historic registers, and the historic district* includes Broad, Main, E. Main, N. Main, Spring,

Court, Bonnell, Mine, William, Brown, Academy, Capner, and Church sts.; Park, Bloomfield, Emery, Maple, Grant, Dewey, Hopewell, Pennsylvania, New York, Central, and Lloyd aves.; and Chorister Place. The county courthouse (northwest corner of Main and Court), with its Greek Revival details, dates to the late 1820s and uses some of the walls from the burned-out courthouse of 1791–93. This building received international attention in 1935 when the trial of Bruno Hauptmann for kidnapping and murdering the aviation hero Charles Lindbergh's baby son was held there. Memorabilia from the trial are on display in the lobby of the courthouse. Across the street from the courthouse is the Union Hotel, rebuilt in 1862 after a fire. (There has been a hotel on this site since the early 19th century.) The hotel was altered again in 1877–78 to produce today's mansard-roofed extravaganza with its towers and deep front porch. Baron Renfrew, later England's Edward VII, is among the celebrities who have signed the Union Hotel's guest register, and during the Lindbergh trial the reporters all congregated here. It is worth looking inside; note partic-

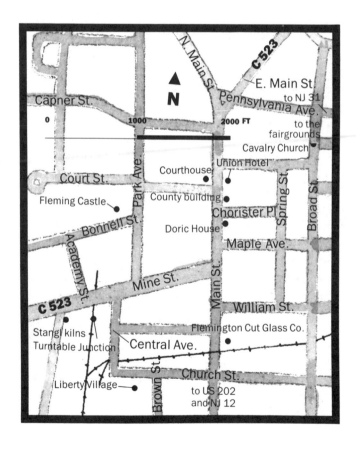

ularly the ceiling, the books on the radiators, and the 1930s mural in the dining room.

Across the street from the courthouse is the Doric House (Maple Ave. and Main St.; 201-782-1091), a Greek Revival structure built by Mahlon Fisher (responsible for many of Flemington's mid-19th-century houses). Formerly a residence, a restaurant, and a church school, it is now the home of the Hunterdon County Historical Society and contains a museum and a library. Among the items in the museum are empire furniture, pier glass mirrors, and a tall case clock made by a Flemington craftsman. Open by appointment.

Fleming Castle (5 Bonnell St.; 201-782-4655, 201-782-6472), now owned by the Daughters of the American Revolution, has served as an inn and a stage depot. Tours by appointment. You may enjoy wandering about the downtown streets, for there are many interesting buildings. Note the Cavalry Church (Broad St. and New York Ave.), built in the 1880s. Henry Beck, the well-known New Jersey popular historian, was rector here 1949–56. The county building at 65 Main St. was once used by the Flemington Children's Choir School, which trained children to sing in choirs from early in this century until 1958. Memorabilia from the choir school can be seen upstairs weekdays, 8:30–4:30.

In 1965 a development began that has changed Flemington considerably. A post–revolutionary war version of colonial Williamsburg, known as Turntable Junction (Mine St.), was built on the site of a former railroad turntable and brick yard. It was followed by Liberty Village (Church St.), which featured weavers, candlemakers, glassblowers, and the like, dressed in period costumes giving public demonstrations of their crafts. Although Turntable Junction and Liberty Village both still exist, they changed owners in the late 1970s, and they now no longer operate as late 18th-century reconstructions but as outlet areas. In fact, since 1980 or so, Flemington has become widely known as an upscale discount center. On weekends as many as 25,000 visitors have been known to appear in this town of 4,000.

Flemington's agricultural heritage can be appreciated at the county fair, where agriculture is still the major focus. Hunterdon County had its first fair in the fall of 1745, and the Flemington Fair (NJ 31) is now the state's biggest and oldest. On grounds built for it in 1846, the fair generally runs from the Tuesday before Labor Day until Labor Day.

From mid-April through November the Black River & Western Steam Railroad (see Ringoes) runs passenger trains between Flemington (from Turntable Junction) and Ringoes, with connections to Lambertville on Sundays, May–October (freight trains run year round). During July and August trains also run Tuesday–Friday. Fee charged.

The annual juried Flemington Festival of the Arts takes place at the end of May.

Forked River OCEAN (US 9) [Lacey Township]

 Located at the head of the Forked River, which empties into Barnegat Bay, the village of Forked (pronounced For-ked) River, like many of the nearby bay towns, was settled before the Revolution and lived off fishing and shipbuilding. Boating and fishing are still important, but the fishing tends to be sport fishing, and the boating tends to center around the Forked River state marina (311 Main St.; 609-693-5045). Many of the older buildings are still standing, some being restored, others showing evidence of the various functions they have served over the years. The Forked River House (Main St.) was frequented by Captain Joshua Huddy during his patrols (Huddy was looking for loyalists; his capture and execution by the British caused a minor incident toward the end of the Revolution); the Captain's Inn (Lacey Rd.) was once a state-licensed gambling casino. South of the marina, off US 9, is the state game farm, which is run by the Corrections Department on an 18th-century estate; the manor house is being restored by the department. Not open to visitors.

Across from the Forked River House is the Old Schoolhouse Museum (Main St.; 609-693-2637), run by the Lacey Township Historical Society. The collection features tools, quilts, and a glass collection showing the history of a Forked River bottling works. Open Memorial Day–Labor Day, Monday, Wednesday, Friday, 1–3, Saturday, 10–12; groups by appointment other times.

Farther south is Jersey Central Power & Light's Oyster Creek Nuclear Generating Station. In a separate building a small museum, the Energy Spectrum (a well-marked turn west off US 9; 609-693-1143), has exhibits that illustrate the history and future of energy. Open Tuesday–Friday, 9–3:30; Saturday, 10–5.

North of Forked River (take 9 north about 5 miles to C 618, Central Parkway, turn left, and continue past the Garden State Pkwy) is Double Trouble State Park,* presently undeveloped. A sawmill was first built on this stretch of the Cedar Creek in the 1760s, and the name Double Trouble was in use by the 1800s. Cranberries were harvested here in the 1830s, and the state is restoring the cranberry workers' houses, the sawmill, and other buildings. In the meantime you can walk on a short trail built by the Youth Conservation Corps, which takes you through typical Pinelands terrain past an old cranberry bog. Plans also call for developing a 20-mile hiking trail westward from here into Lebanon State Forest (see Pemberton), where it will connect with the Batona Trail. It has been said that the Cedar Creek trail will run along the most pristine watershed in the state.

Fort Lee BERGEN (I 95, US 9W, 46, NJ 4, 63, 67, C 505) 32,449

Known to many commuters simply as one end of the George Washington Bridge, Fort Lee sits on the cliffs of the Palisades overlooking the Hudson River. It takes its name from the fort George Washington located there during the Revolution to prevent the British from sailing up the Hudson. Washington was forced to abandon Fort Lee when Fort Washington across the river fell to the British.

From about 1903 to 1920, Fort Lee was a national center of the young motion picture industry; the adventures of Pearl White were filmed here, and D. W. Griffith, Fatty Arbuckle, and Theda Bara, among others, began their motion picture careers in Fort Lee.

In 1931 the George Washington Bridge, considered by many one of the most beautiful suspension bridges in the world, was opened; a second level was added in 1962. A key link in the system of roads bypassing the metropolitan area, the bridge, with 14 lanes and a river span of roughly 3,500 feet, connects with the New Jersey Turnpike and many other major roads. Some 140,000 vehicles use it every business day. The riverwalk that may some day extend along the Hudson to Bayonne will start at the George Washington Bridge.

Since the building of the bridge, Fort Lee's population

has more than tripled. In 1962, Horizon Houses, a group of award-winning high-rise apartments, created the first silhouette on the Palisades skyline. There are more such buildings now.

One-quarter mile east of the original Fort Lee, in Fort Lee Historic Park (Hudson Terrace; 201-461-3956), a revolutionary fort has been reconstructed. Cornwallis's assault path up the Palisades in 1776 can be seen, and at the visitor center exhibits and films explain the British assault. The park, which is run by the Palisades Interstate Park Commission, also sponsors educational programs and special events, including walking tours in the fall. Picnic facilities are available. Grounds open daily year round, 8 to sunset; visitor center open March–December, Wednesday–Sunday, 9:30–5. Parking fee charged mid-April–mid-October. Groups by appointment.

About two miles west of Fort Lee (in the communities of Leonia, Palisades Park, and Teaneck) is Overpeck County Park (Fort Lee Rd., Cedar La., Roosevelt St.; 201-599-6124), over 800 acres with a golf course, tennis courts, playing fields, hiking and bicycle paths, picnic areas, an ice-skating rink (winter only), a year-round horseback riding center (201-944-3253), and a wildlife refuge. You can also fish from the lake shore.

Franklin SUSSEX (NJ 23, C 517) 4,486

Franklin was once the leading zinc-mining town in the United States. In the early 19th century, Dr. Samuel Fowler, a physician and member of Congress, who was largely responsible for the settlement of Franklin, found zinc ores on his land. Perfecting a process for making zinc-based paint in the 1830s, he tried to persuade New York City to ban the use of lead-based paints. He also helped persuade Congress, when it passed a weights and measures law in 1836, to stipulate that the brass used in the weights must contain New Jersey red oxide zinc. Fowler did not profit from these developments, however, for by the time an inexpensive method of extracting zinc from the ore was developed (in 1848), he had died. The New Jersey Zinc Company, which operated the mine on what had been his property, continued to work it for over 100 years, until it was depleted in 1954.

The Franklin area is very rich in minerals (over 300 have been found here). Many of them are fluorescent, and some are not found anyplace else. On the site of the old zinc mine is the Franklin Mineral Museum (Evans St. between Main St. and Buckwheat Rd.; 201-827-3481). Here you can see exhibits of the minerals found at Franklin, in various stages of refinement; an exhibit of fluorescent minerals that lets you see how they glow under ultraviolet light; and, in the old engine house, a replica of a mine, built entirely from materials used in Franklin zinc mines. This is a popular goal of school trips in the spring. The museum also administers the slag heap, known as the Buckwheat Dump, where collectors can look for their own rocks. Picnic sites available. Open July and August, Wednesday–Saturday, 10–4; Sunday, 12:30–4:30; 15 April–30 June and 1 September–15 November, Friday and Saturday, 10–4; Sunday, 12:30–4:30; groups by appointment, Tuesday–Thursday. Admission charged.

Franklin Lakes BERGEN (US 202, NJ 208, C 502) 8,769

 This rapidly growing suburbanized area still has a large number of early Dutch stone houses (drive along Franklin, Pulis, Woodside, Circle, Summit, Mabel Ann, and Ewing aves., Franklin Lake Rd., and Vee Dr.). On Ewing Ave. about one mile south of NJ 208 is the New Jersey Audubon Society's headquarters and its Lorrimer Sanctuary and Nature Center (790 Ewing Ave.; 201-891-2185). There are good observation points for spotting hawks and self-guided nature trails. The center has both permanent and changing exhibits, some of them hands-on, and the society offers many educational programs and tours. Open Tuesday–Saturday, 10–4; Sunday, 1–5. High Mountain, just south of the sanctuary, is also a good spot for viewing hawks.

The Saddle Ridge horseback riding area (Pulis Ave.; 201-848-0844), operated for the county park system, offers lessons Tuesday–Sunday. The area, a former Nike site high on Campgaw Mountain, adjoins the Campgaw Reservation (see Mahwah).

Freehold MONMOUTH (US 9, NJ 33, 79, C 522, 537) 10,020

The seat of Monmouth County, Freehold was settled in 1715 by a group of Scotch immigrants who had traveled inland from Matawan. The center of a rich agricultural area, Freehold was the scene of one of the major battles of the American Revolution, the Battle of Monmouth (28 June 1778). Although this was not a clear-cut victory for the Continental army, it did establish that the newly trained troops could hold their own in conventional open-field fighting. It also created a folk heroine, Molly Pitcher; bringing water to the troops throughout the hot day (102° F.), she, according to tradition, took over her husband's position at his cannon when he was wounded. And because Major General Charles Lee unexpectedly ordered a retreat (Washington arrived and rallied the troops, giving vent to what was for him an unusual display of temper), considerable controversy surrounds the battle.

At Monument Park in the center of town near the spot where the fighting first broke out, a 100-foot tower commemorates the battle. On the top of the monument, which was dedicated in 1884, is a statue of Columbia, and, near the base, there are five bas-relief plaques, one of which shows Molly Pitcher at work during the battle. At 70 Court St. (201-462-1466) near the monument, in a Georgian-style building built especially for the purpose in 1931, are the headquarters and library of the Monmouth County Historical Association (founded in 1898). The museum has exceptional collections of furniture, paintings, and decorative arts, most of which were made in New Jersey or owned by New Jersey residents. The exhibits also feature children's toys and items relating to local history, and the museum owns a copy of Emanuel Leutze's painting of the Battle of Monmouth (Leutze painted the familiar picture of Washington crossing the Delaware). Open Tuesday–Saturday, 10–4; Sunday, 1–4. Admission fee.

The association also runs several historic houses, including, in Freehold, the early 18th-century Covenhoven House★ (150 W. Main St.; 201-462-1466), which was used by Sir Henry Clinton (the British general) as his headquarters the day before the Battle of Monmouth. Using an inventory from 1790, the society has furnished the house to illustrate how a successful farmer lived in the last years of

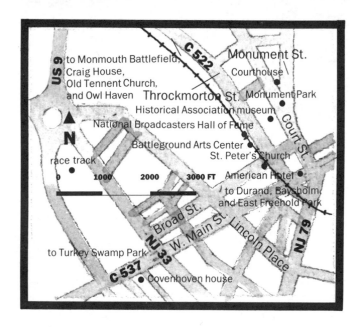

the 18th century. Open June–October, Tuesday, Thursday, Sunday, 1–4; Saturday, 10–4. Groups by appointment other times. Admission fee.

The courthouse dates from the 1950s and replaces four earlier buildings. St. Peter's Episcopal Church (29 Throckmorton St.; 201-431-8383) is a mid-18th-century church that was used as an army storehouse and a hospital during the Battle of Monmouth. Near it (51–53 Throckmorton) is the volunteer fire department's first building (1874)—now a shop featuring memorabilia from the early years of the volunteer fire department—and the Battleground Arts Center's offices (26 Throckmorton; 201-462-8811). The American Hotel (1824) is at 20 E. Main St. (201-462-8019).

At 22 Throckmorton is the National Broadcasters Hall of Fame (201-431-4656), a museum of mementos and tapes of old radio programs. Open Tuesday–Sunday, 12–3. Groups by appointment. Admission fee. Freehold, incidentally, sponsors a cable TV program devoted entirely to local news and run entirely by students. Less directly related to communications is New Jersey Bell's contribution to saving farmland: its award-winning corporate center leases 100 acres of a 177-acre plot to a farmer.

The main battleground for the Battle of Monmouth remains practically as it was in June 1778. Lying northwest of town it now forms part of a state park (C 522, the extension of Throckmorton St., just west of US 9; 201-462-9616). The visitor center (off NJ 33) has exhibits explaining the battle and other interpretive displays. Its 1,500 acres include a variety of habitats, and some 25 miles of trails (many of them unmarked). You can pick up trail maps at the visitor center. About one-quarter of the park is cultivated by local farmers to whom the state leases land. Visitor center open daily, summer (Memorial Day–Labor Day), 9–5; winter, 9–4. Park open daily, summer, 8–8; winter, 8–6.

On park property is Craig House (turn west off US 9, at Schibanoff Rd., north of the intersection with C 522; 201-462-9616). This house, which was built in 1710 and has chunks of local bog iron in its foundation, belonged to John Craig, paymaster for the local militia, and may have been used as a British hospital during the Battle of Monmouth. It has been restored to its 18th-century appearance. Open summer weekends (Memorial Day–Labor Day), 9–4:30, Thursday and Friday by appointment; winter weekends 10–5, Thursday and Friday by appointment.

At the northwestern corner of the park is the Old Tennent Church (1751). Recently renovated, the church still has its original weather vane from the 1690s. In its cemetery are buried many who fell in the Battle of Monmouth.

Also on park property is Owl Haven (C 522, c. 1½ miles west of US 9 on the north side of the road; 201-780-7007), a nature center and licensed raptor rehabilitation center run by the New Jersey Audubon Society. The nature center features displays of live and stuffed animals, and a marked trail begins behind the center. Open Tuesday–Sunday, 1:30–4:30; groups and other hours by appointment.

At the intersection of US 9 and NJ 33 is the Freehold race track (201-462-3800). The oldest parimutuel harness track in the country, it was established in the 1850s by the Monmouth County Agricultural Society (it has not run continuously).

Several county parks are in the area. The East Freehold Park (Kozloski Rd.; take Center St. east about 2 miles from the center of town; 201-842-4000) is a showgrounds, the site of the county fair, held each July, and the Monmouth County Horse Show, held in mid-August and over 90 years old.

The Durand Conservation Area (east on C 537 about 3 miles; turn left or north on Randolf Rd.; 201-842-4000) is a county reservation currently being leased to Freehold Township. Its 90 acres are being left undeveloped as a conservation nature-study area. South of Durand across C 537 (on Burlington Rd.) is the Baysholm Conservation Area (201-842-4000), 70 acres that are also undeveloped and used for hiking and nature observation.

Some six miles southwest of Freehold (within Freehold Township) is Turkey Swamp Park (Georgia Rd.; turn west off US 9; 201-462-7286) and Turkey Swamp Wildlife Management Area. Much of the park's 500 acres is devoted to family camping, but there are also open recreation areas, wilderness camping areas, hiking and nature trails, a fitness trail, and facilities for boating, canoeing, fishing, and picnicking. Camping, March–November. Registration for group use. The wildlife area (west of the park) consists of some 1,800 acres of noncontiguous parcels that include upland woodlands, lowlands, swampy areas, and fields. It is used for hiking and hunting.

Frenchtown HUNTERDON (NJ 12, 29, C 513, 610, 619) 1,573

 Located on the Delaware River between Milford and Stockton, Frenchtown began as a ferry town in the mid-18th century; its strategic importance was considered sufficient to exempt the ferry operator from service in the revolutionary war. In the 1790s the land was bought by a Swiss aristocrat, Paul Henri Mallet-Prevost, wanted by the French for having saved his countrymen in the French Revolution. The town came to be called French's Town, then Frenchtown, after Mallet-Prevost, a French-speaking Swiss.

Thomas Lowrey, from whom Mallet-Prevost had bought his land, had already erected a gristmill and sawmill, both of which continued to operate into the 20th century, grinding corn into feed for the area's poultry industry. (One hatchery in Frenchtown was producing between 5 and 6 million chicks annually in the 1880s; by the 1930s it was up to some 15 million chicks a year.) Today Plessey Frenchtown (established early in the 20th century as the Frenchtown Porcelain plant) is the town's largest employer, and Frenchtown is beginning to attract artists and antiques dealers; many of its buildings are being restored and renovated.

Prevost experimented with growing grapes on his land, and the Delaware grape is the result of crossing some of his vines with native American grapes. In a return to local viticulture, DelVista Vineyards (C 513, 1 mile north of Frenchtown; 201-996-2849), operating on the site of one of the chicken hatcheries, became New Jersey's first farm winery (in 1982 licensing arrangements for wineries were relaxed to allow the establishment of wineries that used New Jersey grapes; the requirement has since been further relaxed to allow farm wineries to purchase up to 49 percent of their grapes outside the state for the first five years). Open summers (Memorial Day–Labor Day), Wednesday–Sunday, 11–5; winters, Wednesday and Friday, 2–4, weekends, 1–5. Tours on weekends or by appointment; charge for tours. Picnic facilities available.

Glassboro GLOUCESTER (US 322, NJ 47, C 536, 553) 14,574

Glassboro was founded in 1775 by a family of German glassblowers, the widow Stanger and her seven sons, who had worked at the Casper Wistar works in Salem County. Although the town derived its name from its glass factories, they have all since been forced out of business by cheaper production methods elsewhere. The Stangers did not themselves prosper from their glassworks, but the works survived, reaching their peak of production in the 1840s when they were under the control of Thomas and Samuel Whitney. The Stangers, were, however, highly influential, and took the style of South Jersey glass they developed to other glass factories throughout the East. You will find many examples of their work in museums that collect decorative arts. In the 1840s the Whitney Glassworks produced an enormously popular bottle, shaped like a log cabin and supposedly modeled on William Henry Harrison's birthplace, which was filled by a Philadelphia liquor distiller named E. C. Booz, leading to the spread of the word "booze" in this country (the use of the word to mean drink, however, can be dated at least as far back as 1732).

In 1849 the Whitney brothers built themselves a mansion★ (Whitney Ave.) on a 55-acre estate called Holly Bush. Of native Jersey sandstone, the mansion may have been designed by John Notman. Now the administration building for Glassboro State College, it became internationally famous in June 1967, when it served as the site of a three-day summit meeting between President Lyndon B. Johnson and Soviet Premier Aleksei Kosygin. A second presidential visit to Glassboro occurred in June 1986, when President Ronald Reagan delivered the high school graduation address. Most of the Glassboro College campus buildings are new, but the college grew out of a state teachers' college founded in 1923. Its performing arts center (609-863-7388) is active during the school year, and the college has a distinguished collection of glass and of the writings of New Jersey historian Frank Stewart. The Hollybush Festival of the Arts (609-863-6043), featuring opera, ballet, concerts, and an art show, is held on the campus (but is independent of the college) each spring.

Another 1840s building of native sandstone with Gothic Revival details, St. Thomas' Episcopal Church★ (Main and Focer sts.), is also tentatively attributed to Notman. It supersedes a frame church that may have been located at Main and Broadway, where many members of the Stanger family are buried.

At the corner of High and Center sts., on land that was once the site of the Whitney Glassworks, is the Heritage Glass Museum (609-881-7468). Housed in a 1926 bank building (when the bank closed in 1931, two of its directors faced embezzlement charges), the museum preserves and exhibits historic bottles, glass, and related items. Open Friday evenings, 7–9, and Saturday, 10–1.

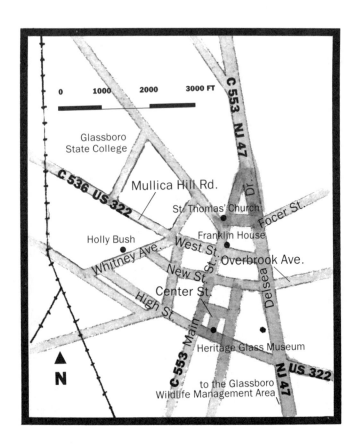

Other buildings of interest include the Franklin House (Main and West); the first tavern on this site was built by Solomon Stanger in the late 18th century. The Whitney-Capie house (29 West St.) is a Victorian house built by a member of the Whitney family during the Civil War; one of its clapboard wings simply incorporates an earlier brick house that stood on the site.

South of the city (access lies off NJ 47) is the Glassboro Wildlife Management Area, one of the earliest such areas (it was started in 1935). The 2,300 acres of woodlands and fields are open to hikers, photographers, bird watchers, and hunters.

Glen Gardner HUNTERDON

(NJ 31)   834

 Situated on the Spruce Run, Glen Gardner was an iron-mining town in the 19th century, and the part of the town lying east of NJ 31 preserves the look of another era, with the houses and balconies right up against the street. Of architectural interest are the Masonic Temple and, coming into town on School St., the iron bridge. If you climb Mt. Kipp on Sanitorium Rd. you will come to a state-run geriatric center, formerly a tuberculosis sanitorium. The road runs through a game refuge and pine forests with wonderful views; the buildings at the center have the look of a European spa or Adirondack sanitorium.

Some two miles east of Glen Gardner is Voorhees State Park (off 31; 201-638-6969), whose 500 wooded acres are particularly lovely in fall. There are picnic sites here, as well as hiking trails and facilities for camping. Stop by at the office for maps of the park. The office is open 8–4:30, the park 8:00 A.M.–9:00 P.M.

Also within the park is the New Jersey Astronomical Association's observatory (Lower Park Rd.; 201-638-8500). The public is welcome Saturday evenings, May–September, and the association holds an annual open house. Call for information on tours of the observatory.

Northwest of Glen Gardner in New Hampton (take 31 north about 2 miles to Musconetcong River Rd. and turn right) is the Township of Lebanon Museum (201-537-6464). Built as a one-room schoolhouse in 1823, the building was enlarged in the 1870s. A 19th-century schoolroom has been re-created on the first floor; on the second are a gallery and a lecture hall. Exhibits, which change roughly every two months, may feature collections of poison bottles or clothespin dolls; there are also arts and crafts shows, regular lecture series, and crafts classes. Open Tuesday and Thursday, 9:30–5; Saturday, 1–5. Groups by appointment.

Green Brook SOMERSET (US 22, C 529) 4,640

According to tradition George Washington in 1777 stood at the site that is now Washington Rock State Park (C 529; 201-754-7940) and watched the British troops on the plain below. At this 45-acre park are an overview, woods to walk in, and facilities for picnicking, with opportunities for sledding in the winter.

Greenwich CUMBERLAND (C 607, 623) 973

Situated on the Cohansey River in the tide-water country of southern New Jersey, Greenwich reached its apogee before the Revolution. For a time it was the largest town in Cumberland County, and for some 10 or 11 months in 1748, it served as the county seat. It is now one of New Jersey's most Brigadoon-like communities.

The town was laid out by John Fenwick, the English Quaker who founded Salem. He envisioned a main street two miles long and 100 feet wide, and by 1684 (the year after his death) Quakers, Presbyterians, and Baptists had begun buying 16-acre lots. Today the Great St. is indeed 100 feet wide and tree lined, and the Greenwich Historic District,★ with its 17th-, 18th-, and 19th-century buildings, extends along the Great St. from the Cohansey River north to Othello.

So prosperous was the shipping at Greenwich that in 1687 the village was named the official port of entry for all ships traveling on the Delaware River, and in 1695 it was chosen as a market town. Market fairs were held twice yearly in Greenwich until the mid-1760s. It was a blow to Greenwich when Bridgeton was chosen as the county seat in late 1748, and by 1800 road travel had become so much easier that

Greenwich's position as a transportation center declined. The town's remarkable 18th-century appearance was discovered after World War II, but although it now attracts many tourists, it has not become a tourist town.

In 1774, when the colonists were boycotting tea as a protest against import duties, a British captain unloaded his cargo of tea in Greenwich, believing it would be safer in the basement of a loyalist merchant there than in Philadelphia, its ultimate destination. The plan was to smuggle it overland to Philadelphia. Ten days later a group of Greenwich men dressed as Indians entered the merchant's shop at night, took the tea, and burned it in a giant bonfire in town. Although seven of them were brought to trial they were never convicted. Like the participants in the Boston Tea Party, these "Indians" were among the most responsible citizens in town. The sheriff who selected the jury (he later became one of New Jersey's first two senators) was the brother of one of the tea burners and the nephew of the foreman. It is claimed that the ringleader was the Reverend Philip Vickers Fithian, a recent Princeton graduate, whose journals were used in the Williamsburg, Virginia, restoration. Other participants included the Reverend Andrew Hunter, who founded Woodbury Academy, and two future governors of the state, Richard Howell and Joseph Bloomfield. In 1908 the state erected a monument commemorating the event.

On the northeast side of the Greate St., just west of the intersection with the Bridgeton-Greenwich Rd., is the Gibbon House (609-455-4055, 609-451-8454), headquarters of the Cumberland County Historical Society. Built in 1730 by Nicholas Gibbon, a shipowner and merchant, the house is operated as a museum. On display are the famous Ware chairs (made just north of Greenwich in Roadstown), children's toys, 19th-century clothing, and mementos of Reverend Fithian. Behind the Gibbon house is the Swedish granary, a c. 1650 cabin built of notched cedar logs (moved to the site from a nearby township) that is an extremely rare example of this early type of building. Open April–December, Tuesday–Saturday, 12–4, Sunday, 2–5 (closed Sundays in August). Tours by appointment. Admission fee for nonmembers. The Pirate House (1734; 609-455-8580, 609-455-4055, 609-455-2020) functions as the society's library; its brick-floored kitchen serves as a crafts room. The library is open April–December, Wednesday, 1–4, Sunday, 2–5. The historical society also arranges tours of

Greenwich (call 609-455-4055 or 609-451-8454; for children's educational tours call 609-451-0002).

Among the many buildings of interest are the Richard Wood house (1785, 1795; northwest corner of Greate and Bacon's Neck rds.) and on the southwest corner, the Wood store—this late-18th-century store is reputed to be one of the oldest in the country—and across from these the Old Stone Tavern (c. 1730), built of fieldstone from Pennsylvania and Maine carried as ballast; the Friends Meetinghouse (1770s; northeast side of Greate St., toward the river); the old schoolhouse (1810; southwest side of Greate St., just southeast of Sheppard's Mill Rd.), possibly the oldest in the county; and the First Presbyterian Church (1835; north on the Greate St., toward Othello), once planted with seeds from Boston Commons elms.

Griggstown SOMERSET (across Millstone River from C 533) [Franklin Township]

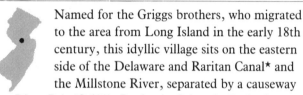

Named for the Griggs brothers, who migrated to the area from Long Island in the early 18th century, this idyllic village sits on the eastern side of the Delaware and Raritan Canal* and the Millstone River, separated by a causeway from River Rd. (C 533). Benjamin Griggs built the first gristmill on the Millstone River before 1733, George Washington marched his troops through the Millstone River Valley after the Battle of Princeton, and John Honeyman, a Continental spy who is given a large part of the credit for the successful surprise attack at Trenton, lived in Griggstown. Honeyman's house still stands on Canal Rd. across from Bunker Hill Rd., and there are many other 18th- and 19th-century houses along Canal Rd. The church dates from 1842. Note also the locktender's house and the barracks used by mule drivers on the canal. The Griggstown Historical Society is restoring the barracks, which will be converted into a museum with exhibits focusing on local history. For hours call 201-873-3050.

In the 1920s Griggstown became a summer resort for Norwegians living in Brooklyn. Their subdivision, which included Bunker Hill, Eriksson, Washington, and Lincoln rds., was followed by another subdivision, Sunset Hill, in which other Scandinavians also participated. After World War II, these summer homes became a year-round settlement, and until fairly recently Griggstown boasted a Scandinavian delicatessen with a considerable reputation.

Griggstown is adjacent to the Delaware and Raritan Canal State Park (see Kingston). This is a particularly lovely stretch of park suitable for walking, fishing, canoeing, and riding.

Delaware and Raritan Canal

Hackensack BERGEN (I 80, NJ 4, 17, C 503) 36,039

 Situated on the Hackensack River and once a busy ocean port, Hackensack was first settled by Dutch traders in the 1640s. The seat of Bergen County, it was until 1921 officially known as New Barbadoes (two of its early landholders came from Barbados). During the Revolution, the Hackensack green was used as a camping ground for both Continental and British regiments. The courthouse complex★ (Main and Essex sts.; 201-646-2472) includes buildings dating from 1910 to 1933. The courthouse is neo-classic, but the jail (designed by the same architect) has medieval turreting. The Administrative Building dates from the 1930s. The public buildings are open weekdays, 8:30–4:30; limited tours by appointment.

Also on the green is the First Reformed Church★ (42 Court St.), built in 1791 and altered in the mid-19th century. The congregation, organized in 1686, had its first building by 1696, and stones from this and the next church (built in 1728) are worked into the building. Many revolutionary soldiers are buried in the graveyard as is General Enoch Poor (a monument to him is just east of the green). George Washington and the marquis de Lafayette attended Poor's funeral. On the northwest corner of Church St. and Washington Place is the Bank House, built in the 1830s for the first bank in Bergen County. Traffic makes it hard to appreciate the green unless you leave your car.

A big treat in Hackensack is the USS *Ling*★ (Court and River sts.; 201-487-9493), a diesel-electric powered World War II submarine commissioned in 1945. After one patrol run, the *Ling* was decommissioned (in 1946), and from 1962 to 1971 she was used as a training vessel at the Brooklyn Navy Yard. Since 1973 the *Ling* has been berthed at the Hackensack River. Renovated, she is open for tours. In the building where you buy your tickets, there are exhibits dealing with the science and history of submarines, and submarine-related memorabilia. Open daily, weather permitting, 10–5 (the last tour starts at 4). Groups by appointment. The *Ling* can also be reserved for birthday parties.

Much of Hackensack's downtown has a 1920s or 1930s flavor. Note the stone Johnson Free Public Library (174 Main St.), built in 1901 and enlarged in 1915 and 1967; the

Oritani Field Club (1887; 18 E. Camden); and the group of 1930s Sears Roebuck stores (436 Main St.), a prototype of post–World War II shopping centers.

Hackettstown WARREN (US 46, NJ 57, 182, C 517)   8,850

Situated in the Musconetcong Valley between Schooley's and Scott's mountains, Hackettstown was known as Helm's Mills until, in the mid-18th century, according to local legend, Judge Samuel Hackett served free drinks to the local citizenry. (Hackettstown is reputed to be the only town in the United States with this name.) Hackettstown grew as the center for the surrounding agricultural area, as a service town for those vacationing on Schooley's Mountain (see Long Valley), and as a center for carriage manufacturing. In the mid-19th century, the Newark Methodist Conference located its Centenary Collegiate Institute, now Centenary College (400 Jefferson St.; 201-852-1400), in Hackettstown. Because of a fire, the campus was rebuilt; many of the imposing buildings you see today date from the late 19th century. The old commercial district is well preserved; note particularly the handsome buildings on Main, High, and Washington sts. and on Grand Ave. The state trout hatcheries, once located here, used to attract many visitors; although there are still fish hatcheries in town, the trout hatchery open to the public is in Pequest (see Oxford). At 106 Church St. in a 1915 house, is the Hackettstown Historical Society museum (201-852-8797), with a collection focusing on local and state history. Open Monday, 9–12; Wednesday and Friday, 9–12, 2–4. Groups and other times by appointment.

In the northeastern corner of Hackettstown is the Stephens section of Allamuchy Mountain Park (C 604; 201-852-3790). This 250-acre state park has picnic facilities, playgrounds, campsites, and hiking trails. In season you can also fish, cross-country ski, and sled.

About two miles north of Hackettstown on C 517 (turn east on unpaved Deer Park Rd.) is the Deer Park Pond Natural Area, 2,500 acres of untouched, undeveloped hardwood forest, old fields in various stages of succession, and Deer Park Pond. You can drive about four miles, park at the barricade, and explore on foot.

About two miles south of Hackettstown on Grand Ave. is the state's Rockport Pheasant Farm (201-852-3461). Children, particularly, might enjoy looking at the deer and the unusual birds to be seen in pens here. Open daily, 8–4. Across the road from the pens is one of the few remaining segments of the Morris Canal. You can take a short walk along the towpath in this beautiful spot.

Haddonfield   CAMDEN
C 573)   12,337

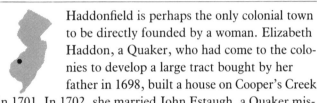

Haddonfield is perhaps the only colonial town to be directly founded by a woman. Elizabeth Haddon, a Quaker, who had come to the colonies to develop a large tract bought by her father in 1698, built a house on Cooper's Creek in 1701. In 1702, she married John Estaugh, a Quaker missionary (to whom, it is said, she had proposed), and in 1713 they moved to the site of Haddonfield. They had no children, and the name died out. Even their house is gone; the so-called Elizabeth Haddon house (201 Wood La.) now on the site was built in the 1840s; theirs had burned some 100 years before. Their story, though, has been immortalized by Longfellow in *Tales of a Wayside Inn.*

The town's location on the main road from Burlington to Salem (the Kings Highway, laid out in 1686 and still the main street) gave it a place in revolutionary history. The Indian King Tavern★ (233 Kings Highway; 609-429-6792) served as a tavern, an inn, a temporary statehouse, and a stop on the Underground Railroad. In it the Continental Congress, the New Jersey legislature, and the Council of Safety all met. Both the great seal of New Jersey and a law substituting the word "state" for "colony" in all official papers were adopted in legislative sessions here. Among those who stopped at the inn were Light Horse Harry Lee, Mad Anthony Wayne, and Lord Cornwallis, and the future Dolley Madison was the innkeeper's niece.

Built as a home in 1750 by a wealthy Philadelphia merchant, the inn was bought by the state in 1903, the first such historic structure to be managed by the state. Much of it is open for guided tours, Wednesday–Friday, 9–12, 1–6; Saturday, 10–12, 1–6; Sunday, 1–6; last tours at 11:30 and 5:30. If a holiday falls on a Monday, it is closed on Wednesday. Closed New Year's Day, Thanksgiving, and Christmas. Groups by appointment.

Although Haddonfield is primarily a suburb of Philadelphia, and a prosperous one at that, it has the feel of a town that had its own identity before it became a suburb. Over 450 colonial, federal, Victorian, and in other ways significant structures are included in its historic district,* which covers almost half the borough's total area. In 1858 on a farm near Haddonfield the first major dinosaur discovery in North America was made. (The dinosaur is now in Philadelphia, but there is a reproduction of it in the State Museum in Trenton.)

The Haddonfield Historical Society has its headquarters in Greenfield Hall* (343 Kings Highway E.); Lafayette and General Howe are both supposed to have stayed here. Most of the building dates from 1841, though the oldest part was built in 1747. Included in the society's collection are Elizabeth Haddon's Queen Anne table and mirror. Open March–December, Tuesday, 9:30–11:30 A.M. Thursday, 2–4, 2d Monday of the month, 7–9 P.M.; groups and other times by appointment. On the same property is the Samuel Mickle House,* often called the hip-roof house (though it actually has a gambrel roof), dated variously 1710 and 1742. There are many interesting buildings in town, many of them with identifying plaques. In addition to Kings Highway, you may want to walk or drive along Tanner, Lake, Grove, Chestnut, Centre, Potter, Clement, and Mechanics sts., Warwick Rd., and Washington, Colonial, Friends, Lincoln, W. Park, E. Park, E. Atlantic, and W. Cottage aves.

The Friends Meetinghouse (Friends Ave.) dates from 1851, and the cemetery wall was built of bricks from the old meetinghouse. Dolley Madison may have worshipped here. In the cemetery is a plaque honoring Elizabeth Haddon as a woman remarkable for "resolution, prudence, and charity." There is a little park around the lake below the meetinghouse.

During the period the Friends were split into two factions, this meetinghouse was used by the Orthodox group. The Hicksite building also dates to 1851 and can be found at Ellis and Haddon sts., entirely incorporated into a supermarket building.

At the corner of Kings Highway and Haddon Ave. is Haddon Fire Company 1 (609-429-2400), formed in 1764 and the second oldest fire company in continuous operation in the United States. (Mount Holly claims to have documents proving that it is the oldest; the Haddonfield company does not accept this claim, but has decided not to fight it.) There is a small museum at the firehouse, organized to suggest what a firehouse would have looked like 200 years ago. In the museum are two old pumpers, one dating from 1818 (it can be seen spraying water on Independence Hall in the movie *Cinerama*), the other from 1873. The collection also includes the fire company's original banner, a window from their original building (this building dates to 1952), and a marvelous collection of old metal toy fire equipment. The museum is open weekdays, 9–5, but you must call for an appointment first (the tour also includes the more modern equipment).

The so-called Elizabeth Haddon house at 201 Wood La. (between Marion and Hawthorne sts.) dates from 1844 and is built of local bricks taken from an earlier house on the site. A two-story brick still, built in 1713 and used by Elizabeth Haddon to produce medicinal whiskey, still stands, possibly the oldest building in Haddonfield.

Among the large houses on the Kings Highway heading north is the splendid Queen Anne-style building of the Bancroft School (at Hopkins La.), a private school specializing in children with mental and physical handicaps. Closer in town note also the former Third Methodist Church★ (301 Kings Highway), now the Haddon Fortnightly clubhouse, and the John Roberts house (344 Kings Highway E.).

Directly south of Haddonfield (take Warwick Rd., C 669) is Tavistock, which, with its 1980 population of nine, is New Jersey's smallest municipality. Basically a country club

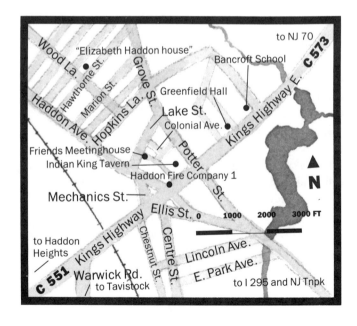

and a few houses, Tavistock managed to incorporate itself as a borough in the 1920s after the members of a country club in Haddonfield, dissatisfied because the club could not sell liquor on Sundays, moved their operation to a new site. Directly south of Tavistock is the borough of Lawnside, once a stop on the Underground Railroad. Established as a black community in 1840, Lawnside remains primarily black today.

In the Haddon Heights Public Library (608 Station Ave.; 609-547-7132) is a "corner museum" run by the Haddon Heights Historical Society (Haddon Heights is directly west of Haddonfield; you can pick up Station Rd. in Haddonfield off Chews Landing Rd., C 573). On display are various artifacts connected with the history of Haddon Heights, including the wooden turbine from a 1740 fulling mill. Open weekdays, 10–5.

Haledon PASSAIC (C 504, 509) 6,607

An excellent example of a streetcar suburb, Haledon developed as a satellite of industrial Paterson after trolley lines from the city were laid in the 1870s. What had been a small rural village became not only a working- and upper-middle-class suburb, but a late Victorian resort as well.

Haledon is the site of the American Labor Museum* (83 Norwood St.; 201-595-7953), one of the few museums in the country devoted to presenting post–industrial revolution history from the point of view of the worker. The museum is located in the house (1908, 1913), now a national historic landmark, of Pietro and Maria Botto, immigrants from northern Italy who came to work in the Paterson silk mills in the 1890s and built their house in 1908. The house is important to American labor history because it served as headquarters for the famous 1913 Paterson silk strike. For seven months in 1913, some 24,000 workers in Paterson, known then as Silk City, stayed off their jobs in an attempt to improve working conditions, and to achieve an eight-hour day and a minimum wage. Because of legal harassment, the workers were unable to meet in Paterson; the mayor of Haledon offered them a refuge in his city and the Bottos offered their house as a meeting place. Every Sunday some 20,000 workers would gather on the front lawn and listen to speeches by members of the I.W.W. (International Workers of the World, known as the Wobblies, who were coordinating the strike), including Elizabeth Gurley Flynn, as well as by the journalist John Reed and the writer Upton Sinclair.

Four rooms of the museum are furnished to reflect the living conditions of immigrants in 1913, other rooms have been converted to galleries for changing exhibitions, and the old-world gardens, including the grape arbor and bocci court, have been restored. The museum's extraordinary collection of photographs and other documents from the peak years of American immigration vividly re-create an important period of American history. The museum also sponsors seminars and other projects. Open Wednesday–Saturday, 12–4; Sunday, 1–4. Closed major holidays.

Just north of Norwood St., off Belmont Ave., is the Kossuth Street School★ (47 Kossuth St.), built at the turn of the century.

Hamilton Township

MERCER   (I 295, US 206, NJ 33, C 533)   82,801

 Considered by some to be a suburb of Trenton, Hamilton Township is actually one of the state's ten largest cities. Much of this growth has been recent, and although parts of the township were settled long ago (some so long ago that Hamilton has been called the richest archaeological site east of the Mississippi), this large (40 sq. miles) township is a city without a center. (Occasionally, though, you may come across reminders of an early crossroads village.)

Celebrating the Indian settlements of Hamilton is the new Early America History Museum (Kuser Rd.; 609-890-3503). The museum is dedicated to the memory of the Lenape Indians, who frequented the area between the Delaware River and Gropps Lake; on display are artifacts that until recently were readily found by anyone walking through that area. Call for hours.

The museum itself is located in Veterans Park (between Kuser and Klockner rds. east of I 295; 609-890-3684) behind the 1730s Abbott House★ (2200 Kuser Rd.; 609-585-1686), where New Jersey tried to sequester the state treasury during the Revolution. Restored and furnished as a house museum by the Historical Society of Hamilton Township, the house retains some of its original hinges and buttermilk paint. Open weekends, 12–5. Groups by appointment. In the 300-acre park are formal gardens, two greenhouses where the flowers used by the township are grown, meadows, woodlands, and a stream and lake where you can fish. There are also athletic fields and what is reputed to be the largest tennis complex in the country. Open daily, dawn to dusk.

West of Veterans Park is the Kuser Farm Mansion and Park (390 Newkirk Ave. or Kuser Ave; 609-890-3630). The mansion was built as a summer home in 1892 and became the Kusers' winter home in the 1920s. The family pioneered in several businesses (Fred Kuser helped finance the forerunner of 20th Century-Fox and was involved with the Roebling family in producing the Mercer car) and sports (tennis and flying), and the furnishings in the lavishly built house reflect their interests. A brochure is available for a self-guided tour of the grounds. The Jersey Valley Model Railroad Club, which houses its displays in the basement, has an annual open house one weekend in early December. Open April–November, Thursday–Sunday, 11–3 (last tour, 2:30). Groups by appointment.

Closer to the river is John A. Roebling Park (just south of S. Broad St.; access from Schiller or Wescott aves.; 609-989-6530), 250 acres of freshwater marsh and a lake. The park is beloved of bird watchers, and you can fish in the lake. There is also a small picnic area, and there are walking paths through the woods and among the shrubs near the picnic area. The oldest house in Mercer County, the Isaac Watson house* (151 Wescott Ave.; 609-882-2062), built in 1708, is the state headquarters for the D.A.R. and can be seen by appointment.

On the old New Jersey State Fairgrounds is the Johnson Atelier, the Technical Institute of Sculpture (60 Ward Ave. Ext.; 609-890-7777). This is a technologically advanced working foundry where artists can maintain control of their work. The atelier casts works by Seward Johnson, its founder, and others, including George Segal, Isaac Witkin, and the late Georgia O'Keefe. The working students can use the facilities for their own pieces after hours. Tours of the facility can be arranged for art students and sculptors interested in using the foundry. The galleries, which have widely varied exhibits, are open to the public Monday–Thursday, 10–4.

Hammonton ATLANTIC (US 30, 206,
NJ 54, C 542, 559, 561) | 12,298

Named for John Hammond Coffin, the son of an early 19th-century glass manufacturer, Hammonton was developed in the late 1850s by Charles K. Landis (see Vineland). Landis encouraged New Englanders and Italians to settle in Hammonton, and the Italian Carnival held on N. 3d St. in mid-July has been a major ethnic and religious festival for over 100 years. Fruit growing is important in the area around Hammonton, and the town serves as a center for the blueberry industry (see Pemberton). The world's largest blueberry plantation is here: 50 employees work on its 1,300 acres year round, 2,000 in season. New Jersey in fact leads all other states in the production of blueberries for consumption fresh (Michigan is first in total production). The Hammonton Historical Society's museum is located behind the town hall on Vine St. Open by appointment only (write J. G. Wilson, 643 Bellevue Ave., 08037). Some northern Jerseyites may be interested to know that US 206 begins in Hammonton.

Hammonton lies just south of Wharton State Forest (609-561-3262), New Jersey's largest state forest (over 100,000 acres) and the largest tract of public lands in the Pine Barrens. The Pine Barrens are a unique New Jersey treasure: 2,000 square miles unlike those anywhere else, the largest wilderness east of the Mississippi in the nation's most densely populated state. Because of the Pine Barrens' particular geological and human history, they contain an unusual variety of rare plants and animals—the barrens represent the southern limit for many northern species and the northern limit for many southern species. Beneath the ground surface lies an enormous reservoir of pure water. The land is generally sandy and much of it is forested with pine and oak, particularly pitch pine, which is better able than other species to withstand the frequent fires. There are cedar swamps and bogs in the barrens; there are forests of pygmy pine; and the rivers are often the color of tea. Seen from a car, the Pine Barrens often look featureless—mile after mile of sand and scrubby trees—but once you leave the paved roads and walk or canoe, you will be struck by the mysterious quiet and beauty. (It is important when hiking, though, to pay close attention to landmarks until you know the area well—it is easy to get lost.) Although much of the Pine Barrens seems devoid of people, there once was considerable industrial activity here: the iron found in the bogs was processed; there were paper mills and glassworks; and sphagnum moss, used by nursery owners to protect plants, and salt hay were gathered. Today, cultivation of cranberries and blueberries is the major economic activity, but what is perhaps most unusual about the Pine Barrens economy is that so many of those who live in the region have chosen not to enter the economic mainstream and support themselves by seasonal work related to the Pine Barrens' natural resources. Although the various grandiose schemes to develop the barrens as a resort area came to naught, large segments are now being used for retirement communities. Remains of old forges and villages are still apparent, varying from those noticeable only to a trained eye to the completely restored iron village of Batsto (see below). The fact that sand quickly obliterates traces of the past has led to the conjecture that the barrens might be serving as a criminal burial ground.

It was the pure water that attracted Joseph Wharton, the Philadelphia industrialist, to southern New Jersey. He had hoped to export water from the barrens to Philadelphia (and to grow and process sugar beets on his land), but the New Jersey legislature forbade the exportation of water, and his large holdings were eventually sold to the state of New Jersey. Included in these holdings was the village of Batsto,* where iron found in the Pine Barrens bogs was once converted to cannons, cannonballs, firebacks, and water pipes. The first furnace was erected here in the 1760s; the last was dismantled in 1858. In between, munitions had been manufactured for the Revolution and the War of 1812, and for a short time the furnace had been used by a glassworks. Batsto is now a historic museum village: the ironmasters' mansion has been restored, as have many of the workers' houses and various outbuildings. Craft demonstrations are given in some of the houses during the summer. The Wharton park headquarters are here, as are a nature center and nature trails; there is also a picnic area. The Batsto grounds are open year round, the buildings Memorial Day–Labor Day, 10–5; call about winter hours, which vary according to the budget. Closed New Year's Day, Thanksgiving, and Christmas.

Within the forest are many miles of hiking trails (including a stretch of the Batona Trail) and bridle paths. The lakes and rivers provide opportunities to swim, fish, and boat. Canoeing the Pine Barrens rivers, among them the Mullica,

Batsto, Wading, and Oswego, is very popular. The Oswego
River goes by the former paper manufacturing town of
Harrisville; there are ruins to explore here. Campsites range
from the primitive to screened cabins; some are accessible

Wharton State Forest

only by foot or canoe. All require permits. The forest also
has picnic areas, and in the winter you can ice-skate and
fish. For information and maps stop at the park headquarters in Batsto or at the ranger's station at Atsion* (US 206),

also a former iron town. Both are open daily (except New Year's Day, Thanksgiving, and Christmas), 8–4:30; April–October, Friday and Saturday evenings, for campers only, until 9. At the Wharton Forest Nature Center (609-561-3170) you will find a few exhibits related to the natural history of the area; guided nature tours can be arranged. Open Memorial Day–Labor Day.

A short distance east of Wharton State Forest is Penn State Forest (east off C 563; 609-296-1114), 3,000 acres with hiking trails and bridle paths, a picnic area, and Lake Oswego, where you can fish and boat.

Many field guides are available to help you explore the Pine Barrens. In planning excursions keep in mind the early 19th-century Batsto-Pleasant Mills United Methodist Church, and the village of Chatsworth (C 532, C 563), often referred to as the capital of the Pine Barrens; see also Pemberton, Tuckerton, Vineland, and Woodbine.

West of Hammonton is the Winslow Wildlife Management Area (access from US 322 and Piney Hollow, New Brooklyn-Blue Anchor, Malaga, and Folsom rds.), over 6,000 acres of woodland bisected by the Egg Harbor River (and the Atlantic City Expressway). These woods are open for hiking, bird watching, hunting, and fishing.

Hancock's Bridge SALEM

(C 606, 658)   [Lower Alloways Creek Township]

Hancock's Bridge is a tiny hamlet now, but the drawbridge over Lower Alloways Creek was considered so important during the Revolution that the militia was stationed there to guard it. In the early morning of 21 March 1778, 300 British troops under Colonel Charles Mawhood massacred some 30 militiamen asleep in Judge William Hancock's house (Main St.; 609-935-4373). This was the only time during the Revolution that a massacre occurred in a house; the building is now a historic house museum run by the state. Built in 1743 of brick in a Flemish-bond pattern, it is notable for the design on one side: the date and the initials of Judge Hancock and his wife, Sarah, are worked into the brick with a zigzag pattern below. Also on the property is a Swedish cedar-plank house (1640–45) moved to the site from the Tyler tract just south of Salem. The planks are of swamp cedar, shaped with an adz and dovetailed at the corners. Open Wednesday-Friday, 9–12, 1–6; Saturday, 10–12, 1–6; Sunday, 1–6.

About a half-mile west of the Hancock House on Poplar St. are the John Maddox Denn house (1725) and the Ware-Shourds house (1730), both of which served as hospitals after the massacre. South on Main St. a short way is the Lower Alloways Creek Friends Meeting House. It still has the original glass in many of its windows and early 19th-century cast-iron stoves made of New Jersey bog iron.

Buried in the local cemetery is Cornelia Hancock, who, as a very young woman, served as a nurse in the Civil War. Much beloved of the troops, she was the first woman to reach the battlefield at Gettysburg.

For an unsettling contrast, continue from Hancock's Bridge south and west on Alloway Creek Neck Rd., following the signs to the Salem Generating Station, an atomic energy installation. The distant sight of the reactor tower rising out of the tideland marshes would probably be striking in any context, but following so close on an 18th-century hamlet, it is eerie. Docked along the Delaware River shore of the property is the *Second Sun* (609-935-2660), a former ferryboat launched in 1901 that ran between Jersey City and New York City until 1967. The boat is now used as a small museum, with exhibits, many of them hands-on, dealing with the history and science of energy, including explanations and demonstrations of how the Salem plant works. Open Wednesday–Friday, 9–4; Saturday, 10–6; Sunday, 12–6. Group tours by appointment. Groups may also arrange tours of the generating facility.

South of Hancock's Bridge (off Alloway Creek Neck and Canton rds.) is the Mad Horse Creek Wildlife Management Area, over 5,800 acres, mostly of tidal marsh. The area, which is rich in waterfowl and frequented by migratory birds including Canada geese, snow geese, hawks, and eagles, is open for bird watching, hiking, fishing, and hunting.

Harrison   HUDSON   (I 280, C 508)   12,242

The population density of this small industrial town is relieved by West Hudson Park (Davis Ave.), a 43-acre county park whose rustic trails are designed to make the rolling land seem rural. In addition to playgrounds, the park contains wooded groves, grassy lawns, three lakes, and wading pools. The abundance of hardwood trees makes the fall colors noteworthy.

Although many of the industries for which it was once known have left, Harrison has kept as its motto "the bee-hive of industry," a designation bestowed on it by William Howard Taft before World War I. In 1987 its mayor had been in office longer than any other mayor in the country.

Helmetta MIDDLESEX (C 615) 955

In the center of Helmetta is the oldest snuff factory still operating in the United States. The present C. W. Helme Snuff Mill district* (Main St., Helmetta Pond, and the area between it and Manalapan Brook) dates from the 1880s, but the operation descends directly from a factory built in 1812. This large brick complex, set directly along the tracks of the old Camden and Amboy Railroad, dominates the western end of the town.

East of the factory, on Main St., note St. George's Church (1894) and the municipal building (1909), once a public school. Note also the plantings along the railroad.

The undeveloped 1,500-acre Jamesburg County Park is an island of Pine Barrens vegetation in a densely populated area. The park is being maintained as a conservation area, but nobody knows what will happen to the Pine Barrens species without the genetic variety of a larger population. You can fish and boat on the lake, and hike along the trails and fire roads; two endangered species live in the area, and the birding is considered excellent. Tours can be arranged by calling the Middlesex County Citizens' Conservation Council (201-846-1825).

Highland Lakes SUSSEX
(C 638) 2,888

This community, centered on Highland Lake, abuts Wawayanda State Park (201-853-4462), 11,000 acres of wilderness, mountains, lakes, and streams. Here you can picnic, fish, swim, hike, and, in season, cross-country ski, sled, and hunt. The several miles of bicycle and hiking trails include a section of the Appalachian Trail. In the park are some natural curiosities, among them the oldest rock to be seen in the Middle Atlantic states and northern white cedar rarely seen elsewhere in the state (here it is at the extreme southern limit of its habitat). The park is known for its display of rhododendron bloom in late June and early July, and for the quality of the fishing in Wawayanda Lake. Two natural areas, Wawayanda Hemlock Ravine and Wawayanda Swamp, occupy over 2,000 acres of the park. Open half-hour before sunrise to half-hour after sunset. Parking fee Memorial Day–Labor Day (except on Tuesday).

East of Wawayanda is the 2,000-acre Abram S. Hewitt State Forest (C 513; 201-853-4462) with extensive hiking trails and some spectacular views.

Directly south of Highland Lakes is Newark's 35,000-acre Pequannock Watershed (accessible from NJ 23 and C 515 and 636), much of it open for recreation. The necessary permits for hiking and skiing, fishing (there are five reservoirs), horseback riding, and hunting can be obtained from the Newark Watershed Conservation and Development Corporation (60 Park Place, Suite 2105, Newark 07102; 201-622-4521, or, within the reserve, 223 Echo Lake Rd., P.O. Box 319, Newfoundland 07435; 201-697-2850).

Highlands MONMOUTH (NJ 36) 5,187

Highlands takes its name from the bluffs that rise 200 feet above the Atlantic Ocean, said to be the first land sighted by ships sailing from the east. On the promontory between the Navesink River and Sandy Hook Bay is the Twin Lights Historic Site★ (Hillside Ave.; 201-872-1814, 201-566-2161), a twin-towered lighthouse decommissioned in 1949. The first twin towers of the Navesink Light Station were built in 1828, although a light was probably manned at this point in the mid-18th century; the present brownstone and brick buildings date from 1862. This was the first lighthouse in the United States to be equipped with Fresnel lenses (1841), and the first to be electrically powered (1898). When electrified, it was the strongest maritime light in the country, visible 22 miles out to sea. At Twin Lights, Marconi demonstrated that wireless telegraphy was commercially feasible: in 1899 he wired the results of the America's Cup yacht race from a ship 15 miles offshore to a receiving mast erected at Twin Lights. Twin Lights is now a museum; exhibits deal with navigation, lifesaving, lighthouse lenses, and telegraphy. A popular site (70,000 visitors a

year), Twin Lights also has a collection of New Jersey boats, soon to be housed in their own building. Also on the property is the lifesaving station from Sandy Hook, built in 1848 (the lifesaving service resulted from the initiative of a New Jersey congressman, William A. Newell; see Allentown). There is an overlook in front of the museum as well as in the towers, and on a clear day you have a wonderful view of Sandy Hook, the bay, the ocean, and the New York City skyline. Picnic sites available. Open daily, 9–5. Group tours by appointment.

138   *Highlands*

Sandy Hook

Beautiful views can also be had by driving along Scenic Drive (Ocean Blvd.) and from Mt. Mitchell overlook (see Atlantic Highlands). For information on beach fees, call 201-872-1515.

Off Navesink Ave. is Hartshorne Woods Park (201-842-4000), a 731-acre county facility with woods that once belonged to Richard Hartshorne, who acquired the land from

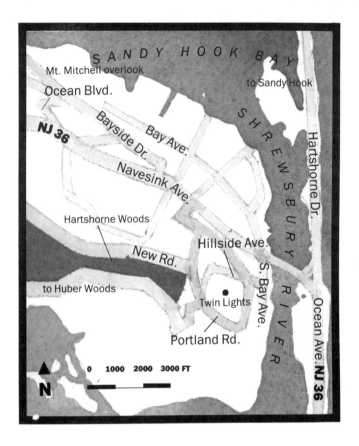

the Proprietors of New Jersey in the mid-17th century. Some of the woods have remained undisturbed, and many of the trees are very old. There are hiking and cross-country ski trails through this undeveloped area.

About three miles west of Highlands is the Huber Woods Activity Center (take Navesink Ave. west to Locust or Monmouth Ave.; from either of these turn on Browns Dock Rd.; 201-842-4000), with over 200 acres of county woods, primarily oaks, beech, and tulip trees, which once formed part of the Huber family's estate. The Monmouth County riding program, including its program for handicapped riders, is located here. Bridle paths and hiking and cross-country ski trails go through the woods. Groups and guided tours by appointment.

At the western edge of Huber Woods (off Cooper Rd.) the Hidden Hollow Hounds often holds its meetings. Visitors are welcome. The season runs from October to the first weekend in April; a midweek and weekend hunt are held, each beginning at 10. For information, call 201-741-9870.

To the north of Highlands is Sandy Hook, a six-mile-long sandspit extending into the Atlantic Ocean and the lower New York bay (to get there take NJ 36 east across the

Shrewsbury River and turn left). On this spit are long stretches of open beach, salt and freshwater marshes, back-dune forests, and a spectacular holly forest, as well as the Sandy Hook unit of the Gateway National Recreation Area, Fort Hancock, and the oldest original operating lighthouse in the United States. The lighthouse,* a national historic landmark, was first lit on 11 June 1764. It was built by a group of New York merchants who were appalled at the losses suffered by ships coming into New York harbor (until 1907 the Sandy Hook channel was the only entrance for large ships) and who sponsored two lotteries to raise funds for its construction. The first use of a steam-powered fog signal took place at Sandy Hook in 1868. When the light-house, a 103-foot octagon tower, was built, it stood some 500 feet from the water; it is now a mile and a half away.

One of the first U.S. Lifesaving Service boat stations was built at Sandy Hook in 1849 (it can be seen at Twin Lights). A Coast Guard unit at the point operates a Loran moni-toring station for the northeast chain of command.

Because of its strategic position, Sandy Hook has always been of military interest. The British and Continental troops fought over it during the Revolution, and the federal government began building a fort there before the Civil War. Fort Hancock,* a national historic landmark, dates from the 1890s, and for many years Sandy Hook was a prov-ing ground. (It was also a Nike missile site, which the army left looking like a dump.) You can still see the massive concrete batteries of the seacoast guns used to fire on ships at sea.

The Fort Hancock buildings,* one of which was designed by Robert E. Lee, have an air of deserted elegance. In the 1899 guardhouse and jail a museum features artifacts, pho-tographs, and other exhibits that show what life at the old fort was like. Open July and August, weekdays, 1–5; week-ends, 10–12, 1–5. The rest of the year open weekends only, 1–5. An officer's house is open weekends, 1–5, mid-May–September, and the Battery Potter, housing for a gun that rose up like the Radio City orchestra to fire and then sank back out of sight, is open weekends, 2–4, mid-May–September. Some Fort Hancock buildings are being used by colleges and other groups for environmental pro-grams. The National Marine Fisheries Service had its sec-ond most important (after Woods Hole) laboratory here until 1985, when 20 years of research were destroyed by a fire that was probably set by an arsonist.

Sandy Hook is heavily used for recreational purposes in the summer (some 2 million visitors a year), but although 75 to 95 percent of the visitors come to use the beaches, the area is also beloved of bird watchers and other naturalists. At the Spermaceti Cove visitor center,* housed in an 1894 lifesaving station, is a small museum. You can see a slide show at the center, and maps and other material to help you tour Sandy Hook on your own are available. A wide range of tours and special events is offered at Sandy Hook, some dealing with the natural aspects of the spit, others with Fort Hancock or the Coast Guard facility. Many of them start from the visitor center; to find out what is available and whether reservations are required call 201-872-0092 or 201-872-0115. Visitor center open daily, 8:30–5. A self-guided nature tour leaves from the center. Notice the prickly pears, the state's only native cactus (often seen with the leaves trimmed by rabbits), and the holly forest with 150-year-old trees that are 50 to 70 feet tall. Parking fee Memorial Day–Labor Day.

Hightstown MERCER (NJ 33, C 539, 571)   4,581

Settled in the 1720s by John and Mary Hight, Hightstown owed its period of greatest prosperity to the railroads. After the Camden and Amboy arrived in 1831, Hightstown became the transportation hub for the surrounding agricultural country, shipping produce to New York and Philadelphia. Growth stopped when the railroad was rerouted farther north to connect with Trenton, but not before the well-off farmers had built the splendid Victorian homes that today distinguish Hightstown. The last passenger train went through in 1939, but considerable railroading interest was generated recently with the discovery of some of the stone sleepers that carried the John Bull, the country's first steam locomotive, into Hightstown.

Peddie Lake, in the center of town, was a popular fishing lake until the construction of the New Jersey Turnpike and Twin Rivers filled it with silt. Recently dredged and stocked, it should be open for fishing soon.

The Peddie School (S. Main St. between E. Ward St. and Etra Rd., C 571), a preparatory school founded in 1864, has a handsome campus; note particularly the white octagonal house. The school runs a theater by the lake in the summer.

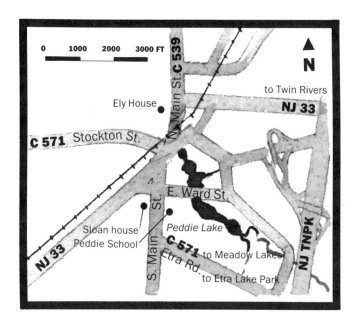

There are splendid houses across the street from the campus, among them the Samuel Sloan house* (1856; 238 S. Main). A characteristic feature of Hightstown architecture is the grillwork on many of the houses; this is particularly in evidence on Stockton St. (C 571) near the intersection with Main St.

The Ely House (164 N. Main St.; 609-443-6527) is the headquarters and museum of the Hightstown-East Windsor Historical Society. The house, which dates from the 1840s, features Indian artifacts, a candlestick holder and other objects belonging to John and Mary Hight, relics from the John Bull locomotive, and period furnishings. Open March–June and September–November, 1st and 3d Sunday of the month, 2–5; 3d Monday, 8–9 P.M. Each spring the society sponsors an antique doll show.

Just east of town on C 571, on the site of a former estate, is Meadow Lakes, a 103-acre community for 400 senior citizens, with a completely staffed medical facility. Farther east on 571 is Etra Lake Park. Recently opened, the park has a two-mile running trail, picnic tables, play areas, an environmental center, a pavilion, and 80 open acres.

A mile or two east of Hightstown on NJ 33 is Twin Rivers, New Jersey's first planned unit development. Nearly half the population of East Windsor Township lives on its 700-plus acres. The community has its own schools and shopping center and a mix of apartments, single-family houses, and townhouses, and has attracted the scrutiny of countless researchers, from sociologists and anthropologists to specialists in energy conservation.

Hoboken HUDSON (Hudson River between Holland and Lincoln tunnels) 42,460

The country's first brewery was established in Hoboken, a community first settled by Dutch from New Amsterdam, in 1642. Beer is no longer brewed in Hoboken—the smell that usually permeates the town is that of coffee from the Maxwell House plant along the Hudson—and Hoboken's current character was shaped more by the Stevens family than by the earlier settlers. Colonel John Stevens, a revolutionary war officer and a famous inventor, in 1784 purchased an estate known as Hobuck Island, which had been confiscated from its Tory owner, and auctioned off lots in what he referred to as the New City of Hoboken. Stevens has been called the father of American railroading, and he and his sons can take credit for many of the events that happened first in Hoboken. Stevens inaugurated the world's first regular steam ferry service (in 1811). He was responsible for the first successful American run of a locomotive (the tracks were near Newark and Washington sts.) and the invention of the T-rail and the ironclad ship. His son John Cox Stevens founded the first yacht club in the United States (in 1844); it was located near 12th St. John Cox Stevens also originated the first America's Cup race. His brother Edwin made possible the founding (in 1870) of Stevens Institute of Technology, one of the first colleges in the country to offer a degree in mechanical engineering (and, many years later, one of the first to require freshmen to have personal computers). Together the two sons built New Jersey's first railroad.

Other Hoboken firsts include the first organized game of what has become modern baseball. In 1846, a uniformed team (only one of the teams wore uniforms) played with stipulated rules on the cricket fields known as the Elysian Fields. What remains of the Elysian Fields can be seen at 10th St. and Hudson, and a commemorative plaque is to be found at 11th and Washington sts. The first international cricket match in which the United States took part was played in 1859 (the United States was badly beaten). And in 1984 Hoboken was the first city in New Jersey to declare itself a nuclear-free zone.

In the early years of the 19th century Hoboken was a popular resort. Visitors came by ferry from New York to frequent the beer gardens, taverns, and boarding houses, and to enjoy the river walks. (Sybil's Cave by the river was a popular meeting place for lovers until a New York salesgirl was murdered there; newspaper accounts of her death inspired Edgar Allen Poe's "The Mystery of Marie Roget.") Washington Irving and Martin Van Buren were among those who visited John Jacob Astor at his villa at 2d and Washington sts.

By the mid-19th century Hoboken was an active manufacturing center, but of the many industrial firms once in Hoboken, only Maxwell House (12th St., near the river) remains. Over the past decade or so the old Keuffel and Esser complex* (3d St., Jefferson, and Grand), part of which dates to the 1880s, has been being converted to apartments. The factory, which used to manufacture precision instruments, is evidently one of the first to be converted into housing. Keuffel and Esser was the first company in the country to manufacture slide rules, and during World War II it raised spiders in Hoboken to supply webs for telescope crosshairs.

At the beginning of the 20th century Hoboken was an important shipping center, and during World War I it was a major port of embarkation for American troops. There were

taverns along River St., and like many other port cities, Hoboken had a reputation as a wide-open town, even during Prohibition. *On the Waterfront* was filmed in Hoboken, and in the 1950s the Port Authority spent considerable sums to refurbish piers, but with the rise in container shipping, shipping activity in Hoboken inevitably declined. The Port Authority, which leases the city-owned marine terminal, plans to create a mixed-use waterfront development at the terminal.

The trans-Hudson train tubes were opened in 1904, and the Erie-Lackawanna's railroad and ferry terminal* (Hudson Place at the river), which also served as a warehouse, was built in 1907. This wonderful building with its striking copper roof is said to have been the first American building with platform train sheds. In 1930, one of the very early electric trains left from this terminal, with Thomas Alva Edison at the controls. Ferry service continued until 1966; it is scheduled to start up again in 1987. The terminal is now the second busiest passenger terminal in the state, and a festival celebrating it and the city is held each year the last Saturday in September.

For a time Hoboken was a wealthy suburb. In the late 1920s it was considered bohemian. At one point there were 20 legitimate theaters in operation, and Christopher Morley, who ran a highly successful theater season in Hoboken, called it "the last seacoast of Bohemia."

The Stevens Institute of Technology demolished John Stevens's mid-19th-century house in 1959, but the view from the building that replaced it makes clear why he built his house on that spot. The gatehouse (1853) from the Stevens estate remains, as does the college's first building (5th and Hudson), designed by Richard Upjohn. At the northern end of the 55-acre campus, fraternities occupy what were once the homes of wealthy commuters. At the college's Davidson Laboratory, named for a Stevens Institute faculty member who towed model ships in the swimming pool to learn how they worked, scientists have worked on the design of America's Cup ships and nuclear submarines. Among the recent ideas being looked into is the development of a high-speed catamaran for ferry service on the Hudson River. In 1985 Stevens Institute made national news when it awarded an honorary degree to Hoboken native son Frank Sinatra, to the displeasure of many students and members of the faculty.

Although the charms of Hoboken have been discovered by New York commuters, and many old-timers worry about overgentrification (you may run into a sign saying, "Speculators, keep out."), the wide main street (Washington) still has an old-time, small-town air. There are no tall buildings on it (tall buildings are, however, gradually appearing, particularly at the northern edge of town), and although the boutiques are coming, you can still find shoe repair shops and dry cleaners and no-meter parking.

Almost every street in Hoboken has interesting buildings, from rows of brownstones to mid-19th-century churches to late 19th-century firehouses to early 20th-century public buildings and hotels. There are also a large number of restaurants for the size of the town. The southern Hoboken historic district includes parts of Bloomfield, Hudson, Newark, River, Washington, 1st, 2d, 3d, and 4th sts. and Observer Highway, but you should also take in Willow Ave., Court, Garden, Jefferson, Park, Clinton, and Grand sts., and the rest of the numbered streets. Particularly interesting are the city hall★ (86–98 Washington St.); the Church of the Holy Innocents (Willow and 6th); the Trinity Episcopal Church (Washington and 6th), another Upjohn design; the public library (Park and 5th); and Our Lady of Grace Church (Willow and 4th), featured in *On the Waterfront.* The strong German influence on Hoboken is apparent along Hudson St.: at St. Matthews Lutheran Church (8th St.) the words "gerichtet 1877" can be seen; the Union Club (6th St.), now scheduled for conversion to condominiums, was the Deutsche Club until World War I.

Ho-Ho-Kus BERGEN (Garden State Pkwy exit 168S, NJ 17, C 502) 4,129

 Ho-Ho-Kus, an early Dutch settlement, has an Indian name, which you will see printed with and without the hyphens. Some of the older buildings remain: along E. Saddle River Rd., for example, are three 18th-century stone houses (at 745,★ 825,★ and 933★). At 335 N. Franklin Tnpk is the Hermitage★ (201-445-8311), a national historic landmark building operated as a house museum. Also known as the Colonel Marc Provost house, it has associations with George Washington, Aaron Burr (he married Theodosia Provost), and the marquis de Lafayette. The nucleus of the house was built in the early 18th century; it was later remodeled, and a wing with Gothic Revival details was added in 1845. The museum has a special program each month, and features a collection of dolls and French costumes. Generally open Wednesday and the 3d Sunday of each month, 1–4, but around the museum's two annual crafts boutiques (one just before Easter, the other just before Christmas) the house is closed, so it is always best to call first. Groups by appointment.

Holmdel MONMOUTH (Garden State Pkwy exit 114, C 520) 8,447

 One of the oldest settlements in Monmouth County, the township of Holmdel was named for the Holmes family, Baptists who came here in the mid-1660s to escape religious persecution in Massachusetts. The first Baptist sermon in New Jersey was preached here in the late 1660s. The township has been growing rapidly, more than doubling its population over the last 25 years. (In the village note the 19th-century Dutch Reformed Church★ at 41 Main St.)

About two miles north of Holmdel village is Holmdel Park (take NJ 34 or Holmdel Rd. north to Longstreet Rd; turn right on Longstreet; 201-946-2669). Within this 330-acre county park is the mid-18th-century Longstreet Farm,★ which is being run by the county parks system as an 1890s working farm. Many of the furnishings in the house, the first part of which dates to the 1700s, were the Longstreet family's original belongings and reflect several periods. You can watch as the park workers go about the regular activities of the farm, and there are self-guided tours. Many special events, such as corn festivals, kite building, and hay rides, are scheduled. Open daily except Christmas. Memorial Day–Columbus Day, 9–5; the rest of the year, 10–4. On weekends and holidays, ½-hour tours of the house from noon until closing. Groups by appointment.

Also within the park is the 20-acre Holmdel Arboretum, with specimen plantings of trees, bushes, and plants suitable for growing in Monmouth County. In the park there are mature stands of American beech, hickory, and white, red, and chestnut oaks; over ten miles of trails (because the terrain is rolling, not all the walks are easy); a fitness trail; tennis courts; an activity center (open weekdays, 9–4; 201-946-2669); picnic areas; shuffleboard courts; and, in winter, opportunities for cross-country skiing, sledding, and skating. This is a popular park (over 1 million visitors a year), and in the spring and fall it sometimes closes for an hour or so because the parking lots are full. Guided nature walks by appointment.

On the edge of the park is the Holmes-Hendrickson House* (Longstreet and Robert rds.; 201-462-1466), a mid-18th-century house run as a museum by the Monmouth County Historical Association. Unusually well preserved when the association acquired it, the house contains excellent examples of mid-18th-century furnishings and working tools of 18th-century farm life. Open June–October, Tuesday, Thursday, Sunday, 1–4; Saturday, 10–4. Admission fee.

Southeast of the park are the Bell Laboratories where Telstar was developed. Over 4,000 people work in the Saarinen-designed building, where in 1962 the first telecast from a satellite was received and in 1964 traces of cosmic energy presumed to have originated in the big bang with which the universe began were recorded for the first time. Not open for tours.

Just south of the laboratories at the intersection of Middletown and Stillwell rds. the Hidden Hollow Hounds (201-741-9870) frequently holds its meets. Visitors are welcome. The season runs from October to the first weekend in April, with regular midweek and weekend hunts, which begin at 10.

North of Holmdel Park is the Garden State Arts Center at Telegraph Hill (Garden State Pkwy exit 116; 201-442-9200). Seating over 5,000 people, this open shell is the scene of concerts in the summer, both popular and classical. The plaza is also used for special events, particularly ethnic celebrations. On either side of the plaza are what's left of the parks that used to be in this spot; there are limited opportunities for picnicking and hiking and a nice view from Telegraph Hill.

Hopatcong SUSSEX (C 602, 607, 631) 15,531

The borough of Hopatcong lies on the western shore of Lake Hopatcong, the largest lake to fall entirely within New Jersey. Reports of monsters in the lake can be found as far back as the 17th century. In the 1750s, the lake was dammed by ironmakers, and in the 1830s, construction of the Morris Canal, which ran from Newark to Phillipsburg, raised its level. Situated over 900 feet above sea level, with 40-odd miles of shoreline and clear water, the lake became a popular summer resort. Before World War I it was known as a haven for burlesque performers—Bert Lahr, for example, was a regular visitor. Over the past 25 years or so, as summer cottages have been winterized and new developments built, Hopatcong has seen its year-round population increase by over 350 percent, and there is some concern about traffic congestion and speeding on the lake as well as possible eutrification.

At the southwestern end of the lake is the very popular Hopatcong State Park (201-398-7010), over 110 acres with facilities for picnicking, swimming, and fishing (a small-boat launch is also available). The lake is considered one of the best spots in the state for ice fishing. Toward the southern end of the park you can see some reminders of the Morris Canal, including the dam, gatehouse, and one of the water turbines that lifted canal boats up the inclined planes. The Lake Hopatcong Historical Society runs a small museum near the basketball courts. Open June–August, Wednesday, 1–4; September–mid-November and mid-March–May, Wednesday, 1–4, Saturday, 11:30–2:30. The park is open daylight hours throughout the year; in the summer an admission fee is charged.

Hope   WARREN   (C 519, 521)   1,468 (township)

Although the nearness of I 80 may soon change Hope's appearance radically, the town today presents a striking concentration of 18th- and early 19th-century buildings, many of them of local bluestone, with little intrusion from later periods. Settled by Moravians from Pennsylvania in 1769, it may represent one of the country's first planned communities. The Moravians bought 1,000 acres from Samuel Green, who had been their host when they passed through the area on missionary trips up the Delaware and had become interested in their church (he even tried to give them the land). The town plan was devised in 1774, and in 1775 the community's name was changed from the original Greenland to Hope. The community began to decline in the 1790s, and in 1807 the inhabitants were ordered by the mother church to sell it; the last service in Hope took place in April 1808.

The first building to be erected (c. 1769–70) was the

gristmill (north side of High St. east of the bridge). It has burned twice but still retains its original walls. Flour was produced here for George Washington's troops when they were quartered at Jockey Hollow, and the mill continued to operate well into the 20th century. At the rear of the mill is the original millrace, cut through solid slate to a depth of 22 feet. The stone bridge that crosses Beaver Brook, although not built by the Moravians, dates to 1807. The little building by the bridge was once the tollhouse. It is now a local museum. Open weekends, 1–4, Memorial Day–Labor Day, and for special events.

If the museum is not open, you can pick up a leaflet that describes a walking tour of the town at many of the local stores. Rye whiskey and beer were brewed at the distillery (1775), and services were held at the Gemeinhaus, or community house (1781), on the southwest corner of High St. and C 519-521. Now a bank, the building has also been a tavern and a hotel, and in 1824 it served as Warren County's first courthouse. The Moravian cemetery (off High St.) dates to 1773; the graves are arranged according to the date of death, and the numbers on the slabs correspond to a chronological list of burials in the Moravian Archives in Pennsylvania. The earliest residence in town (1775) is across from the distillery; the farm manager lived in the house and stored the farm produce in the barn. At the northeast corner of Union St. and Moravian Alley is the American House Hotel (c. 1799–1803), originally a schoolhouse. It is hoped the building can be restored before it is too late. There are several other 18th-century houses and stores in the center of Hope (the historic district* encompasses Union, High, Hickory, and Walnut sts., C 519, C 521, Beaver Brook, and the millrace), and on the outskirts as well—for example, the Israel Swayze house and outkitchen, dating from 1759, on C 519 a little over a mile south of town, and what is often called the Moravian Farmhouse on the west side of the Hope-Blairstown Rd, ¾ of a mile north of town. In addition, St. John's United Methodist Church and St. Luke's Episcopal Church (High St. south of the intersection with Hickory St.) are worth a glance; both date to 1832.

Roughly 5½ miles south of Hope on the west side of C 519 is the Four Sisters Winery (201-475-3671). Associated with a 400-acre fruit and vegetable farm, this relatively new winery gives regularly scheduled tours on weekends and by appointment other times. Open April–December, Monday–Saturday, 11–6, Sunday, 12–6; January–March, Wednesday–Sunday, 11–5.

Northeast of Hope is Jenny Jump State Forest (take C 519 northeast to Shiloh Rd. and turn right; 201-459-4366), 1,000 acres with facilities for picnicking, camping, and hunting, a playground, a lookout point, hiking trails, nature trails, and areas suitable for cross-country skiing and sledding. This is a good place to look at fall foliage.

A mile or two southeast of Hope (take 519 east to C 611 and turn right) is the Land of Make Believe (Great Meadows Rd.; 201-459-5100), a commercial theme park for children. Open daily, 10–5, 3d Saturday in June to Labor Day, Memorial Day weekend and weekends in June, Sundays in September. Admission charge.

Hopewell MERCER (C 518, 569)

2,001 (borough) 10,893 (township)

An attractive small town in the midst of a rapidly growing township, Hopewell was settled in the 17th century. One of its first residents was a son of Richard and Penelope Stout (see Middletown). On the north side of the main street, in a handsome mansard-roofed 19th-century house (with a 20th-century addition), is the Hopewell Museum (28 E. Broad St.; 609-466-0103). Its collection is made up almost entirely of items donated over the last 60 years by Hopewell residents, and rotating exhibits focus on local life from colonial times to the present. Open Monday, Wednesday, and Saturday, 2–5. A little farther west is the Old School Baptist Church (north side of W. Broad St.), a brick and stucco structure first built c. 1747 and rebuilt c. 1825. John Hart, one of the signers of the Declaration of Independence, is buried in the cemetery.

Across the street (19 W. Broad St.) is a pre-1756 (but much altered) clapboard building that housed the first Baptist school of higher education in the state, founded in 1756 by the Reverend Isaac Eaton, the pastor of the Baptist church in Hopewell. Eaton's first pupil was James Manning, founder of Brown University. Other buildings of interest include the railroad station★ (Railroad Place), built in 1876 and recently converted to restaurants and apartments, and the Second Empire-style Valley Inn (E. Broad St.).

Highfields (Van Dyke Rd.), the home of Charles and Anne Lindbergh when their young son was kidnapped (see Flemington), now belongs to the state, which uses it as a home for boys.

The corporate education center of AT&T Technology

(Carter Rd., C 569; 609-639-4500) features in its lobby art exhibits in all media. The shows, which change about every two months, focus on the work of area artists. Open weekdays, 9–4, weekends, 2–5.

Jamesburg MIDDLESEX (C 522) 4,114

Jamesburg's first settlers, Scots fleeing religious persecution, arrived in the late 17th century, and its first mill dates to 1734, but the town's period of greatest prosperity began 100 years later when the railroad came through. Jamesburg eventually had two railroad lines and three depots and became the commercial and social center for the township and the surrounding agricultural area. This prosperity continued until after World War II.

Much of the town's growth can be attributed to James Buckelew, whose great-grandfather had arrived in the area around 1715. In 1832 Buckelew purchased Lakeview* (203 Buckelew Ave.; 201-521-0068), originally a small 17th-century farmhouse overlooking the millpond (now Lake Manalapan), and enlarged it into a 23-room mansion with a colonnaded porch overlooking the lake. Buckelew farmed some 4,000 acres (and was the first in the area to use marl on his land), supplied 700 mules for the Delaware and Raritan Canal, established the Freehold and Jamesburg Agricultural Railroad, and helped establish the First National Bank. Because a black child was excluded from the existing school, Buckelew built another school, open to all, which, at the dedication ceremony, was referred to as the James B. School; James B. eventually became Jamesburg. When President-elect Lincoln was in Trenton on his way to his inauguration, he rode in Buckelew's coach from the Clinton St. station to the capitol. The house, also known as Buckelew's Mansion, is now open as a house museum, and Lincoln's coach is one of the items on display. Among those who helped restore the mansion were students from the New Jersey Training School for Boys. This school was built in 1867 as the New Jersey State Reform School on a large farm owned by Buckelew, which may have been the site of a mid-18th-century French and Indian War stockade. The museum has some period furnishings, items relating to local history, and a high-school memento room. In the front yard are some track from the Camden and Amboy Railroad and several anchoring stones. Special events, including a Christmas program, are scheduled several times a year. Open Wednesday–Sunday, 12–4. Guided tours by appointment.

Although Jamesburg is Middlesex County's most densely populated community (over 4,000 people in less than one square mile), it abuts a county park that is almost as large as the borough. Thompson Park includes Lake Manalapan, where you can fish, boat, and skate; there are also athletic fields, hiking trails (including one accessible to the handicapped), picnic areas, tennis courts, playgrounds, and a small zoo. Part of the park has been designated a bird sanctuary. Several horse and dog shows, as well as two concerts, take place in the summer.

Just west of Jamesburg (take Forsgate Dr.) is Rossmoor, a retirement community built around a golf course. The land was once an early 20th-century estate and dairy farm—the clubhouse was formerly a residence—and each hole on the east course is modeled on a famous hole from a British course.

Jefferson Township

MORRIS   (NJ 15, C 699)   16,413

Located in Jefferson Township, the northwesternmost township of Morris County, is the Mahlon Dickerson Reservation (Weldon Rd.; 201-829-0474). Dickerson, a Morris County native, served as governor of the state, as U.S. senator, and as secretary of the navy under Presidents Jackson and Van Buren. In this large (1,300 acres) county park there are facilities for camping and picnicking, as well as hiking and cross-country skiing trails and a ballfield. From Headley Overlook, 1,300 feet above sea level, you can see the surrounding area, including the northern end of Lake Hopatcong.

Jersey City   HUDSON   (NJ Tnpk exits

14A, B, C, US 1, 9, NJ 440)   223,532

Jersey City, the state's second most populous city, has been the state's first in other ways: the site of the state's first permanent settlement (1660), the first place to be occupied by the enemy in the Revolution (1776). It was one of the first to declare itself a nuclear-free zone, and it can also boast a variety of other, perhaps less significant, firsts: the first automobile tunnel under a river has one end in Jersey City; the first woman elected to the House of Representatives in the eastern United States and the first native-born American to fly a balloon in the continental United States came from Jersey City; the first professional heavyweight fight to produce $1 million in gate receipts and the first mass production of a modern wood-and-graphite pencil took place in Jersey City.

Although there were sporadic settlements in the early years of the 17th century, difficulties with the Indians and with the authorities in Manhattan caused the early residents to leave, and it was not until 1660 that a permanent settlement, known as Bergen (or Bergan), was formed. You can still trace the outline of the original town square—the area bounded by Newkirk, Van Reypen, and Vroom sts. and Tuers Ave., surrounding Bergen Square, south of Journal Square. Alexander Hamilton saw the potential for developing Jersey City as a transportation center and formed an association similar to the one he had established for Paterson. His plans never materialized: he was killed in 1804; until 1834, New York asserted its right to control the Hudson to the low-water mark on the west bank, thus preventing Jersey City from developing its own waterfront; and the railroads came to own the association's waterfront land.

The city nevertheless developed as a transportation and manufacturing center, and some sense of its former prosperity can be seen in the abundance of extravagant architecture; there are any number of architecturally exuberant churches and public buildings to be seen in Jersey City. Like many of the state's other cities, Jersey City suffered an economic decline, but in the 1970s New Yorkers and others rediscovered it as a desirable place to live, and many of the city's brownstones and row houses are being rehabilitated and its commercial buildings converted into condominiums. With plans to convert the National Guard armory into a studio, there are hopes that Jersey City will become a major center for the film industry. At the same time, developers have been working on ambitious plans for the waterfront. Like other rediscovered cities, Jersey City has become involved in the "cargo versus quiche" controversy, a commercial equivalent to the conflict between longtime residents and newcomers in gentrifying neighborhoods: many of the few shipping-related businesses that have managed to survive along the waterfront are being forced to relocate by the more glamorous developments.

There are many different neighborhoods to explore, and within many neighborhoods there are great contrasts between buildings in different states of renovation. The Paulus Hook area is a 19th-century district that includes portions of York, Grand, Sussex, Morris, Essex, Greene, Washington, Warren, and Van Vorst sts. It is bounded on the east by the Colgate factory with its unusual clock tower. Colgate began manufacturing in Jersey City in 1847.

To the west of the Paulus Hook area is the Van Vorst district, with both 19th- and 20th-century structures; it includes Jersey Ave. and Varick, Barrow, Grove, Wayne, Mercer, Montgomery, York, Bright, and Grand sts. Hamilton Square represents a 19th-century residential square, and just east of Hamilton Square is Manila Ave., once Grove St. but renamed in honor of the large Filipino population. Journal Square in the heart of the city boasts the Stanley Theater, a huge 1928 Art Deco building with a large copper sign (it now belongs to the Jehovah's Witnesses); Loew's Jersey, another Art Deco theater, with a terra-cotta façade and an ornate Spanish Baroque interior, built in the late 1920s and one of the first theaters to be engi-

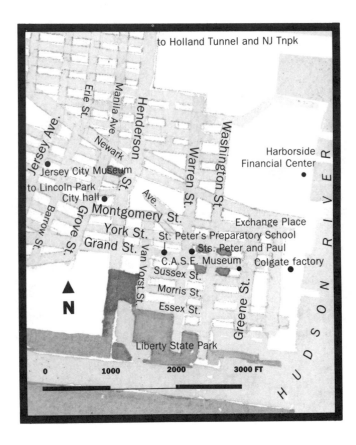

neered expressly for the new talking pictures (Hartz Mountain Industries, its owners, closed it in 1986 and may demolish it); the 15-story office building at 26 Journal Square, with its marble lobby, molded ceiling designs, and ornamental frieze. Just north of Journal Square (Newark Ave. between Kennedy and Tonnele) is an Indian enclave.

The county courthouse (Newark Ave. at Central), a large Beaux Arts building completed in 1910, dominates a city block. Inside are murals painted by Howard Pyle, F. D. Millet, Kenyon Cox, Charles Turner, and Edwin Howland Blashfield. Note also the old Hudson County Jail in the same block. The city hall (1896; Montgomery and Grove sts.), the post office building (Montgomery and Washington sts.), and the main library (1899; 472 Jersey Ave. at Mercer St.) all testify to the size and former wealth of Jersey City.

The Old Bergen Church (the west side of Bergen Ave. at Highland Ave.) belongs to the oldest organized congregation west of the Hudson (it received its charter in 1660). The present building, which dates from 1741 and was built with stones taken from earlier buildings, seems unusually sedate in the context of Jersey City's architectural exuberance—for example, directly across Bergen Ave. is the fanciful brickwork of St. Aedans.

On the top floor of the main library is the Jersey City Museum (201-547-4514), a small museum with two rooms devoted to changing exhibitions, a room devoted to a display of paintings and objects from the permanent collection, and a gift shop. Open Thursday–Saturday, 11:30–4:30; Wednesday, 11:30–8. Closed on Saturday in the summer. If possible, use the stairs rather than the elevator to get to or from the museum; note the swinging gate that can close off upper floors.

The C.A.S.E. Museum of Russian Contemporary Art in Exile (80 Grand St.; 201-332-7962) is housed in a brownstone once used by the city (across the street from the Ukrainian National Center, also an interesting building, now condominiums). Run by the Committee for the Absorption of Soviet Emigrees, the museum features paintings by non-state-sanctioned Soviet artists and Soviet emigrees. Open weekdays, 10–4.

At Jersey City State College (2039 John F. Kennedy

Blvd.; 201-547-6000), the Vodra Gallery shows paintings.
Open weekdays, 11–4. For information on other public
events at the college, call 201-547-3222.

Jersey City

The Jersey City Medical Center★ (Baldwin Ave. and
Montgomery St.) is a large Art Deco complex built in the
1920s. The city removed some of its ornamental grillwork

and will eventually relocate the entire hospital in new buildings, but at least two of its buildings are being converted to rental apartments.

Here are some other buildings you might want to look out for: near the Paulus Hook and Van Vorst districts are St. Peter's Preparatory School, which is over 100 years old; the New Jersey Guarantee Trust Company (Montgomery St.), a splendid late 19th-century extravaganza with the relief of a dog guarding the entrance, now converted to condominiums; Sts. Peter and Paul (near Grand St.); the Congregation of the Sons of Israel (Grove St.), with its lions; the 1888 building at 133 Grand St., with its decorative red tiles (the T. J. Stewart building at 88–92 Erie St. also dates from 1888 and has tiles produced by the Perth Amboy Terra Cotta Company); the Ionic House (1835–40) at 83 Wayne St.; the Grace Van Vorst Church (268 Second St.); the Salem Community Center (northwest corner of Clinton and Crescent aves.), formerly the home of the Jersey City Athletic Club (1886). On John F. Kennedy Blvd. you will find the First Baptist Church (at Fairmount), a small stone castle; Temple Bethel (at Harrison); St. Peter's College (at Montgomery), from which Will Durant received a bachelor's and a master's degree; Jersey City State College (at Audubon), founded in the late 1920s as a teachers' college. Among the larger buildings being converted to housing are the Betz Brewery, the Joseph Dixon Crucible Company complex, the former Baker Chocolate factory (Barrow St.), and Pohlmann Hall. You may also find your eye caught by many of the firehouses; in any case, this list only skims the surface of Jersey City's interesting buildings.

Liberty State Park (exit 14B from the northern extension of the New Jersey Tnpk; Henderson St. and Johnston and Jersey aves. out of Jersey City; 201-435-0736) consists of 800 acres with 2½ miles of shoreline, land that in the early 1970s was an industrial wasteland. Opened in 1976, the park is a tribute to the perseverance of Morris Pesin. A Jersey City native who had fought to save the trees along the John F. Kennedy Blvd. and to save the county courthouse from demolition, Pesin was appalled by how long it took to travel to the Statue of Liberty, which, like Ellis Island, is much closer to Jersey City than to New York City, and spearheaded the drive to create Liberty State Park. At the northern end of the park is the Central Railroad of New Jersey Terminal (1899), a national landmark French château with Neoromanesque details. Historically important because of its connection to Ellis Island, it is used now for special events, and there are plans to open a museum here. Also at this site are a shed for 20 trains (1913–14) and a ferry slip. Ferries ran from here to Liberty and Ellis islands in 1984 and may be reinstated in the future. The Morris Canal basin (Jersey City formed one end of the Morris Canal) still exists at the northern end of the park; plans include using it as a pleasure-boat marina.

An interpretive program, revolving around the park's salt marsh and mud flats, was instituted in 1985; the interpretive center is toward the southern end of the park just north of the Liberty Park Natural Area. The 60 acres of the natural area are predominantly salt marsh, one of the few remaining salt marshes along New York Bay. Since the Clean Water Act of 1972, the area has seen the gradual return of the wildlife driven away by the pollution of the river. The intertidal area serves as a natural nursery for fish; this is also a good area to see canvasback ducks. Programs for the public are scheduled daily in the summer (roughly May–September) and on Saturdays in the winter (roughly October–April). Group tours of the natural area and of the historic aspects of the park can be arranged by calling 201-435-1021. At the southern end of the park are picnic tables, a swimming pool, tennis courts, a boat-launching site, and a display of the flags of all the states. The park is open 8 A.M.–10 P.M. daily, May–September; 8 A.M.– 8 P.M., October–April. The interpretive center is open 8–4 weekdays. Future plans for the park include construction of a four-story Science and Technology Museum. Park authorities expect to break ground by the end of the decade.

Lincoln Park is Hudson County's oldest and largest. (It is also one of the most popular: an estimated 25,000 people use it each summer weekend.) The principal entrance, on John F. Kennedy Blvd. at Belmont Ave., is a formal plaza with a statue of Lincoln, designed by James Earle Fraser, who designed the buffalo nickel. The plaza is the highest point in the park and offers good views to the west. It is particularly lovely in spring, when the bulbs and flowering shrubs are in bloom. Note also the Saint Aloysius complex north of the entrance and the fountain at the circle that ends the formal entrance (the fountain, requiring 365 tons of concrete, is said to be the world's largest concrete monument; it was finished in 1911). The plaza is particularly popular with mothers of young children. In the less formal parts of the park are athletic fields, a playground, a lake for sailing model boats, a driving range, and places to walk and drive. There are plans to develop the underused 100-odd acres between US 1 and the Hackensack River. Jersey City also shares Washington Park (North St. and Central Ave.) with Union City. This smaller park contains tennis courts and other athletic facilities, a children's playground, and an outdoor swimming pool.

Jersey City has continued to be important as a transportation center: the Holland Tunnel starts (or ends) here. Opened in 1927, the tunnel was taken over by the Port Authority of New York and New Jersey in 1931. It is named for its first chief engineer, Clifford M. Holland, who developed its giant ventilating system (the air is completely changed every 90 seconds) and more or less lived in the tunnel, dying in 1924 at the age of 41. Some 26 million cars go through the tunnel each year. Jersey City is also a stop on the PATH trains, which are used by roughly 45 million passengers each year.

Harborside Financial Center (north of Exchange Place), an office complex catering to companies specializing in finance and trade, consists of converted railroad warehouses dating from the late 1920s. These are especially suited to mainframe computers as the buildings were designed with ground floors strong enough to hold railroad cars and upper floors strong enough to hold trucks. A pocket park and a marina will eventually be added here.

Newport City, a 290-acre railroad yard tract on the northern stretch of waterfront, is being developed by Samuel Lefrak, who has built more apartment units in New York City than any other private developer. It will eventually include 9,000 housing units, 1,200 hotel rooms, 4 million square feet of office space, stores, and possibly an aquarium and museum. Its shopping mall will be the first in Hudson County, and a proposed 80-story office tower, if built, will be the tallest building in the state. (In the meantime, the tallest building is likely to be the 30-story office tower scheduled for Exchange Place.) Plans are also being pursued to develop public transportation to cope with the traffic generated by all this construction.

Within Liberty Industrial Park (just north of Morris Pesin Dr. in Liberty State Park) is the site of the Black Tom explosion, possibly the only successful act of sabotage in the United States in World War I. The Germans blew up an ammunition train, resulting in an explosion that was felt as far away as Connecticut and Maryland.

Kearny   HUDSON   (NJ 17)   35,735

An industrial town with a large Scots population, Kearny (pronounced car-knee) was settled in the 17th century. It is named for Philip Kearny, a one-armed American general who fought in five wars, including the Civil War. Kearny Marsh, a flood area in the midst of the Hackensack Meadowlands that is owned by the town, contains one of the largest breeding populations of American coots and pied-billed grebes in New Jersey. It is also one of the few nesting sites in New Jersey for the ruddy duck, and one European species of ladybug is reputed to be so abundant here that it is captured for use by gardeners in less fortunate areas. A meadowlands landfill within Kearny's borders is being converted to a work of art (see New Jersey Turnpike tour, 107 N).

The Kearny Museum (318 Kearny Ave.; 201-997-6911), housed on the second floor of the library, features displays relating to local history, including Kearny memorabilia, period clothes, and household items. Open mid-September–mid-June, Wednesday, 1:30–4, 6:30–8:30; Thursday, 1:30–4; Saturday, 10:30–12:30.

The Public Service generating plant can be visited by groups; call 201-430-5862 between 8:30 and 4 for an appointment.

Keyport   MONMOUTH   (NJ 35, 36)   7,413

Situated on an inlet of Raritan Bay, Keyport has at various times been known for its oyster and shipbuilding industries. (Oysters were being planted in nearby creeks as far back as the early 18th century.) Recreational fishing and boating are important now, and along American Legion Dr. there are lovely views of the waterfront (which, in 1889 Gustav Kobbé described as "a very animated scene"), a fishing dock, a bulkhead used for fishing and crabbing, and a launching ramp. At the corner of American Legion Dr. and Broad St. is the Steamboat Dock Museum (201-264-2102, 201-264-6119), devoted to Keyport history. Located in a building once used by the Keansburg Steamboat Company as a machine shop and winter quarters for the crew, the museum features a variety of exhibits. Among them are a working printing exhibit; artifacts, including a partially refurbished wing section, from the Aeromarine Corporation, one of the country's first aircraft factories, once located in Keyport; 19th-century clothing; exhibits on the oyster and shipbuilding industries; and many other items related to Keyport's early history. Open Sunday, 2–5, from the last Sunday in May through the last Sunday in September. Groups by appointment. While in Keyport note also St. Mary's Church (E. Front St.), built in the late 1870s.

Kingston MIDDLESEX (NJ 27,
C 522) [South Brunswick Township]

Settled early in the 18th century, Kingston was a stop on the stage route between New York and Philadelphia. George Washington paused in Kingston after the Battle of Princeton, making the decision not to go on to New Brunswick and continue the battle, but to retire to winter quarters instead. Many of the houses lining Kingston's attractive main street (Lincoln Highway, NJ 27) date from the 19th century. (Look for the beehives on the porch roof on the north side of 27.) Cook Natural Area (Heathcote Rd.), 50 acres of freshwater marsh habitat, is a good place to hike.

The Kingston Mill historic district★ includes the area where 27 crosses the Millstone River and the Delaware and Raritan Canal.★ The present mill (which is actually in Princeton Township) was built in 1888 (and continued in operation until 1942), but there has been a mill on this site since 1755. The stone bridge dates to 1798. The dam, which backs up the river to form Lake Carnegie, was created in 1911, financed by a gift from Andrew Carnegie. Recently dredged, it is used for Princeton University and national crew races and by local sailors and windsurfers. At this point there is access to the Delaware and Raritan Canal State Park (201-873-3050), a 60-mile linear park that follows the Delaware and Raritan main canal and feeder line through central New Jersey. Opened in 1834, the canal went from Bordentown to Trenton to New Brunswick, the feeder from Raven Rock to Trenton, thereby linking Philadelphia and New York. One of the world's busiest waterways, the canal in its best year (1871) carried more tonnage, much of it coal, than the much longer Erie Canal ever did. Profits began to fall toward the end of the century, and the canal was officially closed in the 1930s. Some parts have been filled in (a stretch under US 1 in Trenton and another under NJ 18 in New Brunswick), but unlike the Morris Canal, most of the Delaware and Raritan Canal still exists. It provides water for several communities in central New Jersey, and its towpath is much beloved of boaters, hikers, joggers, bicycle and horseback riders, bird watchers, cross-country skiers, and those who like to fish. In fact, you can walk, ride a horse or bicycle, and canoe from the US 1 crossing in Lawrence Township all the way to New Brunswick; you can canoe from the west end of Trenton to Bull's Island and, except for a short stretch in Lambertville, walk or ride a bicycle from the west end of Trenton to Milford (the last part of this walk is on an old railroad right-of-way). You are welcome to picnic informally along the path, but more formal picnic areas with tables or fireplaces can be found at Bull's Island (across from Raven Rock, about 4 miles upriver of Stockton), Lambertville, Titusville (at Washington Crossing State Park), Trenton (in Cadwalader Park), Princeton (Basin Park off Alexander St.), Griggstown, and Blackwell's Mills (about 3 miles north of Griggstown). Many of the 17 historic buildings along the canal, which include locktenders' houses and a muledrivers' barracks, have been, or are being, restored (see Griggstown, Lawrenceville, Stockton). For most of its 60 miles the park is narrow (its total area is only 5 sq. miles), but at Bull's Island it widens out, and you can camp on the island. Future plans for the park include instituting a canal-boat ride in the Lambertville area and reinstalling a cable ferry across the Delaware at that point.

Kinnelon MORRIS (C 618) 7,770

 In Kinnelon, a rapidly growing borough in the northern section of Morris County (just south of NJ 23), is Silas Condict Park, a 265-acre county park with scenic overlooks, hiking trails, picnic sites, a playing field, and a seven-acre lake. Silas Condict was a Morris County farmer and surveyor who was a member of the Continental Congress and was elected to the New Jersey Assembly eight times, serving as its speaker in 1792–94 and 1797. The park has facilities for fishing and boating, and in the winter you can skate, ice fish, and cross-country ski.

Lakewood OCEAN (US 9, NJ 88, C 526, 528, 547) 22,863 (CDP) 38,464 (township)

One of the first areas in the United States to be developed as a winter health resort, Lakewood reaped from its fresh pine air and proximity to New York and Philadelphia a long reign as a leading resort. Its golden period lasted from the 1880s to the 1930s, and for most of those years the socially prominent flocked to the hotels and estates of the former mill- and iron town situated on the northern edges of the Pine Barrens.

The abundant forests had drawn sawmills in the late 18th century. The discovery that the soil was rich in iron led to the establishment in the early 19th century of ironworks, first by Jesse Richards, whose family was involved in the Batsto ironworks (see Hammonton), and then in 1832 by Joseph W. Brick. First called Three Partners Mill, then

Georgian Court College

Washington's Furnace, then Bergen Iron Works, on Brick's death the town was renamed Bricksburg in his honor.

The discovery in the 1860s of hard coal close to iron deposits in Pennsylvania put an end to the Pine Barrens' iron industry, but by then Lakewood had begun to build hotels. When in 1879 two New York stockbrokers bought 19,000 acres of land, Lakewood's career as a resort took off. In 1880 the town's name was changed from Bricksburg to Lakewood, but Brick's family is still memorialized in the names of two lakes: Carasaljo (for Brick's three daughters, Caroline, Sally, and Josephine) and Manetta (for his wife).

Many of the hotels were large and lavish, akin to Old World alpine hotels. The Lakewood, for example, covered 14 acres and was used by the federal government as a hospital during World War I. (It was also for a time the winter headquarters of Tammany Hall.) The Laurel House, built in 1880, counted among its guests the Goulds, the Rockefellers, the Vanderbilts, the Astors, the Claflins; Rudyard

Kipling and Oliver Wendell Holmes were frequent visitors. Emma Calvé and Mark Twain spent time in Lakewood; Grover Cleveland built a cottage in town; the Goulds, Rockefellers, and Claflins, among others, built large estates. By the end of World War I, Lakewood had over 100 hotels.

The Depression, the automobile, and inexpensive airline travel combined to end Lakewood's golden years. World War II brought some prosperity, for the town served as a center for nearby military camps. There was a considerable migration of people from the city, and an influx of refugees from eastern and central Europe (including Kalmuks, who built a Chinese temple in nearby Howell Township). The refugees built up an egg-and-poultry business; for many years Lakewood was a leading egg center.

The egg-and-poultry business has also declined, and many of Lakewood's citizens are now commuters. The town fathers have been successful in attracting light industry, and the town is home to several educational establishments, among them Georgian Court College (see below) and the internationally known Beth Medrash Govoha of America (Forest Ave.), a yeshiva founded in 1943 by Rabbi Aaron Kotler, who, with a few students, had arrived in Lakewood the year before as a refugee from Poland. After World War II there was a building boom: housing developments, particularly retirement communities, sprang up, perhaps attracted by some of the same features that brought vacationers, and now roughly one-third of Lakewood's citizens are retired.

The grand old hotels are gone—some burned, others were replaced by motels—but it is still possible to get some idea of what Lakewood must once have been like. One way is to drive around Lake Carasaljo. The area occupied by the Laurel in the Pines (S. Lake Dr.), for example, is now occupied by condominiums, but the scale of the hotel is apparent from that of the condos. Note also St. Mary's Academy (250 Forest Ave.) and the Georgian Court College Music Center. The Castle (Forest Ave.), once a house, has been converted to apartments; behind the façade of the Main Street Bar you can see the 1880s Harrison Drug Building. The Strand Theatre★ (400 Clifton Ave.; 201-367-9595), now the Ocean County Arts Centre and a historic landmark, dates from the early 1920s and the heyday of Art Deco theaters. Pearl Bailey was at its reopening in 1983. Its renovation and the new town plaza at Clifton Ave. and Third St. are part of a program to improve the downtown area and restore it to a late 19th-century appearance.

The best way to recapture Lakewood's past, though, is to visit Georgian Court College★ (Lakewood Ave. and Ninth St.). The college is run by the Sisters of Mercy, who, having outgrown their quarters in Plainfield, in 1924 purchased the estate of George Jay Gould (a son of Jay Gould). The sisters have added buildings and in 1950 they sold some 30 acres along the road, but what they have managed to preserve is remarkable. Reservations are necessary to tour the college; for an appointment call 201-364-2200. Allow at least an hour.

Four of the estate's original buildings remain: the mansion, the stable, the casino, and the small building now used as the chaplain's house. (In addition, Hamilton House, the administration building, which is off the campus proper, occupies a house Gould built for his son.) Started in 1898, the entire estate, grounds and buildings alike, was designed by Bruce Price, the architect of Tuxedo Park and the Château Frontenac. The mansion, built with an extraordinary attention to detail, is an imposing reflection of the styles and characters of several types of European country houses. The casino was the Goulds' recreation building and boasted an indoor race track, a swimming pool, a bowling alley, and squash and tennis courts. The race track has been converted to an auditorium and theater, but the students still bowl in the 1899 bowling alley, swim in the 1899 pool, and dive from its marble platform. The stable area has been adapted to various student activities, but some of the original spaces remain.

On the grounds are an Italian garden, a sunken garden, and a lovely Japanese tea garden. The statuary and the fountains are noteworthy; unfortunately the fountains can be turned on only for special occasions.

Other old estates have been preserved in parks. Ocean County Park* (Ocean Ave., NJ 88, at the east end of town) is the county's largest park and was formerly the John D. Rockefeller estate. Most of the buildings are gone, but included in its 323 acres are magnificent stands of trees planted by the Rockefellers. The park has facilities for hiking, swimming, fishing, and skating, a horticultural center, a visitor center, a pottery shop, and a mobile arts center.

Pine Park, a municipal park (Hope Rd., off County Line Rd., C 526, at the west end of town), is on the site of the Claflin estate, once the Newman School. The buildings are not yet being used.

Also in Lakewood is Lake Shenandoah Park (Clover St.; 201-363-8712), a 143-acre facility with hiking trails, a field sports complex, and facilities for picnicking and fishing. Fishing is also possible in the Metedeconk River (in Carasaljo Park) and in both Lake Manetta and Lake Carasaljo.

Lambertville HUNTERDON (NJ 29, 165, 179, C 518) 4,044

One of Hunterdon County's oldest communities and its only city (Flemington, the county seat, which in 1980 was a little larger, is a borough), Lambertville has seen its fortunes wax and wane. Once a thriving industrial town, it has recently become a magnet for artists, restaurateurs, and those interested in historic renovation.

Situated on the banks of the Delaware River directly across from New Hope, Pennsylvania, Lambertville prospered because of its location. It began as a ferry town; the arrival of the Delaware and Raritan Canal in the 1830s and the Belvidere and Delaware Railroad in the 1850s helped turn it into a flourishing regional industrial and commercial center. Settled in 1705 by John Holcombe, who managed to make sure that the main road from Philadelphia to New York City passed through his land, the town took the name of Coryell's Ferry after Emmanuel Coryell established his ferry service. In 1814 the name was changed to Lambertville when U.S. Senator John Lambert set his nephew up as postmaster. That same year saw the ferry replaced by a wooden bridge; its masonry piers still support today's bridge, built in 1904. (Under that bridge nests the state's largest colony of cliff swallows, an endangered species. When the nests had to be removed recently so that the bridge could be repaired, artificial nests were supplied for the birds.)

George Washington twice (July 1777 and June 1778) made his headquarters in Coryell's Ferry, staying both times at the mid-18th-century Richard Holcombe house (NJ 29 north of the center). At least two other presidents have visited Lambertville: Andrew Johnson and Ulysses S. Grant were both guests at the Lambertville House★ (32 Bridge St.), built by Senator Lambert in 1812. It continued to function as a hotel and restaurant; recently renovated, it is scheduled to reopen in 1988.

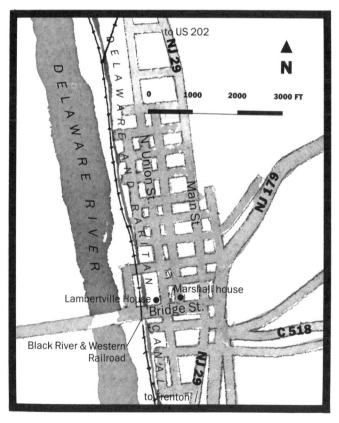

With ready waterpower at Wells Falls, gristmills, paper
mills, cotton mills, and lumber mills were established.
Other industrial enterprises included a railroad machine
shop, rubber plants, ironworks, and a sausage factory. The
population peaked (at 5,100) in the early years of the 20th
century, and there has been little new construction since
then (in 1985 a new hotel was built along the river). Now
the older buildings are being renovated and used for new
purposes: the sausage factory houses restaurants and art galleries; the Pennsylvania Railroad station has been restored
and converted to a restaurant; old warehouse buildings
serve as artists' studios; a private home, which had been
converted to a church, has been converted to an art gallery;
former mansions have become bed and breakfasts.

Another part of Lambertville's past that is reviving is the
shad industry. In 1896 some 19 million pounds of shad were
caught in the Delaware River and Bay; in the 1960s there
were none. Although only one commercial shad fisherman
remains in business in the nontidal parts of the Delaware
(and half of his catch is bought by the state, tagged, and
thrown back), enough fish have returned to the cleaned-up
Delaware (some 4,000 pounds were caught in 1982) that

Lambertville

Lambertville in 1981 decided to celebrate the rebirth of an old industry and held its first annual shad festival. Look for the festival in late April, early May.

Lambertville was the home of James Wilson Marshall, who set off the 1849 Gold Rush, called by some the largest migration in U.S. history, when he discovered gold at Sutter's Mill in California in 1848. His house★ (60 Bridge St.; 609-397-0770), built in 1816 by his father, is operated as a museum by the Lambertville Historical Society. Open May–October, Thursday and Sunday, 1–4. Groups by appointment. The society also sponsors a juried art show each winter.

Lambertville's historic district★ includes the area around NJ 29 (Main St.) and NJ 179. Some of the remnants of Lambertville's importance as a transportation center now serve recreational purposes. There is access to the Delaware and Raritan Canal★ at Lambertville, and there are plans to reinstitute a cable crossing. The Black River & Western Steam Railroad (201-782-9600) runs to Ringoes and Flemington on Sundays, mid-April–November.

Laurel Springs CAMDEN

(US 30)   2,249

This densely populated small borough is perhaps best known because it is where Walt Whitman spent his summers between 1876 and 1881. Indeed, according to one legend, the borough was formed (in 1893) because some of its citizens decided that their connection to Whitman was a marketable commodity. The Whitman-Stafford Farmhouse (315 Maple Ave.; 609-784-1105), an 18th and 19th-century farmhouse where Whitman stayed, has been restored and is furnished with pieces from Whitman's time. In July and August concerts are given regularly on Wednesday evenings, and special events are held occasionally at other times. Open March–December, weekends, 1–4. Groups by appointment during the week.

Lawrenceville MERCER   (US 206,

C 546)   [Lawrence Township]

First settled in 1660 in an area that had been an Indian camp and known until 1816 as Maidenhead, Lawrenceville is perhaps familiar today primarily because it is the home of the Lawrenceville School, one of the country's best-known independent preparatory schools. Much of the school and the town directly across from it on Main St., once the Kings Highway and now part of US 206, form Lawrence Township's historic district.* For two miles along both sides of 206, from the southwest corner of Franklin Corner Rd. (C 546) to just north of Carter Rd., are well-preserved structures from the 18th and 19th centuries. One of the oldest houses, Old Brick (1706), is on the east side of the road in the school's golf course. Wayside (the school side of Main St. opposite Philips Ave.) is perhaps some 30 to 40 years older and was once a tavern. The Presbyterian Church (Main St. north of Gordon St.) dates to 1764, although it was enlarged and altered in the mid-19th century. The 1815 Richard Montgomery Green house (2549 Main St.) was built from stones from the nearby Cherry Grove quarry. Lord Cornwallis was quartered in Lawrenceville in 1776 (and apparently recorded in his journal later that "one night in Maidenhead was more than enough"); on 2 January 1777, Colonel Edward Hand stalled Cornwallis at

Lawrence Rd. (US 206) near Darrah La., thereby preventing Cornwallis from reaching Trenton before dark and thus giving George Washington his chance to escape to Princeton. This event is reenacted every January.

In 1810 the Reverend Isaac Van Arsdale Brown of the Presbyterian Church founded the Academy of Maidenhead; Brown was also a leader in the move to change the town's name, "for reasons of delicacy," from Maidenhead to Lawrenceville in honor of the 1812 naval hero, Captain James Lawrence, of "Don't give up the ship" fame (see Burlington). Brown was a victim of the silkworm craze (also see Burlington), and although his house on Main St. was torn down in the 1940s to make room for the post office, some of the mulberry trees he planted remain. Much of the present appearance of the school dates from the 1880s when a legacy from one of the original graduates made it possible to convert the academy into a boarding school (the trustees looked to the best schools in England for inspiration.) Frederick Law Olmsted drew up the overall plan (which included planting over 300 species of trees and shrubs), and the circle, with its nine Richardsonian buildings, dates from that expansion. Thornton Wilder taught at the school in the 1920s and wrote *The Bridge of San Luis Rey* during his years there. In 1987, the school became coeducational.

The township is expanding rapidly, attracting corporate headquarters and research facilities. Long established in the area is the world-famous Educational Testing Service (entrances on Rosedale and Carter rds.; 609-921-9000), best known for its standardized college-admission tests. (Although ETS has a Princeton address, its campus actually lies within Lawrence Township.) There are art exhibits in Lounge B of Conant Hall (open weekdays, 8:30–4:30) and in the Henry T. Chauncy Conference Center (open daily, 9–9). Shows change every six to eight weeks.

Among the more striking headquarters buildings are those of Lenox (US 206 south of the village) and Squibb (US 206 c. 2 miles north of the village; 609-921-4076). At Squibb there is an art gallery with changing exhibitions. Open weekdays, 9–5; Thursday evening until 9; weekends, 1–5. Like many other corporations with ponds on their lawns, Squibb has been plagued by a superfluity of Canada geese (up to 12,000 Canada geese now winter in the state). The company's attempt to scare off the geese with live swans apparently failed.

Another art gallery open to the public is in the Rider College Student Center (US 206; 609-896-5325). Open Monday–Thursday, 1–10; Friday–Sunday, 1–5. Rider College is an outgrowth of Trenton Business College, founded in Trenton in 1865. Its present campus dates from 1965.

On Lawrence Station Rd. (take 546 east from Lawrenceville past US 1 and I 295) is the 50-acre John Dempster fire-service training center for Mercer County's 24 volunteer fire departments. Most responsible for the center's surreal look is the concrete tower built to resemble a high-rise apartment building. At the center firemen can also gain experience with chemical fires and simulated airplane crashes and house fires. The water used in the exercises is recycled.

The Lawrence Historical Society is restoring the Port Mercer Canal house (Quaker Bridge Rd. at Quaker and Province Line rds.) as a house museum. A Victorian Christmas is celebrated the first two weekends in December, and the house is also open on other special occasions. Tours by appointment (call Frances G. McCarthy, 609-882-2245, evenings).

Lincroft MONMOUTH (Garden State Pkwy exit 109, C 520) [Middletown Township]

The village of Lincroft dates back to the late 17th century. From 1901 to 1932 it was the site of Harry Payne Whitney's racing stable, where the first filly to win the Kentucky Derby was foaled and trained. The Brookdale Breeding and Stock Farm, where Whitney kept his horses, dated to the late 1880s; in the 1890s it became the property of William Payne Thompson who built a mansion on the farm and founded the Monmouth Park Jockey Club. After 1932 the facilities (which included an indoor track) were leased by independent trainers. When Geraldine Livingston Thompson, Thompson's daughter-in-law, died, the 700-acre estate was put to a variety of uses. On this land you will now find Thompson Park, Brookdale Community College, the Lincroft Elementary School, Marlu Farm (a prize-winning dairy operation, soon to become part of Thompson Park), and the Monmouth Museum and Cultural Center.

The Thompson mansion (1893), now in Thompson Park (C 520, Newman Springs Rd.; 201-842-4000), houses a visitor center, which includes an art gallery. The gallery exhibits the work of local artists and features painting and photography shows, which change every four to six weeks.

Open daily, 10–4. A 20-horse barn has been converted to a summer theater, and one of the tracks is now used as a jogging track; there are also athletic fields, a fitness trail, tennis courts, a craft shop, pottery and ceramics studios, and a formal rose garden.

The Monmouth Museum and Cultural Center (Newman Springs Rd.; 201-747-2266) is located on the Brookdale Community College campus (use parking lots 1 and 2). The small museum contains an attractive gallery, with shows that change four or five times a year, and a children's section, with a large hands-on exhibit that changes every two years. Until September 1988 this section will deal with the Lenape Indians. Open Tuesday–Saturday, 10–4:30; Sunday, 1–5. Tours by appointment. Admission charge for nonmembers. Be sure to call before going—if a school group is visiting the children's section you will not be allowed in that section. The college's performing arts center is in the same part of the campus; dance, music, and theater series are presented there. Box office (201-842-3335) open weekdays, 9–5. Phalanx Rd., which cuts through the campus, takes its name from the North American Phalanx, a mid-19th-century Fourier-inspired experiment in communal living. The community, built on over 600 acres, was founded in 1843 and lasted until 1855. Its last remaining building burned in the 1970s. Albert Brisbane, the father of the Hearst writer and editor Arthur Brisbane and one of the prime movers in the colony, interested Horace Greeley (the journalist and political leader, perhaps best remembered for having told a young clergyman, "Go west young man, go west") in the project, and Greeley wrote a regular column about it in the *New York Tribune*. Alexander Woolcott, the man of letters and model for Sheridan Whiteside in *The Man Who Came to Dinner*, was born in the phalanx.

Little Silver MONMOUTH

(C 520)   5,548

Settled in the late 1660s, Little Silver was apparently named for Silverton, the Rhode Island estate of a Mr. Parker, the father of two of the town's founders (Silverton itself may have been named after the town of Little Silver in England). Descendants of these Parkers still live at the 17th- and 18th-century Parker Farm (235 Rumson Rd.), listed in the state register of historic places. In the late 1800s a steamboat dock was built, adding vacationers to the farmers, fishermen, and nurserymen, who until then made up most of Little Silver's population. The Post Office Museum (Prospect St.) is located in Little Silver's first post office building (1875), and the original post office has been recreated in the front of the museum. There are other exhibits of historical interest, and the museum is used for lectures and other community activities. Open April–January, Sunday, 2–4. Other buildings of interest in town include the Embury United Methodist Church (1869; 25 Church St.), St. John's Episcopal Church (1876; Point Rd.), and the railroad station* (1890; Sycamore and Branch aves.).

Livingston ESSEX (NJ 10,
C 508, 527) 28,040

Livingston is named for William Livingston, New Jersey's first governor after the Revolution. Settled early in the 18th century the village for a time supported a considerable shoe industry, supplying many of what shoes the revolutionary army did wear (these shoes, incidentally, fit either foot). One of Livingston's remaining 18th-century houses, the Thomas Force House (343 S. Livingston Ave.), is maintained as a museum by the Livingston Historical Society. The house dates from 1745, with later 18th-century additions, and contains, among other attractions, a buttery, a museum room, and an authentically furnished lower kitchen. Among the Victorian pieces on display is a clothes rack that belonged to General George McClellan, Civil War general, governor of New Jersey (1878–81), and inventor of the notorious McClellan army saddle. Also on the property is a barn museum containing old tools and farm implements and the Condit family cookhouse, which was moved from the Ira Condit farm where the Livingston Mall now stands and is probably one of the oldest buildings in Livingston. Open September–November and April–June, 2d and 4th Sunday of the month, 2–4. Tours by appointment (call Mrs. Bertha Swain at 201-992-2998).

Livingston is also home to Newark Academy (91 S. Orange Ave.), the state's second oldest independent day school (founded in 1774), which moved to Livingston in the

1960s. The New Jersey architects Bernard and Howard Grad and former U.S. Treasury Secretary William Simon are among its graduates. The school sponsors an annual antiques show.

On the site of a former regional missile command center in the heart of the Watchung Mountains is Riker Hill Park (take Eisenhower to Beaufort and watch for signs), named for a family that lived in the area before the Revolution. An unusual feature of Riker Hill Park is its art park, an innovative arrangement in which the county leases space in the habitable buildings to working artists; the hope is that eventually the park will include a gallery in which the work being produced in these studios can be exhibited. The park also includes interpretive nature trails that lead to a dinosaur park, in which you can see fossil remains of dinosaurs.

Long Branch MONMOUTH (NJ 36, 71, C 537) 29,819

Although Long Branch, one of the largest cities on the shore, is enjoying a rebirth, it is hard to realize, looking at it today, that from roughly the 1860s to the First World War it was one of the most glamorous resorts in the country. It was also one of the earliest—a boarding house for summer visitors opened in 1788. At first the resort's clientele came from Philadelphia, then, particularly after the Civil War, from New York as well. Mrs. Lincoln visited in 1861, but it was President Grant's first visit in 1869 that gave Long Branch its cachet. Grant was to visit every summer he was president, and many summers after that. A race track opened in 1870, gambling casinos soon thereafter, and during the 1880s and 90s Long Branch's reputation as a fashionable place was at its height. (It was described at the time as "not a place whither a circumspect parent would take his family for a quiet summer by the sea," and "an object-lesson in certain extreme phases of American life.") A partial list of the people who frequented Long Branch includes such members of society as the Astors, Fisks, Goulds, Biddles, and Drexels, high liver Diamond Jim Brady, General Winfield Scott, actors Edwin Booth, Lily Langtree, and Lillian Russell, painter Winslow Homer, and writers Bret Harte and R. L. Stevenson.

Grant was not the only president associated with Long Branch. James Garfield was a frequent visitor, and after his assassination he was taken here in the vain hope that the sea air would help him recover (a ½-mile railroad spur from the main line to a borrowed cottage was built overnight so that his journey could be more comfortable). Chester A. Arthur, Rutherford Hayes, Benjamin Harrison, William McKinley, and Woodrow Wilson also spent some time at Long Branch.

Although not much of Long Branch's former elegance remains, you can still see the church at which these seven presidents worshipped. Built in 1879 as St. James Episcopal Church, it is now known as the Church of the Presidents★ (1260 Ocean Ave.; 201-229-0600) and is a museum run by the Long Branch Historical Society. Open by appointment.

Seven Presidents Oceanfront Park (Ocean and Joline aves.; 201-842-4000), a 33-acre county park, has facilities for swimming, fishing, and picnicking. A mile-long stretch just south of the park is being converted to a landscaped pedestrian mall and promenade, with benches facing the ocean, and areas for strollers, bicyclists, and joggers. Long Branch also boasts the longest pier in New Jersey, built in 1902, from which you can fish all day long the year round.

Other rebuilding plans include removing the boardwalk and replacing it (at Garfield Park) with a hotel complex, conference center, promenades, and shops, all year-round facilities. A new public beach will also be built; the project is scheduled to be finished in 1988. Just south of the new facilities is Kids World (65 Ocean Ave.; 201-222-0005), a theme park for children. Open weekends in May; daily, June through the first week in September. Mid-June to Labor Day, 10–8; other times, 10–5. Admission charged.

For beach information call 201-222-0400.

Long Valley MORRIS (NJ 24,
C 513, 517) 1,682

 Settled by Dutch and Germans at the turn of the 18th century, Long Valley was known as German Valley until the United States entered the First World War and anti-German sentiment inspired the change of name. The German Valley historic district★ includes portions of Fairview, E. Maple, and W. Maple aves. and Fairmount, E. Mill, and W. Mill rds. On Fairview Ave. note the remains of the Old Stone Union Church, built in 1774 to replace an earlier log church and abandoned in 1832 by the two congregations (Dutch Reformed and Lutheran) that used it. Many of the tombstones in the cemetery are inscribed in German; the oldest goes back to 1765. Next door to the church walls, in an 1830s schoolhouse, is the Washington Township Historical Society museum (201-876-3395). In one section of this local-history museum is a replica of an old schoolroom; other exhibits change every two to three months. Open Sunday, 2–4, except on holiday weekends; other times by appointment. A bit farther up Fairview Ave. is Welsh Farms, a dairy founded in 1891, which still has a major home-delivery business. The last dairy in the state to use glass bottles, it finally abandoned them late in 1985.

Northwest of Long Valley (take 24 west and turn north on Springtown Rd.) is Schooley's Mountain Park (201-876-4294, 201-829-0474), a 375-acre county park. Schooley's Mountain was a popular and fashionable health resort in the 19th century (General Grant was a visitor): not only is the mountain 1,000 feet above sea level, but there are springs here, known to the Indians for the supposed healing qualities of the water, and famous among the colonists at least since the 1770s. The back roads around Schooley's Mountain are worth exploring: the scenery is lovely, occasionally you will see reminders of the elegant resort of the past, and old buildings line many of the roads. The park itself has facilities for hiking, picnicking, boating, swimming, fishing, softball, and many winter activities.

Lyndhurst BERGEN (NJ Tnpk exit 16W, NJ 3, 17, C 507) 20,326

 Situated on the eastern bank of the Passaic River, Lyndhurst is bounded on the east by the Hackensack Meadowlands, some 19,000 acres of salt and freshwater marshes, tidal pools, and uplands that were once thought of as waste land, suitable only for dumping garbage. (Many travelers on the New Jersey Turnpike have been aware of the dumps as the only hills in an otherwise almost flat landscape.) These now-protected wetlands are recovering from past abuse, and some 2,000 acres of them, including the Sawmill Creek Wildlife Management Area, make up the not-yet-completed Richard W. DeKorte State Park. After the dumping has stopped, the county landfill will be landscaped and integrated into the park. This is not a simple task because the decaying garbage generates heat, which

makes it hard for plants to establish themselves unless
moisture is increased. If too much moisture is added,
though, there is a risk of pollutants leaching into the marsh.
It is hoped that the project will serve as a model for land rec-

Hackensack Meadowlands

lamation and wetlands protection in other areas. Already in place is the Hackensack Meadowlands Environmental Center (2 DeKorte Park Plaza; 201-460-8300), a museum and nature center that focuses on environmental problems, which the New Jersey Sports and Exposition Authority, as part of its proposal to build the Meadowlands Sports Complex (see East Rutherford), agreed to help build, finance, and maintain. The road to the center first passes corporate warehouses and offices, and occasionally a house left over from another time, and then arrives at areas covered with trash. As you get close to the center, you can see (and occasionally smell) a steady stream of dump trucks going up and down a mountain of garbage.

The center, which attracts some 10,000 students a year, is solar heated and sits on stilts out over the Kingsland Creek marsh. The area attracts many birds, particularly in May, late August, and early September, and the center has developed a walk around Kingsland Creek (a trail map is available at the center). Exhibits in the environmentally oriented museum focus on such topics as garbage disposal, fish ladders, and weather stations. Many are participatory; in one, visitors are in effect inside a stream. Open weekdays, 9–5; Saturdays, 9–3. Groups by appointment.

Lyndhurst's downtown has some interesting buildings, among them the town hall (Valley Brook Ave.), the library (Valley Brook Ave.), and the railroad station (Stuyvesant Ave.). The Little Red Schoolhouse Museum★ (400 Riverside Ave.; 201-438-0060), dating from the 1890s, is being restored and converted into a museum of local history. Also on Riverside Ave. are two older buildings, the 18th-century stone Jacob van Winkle house★ and the early 19th-century Yereance house. Across Riverside Ave. there is a section of Riverside County Park with tennis courts, picnic groves, playing fields, and a pedestrian and bicycling path.

Madison MORRIS (NJ 24) 15,357

 A colonial town (Mad Anthony Wayne had his headquarters here when the revolutionary army was quartered in the Loantaka Valley), Madison became a spot favored by wealthy commuters in the 19th century. For many years it was known as the rose capital of the country, a huge industry having developed out of what had begun as a hobby of the rich. By the turn of the century, 50,000 roses were shipped from Madison to New York City alone, and at the height of production 25 million roses a year were being grown under 1 million square feet of glass. Advances in refrigeration ended Madison's rose industry; roses today are grown outdoors in the South and shipped in refrigerated trucks.

The Museum of Early Trades and Crafts★ (Main St. and Green Village Rd.; 201-377-2982) is housed in the former public library, a gift of Willis James, a Wall Street commuter. The small stone Gothic building, built in 1900, has an imported-tile roof, leaded handblown-glass windows, forged-bronze chandeliers, stenciled walls and ceilings, and many other remarkable details. The museum was created in 1970 and is devoted to encouraging better understanding of the state's heritage by preserving and exhibiting artifacts showing how people have lived and worked since New Jersey was first settled. The museum is popular with schools— some 1,500 school tours go through each year— and the exhibits generally change monthly. Open Monday–Saturday, 8:30–5; Sunday, 2–5. Closed New Year's Day, Easter, July 4, Thanksgiving, and Christmas Day.

At 36 Madison Ave. (NJ 24) is Mead Hall,★ also known as the Gibbons Mansion. This 1830s building forms part of the Drew University campus. Founded in 1866 as a Methodist seminary on land donated by Daniel Drew, a stock-market speculator, Drew has since become a liberal arts college with a graduate school as well. On its wooded 186 acres are two other buildings from the Gibbons estate, a red-brick former carriage house and Embury Hall, the former granary. The library is the official depository for the United

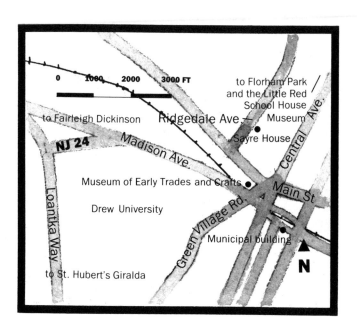

Methodist Archives. The Museum of Archaeology (Embury Hall; 201-377-3000, ext. 546) is open by appointment. The Drew Photography Gallery (University Center, Room 104; 201-377-3000, ext. 456), apparently the only gallery in the state devoted entirely to photographs, mounts shows during the school year. Open weekdays, 12:30–2, 7:30–10:30 P.M. The New Jersey Shakespeare Festival (201-377-4487), a professional repertory company in residence at Drew, performs from late June through late December.

Farther west on Madison is the Florham Park-Madison campus of Fairleigh Dickinson University. Built on 180 acres from the 1,000-acre Twombly estate (the Esso Research Laboratories are also on the grounds of the estate), Fairleigh Dickinson has as its main building a 100-room mansion designed by Stanford White and modeled on one wing of Hampton Court.

There are many buildings of interest in Madison, including several Queen Anne buildings on NJ 24 as you come into town from the east. Note also the United Methodist Church (1730; 120 Madison Ave.); the Daniel Sayre house★ (c. 1740–45; 31 Ridgedale Ave.), possibly Wayne's headquarters; and the elaborate municipal building (Maple Ave.), donated in 1935 by Mrs. Geraldine R. Dodge. Madison is currently sprucing up its downtown, hoping to attract business away from the shopping malls by preserving the classic small-town look of its shopping streets.

St. Hubert's Giralda (575 Woodland Rd.; 201-377-8877), an active animal shelter, contains part of Mrs. Dodge's collection of animal art. Attractively housed in a former cow barn on the Dodge estate (now the site of Schering-Plough and Prudential offices), the museum includes works by Landseer, Bonheur, and Tait, as well as portraits of Mrs. Dodge's own animals. Open by appointment Tuesday–Saturday, 10–4, and without an appointment Saturday, 10–12. Schering-Plough (1 Giralda Farms; 201-822-7000) presents art exhibits in its lobby; these change about every three months. Open weekdays, 10–4.

North of Madison (take Central Ave., C 608, to Ridgedale Ave.), in Florham Park, is the Little Red School House Museum★ (Ridgedale Ave. and Columbia Tnpk, C 510; 201-377-6528, 201-377-6499). Originally a one-room schoolhouse (the basement is a later addition), the mid-19th-century red-brick Gothic building is now a museum of local history, with exhibits of artifacts and period clothes that change three times a year. Open mid-September – mid-December and April – July, Sunday, 2 – 4. Groups and other times by appointment.

Mahwah BERGEN (US 202, NJ 17) 12,127

 Located along the northern border of the state, the township of Mahwah includes within its boundaries both extensive undeveloped areas and many corporate complexes. Bergen County runs two large reservations (each contains over 1,300 acres) in the township, Ramapo Valley County Reservation (US 202; 201-599-6124) and Campgaw Mountain Conty Reservation (Campgaw Rd.; 201-327-7804). Both are wildlife reservations, and both are open year round for hiking and camping (permits are necessary for camping), with marked and rough trails. Guided public hikes and walks are scheduled some weekends, and both parks run nature programs. Fishing is available in a mountain pond in Ramapo Valley; Campgaw has a ski area. Both parks offer picnic facilities. Trail maps are available at the park offices and at the Wildlife Center in Wyckoff. Adjacent to Campgaw is Darlington County Park (Darlington Ave.; 201-327-3500), which has two lakes for swimming and a third for fishing. Open daily Memorial Day weekend to Labor Day (admission is charged). Open limited hours April – Memorial Day and Labor Day – October. There is also a county golf course.

In the Mahwah railroad station (1871 Old Station La.; 201-891-9049), which dates from 1871, is the Old Station Museum. Displays feature railroad memorabilia and items of local history. Open May – October, Sunday, 3 – 5. Groups by appointment.

On the 172-acre site of a Ford Motor Company assembly plant (near NJ 17), which closed in 1980 after turning out close to 6 million cars and trucks, is the largest project ever built in Mahwah. Upon completion it will include the North American headquarters of a Japanese corporation as well as an office and hotel complex, with much of the wooded area left intact. Scheduled to open in the fall of 1987, the complex, with its pools, gardens, and atriums, promises to be architecturally interesting.

There are many 18th- and 19th-century Dutch stone houses to be seen in Mahwah, particularly along Ramapo Valley Rd. (US 202). George Washington is believed to have stayed in one of these houses, and Joyce Kilmer lived for a

time on the southwest corner of Airmount and Armour rds., commuting to his job at the *New York Times*.

The art galleries at Ramapo College of New Jersey (505 Ramapo Valley Rd.; 201-825-1800, ext. 467), located in the college library, house both permanent and changing exhibits. Open weekdays, 11–4; Sunday, 12–4. The college was founded in the late 1960s. Its campus, formerly the Stephen Birch estate, lies on 300 wooded acres in the foothills of the Ramapo Mountains. The college's original building, the late 19th-century Havemeyer mansion, has been augmented by award-winning contemporary buildings.

Bergen County

Manasquan MONMOUTH (NJ 71,
C 524)   5,354

A seaside community near the outlet of the Manasquan River at the southern end of Monmouth County, Manasquan retains in its downtown much of the flavor of another era.

The Indians frequented this area, and the settlement began to grow early in the 19th century. In 1888, before embarking for the South Seas, Robert Louis Stevenson stayed here for six weeks and wrote part of the *Master of Ballantrae*. Note the Holy Trinity Lutheran Church (Main St.), built in 1848, and the railroad station, built in Spring Lake in 1877 and moved to Manasquan a few years later. The town has the reputation for being a family resort in the summer; for information on beach fees call 201-223-0544.

About three miles northwest of Manasquan is the Manasquan River Wildlife Management Area (go south from Manasquan to NJ 35, west on 35 to NJ 34, west on 34 to Ramshorn Dr.), 726 acres open for hiking, trout fishing, and limited hunting.

Margate City ATLANTIC
(C 563)   9,179

A shore community south of Atlantic City (and Ventnor City), Margate City is known today as the home of Lucy,★ the Margate elephant (9200 Atlantic Ave.; 609-823-6473, 609-822-0424). Built in 1881 by a real estate developer as a gimmick to attract potential customers, Lucy is now a national historic landmark. Six stories tall and weighing 90 tons, Lucy was built of wood and covered with a tin skin; she cost about $33,000. Lucy's builder constructed two other elephants, one of which, the Colossus, was 18 stories tall. It burned in 1897. Sold in 1887, Lucy continued her career as a tourist attraction, even serving for a while as a hotel. She began to decline after World War II and was nearly destroyed in the 1960s. Rescued by a citizens committee in the 1970s, she has been relocated; she has also been given a new steel frame, and her exterior has been restored. Special events are held to raise money to restore the mosaics and other aspects of her interior and to landscape the grounds she stands on. There is a fine view from her howdah. Open for visits daily, 21 June–Labor Day, 10–4:30 (until 9 P.M. in July and August); weekends,

Memorial Day–20 June and Labor Day–October,
10–4:30. Group tours by appointment. Admission charged.
For information on beach fees, call 609-822-0424.

Matawan MONMOUTH (Garden State Pkwy
exit 117, NJ 34) 8,837

Matawan, originally settled by Scots and
known as New Aberdeen, has seen its population quadruple over the last 50 years. It was the
home of Major John Burrowes, who organized
the first New Jersey company of militia. His
fish-scale-shingle house* (94 Main St.), built in 1723, has
served as a restaurant but is now operated by the Matawan
Historical Society. Open March–December, 1st and 3d
Sunday of the month, 2–4. Tours by appointment.

West of Matawan is Cheesequake State Park (Garden
State Pkwy exit 120; 201-566-2161), 1,000 acres of rolling
land, 450 acres of which are a salt marsh (the Cheesequake
Marsh Natural Area). The area exhibits a wide diversity
of plant communities, including Pine Barrens vegetation
typical of the southern part of the state, deciduous forests
typical of the northern part, a cedar swamp, white pine
stand, freshwater swamp, and flood plain. In the spring the
display of wildflowers, particularly the pink lady's slippers,
is spectacular. The extensive trail system goes into the
marsh to an abandoned landing on the Cheesequake River,
where once bricks made from local clay, salt hay harvested
from the marsh, and agricultural products from nearby
farms were loaded for transportation elsewhere. The park
also has facilities for swimming, camping, and fishing. It
can be crowded in the summer. Open daily, 8–8, in summer (Memorial Day–Labor Day); 8–dusk in winter. Parking fee in summer.

Mauricetown CUMBERLAND
(C 744) [Commercial Township]

Although the first settlers arrived in what
is now Mauricetown in the early 18th century,
the town was not really developed until the
early 1800s. It thrived as a fishing port during
the 19th century, when fleets of boats worked
the Delaware River, and in the mid-1800s attracted captains of three-masted schooners, who built houses in town.

Mauricetown is an unusually well-preserved entity, with most of the houses dating from 1815 to 1870 (but note the 1714 Caesar Hoskins house at the foot of 2d St.). Most of the residents commute to Philadelphia, although there is a sand works outside town. There are plaques on many of the houses, giving their dates, and often identifying them as captains' houses. The Greek Revival Mauricetown Academy (High St.), a two-room elementary school from 1860, was used as a school for over 100 years; it now serves as a community center. The Elizabeth Compton house (Front St.; 609-785-1137, 609-785-1391), built in 1862, is being restored by the Mauricetown Historical Society and will function as a library and museum. The Methodist Church (Noble and 2d sts.) dates from 1880; its high spire once served as a navigational aid. Note also the 1888 drawbridge (foot of High St.).

The historical society sponsors an annual house tour, usually in December, and a concert the Sunday before Memorial Day. It also arranges group tours by appointment. The fire company sponsors four antiques shows each year (the first weekends in March, June, August, and December), as well as an annual crafts show in November, and a seafood festival in October, which draws some 2,500 people. Statewide oyster-shucking contests have been among the events taking place at the seafood festival, and if you continue on to Bivalve (take Noble St. which becomes C 548 to High St. and turn left), you will come to the heart of New Jersey's oyster industry, which has been devastated by a parasite that has drastically reduced yields. Before the parasite hit Delaware Bay in the late 1950s, 10 million bushels of oysters a year were harvested, but now the industry's biggest crop is quahog clams. The Rutgers Shellfish Research Laboratory in Bivalve is actively engaged in research that it hopes will find a way to overcome the parasite.

Mays Landing ATLANTIC (US 40, 50, C 552, 559) 2,054

Located at the head of Great Egg Harbor River, Mays Landing has been the county seat since Atlantic County was formed in 1837. The original red brick courthouse (1838) remains the center of the greatly expanded county buildings. The smallest county seat in the state, Mays Landing was founded in 1760 by George May, a trader from Philadelphia. It is an attractive spot, with large trees and a common. Note the Presbyterian Church* (1841) at the corner of Main St. and Cape May Ave. Along the river in the heart of town is Gaskill Park, a ten-acre county facility where you can fish, boat, and picnic. In the summer the shell is used for concerts. Guided tours by appointment (609-645-5960).

Northwest of the center of town (on US 322) is Atlantic Community College (609-646-4950). From September to May tours of the campus can be arranged, and the college's Culinary Institute runs a restaurant that is open to the public by reservation. The college runs an active performing-arts program that is also open to the public (call 609-343-4984 for the schedule).

To the west of the center of town is Lake Lenape; the county is currently developing an 1,800-acre regional park that includes the lake.

Three miles south of Mays Landing on NJ 50 is Estell Manor Park (609-625-1897), a county facility with 1,672 acres located primarily on the site of the World War I Bethlehem Loading Company plant. Built in 1918 the plant ceased operations in 1919. All the usable steel and iron was removed, and all that remains now are concrete foundations and rail beds (the nature trail goes along the rail bed, and chunks of coal, slag, and cinders can be seen, although the forest has almost reclaimed the site). Also in the park are the remains of the Estellville Glassworks, which dates from the 1830s and is remarkable for being built of local sandstone. The works operated until the late 1870s; window glass was the principal product. The park has a nature education center with a passive solar envelope design. Inside are exhibits focusing on the history and the plant and animal life of the Pinelands. The park also has facilities for fishing, boating, picnicking, hiking, biking, and cross-country skiing, as well as a fitness trail and a nature trail (a brochure describing this trail is available at the nature center). Many special programs are offered for school groups and the general public, including orienteering, canoe trips, and environmental education programs. Guided nature and history tours are available by appointment to groups of ten or more. In summer (May–September) the park is open weekdays, 7:30–7, weekends, 9–8, and the nature center is open daily, 9–5. In winter (October–April) the park is open weekdays, 7:30–4, weekends, 9–5, and the nature center is open weekdays, 7:30–4, and weekends, 9–5. An annual Pinelands festival is held in the park the first weekend in

August, with craft demonstrations (including dulcimer and broom making), military encampments, folk music, and dancing.

Among New Jersey cities, Estell Manor is second in area only to Vineland. Over the years the city has supported a wide variety of trades, from shipbuilding to glassmaking to piracy. The historical society is restoring the 1913 Risley schoolhouse (Cape May and Cumberland aves.) to serve as a research library and museum of local history. The museum is expected to open in 1988.

Medford BURLINGTON (NJ 70, C 541)
[Medford Township]

 The village of Medford is a tiny dot at the edge of what used to be pine barrens in the midst of an extremely fast-growing township. (The population of Medford Township more than quadrupled between 1960 and 1980, more than doubled between 1970 and 1980.) This was Indian territory before the first settlers began arriving, possibly late in the 17th century, more definitely early in the 18th, and the excavations for the many housing developments keep turning up artifacts. C 541, in fact, follows an old Indian path to the sea (NJ 70 follows an old Camden and Atlantic Railway route).

The first real community probably didn't develop until the mid-18th century (the oldest gravestone reads "M. S. 1759"), and from the 1760s to the 1780s Medford profited from the nearby Etna and Taunton bog-iron furnaces. The first machine to manufacture cut nails was built in Medford by Mark Reeve, who arrived in town in 1800; however, he did not patent his invention. According to legend, he was so impressed with Medford, Massachusetts, that he urged changing his adopted town's name from Upper Evesham to Medford. His former factory can be seen on Jennings Rd. off NJ 70.

When the railroad arrived in 1869, Medford was a prosperous village with sawmills, a gristmill, and a glass factory. The area was, and is, an important cranberry-growing region. The many lakes that have made it into something of a resort area result from the damming of the streams and the draining of some of the cranberry bogs.

A famous native son was James Still, known as the Doctor of the Pines. Born in 1812 to freed slaves from Maryland, he managed somehow to educate himself, and surmounting incredible obstacles built up a practice, based mainly on herbal remedies, that enabled him to die (in 1882) the largest property holder in the area. A modern housing development sits where his house once sat, but his office, with its double fireplaces in the basement for boiling syrups, is still standing (Church Rd. just east of 541, north of the village).

Many of the village's buildings date from the 19th century. The Stage Coach Inn (Main and Union sts.), which now houses shops and a luncheonette, was built in 1810. Braddock's Tavern (Main St.) is on the site of the old Medford House, which had pillars cast at Batsto. The Quakers still use both their meetinghouses—the Hicksite (1842; off Main St. at South St.) and the Orthodox (1814; Union St.)—as well as a former school from the same era. The former St. Peter's Episcopal Church (Union St.), a 19th-century Gothic structure, has been converted to doctors' offices. The former Methodist Episcopal Church (1854; 1896; Branch and Filbert sts.) is now the Faith Bible Church; the First Baptist Church (Bank St.) dates from 1893. Note also the Reily house (53 S. Main St.) and the Braddock house (70 S. Main). The Medford Historical Society (609-654-7767) sponsors house tours every other December, as well as a quilt show the first weekend in June and an apple festival the second Saturday in October.

The Kirby's Mill Museum* (Church and Fostertown rds.; take 541 north out of the village to Church, C 616; 609-654-7767) is in an old gristmill (the foundations date to

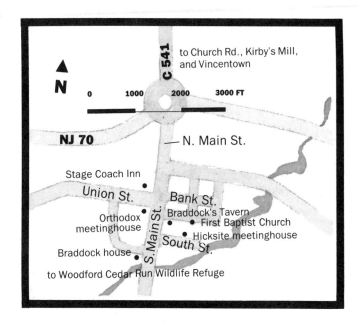

1788, and a sawmill was on the site before that) that operated with water power until 1961 and with combined water power and electricity for a short period more. The historical society is gradually restoring the mill and plans to return it to working condition. A blacksmith's shop on the property will also be restored. In the museum are the mill's stones and wheels, farm tools, woodworking equipment, and a collection of period clothes and costumes. Both the quilt show and the apple festival are held at the mill. Open July and August, Sunday, 1–4; other times by appointment.

If you continue from Kirby's Mill on C 616 about three miles, you will come to Vincentown. In this small village are two museums, the Vincentown-Tabernacle Telephone Museum (17 Mill St.) and a one-room schoolhouse (Race St. at the millpond). The telephone museum, in a c. 1898 building, has a working 1910 switchboard and old telephones; eventually a Southampton Township history museum will be installed in the same building. The schoolhouse, c. 1860, is furnished as an 1860s schoolroom, and visiting schoolchildren are treated to lessons using the materials and methods of the 19th century. Both museums open by appointment (609-859-9503, 609-859-3154).

About two miles north of the village (take 541 to Brace Rd. and turn left, or west) is the Medford Wildlife Management Area, 200 acres of fields and hedgerows open for hiking, bird watching, and hunting.

Seven miles southwest of the village (6 Sawmill Rd.; 609-983-3329) is the Woodford Cedar Run Wildlife Refuge. In addition to serving as a wildlife refuge, these 150 acres of pine barrens support a rehabilitation center for wounded animals, bird studies, and an environmental education center. A one-mile nature trail circles Cedar Lake. Visits by appointment only.

Mendham MORRIS (NJ 24, C 510)   4,899 (borough)

 A region of rich soil and abundant water power, the Mendham area was first settled in the early 18th century. At least three stories have grown up to explain its name: it derived from an Indian word, from a town in England, or from a clergyman, who, when apprised of the settlers'

bad habits said, "Don't worry, I'll mend 'em." Although like much of Morris County it has grown considerably over the last 25 years, more than doubling its population, a lot remains from the 18th and 19th centuries. The Black Horse Inn (Main St.) has been in continuous operation since 1742, and on the other side of the street another 18th-century hotel, the Phoenix House★ (Main St. and Hilltop Rd.) now contains municipal offices. On Hilltop Rd. is the First Presbyterian Church (1860), the third church built by a congregation that goes back to the 1730s. When the church celebrated its 150th anniversary in 1888, it is supposed to have coined the word "sesquicentennial," used later by Princeton University to celebrate its 150th anniversary.

The Patriots' Path, Morris County's linear path to Hanover Township, starts here. You can enter at Ironia or Pitney rds. and Mountain Ave.

About one mile west of Mendham is the historic district of Ralston★ (NJ 24 and Roxiticus Rd.; the community was formerly known as Rocksitious or Roxiticus). At this corner are the general store and manor house, both dating from the 1780s. The general store was still in business in the 1920s, and the building served as the Ralston post office from 1892 to 1941. The store is now operated as a small museum and contains household and other items of historical interest. Open Sundays and holidays, Memorial Day–Labor Day, 2–5. Tours by appointment (201-543-4347).

Another mile or so southwest off 24 is Mount Paul Memorial Park (East Fox Chase Rd.), an undeveloped county park of 251 acres, where you are welcome to hike.

About three miles southeast of the town center (take 24 east to Tempe Wicke Rd. and turn right) is Jockey Hollow Environmental Studies Center (Leddell Rd.; 201-538-4936), run by the Morris Area Girl Scout Council. There are over 200 acres, with woods and a river running through the property. Although the center is primarily designed to offer environmental education programs to groups, individuals are welcome to hike and camp as long as they make arrangements with the office (which will supply trail maps) before coming to the center. Hiking is also possible at the nearby Mendham Township Buck Hill (or Dos Passos) Park (west of Tempe Wick Rd. north of Corey La.) and at the Dismal-Harmony Natural Area (Woodland and Mt. Pleasant rds.), a 150-acre township preserve about three miles northeast of the town center (take 24 east to Cherry La. and turn left, or north; Cherry La. turns into Woodland Rd.).

Metuchen MIDDLESEX (NJ 27, C 501, 531) 13,762

Settled in the late 17th century by Dutch and English settlers, Metuchen became a commuters' town in the 1830s. It remained rather an exclusive community until the rapid growth of neighboring Edison Township after World War II. Because it attracted many literary and intellectual figures, it gained the nickname "Brainy Borough." Its older buildings are generally well preserved. Note in particular the Franklin Meeting House (291 Middlesex Ave.), built in 1805, used as a school from 1807 to 1872, and since then serving a variety of civic purposes; and the railroad station (off Main St.), dating from 1888. St. Luke's Episcopal Church (Middlesex and Oak aves.), a charming frame building with vertical siding and Gothic Revival details, dates from 1868 and was designed by Richard Upjohn. Joyce Kilmer was married in St. Luke's, and Mark Twain, William Dean Howells, Helen Keller, and Ogden Nash have been among its visitors.

The ten-acre Dismal Swamp in the northwestern corner of the borough is being preserved as open space. The borough may eventually put formal trails through the area, but you are welcome to walk here now (access from an unpaved road off Durham Ave. between Weston Ave. and Lisa La.).

Middletown MONMOUTH (NJ 35) 61,615 (CDP)

The village of Middletown, set in the middle of a rapidly growing and densely populated township, is one of the state's oldest continuously settled communities. Dutch settlers were among the first, followed in the 1660s by Baptists seeking freedom from the religious intolerance they had experienced on Long Island. Among the early settlers were Richard and Penelope Stout. He was one of the founders of the Middletown Baptist Church and a recipient of the Monmouth Patent; she was a Dutch immigrant who early in the 17th century had been attacked by Indians, who left her for dead. Nursed to health by other Indians, she found her way to New York (then New Amsterdam), where she met and married Stout. Eventually they settled in

Middletown and had ten children; at her death at 90 she reputedly had 492 descendants. The large family gathers each year for a celebration.

The Kings Highway historic district* (the intersection of Kings Highway with NJ 35) is an 18th- and 19th-century neighborhood, and it is even possible to find a 17th-century structure or two by wandering about the village. (The Kings Highway was supposedly built wide so that horses could be raced along it, and there is a record of a race being run as early as 1699.) The best known is Marlpit Hall (137 Kings Highway), a one-room Dutch cottage (1685), which was "enlarged in the English taste" (c. 1740) by John Taylor, a Tory merchant. The house remained in the Taylor family's hands until 1936, when it became the property of the Monmouth County Historical Association. The house retains most of its original paneling, hardware, and doors, one of which has bull's-eye panes, and has been furnished to reflect life in Middletown over several generations. The dining room is particularly gracious. Open April–December, Tuesday, Thursday, and Sunday, 1–4; Saturday, 10–4. Closed July 4, Thanksgiving, December 24 and 25. Group tours by reservation. Admission charged.

Middletown's Baptist Church was the first in the state. The congregation was organized in 1668; the present building (69 Kings Highway) dates from 1832. Christ Episcopal Church (92 Kings Highway at Church St.) was organized in 1702; this building dates from 1835. Part of the church's funds derive from money left to it by William Leeds, a convert who had been a member of Captain Kidd's pirate crew. Note the octagon house (1885) on Church St. and the blacksmith's shop (1825).

On Leonardville Rd. between Chamone and Bellevue aves. (in the Leonardo section of the township) is Croydon Hall, once the home of Melvin A. Rice, a wealthy dairy farmer who served as a roving ambassador for Woodrow Wilson. The turn-of-the-century building, which actually may have been the expansion of an old small farmhouse, for many years housed a private school and is now used by the Middletown Township Historical Society for its museum. Both the changing and permanent exhibits feature local history, and the library has many items going back to the 1660s. Open weekends, 1–4.

South of the Kings Highway on Red Hill Rd. (or c. 1½ miles east of Garden State Pkwy exit 114) are two county parks. Deep Cut Park (201-671-6050) consists of 40 acres of greenhouses and gardens that have been planned to serve as "a living catalogue of cultivated and native plant material." The park is on property that was under cultivation during the Revolution, though the old house burned in 1948, and the house that serves as the activity center dates from 1954. The park sponsors educational programs and has a reference library devoted to horticultural materials, classrooms, and a shop that features rare horticultural items.

Directly across Red Hill Rd. is the entrance to Tatum Park (201-671-2670), 365 acres of rolling hills, open fields, and woods. There are hiking trails and open play areas, and the activity center (formerly a radio-wave generation center for the U.S. Army) features cultural programs open to the public.

South of the village on Oak Hill Rd. (east off NJ 35) is Poricy Park Nature Center (201-842-5966). On the property are an 18th-century farm listed in the state historic register, a 250-acre nature preserve, a 65-million-year-old fossil bed, a 20-acre pond, and four miles of trails that wander through fields, forests, and marshlands. Educational programs concentrate on the environment and colonial history. Nature center open weekdays, 9–4; Sunday, 12:30–3:30. Groups by appointment.

Milford HUNTERDON (C 519, 619, 627) 1,368

Like many other Delaware River towns, Milford began as a ferry location. Although there was a sawmill here in the mid-18th century, real development came toward the end of the century with the establishment of three mills and the ferry. The town was known first as Burnt Mills (after fire destroyed an early mill), then Burnt Mills Ferry, then Mill-ford Ferry. Milford lost its ferry in 1842 when the first bridge was built. Today's bridge, dating from 1933, was built on the concrete and rubble abutments from the original wooden bridge.

Today Milford is a lovely river town with many old buildings, antiques shops, inns, and restaurants. It has attracted artists, among them Clarence Holbrook Carter and Wanda Gag, the children's book writer and illustrator. Many of the old buildings have been converted to other uses: the Old Mill (1798) serves as an antiques shop, the railroad station has shops and a restaurant, some of the houses have been converted to bed and breakfasts. The Riegel Paper Company (now part of the James River Corporation), which be-

Volendam Windmill

gan up the river in Finesville, has one of its largest plants in Milford.

The last two miles of 627 heading into Milford are particularly beautiful. The road, in many places only wide enough for one car, goes right along the Conrail tracks and the Delaware River.

The Volendam Windmill Museum (Adamic Hill Rd.; 201-995-4365) can be reached off 627 about 3½ miles southwest of Milford. (Take Crabapple Hill Rd. to Alfalfa Hill Rd. and watch for signs. You can also take Mt. Joy Rd., farther north on 627, to Adamic Hill Rd., or approach from 519 and go west on Anderson Rd., jog left when it ends, and turn right on Adamic Hill Rd.) The roads climb through lovely woods. The windmill, which stands near a splendid

18th-century house, is a replica of a Dutch or Danish wind-driven grain mill. Open May–September, weekends and holidays, 10–12:30, 1–4; other days and times by appointment. Tours hourly except at noon. Admission fee.

Millburn ESSEX (NJ 24, 124, C 527, 577) 19,543

Settled early in the 18th century, Millburn became a wealthy commuter town in the 19th. Within the township is Short Hills, established in 1877, which, for many, typifies the affluent suburb. The Short Hills Park historic district★ encompasses 19th- and 20th-century buildings in the area roughly between Hobart Ave. and Parsonage Hill Rd. At the eastern edge is the Wyoming historic district, listed in the state register of historic places, also with 19th- and 20th-century buildings, roughly bounded by Sagamore Rd. and Wyoming Ave.

Just east of the Short Hills railroad station is the Cora Hartshorn Arboretum and Bird Sanctuary (324 Forest Dr. S.; 201-376-3587), over 16 acres of natural woodlands with three miles of trails. The arboretum was founded in 1923 by Cora Hartshorn, the daughter of the founder of Short Hills, on land given her by her father. Stone House, built with traprock and oak from Hartshorn property, houses a small museum with changing nature exhibits and a small collection of live animals; there is also a library. Trails open daily. Museum open Tuesday–Thursday, 2:30–4:30; Saturday, 9:30–11:30; Sundays in May and October only, 3–5. Tours by appointment.

Part of the South Mountain Reservation is in Millburn. This 2,000-acre park has many miles of trails, many lookout points, picnic areas, and a wildlife preserve (see also West Orange). At the entrance to the reservation is the Paper Mill Playhouse (Brookside Dr.; 201-376-4343). Originally housed in a converted 18th-century mill, which continued to produce paper until after World War I, the theater now has a new building (1982); only fragments of the mill remained after a fire in 1980.

At the railroad station you can pick up the Lenape Trail and follow it for 17 miles to Newark.

Tiny in area as well as population (it occupies 0.6 sq. mile), this picture-book village and former agricultural center situated on the Millstone River and the Delaware and Raritan Canal★ was once called Somerset Courthouse because for almost 50 years in the mid-18th century it was important enough to be the county seat. (After the British burned the courthouse in 1779, the seat was moved to Somerville.) Millstone's 19th-century historic district★ includes Ann, S. River, West, and Main sts., Alley Way, and the Amwell Rd.

The Old Forge Museum (C 533; 201-359-7221) is in what was once a blacksmith shop, which may date to the late 17th century. The Millstone Dutch Reformed Church (Main St. and the Amwell Rd.) dates from 1828. Troops came through Millstone during the Revolution, and George Washington stopped at the John van Duren house (1754; W. River Rd., 1 mile south of the Amwell Rd.) after the Battle of Princeton; he may also have made it his headquarters on other occasions.

Across the water is East Millstone, even smaller but also picturesque. Its 18th- and 19th-century historic district★ includes the area along the Amwell Rd. and the canal. The white frame Van Liew house (c. 1834; north side of the Amwell Rd. by the canal) served for many years as a tavern and hotel and may have been used by British troops as their headquarters in 1777. About a mile east of the village on the south side of the Amwell Rd. is the 125-acre Hutcheson Memorial Forest, formerly Mettler's Woods, a national natural landmark. This is one of the oldest undisturbed stands of oak-hickory forest remaining in the United States. Although not virgin forest, it has apparently never been cut over, and has not burned since the early 18th century. The original 90-acre tract was bought by the United Brotherhood of Carpenters and Joiners of America and given to Rutgers University, which uses it as a laboratory for ecological and biological research. The woods have been described as a living museum of the eastern United States as it was 200 years ago, and "the most intensively studied primeval woods on the continent." Open for guided tours by appointment only (write Director, Hutcheson Memorial Forest, Department of Botany, Rutgers University, New Brunswick 08903).

On the north side of the Amwell Rd. is Somerset County's 467-acre Colonial Park (Mettlers Rd., with access from the Amwell Rd. and Elizabeth Ave.; 201-722-1200, 201-873-8716). In the western section are a 5½-acre arboretum and the Rudolf van der Goot Rose Garden, with over 4,000 plants and a sensory and fragrance section for the handicapped. The western boundary of the park includes frontage on the canal and the river. Park facilities include a canoe-launching ramp as well as family and group picnic sites, playgrounds, fishing ponds, open playing fields, a bicycle path, hiking and bridle trails, and tennis courts. The Spooky Brook Golf Course (Elizabeth Rd.; 201-873-2241) is at the eastern end of the park. Both open daily, dawn–dusk.

Milltown MIDDLESEX (off US 1) 7,136

 Known in the early 19th century as Bergen's Mill after Jacob I. Bergen, who built a gristmill on Lawrence Brook, Milltown for a time was the center of the nation's rubber industry (at the end of the 19th century the industry shifted to Trenton and in the 20th century to the Midwest). In 1843 the Meyer Rubber Company built a plant* on Bergen's mill site (Main St. at Mill Pond); the plant was later run by the India Rubber Company and the International Rubber Company before the Michelin Tire Company bought and expanded it in 1907. At peak production the Michelin plant employed as many as 3,000 people. The company stopped producing rubber in Milltown in the 1930s, and parts of the large complex have been converted to other uses.

The Milltown Museum (116 S. Main St.; 201-828-0458) occupies a c. 1860 farmhouse. Its rooms are traditionally furnished, and the collection includes artifacts from Milltown. Rotating exhibits feature Stangl pottery, wedding gowns, and quilts. Open September–December and March–June, Wednesday, 1–3. Group tours by appointment.

Next door to the museum and behind the red, fish-scale-shingle firehouse is the Eureka Fire Museum (201-828-7207). In an 1899 building, the museum has early fire-fighting equipment, with rotating exhibits of old apparatus, extinguishers, helmets, and the like. Guided tours by appointment.

A walk along Main St. will reveal many mid- and late 19th-century buildings. Some, like the hardware store at Main and W. Church St. or the funeral home at 170 Main, have been converted from homes to other uses. Note also the police department's informal duck-crossing sign. A walking-tour brochure is available from the Middlesex County Cultural and Heritage Commission (201-745-4489).

Millville CUMBERLAND (NJ 47, 49, C 555) 24,815

 Situated at the head of the tidewater of the Maurice River, Millville was settled as a shipping center around 1720. Word of vast sand deposits led to the establishment, in 1739, of Millville's first successful glassworks. Over the years glassmaking became Millville's major industry; it remains that today, followed by aircraft repair.

Wheaton Industries, the largest family-owned glassworks in the world, descends from a firm founded in 1888 by Dr. T. C. Wheaton, who arrived in Millville in the 1880s intending to establish both a medical practice and a pharmaceutical business. The need for pharmaceutical bottles led him to buy into a recently established glassworks. Wheaton Industries today employs 3,000 people in Millville alone.

Wheaton Village (Glasstown Rd., off Coombs and Valley rds. between NJ 55 and Wheaton Ave; 609-825-6800) is a re-creation of an 1880s South Jersey town. Founded some 20 years ago by Frank H. Wheaton, Jr., T. C. Wheaton's grandson, it centers on the Wheaton Museum of American Glass and a replica of his grandfather's first factory. The museum contains one of the world's largest collections of American glass, with the style of the rooms designed to reflect the era of the glass on display. The museum has rescued chandeliers from the Roxy Theater in New York City and the Traymore Hotel in Atlantic City. Large collections of bottles, decorative glass, paperweights, and lighting devices are some of the items on display.

The glass factory has been re-created following early photographs and partial blueprints (but with modern precautions against the fires that plagued 19th-century glassworks). You can watch the glassblowers while they work; at certain times of the day they give a set talk explaining what they are doing. Ask at the gatehouse for the day's demonstration schedule. (You can also arrange in advance to blow your own paperweights.) The village contains a Crafts and Trades Row, where potters, a decoy carver, and a lamp-worker demonstrate their crafts; a miniature railroad; a playground; and various old buildings, shops, and restaurants. Open daily, 10–5 (the last glass demonstration is at 3:30); weekday hours vary January–March, and not all attractions are open in the winter, so it is best to call ahead. Closed New Year's Day, Easter, Thanksgiving, and Christmas. Admission charge (except for the stores and restaurants). Group tours by appointment.

Millville is also the home of the largest American-holly farm in the United States (the English-holly farms in Oregon are bigger). American Holly Products, Inc. (NJ 49, 4 miles east of Millville; 609-825-4959) grew out of the president of the New Jersey Silica Sand Company's aversion to sending liquor as a Christmas gift to his customers and employees. In 1926 he began sending boughs of holly, and in 1939, after frost had killed the native trees, he planted 2,800 trees. The farm has passed through various hands, and now there are 4,400 trees, representing 40 varieties, planted on 50 acres. Between mid-November and mid-December 1985, the firm shipped 25,000 pounds of holly. The small museum, featuring an outstanding collection of holly-motif china, as well as furniture made from holly wood and other holly-related items, was closed to the public in 1985.

Several wildlife management areas lie close to Millville. Northwest of the center of town is the Union Lake area. Union Lake, the largest freshwater lake in southern Jersey, was created in the 1860s (by damming the Maurice River). The lake has long had a reputation as a good place to fish (in 1978 a 27-pound striped bass was caught here), and you can hike in the surrounding area.

South of Millville on C 555 is the Edward G. Bevan Wildlife Management Area (formerly the Millville Wildlife Management Area). One of the oldest such areas in the state (it was started in 1932), it contains over 12,000 acres of woodlands and fields and is a good place for hiking, fishing, and hunting. You can also fish in the Menantico Ponds Wildlife Management Area, just east of Millville off NJ 49. The access road, just after the Menantico Creek crossing, is suitable for walking. Some seven miles east of Millville on NJ 49 is the Peaslee Wildlife Management Area. Its 14,000 acres make it one of the largest such areas in the state. It consists of pine-oak woodlands and lowlands, and it is bordered on the west by the upper reaches of the Tuckahoe River. It has a field-trial course and is open for hiking, fishing, and hunting.

Montclair ESSEX (Garden State Pkwy exit 151, C 509) 38,321

 Although Montclair was first settled in the 1660s, today's community took shape in the 1860s, when Montclair broke away from Bloomfield in a dispute over the routing of a railroad line. Frank and Lillian Gilbreth, the efficiency experts about whom *Cheaper by the Dozen* was written, raised their large family (12 children) on Eagle Rock Way, and a junior high school is named after the painter George Inness, who lived in Montclair for a time.

Like many of the early suburbs, Montclair suffered a period of population decline, but the community is now engaged in a vigorous program to revitalize its downtown. The Montclair railroad station★ (Lackawanna Plaza), for example, designed in 1913 by William H. Botsford, who also designed the railroad terminal in Hoboken, is being converted into a restaurant. A nearby school from the same era (Baldwin St. and Glen Ridge Ave.), with its 12-foot-high windows and all, is being converted into apartments. At the same time, residents are worried that skyrocketing real estate prices and the gentrification of older buildings will destroy the city's economic and racial heterogeneity.

The Israel Crane House★ (110 Orange Rd.; 201-744-1796) was built in 1796 by Israel Crane. A direct descendant of one of Montclair's original settlers (part of today's Montclair was once called Cranetown), Crane was a highly successful businessman who engaged in a wide variety of enterprises from cider, cotton, and woolen mills to turnpikes and quarries; the writer Stephen Crane (1871–1900) was a descendant of this family. The house, which was altered in the mid-19th century, is now run as a house museum by the Montclair Historical Society. The only building remaining in Montclair with connections to the early settlers, it has been furnished to reflect changing styles from 1740 to 1840. The house is specially decorated at Christmas, and the society offers crafts classes in the winter and spring. Open Sunday, 2–5; groups by appointment other days.

The Montclair Art Museum (3 S. Mountain Ave.; 201-746-5555), housed in a Greek Revival 1914 building, has an unusually fine permanent collection for a town the size of Montclair. The collection specializes in American painting and sculpture from the mid-18th century to the present and also includes American Indian art. The museum puts on changing exhibitions and sponsors classes, workshops, lectures, and other special events; gallery talks take place Sunday at 2:30. Open September–July, Tuesday, Wednesday, Friday, and Saturday, 10–5; Thursday, 2–9; Sunday, 2–5. Donation requested except on Thursday.

The fine and performing arts are stressed at Montclair State College (Normal Ave. and Valley Rd.; 201-893-4333). The college, established in 1908 on a 200-acre campus, sponsors an annual independent film-makers' festival and a professional summer theater program. These are open to the public, as are its art galleries (Gallery One, weekdays, 9:30–4:30; the College Art Gallery, weekdays, 10–4). The Montclair-Kimberly Academy (Bloomfield Ave. and Lloyd Rd. campus; 201-746-9800) also sponsors a professional summer theater, and the Whole Theater Company (544 Bloomfield Ave.; 201-744-2989) is active in the winter months.

For such a densely settled area, the amount of open space is surprising. At the northwestern end of town are Mills Reservation (Reservoir Dr.; 201-482-6400) and Mountainside Park (500 Upper Mountain Ave.; 201-744-1400). The former is a 157-acre county facility with a wildlife reserve, a lookout point, and three miles of trails, the latter a town facility with the world-famous Presby Iris Gardens★ (1927), which from roughly the last week of May through the first two weeks of June have a spectacular display of 4,000 kinds of iris.

The opportunities for bird watchers are also remarkable. In the northwestern area is the Montclair Hawk Lookout (Edgecliff Rd.; take Upper Mountain north to Bradford, turn left on Bradford, right on Edgecliff), a New Jersey Audubon Society sanctuary and a national natural landmark situated on an outcropping on the first Watchung ridge. Because of the ridge, there are updrafts, essential to hawks on their long migrations. The season runs from mid-September through November, with the peak during the first four weeks. In mid-September you can see as many as 2,000 broad-winged hawks in a few hours, and, although it doesn't happen often, there have been days when 10,000 hawks have been spotted. Farther east is the town's Alonzo F. Bonzal wildlife preserve (Riverview Dr. off Alexander Ave.), 23 acres of natural area with trails.

On the eastern edge of town is Brookdale Park (Bellevue Ave.; 201-482-6400), which Montclair shares with Bloomfield. This 121-acre park is one of the many Essex County parks to have been designed by the noted Frederick Law Olmsted firm. It has a fitness and interpretive trail, playgrounds and playing fields, tennis courts, and facilities for fishing and picnicking.

Moorestown BURLINGTON (NJ 38, C 537) 13,695 (CDP)

A Quaker town that was laid out in the 1720s, Moorestown is the home of the well-known Moorestown Friends School.★ Founded 200 years ago, the school has grown and now occupies a complex off W. Main St. in the center of town. Several buildings in the town center are of particular interest. Note the old town hall★ (40 E. Main St.) and the First Baptist Church (1877; 19 W. Main St.), connected to a 19th-century brick building, once the parson-

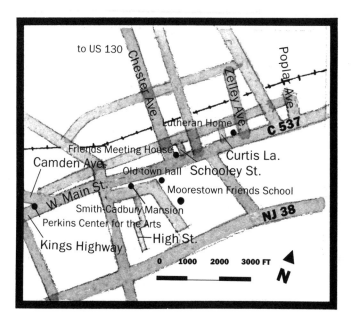

age, now used by Family Services of Burlington County. The Smith-Cadbury Mansion★ (12 High St.; 609-234-9087, 609-235-1592), c. 1738, serves as the headquarters of the Moorestown Historical Society. The house has been furnished almost entirely by donations and concentrates on the period 1830–40. The collection also includes period clothes and some Moorestown memorabilia. Open Tuesday, 1–3, and by appointment. (The historical society, which has published walking tours of Moorestown, has plans to expand the hours soon.) Taking Main St. (C 537) west out of town takes you through a particularly lovely stretch of houses. At 436 E. Main St. (just west of Poplar Ave.) is the bondsman's house, c. 1780, which is one room wide and two rooms deep, with 12-inch-thick stone walls.

Moorestown was the home of the noted suffragette Alice Paul (1885–1977). Trained as a sociologist, Paul helped revitalize a faltering women's suffrage movement, continuing her fight for women's rights after the 20th Amendment was passed. She drafted what is believed to be the earliest version of the Equal Rights Amendment.

A well-known worshipper in the Friends Meeting House (1802; E. Main between Chester Ave. and Schooley St.) was Samuel Allen, inventor of the hand cultivator, a manure spreader, and the Flexible Flyer sled. The Lutheran Home (E. Main St. between Zelley Ave. and Curtis) was his house, which, according to legend, the meeting considered too ostentatious for a Friend. In 1920 it was bought by Eldridge R. Johnson, founder of the Victor Talking Machine Co. (later part of what is now RCA; see Camden); it was bought by the Lutherans in 1946.

The Perkins Center for the Arts★ (Camden Ave. and Kings Highway; 609-235-6488), located in a 1910 Tudor house on the site of a nursery that specialized in ornamental trees as far back as 1815, features fine arts and crafts exhibits, special events, and classes. Exhibits change roughly every other month, and gallery hours change with each show. Call for hours. The center sponsors an annual juried photography show.

Morristown

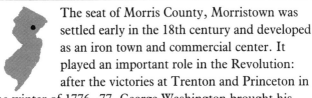

The seat of Morris County, Morristown was settled early in the 18th century and developed as an iron town and commercial center. It played an important role in the Revolution: after the victories at Trenton and Princeton in the winter of 1776–77, George Washington brought his tired troops here to spend the winter. While the troops encamped in the Loantaka Valley, Washington made his headquarters at Arnold Tavern in the center of town. He returned again in 1779–80; this time he stayed at a substantial private house in Morristown while the troops were quartered at Jockey Hollow, some six miles southwest of town. The strategic location of Morristown was such that there were always soldiers stationed here during the war, and the British army never went through Morristown. After 1838, when the Morris and Essex Railroad provided connections to Newark, the town attracted large numbers of wealthy residents, and it developed a reputation for having the densest concentration of millionaires in the state. Because of the Depression, many owners of large estates and houses could no longer maintain them, and you will come across several public buildings in Morristown that once were private homes.

Morristown now finds itself the center of an explosive growth in corporate headquarters. Much of that growth is taking place in the surrounding townships, but there are some striking signs of it in town as well, the most obvious being Headquarters Plaza. Despite these taller buildings and the enormous increase in traffic, the look of Morristown is still dominated by its large green, which was laid out in 1715 and is one of the few surviving town greens in the state. It is also interesting that Morristown has the feel of a city rather than of a town; in fact, its population is not that large and has hardly increased at all over the last 50 years.

Morristown's historic district* includes Green, South, DeHart, Elm, Wetmore, Madison, and Pine sts., Macculloch, Maple, and Colles aves., and Farragut and S. Park places. This is primarily a 19th- and 20th-century area, but there are still some 18th-century buildings to be seen in town, among them the Condict house* (51 South St.), now the Women's City Club, and the Timothy Mills house★ (27 Mills St.), c. 1740. Note also the courthouse★ (Washington St. between Court St. and Western Ave.), built in 1827; the Presbyterian Church (65 Park Place), from 1895; and the town hall (South St.), built in 1918 as a private house. If you happen to notice an unusual number of seeing-eye dogs as you wander through the center of town, this is because Seeing Eye, Inc., which trains the dogs, has its headquarters on Maple Ave.

Several sites and buildings related to Washington's second time in Morristown make up the Morristown Historical National Park, the first historical park established by the federal government (in 1933). (Arnold Tavern, where Washington stayed the first time, was moved in 1886 to make way for an office building; it later burned and had to be torn down.) In addition to the Ford Mansion (230 Morris St.; 201-539-2085), where Washington had his headquarters, and the Jockey Hollow Encampment Area, where the troops were quartered, the park includes a museum (located behind the Ford house) and the site of Fort Nonsense. Jacob Ford, Jr., was a wealthy Morristown merchant and powder maker who died early in the Revolution; his widow offered Washington the use of her beautiful Georgian house, built earlier in the 1770s. The house has been furnished to look as it did when Washington was in residence (this means much of it is quite sparsely furnished as Mrs. Ford was concerned that her belongings not be pilfered by colonial troops). Adjacent to the Ford Mansion is the Historical Museum and Library, with displays relating to the 1779–80 encampment and other artifacts and memorabilia of Washington and the Revolution.

To reach the Jockey Hollow area take Western Ave. south for about six miles. On your way you will pass the entrance to the site of Fort Nonsense, an earthwork built on a 600-foot hill, fortified on Washington's orders in 1777. Nothing remains of the fortification, but there is an explanatory plaque and a view of the town that will give you a sense of why—situated as it is on a shoulder of Mt. Kemble with the Normandy Heights and the Watchung Mountains to the east, Gillespie Hill to the west, and Horse Hill to the north—Morristown was a strategically advantageous location. The fort's name is supposed to have developed because people forgot why the fort had been built and assumed it must have been created to make work. (Frank Stockton, who lived in Morristown for a while, accepted this theory, and in "The Story of Fort Nonsense" he offers it as evidence for Washington's astute understanding of the need to keep his troops feeling useful.)

Some 10,000 troops were quartered at Jockey Hollow in 1779–80 and endured a winter worse than the one at Valley Forge. Model huts, like those the soldiers built for themselves, were re-created during the 1930s by the Civilian Conservation Corps, and the various areas used by the troops have been delineated and are clearly marked. Also at Jockey Hollow is the Wick House, a mid-18th-century farmhouse and garden, which have been restored to show how a prosperous farmer would have lived. According to legend, the Wick daughter hid her horse in the house to prevent the soldiers from appropriating it. You can pick up maps at the visitor center and take your own tour of the park, and there is usually someone around to answer questions. The park also has miles of trails for hikers, riders, and cross-country skiers, and there are picnic facilities and lake swimming in the adjacent Lewis Morris Park (see below).

The park schedule has been changing because of budgetary problems, so it is best to check before you go. The park area at Jockey Hollow is open daily, dawn–dusk, and the

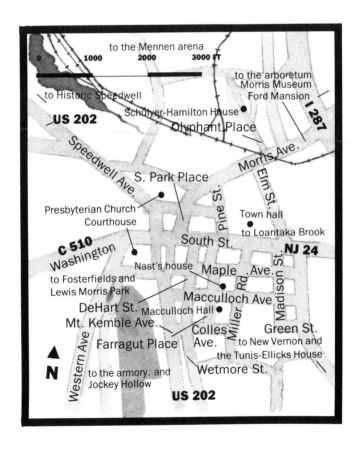

visitor center and Wick House, as well as the Ford Mansion and the museum, are open 9–5, Wednesday–Sunday. In summer (Memorial Day–Labor Day), the Ford Mansion and the museum may be open Monday and Tuesday as well. Closed New Year's Day, Thanksgiving, and Christmas.

While Alexander Hamilton, who accompanied Washington to Morristown, was staying at the Ford Mansion, he courted and became betrothed to Elizabeth Schuyler, then visiting her aunt at what is now the Schuyler-Hamilton House (5 Olyphant Place; 201-267-4039). This colonial clapboard house has been lovingly restored with period furnishings by the D.A.R. and features a re-created colonial garden. Open Tuesday and Sunday, 2–5. Admission charged.

One of the local ironworks was Stephen Vail's Speedwell, which, in the early 19th century, built most of the machinery for the S.S. *Savannah*, the first transatlantic steamship. The ironworks was converted to a cotton factory in the 1820s. The first public demonstration of the telegraph took place at Speedwell in 1838: Vail's son had worked with Samuel F. B. Morse in developing it. Much of the Vail homestead has been preserved and forms the backbone of Historic Speedwell★ (333 Speedwell Ave.; 201-540-0211), a national historic site. On the site are several 18th- and 19th-century buildings, including the Vail factory, now a national historic landmark. Not all the buildings were originally part of the Vail homestead. Exhibits in various of the buildings deal with early ironworks, the development of the telegraph, farm tools, and the like. Open May–October, Thursday and Friday, 12–4; weekends, 1–5. Groups by appointment. Admission charge.

Another of Morristown's 19th-century residents who influenced the development of the state was George P. Macculloch, the driving force behind the construction of the Morris Canal. His house, started in 1810, and now the Macculloch Hall Historical Museum (45 Macculloch Ave.; 201-538-2404), is furnished with period pieces. Among its collections are fine china, oriental rugs, and prints and drawings by Thomas Nast (see below). The gardens have been restored; of particular note is the wisteria, apparently brought from Japan by Commodore Matthew C. Perry. Museum open April--November, Sunday, 2–4:30. Groups by appointment. Admission charged. Gardens open daily.

One of Morristown's renowned citizens at the turn of the

century was Thomas Nast, remembered today for having invented the donkey and elephant as symbols of the Democratic and Republican parties and for popularizing the image of Uncle Sam in striped trousers and tall hat and, possibly, that of Santa Claus suggested by Clement Moore's "'Twas the Night before Christmas." To his contemporaries, however, he was known for his crusade against the corruption of Boss Tweed and Tammany Hall. His house,★ known as Villa Fontana (Macculloch Ave. and Miller Rd.), built in the 1860s, is a national historic landmark.

The Morris Museum (6 Normandy Heights Rd.; 201-538-0454) is a general museum with permanent and changing exhibits in the arts and sciences. Among the collections are dolls, toys, early American and Indian artifacts, and dinosaurs and fossils. Located in the former house of Peter H. B. and Adaline Frelinghuysen, the museum also sponsors concerts and educational programs. Open Tuesday–Saturday, 10–5; Sunday 1–5. Admission charge.

Acorn Hall★ (68 Morris Ave; 201-267-3465), an Italianate house built in 1853 and the headquarters of the Morris County Historical Society, is also a museum. Many of the furnishings have been in the house since it was built, and the gardens have been restored to represent a Victorian garden from the 1853–88 period. Gardens open daily until dusk. House open March–December, Thursday, 11–3 (last tour, 2:30), Sunday, 1:30–4 (last tour, 3:30). Closed major holidays. Groups by appointment. Admission charge.

On Whippany Farm, built in 1891 as a summer home for George Griswold and Sarah Ballantine Frelinghuysen, is the Frelinghuysen Arboretum. The Morris County park commission uses the Colonial Revival house★ as its administrative headquarters, but the extensive arboretum (127 acres) is open to the public. Among its attractions are a rose garden, a crabapple collection, a lilac garden, two self-guided trails, and a braille nature trail. You can pick up maps and guides at the administration building.

About a mile west of the center of town (take Washington St., NJ 24, to Kahdena Rd.; 201-644-0342) is Fosterfields Living Historical Museum. This museum is actually a working farm, used to demonstrate farming methods from 1880 to 1910. The mid-19th-century main house was built by the grandson of Paul Revere, and for a short time in the 1870s it was rented to Bret Harte. There are several outbuildings and barns, and plans call for more animals and a transportation museum. Open April–November, Thursday–Saturday and holidays, 10–5; Sunday, 1–5.

On a hill with lovely views into town is the campus of the Rabbinical College of America (Sussex Ave., off Speedwell Ave.), said to be the world's largest campus for the study of Hasidic Judaism. The original buildings were once the campus for a Catholic girls' reform school.

Adjacent to Jockey Hollow is Lewis Morris Park (also accessible from NJ 24; 201-829-0474), the first park in the Morris County park system. Named for the first governor of New Jersey, the park contains facilities for picnicking, swimming, boating, fishing, and camping. There are also several miles of hiking and cross-country ski trails, fields, open woods, and playing fields.

South of town are the Seaton Hackney Stables (South St.; 201-267-1372), part of the Loantaka Brook Reservation (201-829-0474). The park stretches southward to include the Helen Hartley Jenkins Woods. In addition to the stables, there are picnic facilities, softball fields, and trails suitable for bicycling, horseback riding, and hiking.

North of the center of town is the William G. Mennen Sports Arena (E. Hanover Ave.; 201-267-0750), a skating rink with a year-round schedule.

The county is also developing Patriots' Path, a linear park along the Whippany River. Within Morristown there are entry points at Lake Rd., Speedwell Ave., and the Abbett Ave. playground. You can also pick it up in the arboretum and at the end of Lindsley Rd.

The New Jersey Flower and Garden Show is held every spring in the National Guard Armory (Western Ave., roughly midway between Fort Nonsense and Jockey Hollow, about 2 miles southwest of the center of town; 201-538-7778). The show occupies about an acre and is seen by some 50,000 people each year.

About four miles south of Morristown (take James St. out of town to C 663) is the village of New Vernon. Its historic district* includes Lee's Hill, Village, Millbrook, and Glen Alpin rds. The Tunis-Ellicks House (Village and Millbrook rds.; 201-267-8000), a c. 1800 farmhouse run as a house museum by the Harding Township Historical Society, has a restored kitchen wing used for demonstrations of open-hearth cooking and an 1840s herb garden with labeled plants. House open October, November, and February–April, 1st Sunday of the month, 1–4; garden open daily. Groups other times by appointment.

The Spring Valley Hounds hunts out of New Vernon early Tuesday and Thursday mornings from Labor Day to mid-January. For information call 201-377-5668.

Mountainside UNION

(US 22) 7,118

First settled in the late 1660s by a group of miners from Cornwall, England, who were looking for mineral deposits in the Watchung Mountains, Mountainside is primarily a residential community. A large portion of Union County's 2,000-acre wooded Watchung Reservation falls within its borders. Within the reservation is the Trailside Nature and Science Center (Coles Ave. and New Providence Rd.; 201-232-5930), a complex containing a visitor center, museum (built in 1941 and apparently the state's first nature center), and planetarium. The visitor center, a Michael Graves building dating to 1974, has permanent exhibits that focus on the history, both human and natural, of the reservation, pond life, and reptiles, and changing exhibits of artwork and photographs; it also displays various private collections. Open daily (except New Year's Day, Easter, July 4, Thanksgiving, and Christmas), 1–5. The

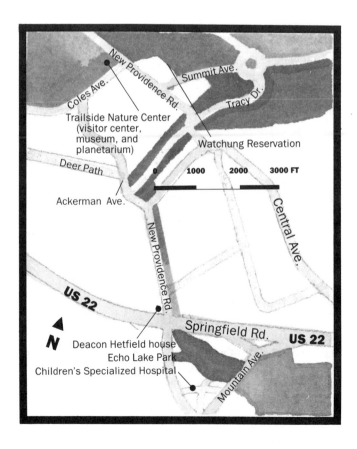

museum's exhibits include taxidermy, birds of prey, habitats, fossils, a weather station, and a butterfly garden. Open daily, 1–5, April to the fourth week of November and during Christmas and other winter school vacations. Open weekends, 1–5, the fourth week of November through March. Closed the same holidays as the visitor center. The planetarium, opened in 1969, has regular weekend afternoon programs, as well as weekday programs during the summer and school vacations. Groups by appointment. The center supplies information and referrals on plants and animals including injured and orphaned wildlife. In January the center offers cross-country ski instruction, and all the trails of the reservation are open for skiing.

Within the reservation are over 13 miles of marked hiking trails, several nature trails, and nearly 30 miles of bridle trails. Stop at the visitor center for maps. The Watchung Riding Stable (Summit Ave.; 201-654-9404) offers classes for adults and children, sponsors shows and a drill team, and rents horses by the hour. Open Tuesday–Sunday, 9–5 (rental hours are more limited). Closed Memorial Day, Thanksgiving, and Christmas. You can explore the deserted village of Feltville,* a factory town dating from 1841, and fish in Seeley's Pond and Blue Brook. The houses in Feltville are being restored, and the village is expected to become a major attraction. You can still fish and boat (with permission from the parks department) in Surprise Lake, despite the damage caused by runoff from the construction of I 78. The lake will eventually be dredged and restored. The reservation also has a rhododendron display garden and the county nursery.

Also partially in Mountainside is Echo Lake Park (Mountain Ave; 201-352-8431, 201-232-9819), one of the many parks in Union County designed by Frederick Law Olmsted. Its 140 acres offer opportunities for boating, fishing, and ice-skating. There are athletic fields, a playground, and picnic facilities, as well as a fitness course that includes a ten-station course for people in wheelchairs.

The reception area of the Children's Specialized Hospital (New Providence Rd. south of 22; 201-233-3720) is in a 1750 farmhouse built by Jonathan Crane. The house was purchased in 1875 by Thomas Drew, who was related to the Barrymore family of actors, and, according to local legend, John, Ethel, Lionel, and Maurice Barrymore all stayed there. Although the hospital, which purchased the property in 1896, has altered the house considerably, it tries to maintain the look of a late 19th-century mansion in the reception area. Open weekdays, 8–4:30.

Also on New Providence Rd. (on the westbound side of 22) is the Deacon Hetfield house (1755), moved ½ mile along 22 in 1985. This house, which retains its original floors, plaster, beams, and mantels, was the writer McKinlay Kantor's home in the 1930s. It is being restored as part of a borough cultural center, museum, and meeting place. (For information call Fern Hyde, 201-232-3834.)

Mount Holly BURLINGTON (C 530, 537, 541, 612, 628) 10,818

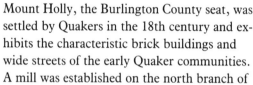

Mount Holly, the Burlington County seat, was settled by Quakers in the 18th century and exhibits the characteristic brick buildings and wide streets of the early Quaker communities.

A mill was established on the north branch of Rancocas Creek in the 1720s and an ironworks and clothing factory in the 1730s. (The clothing factory was set up by Josiah White, ancestor of the Josiah White who realized the importance of coal as a fuel and formed the Lehigh Coal and Navigation Company, and of Joseph C. White and Elizabeth C. White, who developed New Jersey's cranberry and blueberry industries respectively.) Also in the 1730s, Benjamin Franklin published in the *Pennsylvania Gazette* an account of a Mount Holly witch trial in which two witches were accused of making the livestock sing and dance; accusers and accused had to stand trial together, and only the accused sank in the trial by water. It has been suggested that this may be the first New Jersey joke.

By the late 18th century, Mount Holly was important enough to be made the county seat. The Burlington County Court House (west side of High St. at Union St.), a beautiful two-story brick Georgian building dating from 1796, may be the oldest courthouse in the United States still used for its original purpose. The two flanking buildings date from 1807.

Until its conversion into a museum in 1966, the Burlington County Prison Museum (128 High St.; 609-261-5068) was probably the oldest operating jail in the United States. Designed by the architect of the Washington Monument and built in 1810 according to the most modern principles

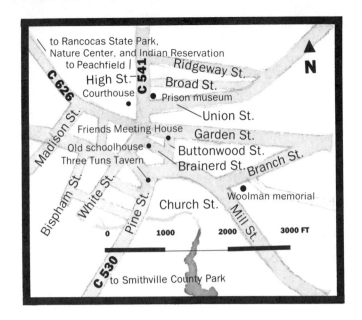

to Rancocas State Park, Nature Center, and Indian Reservation
to Peachfield
to Smithville County Park

of penal practice (prisoners had individual cells and could
learn a trade in the prison workshop), the stone jail may
have been the first fireproof building in the United States.
The building is now a national historic landmark. Guided
tours Wednesday and Saturday, 10–4.

What is probably the state's oldest surviving schoolhouse
is to be found at 35 Brainerd St. (609-267-4337). The one-
room brick building, dating from 1759, is run as a museum
by the New Jersey chapter of the Colonial Dames of
America. Open May–October, Wednesday and Sunday,
1–4; other times by appointment. And what may be the
oldest volunteer fire department in the state—it dates from
1752—is to be found at 15 Pine.

John Woolman, the Quaker whom many have credited
with beginning the antislavery movement in this country
and whose journal remains a well-loved and much-read
book (the second book chosen for the Harvard Classics),
was born nearby and moved to Mount Holly in 1740. The
house he built for his daughter (99 Branch St.; 609-267-
3226) in 1771 (the "i. e. w. 1783" visible on the south eleva-
tion refers to Jabez Woolman and his wife, who bought the
house that year), with two acres surrounding it, once Woolman's orchards, has been preserved as a memorial. There
is a lovely garden, and in the peaceful room (used for the
Mount Holly Quaker meetings January–April to save heating the big house in town) are a few mementos of Woolman

and his times, among them his chair and a fragment of his handwriting. Open daily, 10–4; groups by appointment.

Woolman's grandfather, Henry Burr, in 1695 purchased Peachfield Plantation from the widow of John Skene, the first Freemason resident in America. Burr built a new, ironstone house on the property in 1725; a wing was added in 1732. The property remained in the Burr family until the late 1920s, when the house was severely damaged in a fire. Restored and handsomely furnished with 18th- and 19th-century pieces, Peachfield* is run as a house museum by the Colonial Dames of America; the Peachfield land is still being farmed. Open May–October, Wednesday and Sunday, 1–4; other times by appointment. Admission charged.

John Brainerd, the famous missionary, was also active in Mount Holly, preaching here from 1767 to 1775, preaching at the Indian reservation in nearby Brotherton (now Indian Mills), and founding the Mount Holly Presbyterian Church. He sold the land on which the Friends Meeting House (1775; Main and Buttonwood sts.) stands. The house was used by the Hessians as a slaughterhouse in December 1776 (apparently, the marks of their cleavers can still be seen on the benches) and by the state legislature in 1779.

The Mount Holly historic district* encompasses much of the town's center and includes 18th- and 19th-century buildings on Mill, Pine, High, Garden, White, Union, Bispham, Madison, Buttonwood, Branch, Church, and Ridgeway sts., as well as Park Dr. and Commerce Place. At 211 Mill St. is the Stephen Girard house (c. 1779). The American financier who was later to be prominent in financing the Revolution and who founded Girard College in Philadelphia lived here for a year or two. The Three Tuns Tavern (Pine and Mill sts.) dates from 1723. Off Pine St. is Mount Holly Park, situated on the holly-covered hill that gave the town its name.

Two miles east of Mount Holly (C 530 or 621 to the Smithville-Jacksonville Rd.; turn left off 530, right off 621) is the Smithville County Park* (609-261-5068, 609-261-3780). In the 1850s Shreveville (as Smithville was then called) was the site of a large industrial complex, where cotton was spun, woven, and printed. The enterprise failed, and between 1858 and 1865 Shreveville lay dormant. In 1865 the complex was purchased by Hezekiah Bradley Smith, a machinery manufacturer from Lowell, Massachusetts. Smith converted the various cotton factories and began producing woodworking machines; eventually, the H. B. Smith Machine Company would produce one-quarter

of the country's woodworking machinery. Its Star bicycle
also proved highly successful. Smith renovated the workers'
houses, built new ones, and added a boardinghouse with a
dining room and theater. Three hundred acres of farmland
were added to the complex, supplying much of the town's

Mount Holly

food. He expanded the Shreves' mansion, adding, among other amenities, a billiard room and bowling alley. After Smith's death the company continued, and one of its most remarkable achievements was the Bicycle Railway, intended to carry employees from Mount Holly to Smithville. Workers glided along a rail on special self-propelled bicycles, reaching a maximum speed of 18 miles per hour, but since a second rail was never built, there were always delays when a rider approached from the opposite direction. Although the Smithville company was a victim of the Depression, descendants of the family continued to live in the mansion until 1962. Since 1975 it has belonged to the county, and the facilities currently include the orientation and exhibit center, the Victorian house museum, the casino annex and art gallery, and the formal gardens and grounds. You can also take a self-guided walking tour. Open April–November, Wednesday and Sunday. Groups by appointment.

Northwest of Mount Holly on C 626 is Rancocas State Park (609-726-1191), 1,200 acres of largely undeveloped land, suitable for fishing, hiking, and informal picnics, with a natural area along the Rancocas Creek. The Audubon Society's Rancocas Nature Center (609-261-2495), at the eastern end of the park, encompasses 200 acres of fields, woodlands, and freshwater tidal marsh, with self-guided nature trails. The center also sponsors a variety of programs. Open Tuesday–Sunday, 9–5. A little farther west off 626 is the Rancocas Indian Reservation (609-261-4747), 250 acres the Powhatan Indians have leased from the state for 25 years. A so-called grandfather's house, a two-story four-headed turtle with museumlike exhibits, is scheduled to open in the summer of 1987.

Mount Laurel BURLINGTON
(NJ Tnpk exit 4, I 295, NJ 38, 73)   17,614

 Composed of several old communities, the modern township of Mount Laurel has seen its population more than triple over the last 25 years. The name of the town is familiar to many in New Jersey because of the 1975 and 1983 court decisions requiring the town to provide a certain amount of middle- and low-income housing, a decision that has had repercussions in most other growing New Jersey communities.

The Evesham Friends' Meetinghouse★ (Moorestown-Mt. Laurel Rd.) dates to 1760 and replaced the original 17th-century building. The eastern end was built, with the help of Indians, from sandstone quarried across the street. The western end was added in 1798. The church, which is only used in the summers now, served as a barracks for the British in 1778. Note also the Farmers Hall* (Hainesport-Mt. Laurel and Moorestown-Mt. Laurel rds.), built in the 1860s.

PAWS Farm (Hainesport-Mt. Laurel Rd., east of Hartford Rd.; 609-778-8795) is an 18th-century farm sheltering wild and domestic animals. The farmhouse, smokehouse, and dairy barn are open to visitors, and there are nature displays, an archaeological trail, and a self-guided nature trail. The farm sponsors a visiting pet program as well as various special events and educational programs. Open Wednesday–Sunday, 10–4. Groups by appointment. Admission charge.

Mullica Hill GLOUCESTER (NJ 45, 77, C 322, 581) 1,050

Mullica Hill, located in the center of one of the largest fruit-growing regions in New Jersey, was settled in the late 17th century by four Finns, the brothers Eric, John, Olaf, and William Mullica. (Because Finland was controlled by Sweden at the time, they are often identified as Swedes.) There were also many Quakers among the early settlers, and the town is reputed to have sent an all-Quaker company to the Civil War. The Friends Meeting House (c. 1806; Main St.) stands on land purchased from the first person to settle on the south side of Raccoon Creek. Many of the older buildings have been converted to crafts and antiques shops, and there are some 80 crafts and antiques dealers in Mullica Hill. A crafts show is held the first weekend in May and an antiques open house the third weekend in October. Because of the orchards, the area is particularly lovely in spring.

The Old Town Hall Museum (S. Main St., NJ 77, and Woodstown Rd., NJ 45; 609-478-4949, 609-478-4646) occupies the former town hall, built in 1871 by a private stock company. The museum includes a re-created country store and 19th-century classroom, as well as permanent and changing exhibits. The exhibits usually focus on South Jersey; past ones, for example, have dealt with agriculture, Quakerism, and images in art of southern New Jersey. Open March–May and October through the first week in December, Saturday, 11–4; Sunday, 1–4.

National Park GLOUCESTER

(Delaware River, west of Woodbury) 3,552

The site of an important battle in the revolutionary war, Red Bank Battlefield,* a national historic landmark, is in the borough of National Park (so named because Congress in 1870 authorized the purchase of a portion of the battlefield). Fort Mercer was hastily erected here in the apple orchard of James and Ann Whitall (he was a wealthy Quaker farmer and merchant) to protect the river approach to Philadelphia. Troops under Christopher Greene built a trick wall in the earthworks and withheld their fire until the Hessian troops, who outnumbered them more than two to one, were so close that they ended up with wadding in their chests. Most historians believe the American victory helped delay the British navy's entrance into Philadelphia and helped convince the French to enter the war. Count von Donop, the Hessian commander, was fatally wounded in the battle.

After the engagement the James and Ann Whitall house (100 Hessian Ave.; 609-853-5120) was used as a hospital for wounded Hessians and Americans. It is said that during the fighting Ann Whitall, whose nine children had retired to Woodbury for safety, continued her spinning, and when a cannonball came through the house, she picked up her spinning wheel and resumed spinning in the basement. After the battle she nursed both Hessians and Continentals. A brick building (1748) with a stone wing, the house, recently restored, bears scars from the battle. It now contains the Gloucester County park system's offices and a county-run museum. The rooms have period furnishings, and displays change periodically. Plans include introducing more features of a living museum. Open April–October, Wednesday–Sunday, 9–5. Winter months and groups by appointment. The battle is restaged annually on the Sunday closest to 22 October, the date of the battle, and the event includes a crafts show and crafts demonstrations. The 20-acre park, which also has a picnic pavilion for groups with reservations, is open daily, 9–dusk.

Nearby (100 Grove Ave.) is the James Whitall, Jr., house,* built in 1766 by one of the Whitall sons.

Neptune MONMOUTH (Garden State Pkwy exit 100, NJ 18, 33, 66) 5,276 (borough) 28,336 (CDP)

The birthplace of actor Jack Nicholson, Neptune is the site of Monmouth County's first county park, the 580-acre Shark River Park (Schoolhouse Rd.; 201-922-3868). The park is hilly, and there are pitch-pine and oak forests with a dense understory of sheep laurel, ferns, pepperbush, and blueberries. The Shark River goes through the park, and because of the cedar swamps and sphagnum bogs, the trails can be wet. In addition to its hiking, cross-country skiing, and nature trails, the park contains picnic facilities, a pond for fishing and skating, shuffleboard courts, and horseshoe pitches. Guided nature walks by appointment (201-842-4000). A county golf course (Old Corlies Ave.; 201-922-4141) abuts Shark River Park to the east; its clubhouse (1918) is of interest.

The Neptune Historical Museum (25 Neptune Blvd.; 201-775-8241, 201-775-8243), housed on the second floor of the public library, contains exhibits concentrating on local history. Open Tuesday, Friday, 10–1, 2–5:30; Thursday, 1–6, 7–9. Other times by appointment.

South of Neptune (in Wall Township across from the municipal building) is the Allgor-Barkalow Homestead Museum (1701 New Bedford Rd.; 201-681-3806). The museum contains period furnishings and an old-style country store and sponsors several special events each year. Open Sunday, 1–4; groups by appointment.

Newark ESSEX (NJ Tnpk exit 14, I 78, 280, 287, US 1, 9, 22, NJ 24) 329,248

New Jersey's largest city, and one of the first to be settled by the English, Newark was founded in 1666 by a group of about 40 men, women, and children who left Connecticut to seek a place where they could live as they chose, which meant a place where the church would have ascendancy over the state. They settled near the intersection of Broad and Market sts. and were soon joined by other families from Connecticut. Toward the end of the century the settlement became known for its apple cider, which was thought to be of higher quality than that produced in other colonies.

Eventually the religious monopoly was broken, but the community continued to grow very slowly until the end of the 18th century, when small-scale manufacturing began to appear: hat factories in the 1780s, shoe factories in the 1790s. In the 1830s the coming of the Morris Canal and the railroads connected Newark more readily to raw materials (particularly coal and iron from the west) and markets (particularly in the south). The city became a leading center for all types of leather goods, for jewelry, and for carriages. Brewing, established in Newark in the 1840s, remained one of the city's largest industries until very recently (only one brewery, its copper vats and steaming smokestacks familiar to those who use the Newark Airport, is in operation today). Financial services also appeared early—the first bank in 1804, the first insurance company in 1810. Newark's development as a transportation center continued with the opening of Port Newark in 1915 and of Newark Airport in 1927. Although Newark has been losing population since World War II, and has suffered most of the problems faced by older cities all over the country, it remains a center for financial services and transportation, it is becoming a center for education, and it is attracting a considerable number of artists. Some of Newark's largest companies are engaged in major construction projects, primarily in the area of Penn Station and on the Passaic River (before the turn of the century a popular spot for recreation). Port Newark, with Port Elizabeth, is a major facility for container ships, and the airport (the busiest domestic airport in the metropolitan area), is the fastest-growing airport in the nation, handling some 30 million passengers a year. Newark has not conquered all its problems, not the least of which is its financial situation—with all the cultural, medical, and educational facilities, not to mention federal, state, and county courts and offices, some two-thirds of Newark's institutions do not pay property taxes—but most people seem to feel the corner has been turned.

The list of famous people connected with Newark is long. One of the most remarkable is Seth Boyden, who came to Newark around 1815 and, except when he took part in the Gold Rush, spent the rest of his life in the city. Boyden invented the process for making patent leather, developed a way to make malleable iron and to refine zinc from New Jersey ores, designed a train that could go up grades, invented machines to make nails and form hats, improved the daguerreotype process, and, at the end of his life, developed a giant strawberry. He profited from none of his inventions and spent his last days in a small house purchased for him by some of the men who did (he died in 1870). Another Newark resident, Hannibal Goodwin, the pastor of the House of Prayer (407 Broad St.), invented the flexible film used by Edison in the development of motion pictures.

Among the writers Newark can claim are Stephen Crane, best known for *The Red Badge of Courage*, born here in 1871 (his birthplace on Mulberry Place was torn down in 1940); Mary Mapes Dodge, the author of *Hans Brinker, or the Silver Skates*, described by one Dutch bookseller as the best book ever written about Holland, although Dodge did not visit the Netherlands until many years after the book was published; Howard Garis, the author of the Uncle Wiggily tales, which first appeared in the *Newark Evening News;* the playwright Imamu Amiri Baraka (Leroi Jones); the poet Allen Ginsberg, who later lived in Paterson where his father taught English at the high school; the novelist and dog fancier Albert Payson Terhune; and the novelist Philip Roth.

Musicians and entertainers connected with Newark include the opera singer Maria Jeritza, who moved to Newark in the 1940s; Jerome Kern, who graduated from Newark High School in 1902; and Sarah Vaughan, Jerry Lewis, Samuel Augustus Ward (he wrote the music later used for "America the Beautiful"), and Dore Schary, all born in Newark. And Moe Berg, presumably the only professional baseball player who ever served as an undercover agent (in World War II), was raised in Newark.

The state's first daily newspaper, the *Daily Advertiser*, was started in Newark in 1832; the first regular radio station on the eastern seaboard, WJZ, which was the first to broadcast a world series (in 1921), was a Newark station; the first municipally supported summer school was established in Newark in 1886; the first blackout test in World War II took place in Newark.

A tour of Newark's downtown should include the late 18th-century Old First Presbyterian Church★ (820 Broad St.), the direct descendant of the church built by Newark's original settlers. From the 1760s until 1986, Old First owned the prime real estate across from it on Broad St.

North of Old First, at Washington Park, is the Newark Museum (49 Washington St.; 201-596-6550). As part of a plan that will double its floor space, the museum is adding on to its 1920s building. A pioneer in the recognition of folk

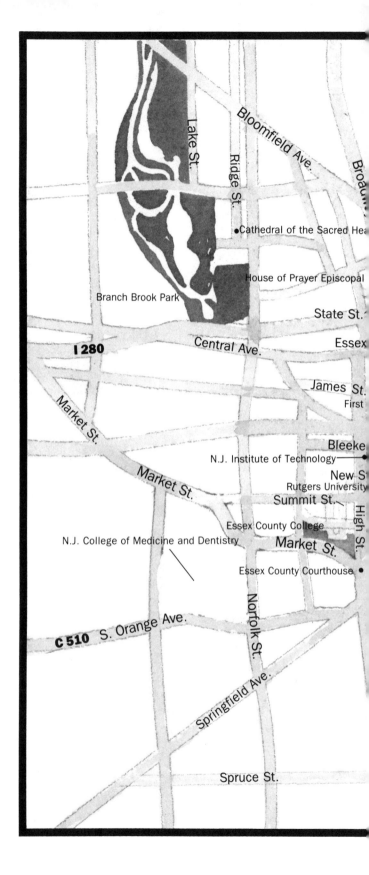

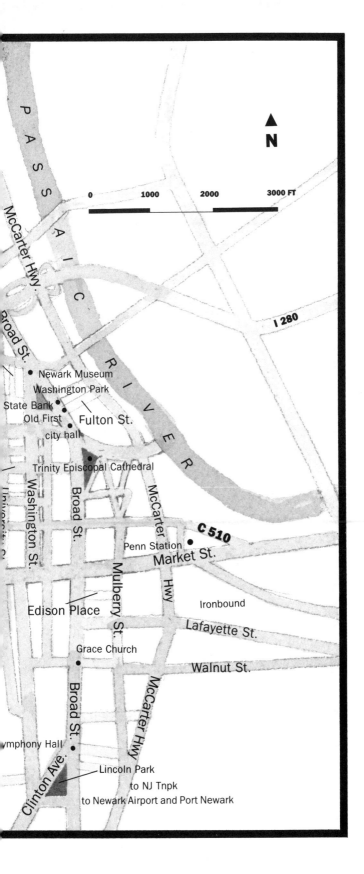

PASSAIC RIVER

McCarter Hwy.

Broad St.

0   1000   2000   3000 FT

N

I 280

• Newark Museum
Washington Park
State Bank •
Old First • Fulton St.
city hall

Washington St.

University S.

Broad St.

Trinity Episcopal Cathedral

McCarter

C 510

Penn Station •
Market St.

Mulberry St.

Hwy

Ironbound

Edison Place

Lafayette St.

Grace Church •

Walnut St.

Broad St.

McCarter Hwy

ymphony Hall •

Clinton Ave.

Lincoln Park
to NJ Tnpk
to Newark Airport and Port Newark

art, the museum is known for its collection of American painting and sculpture. It also has a large collection of decorative arts. In its garden is a sculpture collection that includes works by David Smith, George Segal, and Tony Smith, all, incidentally, New Jersey artists. Also in the garden are the Old Stone Schoolhouse,* 1784, one of Newark's oldest buildings, which was moved to the museum grounds, and, in an old carriage house, a small fire-fighters' museum. Attached to and part of the museum is Ballantine House,* a national historic landmark built in 1885 by John Ballantine, the son of the founder of Ballantine Brewery. Built with Victorian abandon in a variety of styles and with considerable attention to detail, the building is the only mansion remaining around Washington Park (Washington and Broad sts.), once a fashionable residential district. (The park was laid out as a marketplace in 1667; note the statue of Seth Boyden.) In Ballantine House, the library, drawing room, reception room, hallway, and dining room are open to the public; the museum is gradually restoring other rooms. Special Christmas holiday exhibits are held in Ballantine House. Also part of the museum is the planetarium (201-596-6611), which offers public programs weekends, at 2 and 3, Wednesdays at 3, September–June; Wednesdays at 3 and Fridays at 12:15 in July and August. Family programs are offered Saturday at 1, October–May; Friday at 2:30, July and August. Groups by appointment (201-596-6615). Admission charged. (Because of the renovation, the planetarium schedule may change, so it would be best to call for confirmation.) There is also a junior museum with many special programs. The main building and Ballantine House open Tuesday–Sunday, 12–5; the fire-fighters' museum open Tuesday–Sunday, 12–4:30.

Near the museum is the Newark Public Library (5 Washington St.; 201-733-7800). Its splendid early 20th-century Renaissance building houses a large collection, and the library continues its long tradition of civic involvement with concert, film, and lecture series, as well as art exhibits.

Military Park (Broad St. and Park Place), once a training ground for the militia, was laid out in 1667 by Newark's original settlers. In 1776 it was used by George Washington's troops as a camping area; it was during this encampment that Thomas Paine wrote "The Crisis" ("These are the times that try men's souls"). The park contains *The Wars of America*, a large bronze group done by Gutzon Borglum, the sculptor of Mt. Rushmore. Also in the park is Trinity

Episcopal Cathedral,* 1744–46, possibly the only church in New Jersey to be situated in a public park. This church is said to owe its origins to the decision of one of the stalwarts of Old First to harvest his hay on a Sunday because rain threatened; the ensuing argument with Old First led him to help found Trinity.

Walking along Broad St. (first paved in 1852) notice (at State St.) the House of Prayer Episcopal Church* and rectory* (Plume House), in which Goodwin invented flexible film; the 19th-century North Reformed Church* (510); the First Baptist Peddie Memorial Church* (at Fulton), from the late 1880s; the Griffith building* (605) from the 1920s; First National State Bank* (810), 1912; Old First and City Hall; and Richard Upjohn's Gothic Revival Grace Church* (at Walnut).

West of Washington and Military parks on the way to the new concentration of educational institutions is the James St. Commons historic district* (University, Bleeker, New, Linden, James, Essex, Burnet, Washington, and Summit sts., and Central Ave.). Among the educational institutions to be found in Newark are Rutgers University, the New Jersey College of Medicine and Dentistry, the New Jersey Institute of Technology, Seton Hall Law School, and Essex County College. The Rutgers unit was formed in 1946, when the University of Newark, itself an amalgam of several colleges, was incorporated into Rutgers. Its Paul Robeson Center Gallery (350 Martin Luther King, Jr., Blvd.; 201-648-5970) is open weekdays, 10:30–4. The New Jersey Institute of Technology, founded in 1881 as the Newark Technical School, has offices in Eberhardt Hall* (High and Bleeker sts.), once an orphanage and now a national historic landmark.

Across Market St. from Essex County College is the Essex County Courthouse* (470 High St.), designed by Cass Gilbert and opened in 1907. On the steps of this impressive marble building is a seated statue of Lincoln, also by Borglum. This courthouse replaced an earlier Egyptian-style one (1836).

Penn Station* (Raymond Plaza W.), built in the 1930s, has recently undergone extensive renovation. The station serves New Jersey Transit, Conrail, Amtrak, and PATH trains, altogether about 450 freight and passenger trains each day, and there are plans to link the station to the airport by means of a monorail. Roughly 50,000 people, two-thirds of them commuters, pass through this Art Deco building every day, some 12,000 heading for the buses, perhaps 12,500 for the subways. The subway runs on trolley tracks laid 50 years ago in the old Morris Canal bed; it comes up at Branch Brook Park. Note the sculpture of seven life-size figures outside the subway entrance done by Grigory Gurevich and students at the Newark School of Fine and Industrial Arts.

Near the station is Clinton Plaza (207–215 Market St.), once the Newark News building (the paper folded in 1972), now condominiums. The oldest structure in the complex dates to 1915; some of its ceilings are 12 feet high. Nearby St. Joseph Plaza★ (233 Market St.) is an office, dining, and physical fitness center in what was once St. Joseph's Church, built in 1880 to serve the Irish immigrant community.

Also near the station is the Gateway Center office complex, a multibuilding project that the Prudential Life Insurance Company, the nation's largest insurance company (established in a Broad St. storefront in the 1870s), became involved in when a company for which Prudential held the mortgage went bankrupt. The 26-story headquarters of the Public Service Enterprise Group Inc. is on Park Place, as is the former home office building of the Fireman's Insurance Co.,★ which dates from the 1920s.

One of the new building projects along the river is the Newark Legal and Communications Center, which will be linked to the satellite communications center on Staten Island by fiber optic cable. The riverfront development also includes offices, a hotel, shops, a garden, and pedestrian walkways.

The Lincoln Park historic district★ includes the park and parts of Spruce, Broad, and Washington sts. and Clinton Ave. The Cathedral Evangelica Reformada★ (27 Lincoln Park at Halsey St.) was once the First Reformed Church, dedicated in 1872. The South Park Cavalry United Presbyterian Church★ (1035 Broad St. at Lincoln Park), was built in 1853.

Just north of Lincoln Park is Symphony Hall★ (1020 Broad St.). It was built as the Salaam Temple in 1925 (at a cost of $2.5 million, a considerable sum in those days), and later became known as the Mosque Theater. Second in size on the east coast only to Radio City Music Hall, it has recently undergone extensive renovation. Among the organizations that use Symphony Hall are the New Jersey Symphony Orchestra and the New Jersey State Opera.

East of Symphony Hall, in the Ironbound section, fashionable today because of its ethnic restaurants, are the only catacombs in the United States. Modeled on those in Rome, they are in a former church (now used by the board of education as an annex of the Lafayette St. School) and are run by the Immaculate Heart of Mary Church (212 Lafayette St.). Open Monday–Saturday, 9–12, 2–6 (ring rectory door bell at 114 Prospect). Also in the Ironbound section note the Ironbound Education and Cultural Center* (178–184 Edison Place), built in 1848 as the Second Reformed Dutch Church (later Our Lady of Mount Carmel).

Newark's Branch Brook* (Clifton Ave.), dedicated in 1895, is the first county park in the United States. Situated on a marsh once known as Old Blue Jay Swamp and used as an army training camp in the Civil War, the park was designed by the Frederick Law Olmsted firm. The Beaux Arts entrance gate (Lake St.) was a gift from Robert Ballantine, and the turn-of-the-century stone lions at the concert mall once guarded the entrance to the Prudential Building. In 1910 the world's largest water fountain was installed, but it had to be abandoned because it endangered the city's water supply. Branch Brook is perhaps best known for its Japanese cherry trees, first planted in 1929. In the spring, when 2,700 of them are in bloom, the park's display surpasses that in Washington, D.C. Half a million people visit the park in April, and the park commission sponsors various special events, including the ten-kilometer Cherry Blossom Run.

East of Branch Brook is the Gothic Revival Cathedral of the Sacred Heart* (89 Ridge St.), started in 1899, but not completed until 1954. This huge cathedral is modeled somewhat on that at Rheims. Among its noteworthy features are 200 stained-glass windows, woodwork of Appalachian white oak, and the angle of the wings of the façade. It is also said to be the first cathedral in the United States to have its own symphony orchestra. Near the cathedral is the Essex County Park Commission Administration Building* (115 Clifton Ave.), built in 1914.

Also east of Branch Brook are the headquarters of the New Jersey Historical Society (230 Broadway; 201-483-3939). Founded in 1845 (in Trenton), the society sponsors a variety of exhibits and educational programs. Its Georgian-style building dates from the mid-1930s and houses a library (used by over 3,500 people in 1985), museum, galleries, and publication and education departments. Museum and library open Tuesday–Saturday, 10–4:30.

South of downtown is Weequahic Park (Elizabeth Ave.; 201-482-6400). The park, also designed by the Olmsted firm, contains a lake for boating and fishing, a rose garden, a trotting track (once known as the Waverly Fair Grounds), and a golf course (201-923-1838). Note the fieldhouse (1907) and the Gothic comfort station (1916).

Newark Airport is east of Weequahic Park. Opened in the late 1920s, the airport for a time was the only one serving the New York metropolitan area. North Terminal, now considerably remodeled, was the original terminal (but for period flavor, note, at the northern end of the airport, the administration building,★ Brewster hangar,★ and the medical building,★ all dating from the late 1920s). Operated by the Port Authority of New York and New Jersey, the airport currently generates almost $1 billion in economic activity each year. Tours of the facilities can be arranged for groups (201-961-2066), but they must provide their own transportation.

Adjacent to the airport on Newark Bay is Port Newark. It and Port Elizabeth, directly to the south, together constitute one of the busiest container ports in the world, handling 12 million tons of cargo annually. Although they are considered among the most modern facilities in the world, they are already threatened by the newest generation of container ships. These latest models carry as many as 4,000 20-foot containers and have a 40-foot draft, which means that when fully laden they must wait for the proper tide (the channels in this port are currently dredged to 35 feet). (They are also computer loaded and can turn around in a day.) On the 2,100 acres are storage sheds, warehouses, offices, cranes, railroad tracks, and roadways. Tours of the New Jersey marine terminals can be arranged by appointment (call the facility staff assistant at 201-589-7100), but you must provide your own transportation.

New Brunswick MIDDLESEX
(US 1, NJ 18, 26, 27, 91, 171, 172, C 514)   41,442

The settlement of New Brunswick goes back to the 1680s when a group of Englishmen from Long Island, among them John Inian, purchased some 10,000 acres along the Raritan River. Inian established a ferry across the river in 1686, eventually adding an inn, docks, and a road to Trenton; in 1697 he gained exclusive rights to the crossing.

The settlement, originally known as Pridmore's Swamp, came to be called Inian's Ferry, but early in the 18th century it was again renamed, becoming New Brunswick, in honor of the English royal house of Brunswick.

New Brunswick developed as an active shipping center during the 18th century and saw considerable action in the Revolution. The Continental army retreated here after the defeat at Fort Lee, and Alexander Hamilton commanded an artillery battery that stalled the British while George Washington moved south toward the Delaware River. Between 29 November and 1 December 1776, Washington made his headquarters at Cochrane's Tavern, at the corner of Neilson and Albany sts. In all, Washington visited New Brunswick five times. The third reading of the Declaration of Independence in the colonies took place here on 6 July 1776. Although many from New Brunswick were accused of favoring the loyalists, local merchant shippers successfully harassed British shipping.

New Brunswick continued as a transportation center during the 19th century (and hence its nickname, Hub City), but the coming of the railroads shifted the action from water to land. The city also developed industrially. Its preeminence as a pharmaceutical town dates to c. 1885 when the Johnson brothers moved their adhesive tape and gauze business (founded in 1873) to an old mill in New Brunswick. Incorporating as Johnson & Johnson in 1887, the firm recruited workers from Hungary, giving New Brunswick the largest Hungarian population of any city in the United States. (A Hungarian festival is held each June; 10,000 people attended in 1985.) Joyce Kilmer (1886–1918), New Brunswick's best-known poet, was the son of the scientific director at Johnson & Johnson. Other industries that have been important to New Brunswick include rubber, hosiery, and musical instruments. The New Jersey Rubber Shoe Company, later part of US Rubber, was founded here in 1839, and the National Musical String Co.* (1898; 120 Georges Rd.), a manufacturer of steel strings, was the first firm in the United States to make harmonicas. Of these only the pharmaceutical industry remains as a major presence (Johnson & Johnson was later joined by E. R. Squibb).

Another major presence in the city is, of course, Rutgers University. The eighth college to be founded in the colonies and the only state university to have existed before the Revolution, Rutgers was chartered in 1766 as Queen's College, its mission the training of Dutch Reformed ministers. In 1771 it opened in a New Brunswick tavern, the Sign of the Red Lion, with one instructor, Frederick Frelinghuysen, one sophomore, and a handful of freshmen. In 1774 it graduated its first student, Matthew Leydt, whose clergyman father was a trustee and founder of the college. Its early years were rocky, but in 1825 it changed its name to Rutgers College in honor of Colonel Henry Rutgers, a New York philanthropist who had fought in the Revolution and been a trustee of the college. He gave the college some modest financial assistance and the bell that still hangs in the cupola of Old Queens (it is the oldest bell in Middlesex County). Rutgers became a land grant institution in 1864, and over the years various colleges, among them agriculture, engineering, pharmacy, Douglass College for women (the largest women's college in the United States), and education, were added. In 1924 Rutgers College became Rutgers University, and in 1945 the state university. It now enrolls some 47,000 students in its 25 schools and colleges on three campuses (Camden, Newark, and New Brunswick; the university's general information number is 201-932-7799).

Now considered a major university (its library, for example, is ranked among the top 25 in the country), Rutgers is also widely known for the Rutgers tomato (developed in 1934) and streptomycin, the first broad-spectrum antibiotic (developed by Selman Waksman in 1943). The first intercollegiate football game (Princeton vs. Rutgers) was played at New Brunswick in 1869, the Princeton team arriving by train. Rutgers won, 6–4. The faculty apparently disapproved of football, but the captain of the Princeton team went on to become chief justice of the New Jersey supreme court, and the captain of the Rutgers team became a leader in the Dutch Reformed church. Rutgers was not to beat Princeton again until 1938 at the game dedicating the new stadium.

Two other large institutions also shape New Brunswick. As the county seat, it is home to the county courthouse (1 John F. Kennedy Sq.) and a host of county agencies. It is also home to two teaching hospitals, St. Peter's Medical Center (254 Easton Ave.) and Robert Wood Johnson University Hospital (180 Somerset St.), founded in 1884 by a group of concerned lay people. New Brunswick, incidentally, had been a leader in colonial medicine—the country's first professional medical association, the Medical Society of New Jersey, was founded here in 1766.

Like many other cities of the northeast, New Brunswick suffered a decline after World War II, and in 1975 a coalition of business, university, community, and government leaders formed to reverse that decline. In part through their efforts downtown New Brunswick has a new look: the central business district was redesigned by I. M. Pei Associates, Johnson & Johnson has a new headquarters, a new hotel has been built, and new office buildings are rising. The New Brunswick Cultural Center (Livingston Ave. and George St.) is being shaped out of four existing buildings (a department store, a 1921 theater, a YMCA building, and a warehouse). The center will include two professional repertory theaters, three stages, and a home for various organizations, including Designer Craftsmen of New Jersey, Young Audiences of New Jersey, the Princeton Ballet, the Garden State Symphonic Pops Orchestra, the Opera Theater of New Jersey, and various units of the university's Mason Gross School of the Arts. Eventually George Street will be closed to all vehicular traffic except the university's shuttle buses. Plans for redeveloping the waterfront have also been formulated; they include a new dock for fishing and boating and bicycle and walking paths along the river; the park on the concrete deck over NJ 18 has already been built.

Despite all the rebuilding, which has involved considerable demolition, there are still a remarkable number of historic buildings to be seen in New Brunswick. (A walking tour of the city is available from the Middlesex County Cultural and Heritage Commission; 201-745-4489.) The old Hiram Market commercial district encompasses parts of Albany, Bayard, Church, Dennis, Hiram, Neilson, Paterson, Peace, and Richmond sts. and Memorial Parkway. Nineteenth-century rubber factories were located here (Daniel Webster won a patent case for one of them), and the area includes two old churches (one English, one Dutch, reflecting part of the city's history—Dutch settlers arrived in 1730). Middle-income townhouses will soon be added to this area. Middlesex County's oldest church (1812; the clock dates to c. 1830, the interior was rebuilt in 1847 and 1862), the First Reformed Church of New Brunswick, is on the west side of Neilson St., opposite Hiram Ave. (201-545-1005). In the cemetery are graves going back to 1746. Open September–June, Tuesday–Friday, 9–1; July and August, Thursday, 9–1; guided tours by appointment.

Christ Episcopal Church is also on the west side of Neilson St. between Church and Paterson sts., and it too has a prerevolutionary cemetery. The building dates from

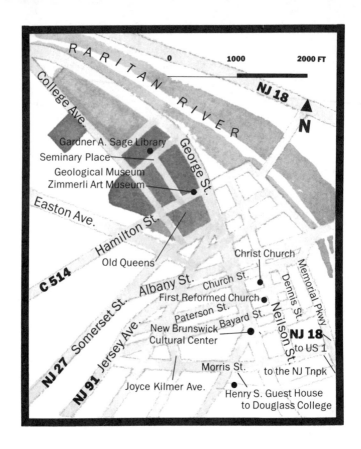

the 1850s (with later alterations and additions) and uses the stone from the original church built 100 years earlier.

Buccleuch Mansion★ (Easton Ave. in Buccleuch Park; 201-745-5094, 201-846-1063) is an 18th-century house (c. 1739) built by Anthony Walton White, a cavalryman who married Lewis Morris's daughter. In 1821 the house was acquired by Col. Joseph Warren Scott, son of the surgeon-general of the Continental armies and himself a noted New Jersey lawyer, who named it after a Scottish ancestor, the duke of Buccleuch. His grandchildren gave the house to the city in 1911, and it has been operated as a museum since 1915. The recently renovated house has 16 rooms, which have been furnished to show how styles have changed over its lifetime; particularly noteworthy is the hand-blocked wallpaper, with scenes of Paris and of Indian tiger hunting, dating from 1815. The saber and spur marks made by the Enniskillen dragoons, who were quartered in the house in 1776–77, are still visible. Open weekends, 3–5, from the last Sunday in May to the last Sunday in October. Buccleuch Park itself (George St. and Easton Ave.; 201-745-5094) consists of 78 acres overlooking the Raritan River.

The Henry S. Guest House* (Livingston Ave. and Morris St.; 201-745-5108) was built c. 1760 (the front doorway and porch were added c. 1825 and the house moved to its present location 100 years later). Guest was a whaler and tanner, and among his guests were John Adams, Thomas Paine, and Lafayette. Paine, in fact, was hidden from the British in Guest's house. The house has exhibits of shawls and old lace and a room with Japanese items. There are occasional art shows. To visit the Guest house, ask at the public library next door, weekdays, 9–4:30. Driving south on Livingston Ave. toward US 1, you will see a considerable number of substantial late 19th- and early 20th-century houses.

The university's Queen's campus* (part of the College Ave. campus) combines 18th- and 19th-century buildings, and Old Queens itself (north side of Somerset St. between George St. and College Ave.; 201-932-7823) is a national historic landmark. A three-story brownstone built between 1808 and 1825, it was intended to serve the needs of a grammar school, a college, and a theological college of the Dutch Reformed church with living quarters for two professors. The architect, John McComb, Jr., was also the architect of New York's City Hall, designed at about the same time. University administrative offices are here, including the president's office. One of the fireplaces has a preserved Dutch oven, and some of the windowpanes are handmade. Open weekdays, 8:30–4:30; group tours by appointment.

The College Ave. campus has an unusual sense of space for an urban campus, and many fine old houses are scattered throughout the area. West of Old Queens is the Rutgers University Geological Museum (201-932-7243). Open weekdays, 9–4. The Daniel S. Schanck Observatory (c. 1865–66), two octagons connected by a one-story passage, was the first building intended exclusively for scientific purposes to be erected at Rutgers; it is now used to store equipment. North of Old Queens is the Jane Voorhees Zimmerli Art Museum (George and Hamilton sts.; 201-932-7237). Portions of the permanent collection, which includes a nationally renowned print collection particularly strong in 19th-century French prints, are exhibited in the lower wing; temporary exhibits are shown in the other galleries. Open Monday, Tuesday, Thursday, Friday, 10–4:30; weekends, 12–5. Tours by appointment (201-932-7096).

At the northern end of the College Ave. campus is the statue of William of Orange, founder of the Netherlands, and the New Brunswick Theological Seminary, founded in 1784. The Gardner A. Sage Library (21 Seminary Place; 201-247-5243) was built in 1875; the archives of the Reformed Dutch church repose there. There are also changing exhibits. Open Monday–Thursday, 9 A.M.–10 P.M., Friday, 9–5, Saturday, 10–2. Note also the Doolittle-Demarest house (southwest corner of George St. and Seminary Place), 1850–70, and the painted Suydam statue. The red-brick former headquarters of Johnson & Johnson are visible toward the river.

At 101 Somerset St. is Alexander Johnston Hall (1830, 1870) once the home of Rutgers Preparatory School,★ one of the 12 oldest schools in the country. Joyce Kilmer's birthplace (17 Joyce Kilmer Ave.; 201-745-5117), a modest 18th- and 19th-century farmhouse, is used as an office by the New Brunswick Dial-A-Ride. The house contains some period furniture and pictures of members of the Kilmer family. Tours by appointment.

On the Douglass campus (southwest of the College Ave. campus) is the Levi D. Jarrard house,★ a mid-19th-century brownstone. The Cook College campus (south of the Douglass campus) includes the university farm. Although much high-technology work occurs on this campus, its appearance has a period quality. On the east side of US 1 are the university's display gardens (Ryders La., about 1 mile south of NJ 18). This lovely area is open daily, 8:30–dusk.

Newton SUSSEX (US 206, NJ 94, C 519) 7,748

 Newton, the seat of Sussex County, was settled in the mid-18th century. Until recently it was the center of a bustling farming community providing the legal, financial, and medical services associated with a county seat, but it is becoming more of a bedroom community for Morris County and even New York City commuters.

Much of Newton retains its 19th-century air, and if you can ignore the cars, you can get a strong sense of earlier times. Try to walk around the central square and Main St., with its well-preserved line of 19th-century shops, and drive along the streets off the square. The county courthouse★ (High and Spring sts.), built in 1847, replaces the first one (1765), which burned. A Greek Revival building with six Doric columns, it is strikingly sited on a steep hill. Note the inn at Main and Spring sts.: in 1782 George Washington stopped here on his way to Newburgh, N.Y. The First Presbyterian Church (High and Church sts.) dates from the 1860s and is listed in the state register of historic buildings.

The Hill Memorial Building (1916) at the corner of Church and Main sts. houses the Sussex County Historical Society's headquarters and museum (201-383-6010). The building was built in 1916 specifically for the society, and contains a fireplace with stones taken from various buildings and sites of historic interest. Displays are changed throughout the year. Open Friday, 9–4.

The Newton Fire Museum (150 Spring St.; 201-383-0396) is housed in the department's first station and includes old equipment (an 1863 hand pumper, an 1873 steamer, and the like), memorabilia, and photographs. Open July and August, Tuesday–Saturday, 9–3; September–June, Friday and Saturday, 9–3. The department, incidentally, gave up its horses in 1923.

The Merriam house* (131 Main St.) is a particularly splendid example of Queen Anne architecture. Built in the 1880s for the founder of the Merriam Shoe Company, it is now a rest home. The factory itself, which once employed some 750 people, is being converted to other uses. About one mile south on US 206 is St. Paul's Abbey. The original structure (now the right wing) dates from 1840, the rest from 1932.

Some two miles south of Newton off 206 (head west on Fredon Rd., C 618, across from the Newton Airport) is the

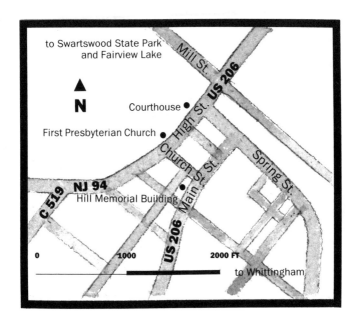

Merriam House

Whittingham Wildlife Management Area. Of the area's
1,500 acres, 400 are left as a refuge in which live beaver, ot-
ter, and many species of waterfowl. On the limestone cliffs
in this northern swamp and flood-plain forest you can see
rare species of fern. The open places are kept open, which
makes this a good spot for watching butterflies, and there
are dirt roads to walk on. It is possible to canoe into the area

from the community of Springdale (at the intersection of 206 and C 611). You can also hunt and fish here.

About five miles west of Newton on C 622 is Swartswood State Park (201-383-5230), almost 1,500 acres with facilities for picnicking, swimming, boating, hiking, and in season hunting, cross-country skiing, and skating. Open 8–sunset in summer (Memorial Day–Labor Day), 8–4:30 in winter. Parking fee in summer, Wednesday–Monday.

West of Swartswood at Fairview Lake (off Fairview Lake Rd., C 624 at that point) is the Fairview Lake YMCA camp and conference center (201-383-9282). Trails here are open to the public for cross-country skiing.

North Bergen HUDSON (I 495, US 1, 9, C 501, 505) 47,019

Louis XVI once had a garden here, and it is said that the country's first Lombardy poplar trees were introduced into this garden by André Michaux, the king's official botanist. At the eastern end of the township is North Hudson Park (John F. Kennedy Blvd. E. and Bergenline Ave.), a 167-acre county park. Part of it lies on the Palisades, offering views of the Hudson River and New York City, and a scenic path goes down steps to the river valley. West of the boulevard the land is more rolling, and the park contains a lake, with fishing, boating, and skating. Other facilities include a children's playground, athletic fields, picnic areas, and tennis courts. There are also woods, rare in Hudson County.

At Flower Hill Cemetery (John F. Kennedy Blvd. at 55th St.), there is a splendid view of the wetlands to the west, and the architecture of the gatehouse and the mausoleum with the gray stone windows is worth a look. Note also the mid-19th-century Egyptian-Revival sphinxlike creature guarding a crypt.

Wandering around in North Bergen you will come across many interesting buildings: the 1920s eclectic Embassy Theater or the 19th-century Cameron Button factory, now condominiums. Schuetzen Park (3167 John F. Kennedy Blvd.), now used for banquets and weddings but once an opera house, and the Fritz Reuther Altenheim (3161 John F. Kennedy Blvd.) tell us something of North Bergen's ethnic past.

Nutley ESSEX (Garden State Pkwy exits 150, 151, NJ 7, 21) 28,998

Settled in the 17th century by colonists from Newark, Nutley was once known as Franklinville after William Franklin, New Jersey's last royal governor (and Benjamin Franklin's natural son). The town still boasts one house dating from the beginning of the 18th century (the Vreeland house, now used by the Woman's Club of Nutley, 216 Chestnut St.; the town hall across the street was once a textile mill). After the Civil War, it attracted a colony of artists and writers, many of whom lived in the Enclosure historic district* (Enclosure and Calico las.). Mark Twain was a frequent visitor here (the editor of *Puck* was his host), and Frank Stockton wrote his most famous story, "The Lady or the Tiger?", at his home on Walnut St. Annie Oakley was another famous resident. Near the Enclosure is Memorial Park, a lovely linear park along the Third River.

Tradition has it that Mussolini once owned a one-acre tract in Nutley, now the site of the Amvets Memorial Post 30 clubhouse. He was the only creditor of a local bank that tried to pay him before declaring bankruptcy, but the bank didn't wait long enough, and the draft didn't clear. Since 1928 Hoffman-LaRoche has had a plant here (340 Kingsland St.), sometimes employing as many as 6,000 workers.

The Nutley Historical Society museum (65 Church St.; 201-667-5239, 201-751-8847), housed in an attractive brick

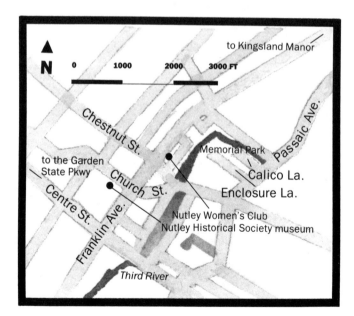

building, features local history, including exhibits of Annie Oakley memorabilia. Across the street is the Franklin Reformed Church, an attractive wooden building.

Kingsland Manor★ (3 Kingsland St.; 201-661-3410, 201-667-2800), a sandstone structure built by a mill owner, most of which dates to the late 18th century (a portion was built earlier, and the structure was altered in the 19th century), is being restored as closely as feasible to its original condition. Open September–June, 3d Sunday of the month, 2–4, and for the annual Christmas fair the 1st Saturday of December. Other times and groups by appointment.

At 4 Franklin Ave. is Villa Capri, a small house almost hidden behind a collection of architectural fragments that fill up the yard, climb up the willow tree, spill out onto the sidewalk. The fragments making up this surreal landscape vary from well-preserved larger-than-life heads to truncated fluted columns to pieces of polished marble.

Oakland BERGEN (US 202, NJ 208)

13,443

Oakland is one of Bergen County's older communities, and several early stone houses remain, particularly along Ramapo Valley Dr. (US 202), to remind us of that past. One of these, the Van Allen House★ (Franklin Ave. and Ramapo Valley Rd.; 201-337-5721), is maintained as a museum by the Oakland Historical Society. This 18th-century structure, which for a brief period served as George Washington's headquarters when he was traveling from Morristown to West Point and other northern spots, and for another brief period functioned as the Bergen County courthouse, has exhibits of clothing and colonial furnishings intended to convey the atmosphere of a Dutch colonial household. Open the 1st and 3d Sunday of the month, 1–4; other times by appointment (201-337-0247). (A former architectural attraction, Oakland's diner, was transported to Baltimore, where it served as the principal set for the movie *Diner*.)

Northwest of Oakland (take W. Oakland Ave. to Skyline Dr.; turn right; you can park near the creek) is Ramapo Mountain State Forest (201-962-7031), a 2,800-acre preserve that includes the 1,800-acre Ramapo Lake Natural

Ocean City CAPE MAY (NJ 52,
C 619, 623, 656)   13,949

Founded in 1879 by three brothers, Methodist ministers looking to create a wholesome year-round family resort, Ocean City is still a dry community that has maintained its reputation as a family-oriented place. With its well-kept look, eight miles of beach, over two miles of boardwalk, including a music pier on which summer concerts are given, and a new Australian-hardwood promenade, Ocean City can find its population swelling to 150,000 during the summer months. Until recently the town was not only dry but closed on Sundays; partial blue laws may well be reintroduced. The community sponsors many special events in the summer, including a hermit-crab race, a baseball card and sports memorabilia show, an antique car show, a sand-sculpting contest, and surf-fishing contests.

The Ocean City Historical Museum has for many years been located in a c. 1910 school (409 Wesley Ave.; 609-399-1801), but hopes soon to move, with the arts center and the library, to a new building on 18th and Simpson. Note on the museum's grounds the pumper under glass and the dog fountain, a memorial to a mascot. In the museum are Victorian rooms and exhibits of dolls, Indian artifacts, apparel, and items related to the history and natural history of Ocean City. Of particular interest is the Sindia Room, with mementos of the four-masted bark that went aground on the Ocean City beach in 1901. (The wreck is said to be visible at the foot of 15th St.) There are special exhibits for the Christmas season. Open mid-June–mid-September, Monday–Saturday, 10–4; mid-September–December and March–mid June, Tuesday–Saturday, 1–4. Groups by appointment.

The Ocean City Arts Center (3601 Bay Ave.; 609-399-7618) is temporarily located in an old rescue squad building (it used to be on the second floor of the school used by the museum). The center's gallery exhibits change roughly every month; the center also offers a variety of classes and other programs. Open weekdays, 9–4; Saturday, 9:30–12.

Corson's Inlet State Park (Ocean Dr.; 609-861-2404) is off the southern end of Ocean City. The park's 300-odd acres offer opportunities for fishing, boating, picnicking, and hiking. The park administration's policy of letting the beach develop without interference means that you can get a good sense of what the island on which Ocean City was built looked like before the community was developed. This is a very popular park in the summer, although flies and poison ivy can be problems. The inlet is surrounded by the Marmora Wildlife Management Area, over 6,000 acres, most of it salt marsh, with excellent opportunities for boating and bird watching.

About five miles from Ocean City in Palermo (take Bay Ave. to Roosevelt Blvd. to US 9 and turn left) is the Friendship School (Ocean Ave. and Shore Rd.), a reconstruction and restoration of an 1830s school. Open Sunday, 1–4.

Ocean Grove MONMOUTH

(NJ 33, 71)   [Neptune Township]

Founded in 1869 by Methodists as a religious summer colony, the town of Ocean Grove was for 100 years run by the Methodist Camp Meeting Association. In 1979 the state supreme court declared Ocean Grove's government unconstitutional, and Ocean Grove became part of Neptune Township. At that point most of the community's strictly enforced blue laws, which included Sunday prohibitions against driving (the gates leading into the community were closed at midnight Saturday), bicycle riding, boating, swimming, and hanging laundry outside, no longer applied. It is still the case, however, that no alcoholic beverages can be sold or served, and that no one is allowed on the beach on Sundays until the church service is over. Many residents of the community, which has a population of about 6,000 in winter and 30,000 in summer, are supporting movements either to secede from Neptune or to get the township to issue special ordinances that apply only to Ocean Grove.

Ocean Grove's historic district★ (the area between Main St., the Atlantic Ocean, and Wesley and Fletcher lakes) is

Ocean Grove

distinguished by its generally homogeneous Victorian look.
Permanent tents (actually houses extended in the summer
by tents) are clustered around the Great Auditorium; there
are fine old hotels with porches on Ocean Ave.; the street
signs are made of tile. The auditorium (54 Pitman Ave.;

201-988-0645), a magnificent pile built in 1894 and now a national landmark, seats over 7,000; each summer a series of concerts ranging from classical to popular to barbershop quartets is held there. The Historical Society of Ocean Grove sponsors a house tour each summer; for information call 201-774-4736.

For information on beach fees call 201-988-5533.

Forsythe National Wildlife Refuge

Oceanville ATLANTIC (US 9)

[Galloway Township]

About one mile east of the center of Oceanville is the headquarters of the Edwin B. Forsythe National Wildlife Refuge (Great Creek Rd.; 609-652-1665), named in honor of a conservation-minded congressman. This is the refuge's Brigantine unit, founded in 1939, primarily to protect the Atlantic Flyway. Its 20,000 acres contain a variety of habitats: marshes (salt, brackish, and fresh water), creeks, ponds, upland fields, shrubby areas, and forests.

Over 200 species of birds are known to frequent this spot. Some 1,600 acres have been impounded, creating fresh-water habitats. One of the high points of this popular refuge (some 125,000 people visit it each year) is an eight-mile car trail along the impoundment dikes that gives you a view of the fresh-water ponds, the salt marshes, and the mud flats (not to mention an eerie view of the Atlantic City skyline across the bay). There are 14 stops along the auto trail, and many of the birds have become accustomed to the cars so that they go about their business (cracking clam shells on the highway, leading their young across the road) as if you weren't there. There are also two short self-guided nature trails through the fields and woods and limited hunting, fishing, and crabbing. For leaflets describing the auto trail and the two nature trails, as well as information on hunting permits, stop at the headquarters building, which also contains some natural history exhibits. The refuge is open daily, dawn to dusk, the office 8–4 weekdays, 9–3 weekends during the spring (April and May) and fall (October and November) migration only. Group orientation programs by appointment.

Mid-March to mid-April is the peak of the northbound waterfowl migration. To see young birds come in mid-April through May for the Canada geese and mid-June to mid-July for the ducks. (The end of May is also a good time to see a major display of dragon's mouth orchid and grass pink on Great Creek Rd., about ½ mile west of the entrance to the refuge.) The first ten days in November usually produce spectacular concentrations of ducks, geese, and brant in the pools—over 100,000 birds congregate on 1,600 acres. Mid-November to mid-December is the best time to see snow geese.

The other side of Lily Lake is southern New Jersey's first art museum, the Noyes Museum (Lily Lake Rd.; 609-652-8848). Opened in 1983, this lovely building is beautifully situated; its own collection is displayed in one gallery, and in other rooms there are special exhibitions. One gallery has a permanent collection of decoys, and demonstrations of decoy carving are given at 2, Wednesday–Sunday. The museum also sponsors concerts and other special events. Open Wednesday–Sunday, 11–4.

Oldwick [Tewksbury Township]

Oldwick, situated in the rolling hills of northeastern Hunterdon County, was settled by German immigrants from Philadelphia in the mid-18th century. Originally called New Germantown, the town changed its name during the World War I days of pervasive anti-German sentiment. Strikingly untouched by the 20th century, Oldwick today is a beautiful village set in the midst of beautiful agricultural country.

In the center of the village is the Zion Lutheran Church, said to be the state's oldest Lutheran church in continuous use. Built in 1749, but altered considerably during the course of the 19th and 20th centuries, the church housed what was apparently New Jersey's first organ. On the west side of High St., a bit farther south, is the Oldwick Methodist Church; it dates from the mid-1860s. The community center and town library (west side of High St. opposite Joliet St.) dates from 1807 and was given to the town by Dr. Oliver Barnet (his house, built in 1771, lies on the eastern continuation of Church St.) to serve as a classical academy and meetinghouse. It remained in the public school system until 1951 and has served as the community center since the mid-1950s.

Just north of Church St. on C 517 is the Cold Brook Preserve (formerly the Van Doren farm), 298 acres of rolling fields, orchard, and old pastures, administered by the county park system. Part of the land is still being farmed, and it is hoped that this unusual combination of farm area and adjoining conservation easements will help preserve some of Hunterdon County's rural heritage. There are also hopes of being able to open a small theater and art gallery in the barn. You are welcome to walk in the park, but you are asked to respect the farmer's fields. Open to limited hunting.

On an old farm a few minutes out of Oldwick is the Tewksbury Wine Cellars (Burrell Rd.; take 517 north out of Oldwick c. 3½ miles; turn left on Saw Mill Rd. and continue c. ½ mile; bear right at the fork onto Burrell Rd.; continue c. ½ mile; 201-832-2400). Opened in 1979 by a veterinarian who converted his mid-18th-century barn (al-

ready converted into a hospital for horse surgery) into a
winery, Tewksbury is devoted primarily to vinifera grapes
grown on its own slopes. The views from the slopes out

Hunterdon County Vineyard

across the countryside are spectacular. Open for tours
Saturday, 11–5, Sunday, 1–5, and by appointment.
Picnic facilities.

Oradell BERGEN (Garden State Pkwy exit 165, C 503) 8,658

One of Bergen County's many Dutch settlements, Oradell still has some of its early stone houses, particularly along Kinderkamack and Paramus rds. The hometown of Walter Schirra, the astronaut who orbited around the earth six times in 1962, Oradell is also the home of the Hiram Blauvelt Wildlife Museum (637 Kinderkamack Rd.; 201-261-0012), an unusual museum devoted to a personal collection focusing on wildlife. Housed on the upper level of the former carriage house of the late 19th-century Blauvelt mansion (the dark house with turrets and towers that looks like a haunted house in a Grade B movie), the collection includes examples of animals from around the world, as well as paintings and sculpture related to wildlife themes. Among the holdings are rare Audubon editions. Open Thursday, 10–3. Groups by appointment other times.

Oxford WARREN (NJ 31, C 624, 625, 631) 1,587

Situated on the slopes of Scott Mountain, Oxford became an important iron town in the 1740s, producing cannonballs for the revolutionary army. It was the first ironworks in the United States to use the hot blast method (1834), which revolutionized iron making in this country. A variety of iron products was made here, including railroad wheels and firebacks, until the furnaces were blown out in the 1880s. The remains of the Oxford Furnace★ can be seen on the west side of Washington Ave. (between Belvidere Ave. and Cinder St.); there are explanatory plaques at the site. Farther up the hill on Belvidere Ave. is the Shippen Mansion★ (1744), now being restored. During one period in the mid-18th century, the Oxford ironworks were owned by the Shippen brothers from Philadelphia; their niece Peggy Shippen, who became Benedict Arnold's wife, visited Oxford frequently to take part in its active social life. Oxford's historic district, which includes Washington and Belvidere aves., is listed in the state register of historic places.

North of Oxford on the south side of US 46, a little less than three miles east of the intersection with NJ 31 (the approach is well marked) is the Pequest Trout Hatchery and Natural Resources Education Center (201-637-4125). Located in the northeast quadrant of the Pequest Wildlife Management Area, this facility opened in 1982. The area was chosen for the hatchery because of the exceptionally high quality of the water in the Pequest Valley. The hatcheries produce some 700,000 brook, brown, and rainbow trout each year for stocking the roughly 200 streams and lakes open for public fishing. (There are about 200,000 licensed anglers in the state, who apparently take 150,000 children fishing along with them each year.) This is basically a put-and-take operation, as very few New Jersey streams can support trout naturally. Visitors can look into the nursery rooms and watch the upper raceways from an observation ramp. The handsome new educational center (it opened in 1985; children will probably be fascinated by the sinks in the restrooms) will eventually house exhibits and displays relating to the Pequest watershed, the management of natural resources, and the nature of trout. At present there is a live fish pond with specimens of brook, brown, and rainbow trout, and a display tank that imitates a cross-section of Sussex County's Flat Brook. Popular with visitors (1,000 a week in its first year) the center operates programs for school groups, conservation organizations, and casual visitors. There are slides shows at 11 and 2, with guided tours after each show. Open Friday–Sunday, 10–4; groups by appointment Wednesday and Thursday. On the grounds are also a fishing education pond and facilities for picnicking. Five hundred acres of the wildlife management area are leased to local farmers who grow small grains and corn to attract game birds and deer; within designated areas you can hike, hunt, and fish.

Paramus BERGEN (Garden State Pkwy exits 163, 165, NJ 4, 17) 26,474

Settled in the mid-17th century by Dutch emigrants, Paramus may have derived its name from the Indian word "permessing," for "abundance of turkeys." Fifty years ago the town was described by the WPA guide to New Jersey as "an old Dutch farm community . . . growing vegetables for the city markets." You can still find a half-dozen or so old Dutch stone houses (drive along Paramus and E. Ridgewood aves.), but any sense of being in anything as compact as a farm community is gone (and the turkeys, of course, disappeared long ago).

In fact, Paramus is noted among historians of the city for having led in the development of the post–World War II shopping mall. (It has even been described as the mecca of malls.) The Garden State Plaza (NJ 4 and 17), which opened in 1957, was an early example of the open mall that served several regional community functions (it has since been converted to a closed mall), and the Paramus Park Mall (Garden State Parkway and NJ 17) is an early example of the newer type of enclosed mall that for many has taken over some of the functions of the city's downtown. Paramus Park Mall is architecturally interesting; the exterior is severe, yet the interior, with its waterfall, fountain, hanging shrubs, and diagonally intersecting skylights, is open and light.

The Bergen Museum of Art and Science (327 E. Ridgewood Ave. at Fairview in the Bergen County Community Services building; 201-265-1248) is housed in a mid-19th-century pink-brick building, once the Bergen County

Paramus Park Mall

Almshouse (1852–1930) and the County Old Folks Home (1930–67). The museum has a small but extremely well laid out nature exhibit, which features a well-known mastodon skeleton unearthed nearby and a discovery room for younger children. Art exhibits change every six months (there is also a small permanent collection), and the museum has an active schedule of special programs. Open Tuesday–Saturday, 10–5, Sunday, 1–5. Groups and gallery tours by appointment. Donation requested.

Behind the museum in the same county complex is the award-winning Norman Bleshman State Regional Day School for the Handicapped, designed so that everything will be not only convenient but pleasurable for someone in a wheelchair. The horticultural center in the same area, part of the county's vocational and technical school facilities, includes an old barn, a modern airplane-type windmill, buildings with solar panels, greenhouses, and a wood silo.

Van Saun Park (Forest, Continental, and Howland aves.; 201-262-2627), one of Paramus's two county parks (it shares Van Saun with River Edge), is one of the county's most popular parks and can be crowded in the summer. Its five-acre zoo features some 300 animals representing 80 species from North and South America. In the zoo is a 4,000-square-foot aviary made like a circus tent and covered with netting, which replicates the environment of the Meadowlands. A boardwalk goes through the aviary over a 9,000-gallon artificial pond, which contains aquatic species from the Meadowlands. The zoo offers educational programs and tours by appointment (201-262-3771). During the summer months (roughly mid-April–mid-October) a train (201-262-2627) runs around the zoo and a mid-19th-century farmyard scene, with a replica of an old Dutch farmhouse (used as an office building) and outbuildings, antique farm implements, and old-fashioned flower beds. Another garden, a shaded one, is found around Washington Spring Park (between Van Saun's areas M and L), so called because Washington's army camped near here in 1780 and according to legend took water from the natural spring. There are also picnic grounds, a lake and boat basin, a bicycle-pedestrian path, sledding slopes, and a tennis center (201-265-1028). The zoo and aviary are open mid-April–mid-October, Tuesday–Sunday, 10–5; the rest of the year only the zoo is open, Tuesday–Sunday, 10–4:30.

One section of Saddle River County Park is on Dunkerhoof Rd. (off Paramus Rd.); here are a wooded picnic area and one section of the trail that will eventually continue for

5½ miles along the Saddle River. Bergen County Community College, on the site of a former golf course, is a compact campus joined by covered walks.

Along the Saddle River at the southwestern corner of the borough (Red Mill Rd., just south of 4 and east of Saddle River Rd.) is the Easton tower and water wheel, built on the site of an 18th-century mill that produced blankets for the army in the Civil War.

Park Ridge BERGEN (Garden State Pkwy exit 172S, C 2, 111) 8,515

 Like much of Bergen County, Park Ridge (hometown of the singing group the Roche sisters) was settled by Dutch farmers, and there are old Dutch stone houses to be seen on Pascack and Rivervale rds. At 13 Pascack Rd., for example, is the Wortendyke Dutch Barn★ (201-646-3396, 201-599-6151), an 18th-century barn with a typically Dutch shape: wider than it is deep and with side aisles for the livestock. Inside the barn is a collection of 18th- and 19th-century farm implements; there are also changing exhibits. Open May–October, Wednesday and Sunday, 1–5. Groups by appointment. Directly across the road (12 Pascack Rd.) is the mid-18th-century Frederick Wortendyke house.★

From about 1775 until 1889 Park Ridge was the site of a wampum mint. Wampum, manufactured here by John W. Campbell and his descendants, was used by the United States government and by fur traders (John Jacob Astor bought wampum from the Campbells) in their dealings with the Indians in the West. Most wampum was manufactured by hand, but the Campbells invented a machine that could drill holes in six shells at once. They are reputed to have given picnics at which one could eat all the shellfish one wanted without charge as long as the shells were not broken. Their machine, thought to be unique in the world, is on exhibit at the Pascack Historical Society Museum (19 Ridge Ave.; 201-391-4358), along with other tools from the mint and collections of old instruments, cabinetmakers' tools, paperweights, and many other items. The museum, housed in an 1873 Congregational church building, concentrates on exhibits that highlight life in the Pascack valley. The central exhibit changes each year. Open May–September, Sunday, 2–5; groups other times by appointment.

Paterson PASSAIC (I 80, NJ 4, 20) 52,463

First settled by the Dutch in the late 17th century, Paterson remained an agricultural community until late in the 18th century. It was an unusually early tourist attraction—the 77-foot-high Great Falls of the Passaic River drew visitors from as far away as New York when it took three days to get to the site. During the Revolution, George Washington, Alexander Hamilton, and the marquis de Lafayette had stopped to eat lunch at the Great Falls, and Hamilton had been struck by the power that lay in them. He believed that the success of the young country depended on its establishing its own industrial base, and 12 years after his visit to the Great Falls, as secretary of the treasury, he proposed to Congress the establishment of an industrial district. When Congress was unenthusiastic about funding the project, he arranged private support for what was in effect the country's first planned industrial city. Thus was the Society of Usefull Manufactures (S.U.M.) born in 1791. Pierre l'Enfant, later to design Washington, D.C., was hired to design the city. His scheme proved too expensive, although the raceways were laid out according to his plan, and the work was taken over by Peter Colt, a member of a family that had much to do with the S.U.M. and Paterson's development. The area surrounding the falls was named Paterson in honor of the then governor of the state and signer of the Declaration of Independence, William Paterson. The society, which was granted many financial and legal privileges by the state, continued to operate until after World War II.

Over the course of the 19th century Paterson became a leading industrial city, known as the home of the Colt revolver ("The gun that won the West") and the submarine, as a leading producer of cotton and the home of cotton duck sails, as Silk City, as a major producer of locomotives and then airplane engines, as the scene of momentous labor struggles. It was also a major stop on the Underground Railroad. By 1900 it had become the 15th largest city in the United States. Many famous people were Paterson natives, among them Nicholas Murray Butler, the president of Columbia University for over 40 years; Garret A. Hobart, vice-president during McKinley's first term; Albert Sabin, discoverer of the oral polio vaccine; Larry Doby, the first black in the American Baseball League; Allen Ginsberg, the poet; and Lou Costello, the comedian. Perhaps less well remembered today is Sam Patch, a cotton spinner who jumped into the falls when drunk one night. He survived and started a second career as "the Great Descender," achieving a successful jump at Niagara Falls. (He died in the Genessee Falls.) Although not a native (he came from Rutherford), the poet William Carlos Williams is forever associated with Paterson because of his long poem of that name.

The first factory was in operation by 1794, producing calico goods, and cotton was Paterson's first important product. In the 1830s Sam Colt began manufacturing his revolver in what is still called the Gun Mill. The venture was not successful, and he sold the factory. When the government decided it wanted to order the revolver (apparently because of a recommendation by the Texas Ranger Sam Walker, who had used it in 1838), Colt had no model at hand. In one version of the story, he paid an exorbitant price to buy someone else's gun; in another he redesigned the gun. In either case, there is agreement that he made his fortune from the gun, but this time the factory was in Connecticut.

At about the same time that Colt first made his revolver, Thomas Rogers manufactured the country's first steam locomotive, the Sandusky. Over the next 50 years four companies were manufacturing locomotives in Paterson and among them produced roughly 40 percent of the nation's locomotives. Paterson also produced most of the rotary snowplows used on locomotives.

The silk industry began in Paterson in the 1840s, cotton by then having moved to New England, and by the 1880s Paterson was called Silk City. Every stage of production, except growing the silkworms, took place in Paterson, and unlike the other industries mentioned, silk continued as a prominent industry into the 20th century. In fact, the famous silk workers strike of 1913 (see Haledon) took place when the industry was still vital to the city. Silk ceased being important to the city when synthetic fibers were developed.

A Paterson schoolteacher, John P. Holland, developed the first successful submarine in 1878 and tested it in the Passaic River. Although Holland's ideas lay behind today's atomic submarines, for years the navy did not take him seriously, even when he surprised a navy ship on a secret maneuver.

Paterson

After World War I the Wright Aeronautical Corporation, manufacturers of airplane motors, moved to an old silk factory in Paterson, where they made the engine for Charles Lindbergh's *Spirit of St. Louis*. For a time this was Paterson's dominant industry, but it moved elsewhere after World War II.

Although Paterson is no longer a leading industrial city and has lost more than half its population over the last 50 years, it has found creative ways to reuse its remaining 19th-century industrial buildings and is experiencing new vitality as a different sort of city. The S.U.M. historic district* (encompassing W. Broadway; Ryle, Wayne, and McBride aves.; Grand, Morris, Barbour, Spruce, Market, Mill, Van Houten, Curtis, River, Oliver, and Reservoir sts.; and the Passaic River) is a national historic landmark. The buildings here date from the 18th to the 20th century, and many of the industrial buildings have been converted to a variety of uses. In the Rogers Locomotive Erecting Shop (1874), for example, is the Paterson Museum (2 Market St.; 201-881-3874), dedicated to preserving the industrial, technological, and geological history of Paterson. There are both changing and permanent exhibits. Among the permanent displays are ones relating to l'Enfant's system for harnessing water power and the aircraft engine industry, as well as one of Holland's submarines. Open weekdays, 10–4:30, weekends, 12:30–4:30. Admission charge. The Great Falls Tour Office (201-279-9587) is also in the Rogers Building. Tours can be arranged in advance, or you can pick up a map here for a self-guided tour.

Wandering through the district you will see not just old mills but workers' houses, the raceways, churches, even the bar (Cianci and Van Houten sts.) that served as I.W.W. headquarters during the silk strike. Some of the mills have been converted to living quarters: the Phoenix Mill complex (Van Houten St.), 1815–70, has been made into cooperative apartments, the Essex Mill (Mills St.), 1807–72, which used to manufacture mosquito netting, to subsidized apartments for artists. The People's Republic of China has even purchased an old paper mill.

The falls, 77 feet high and 280 feet wide, have been declared a national natural landmark, and their energy is scheduled to be harnessed again in 1987. They are best observed from Overlook Park (McBride); from there you can also see much of Paterson's geological history in the rocks.

A visit to downtown Paterson, which is close to the Great Falls district, is also rewarding. Note particularly the Cathedral of St. John the Baptist* (Main and Grand sts.), 1865, a national historic landmark; the Passaic County courthouse annex, originally the post office (Hamilton St.), built at the turn of the century as a copy of the medieval Haarlem Guild house (to honor the first settlers of Paterson); the late 19th-century city hall (155 Market St.), modeled on that in

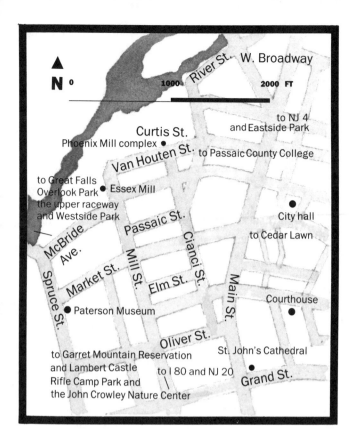

Lyons, France (also a silk-producing city); and the county courthouse, 1903 (Clark St.).

Another aspect of the silk industry can be seen in Lambert Castle,* also known as Bella Vista (Valley Rd.; 201-881-2761), a pretentious late 19th-century stone mansion built by one of the leaders of the industry, Catholina Lambert. The Passaic County Historical Society runs a museum here. Although Lambert was forced to sell his art collection (it included works by Rembrandt, El Greco, Renoir, and Monet), a few pieces and some of his furnishings remain, and there are many items of local history, as well as changing exhibits, on view. The house itself is of interest: note the hand-carved oak structure that places anyone descending the steps in a picture frame, and be sure to take in the view from the terrace. Open Wednesday–Sunday, 1–4. Admission charge.

Lambert Castle is located in Garret Mountain Reservation, a county park with open fields, a fishing pond, a three-mile cross-country track, an overlook, and picnic areas. Garret Mountain has an unusual number and variety of rare minerals and is a national natural landmark because of the volcanic activity associated with its creation. It is also a good place to watch for hawks.

South of Garret Mountain in Rifle Camp Park (Rifle Camp Rd.) is the John Crowley Nature Center (201-523-0024). The center, which includes an observatory, a seismograph, and a weather station, sponsors a variety of programs and has changing nature displays. At the center you can pick up maps and brochures for the self-guided trails. Group tours by reservation. Open daily, 9–5, except New Year's Day, Thanksgiving, and Christmas. At the park there are also picnic areas, including one set up for paraplegics, and a fitness course.

Holland's first successful submarine is on exhibit at Westside Park★ (112–242 Totowa Ave.), a turn-of-the-century park. The 19th-century Van Houten house is also at the park.

Many of Paterson's distinguished citizens, including Lambert, Rogers, Hobart, and Butler, are buried in the Cedar Lawn Cemetery (McLean Blvd., NJ 20), opened in 1867. This cemetery, which includes a Greek Revival temple for Hobart designed by Henry Bacon, who designed the Lincoln Memorial, is rich in examples of Victorian funerary architecture. North of Cedar Lawn (take McLean Blvd.), in what was Paterson's wealthy area, is Eastside Park, laid out in the 1890s. There is a splendid view here, and some of the mansions from Paterson's days of glory surround the park.

At Passaic County Community College (College Blvd.) there is a large mural depicting the history of the city from the time of Hamilton to the visit of Martin Luther King, Jr., in 1968. (King's visit took place shortly before his assassination.) Also to be seen on campus is a life-size brass-and-copper statue of King. The arts center (201-684-6555) sponsors programs that are open to the public.

Paulsboro GLOUCESTER (NJ 44) 6,944

 Settled in the 1680s, Paulsboro is named for one of the first families to arrive in the area. Fort Billings Park (Delaware River, Billingsport Rd. at 3d St., Clonmell Rd., N. Delaware St.), listed on the state historic register, commemorates the fort, which was built by the U.S. government in 1776 to keep the British from getting to Philadelphia. The land bought for Fort Billings represented the new government's first land purchase (the Pauls were the sellers), and the fort was designed by Tadeusz Kosciuszko, the Polish patriot. The Gill Memorial Library (Broad and Commerce sts.) is in a stone house built c. 1810 by John Clark and named in honor of Matthew Gill, a prominent 19th-century Paulsboro man, who, among other charitable activities, in the 1870s gave the land on which the Episcopal Church stands. (The current building dates to 1910.) The Samuel Philip Paul house (212 E. Broad St.), like the library, dates to 1810, although the back portion may be much older. The Mobil refinery just south of the park (known as the Paulsboro plant, it is actually in Gibbstown) opened in 1917 and manufactures gasoline, lubricating oil, and motor oil.

Peapack and Gladstone

SOMERSET   (US 202, 206, C 512)   2,038

 Situated in an area of rolling hills and large estates, Peapack and Gladstone (together they form a single borough) are both attractive villages. Many of the estates have been converted to other uses—the former Blair mansion, for example, a French château built in 1903 that overlooks Ravine Lake, is now St. Joseph's Villa, a religious retreat. The former Ladd estate was bought by King Hassan II in 1983 in what was then the largest domestic real estate transaction in the state's history ($7.5 million). Hamilton Farms, a former estate with very elegant stables, now serves as the headquarters of the USET (United States Equestrian team; Pottersville Rd., C 512, just west of US 206; 201-234-1251). Here the team trains for international events, and master classes and competitions are held. Open to the public Monday–Saturday, 9–1, and for special events (call for information); admission is sometimes charged for the special events.

A little north of Gladstone are two Morris County facilities, both on former, albeit more modest, estates—

Willowwood Arboretum and Bamboo Brook Outdoor Education Center (continue on 512 past Hamilton Farms to Union Grove Rd., right on Union Grove, left on Longview; the second driveway on the left leads to Willowwood, the third to Bamboo Brook; 201-829-0474). On 130 acres of rolling farm land in the Hacklebarney Hills, Willowwood contains some 3,500 kinds of native and exotic plants, including one section of undisturbed forest. There are impressive collections of lilacs, ferns, magnolias, and hollies, and a hillside of pink lady's slippers. Near the house, which dates from 1792, are two small formal gardens, but most of the paths wind through open areas and woodland. Classes, tours, and workshops are held here.

Bamboo Brook, formerly Merchiston Farm, was for many years the home of Martha Brookes Hutcheson, one of the first women to be trained as a landscape architect in the United States. On the center's 100 acres are fields, forest, and a five-acre formal garden designed by Hutcheson. The earliest section of the house dates from the 1720s; the lecture hall is a music room added in the 1920s. The gardens include a cedar arbor, pool garden, and ha-ha. As in the Willowwood Arboretum, trails here wind through the fields and along the brook. Educational programs, including tours and workshops, are offered on gardening and botanical subjects throughout the year at Willowwood, in spring, summer, and fall at Bamboo Brook. The grounds in both parks are open dawn–dusk, the buildings for those registered in programs; at Bamboo Brook, the buildings are also open the 3d weekend of the month.

Because the two facilities are in different geological sections—Willowwood is in the Piedmont and much of Bamboo Brook in the Highlands—the contrast between the two adjacent sites is of interest. The wooded area between them contains examples of Roxbury pudding stone.

In the winter of 1986 the Peapack ski area (US 206), first opened in 1939, closed because of insurance problems.

Near Peapack-Gladstone on US 206 is the Beneficial Management Corporation headquarters. Seen from the highway it looks something like an Italian hill village. Occupying 30 acres of an 850-acre tract, the buildings are linked by arcades, there are formal gardens and landscaped courts, and dominating all is the 88-foot campanile.

Pemberton BURLINGTON
(C 530) 1,198

This small Pine Barrens community, just a few miles west of Fort Dix and McGuire Air Force Base, was settled by Quakers in the late 17th century and named in the 19th century for James Pemberton, a Philadelphia merchant. An early 19th-century house and mill* can still be seen where Rancocas Creek crosses Hanover St.; note also the North Pemberton railroad station,* also on Hanover St. (An 18th-century Quaker meetinghouse* still stands in Arneys Mount, north of Pemberton.) Burlington County College is south of the borough on the Pemberton-Browns Mills Rd. (C 530).

If you continue on C 530 and turn right on New Lisbon Rd. (C 646), after about four miles you will enter Lebanon State Forest (609-726-1191). The state began acquiring this forest early in the century; it now covers almost 30,000 acres. Two units of the CCC (Civilian Conservation Corps), one all black, were active here in the 1930s, developing 60 miles of road; building shelters and cabins, five of which are still in use; creating Pakim Pond out of a former cranberry reservoir (the pond is near the site of the Lebanon Glass Works, active for a few years in the 1860s, which gave the forest its name); and planting over 3 million seedlings. Today, the lumber used in the forest for repairs and signs comes from those trees. Among the many attractions of this Pine Barrens tract is the Cedar Swamp Natural Area, an Atlantic white-cedar swamp surrounded by a pitch-pine forest, in which can be found many of the unusual plants that thrive in the Pine Barrens. This is the northern limit of commercially useful white cedar. Hikers can find many miles of unmarked sand roads as well as a section of the Batona Trail, which begins in the forest at Ong's Hat and ends in Wharton State Forest (see Hammonton). Horseback riders will also enjoy the sand roads. The forest is open for picnicking, camping (March–November), and hunting, and lifeguards are at the beach in Pakim Pond between Memorial Day and Labor Day. Nature programs, ranging from plant hikes to motor tours in search of deer, are offered during the summer. For information and trail maps stop at the office (the entrance is off NJ 72, one mile south of the NJ 70–72 intersection). Parking charge weekends and holidays.

If you continue on C 530 past New Lisbon Rd. (at Browns Mills 530 turns right and becomes Lakehurst Rd.), about 4½ miles east of Browns Mills, you will reach Whitesbog Rd. Turning left here takes you to the community of Whitesbog, developed in the 1860s by Joseph J. White, a cranberry cultivator who discovered the value of flooding cranberry bogs and became known as the cranberry king. His eldest daughter, Elizabeth C. White, was responsible for developing the commercial blueberry from native huckleberries. In 1916, five years after she began her cooperation with a U.S. Department of Agriculture scientist, she marketed her first commercial crop. White maintained her interest in the development of the blueberry all her life, and donated land for further work. (She also maintained a lifelong interest in and concern for those who tended the plants.) New Jersey now leads the nation in the production of blueberries for consumption fresh (30 million pounds in 1985), is second in overall production, and third in acreage (7,700 acres in 1985). (The acidic soil of the Pine Barrens, combined with the blueberry's low fertility requirements, make this the ideal place to grow them.) At one time the White plantation employed 80 full-time and 600 migrant workers. Although cranberries and blueberries are still grown commercially around Whitesbog, much of the community was neglected for a time. The Whitesbog Preservation Trust (609-893-4646) is restoring the 26 remaining buildings, and there are plans to turn the packing house into a museum devoted to the state's cranberry and blueberry industries. A conservation and environmental studies center is also located in Whitesbog. This is a wonderful area to walk in, but as in all hikes on unmarked Pine Barrens roads, it is easy to get lost unless you take care to watch for distinguishing landmarks.

Pennington MERCER (NJ 31) 2,109

Although Pennington's population has increased more than 50 percent over the last 50 years, it has remained relatively stable over the last 20. Occupying only 0.9 square mile, the town is 95 percent developed, leaving no room for expansion. First settled late in the 17th century, Pennington was named Queenstown in honor of Queen Anne, but came to be called Penny Town, possibly because it was so small. By the mid-18th century, the name had solidified as Pennington.

In 1776 Pennington was occupied by British and Hessian troops, who apparently used the town as a base for raids on Trenton. Lord Cornwallis had his headquarters here for a time, and members of the British cavalry are said to have jumped their horses over the wall in front of the First Presbyterian Church. (The present building on Main St. dates to 1875; the earlier building burned.)

Pennington today is much admired for its well-preserved look. The Pennington School (112 W. Delaware Ave.), founded in 1838, is the oldest Methodist secondary school in the United States. Established as a Methodist Episcopal male seminary, in 1854 it became coeducational. Reverting to a boys' school in 1910, it went coed again in 1972. Among Pennington's many attractive buildings note the 18th-century John Welling house* (52 E. Curlis Ave.), with its fish-scale shingles, and the railroad station* at the corner of Green St. and Franklin Ave. (c. 1882).

On Titus Mill Rd. east of the center of town is the Stony Brook-Millstone Watersheds Association (609-737-3735), a conservation organization that operates out of a farmhouse on over 500 acres. Also on the property are a pondhouse, an organic farm, and eight miles of trails suitable for hiking and cross-country skiing. Maps are available for self-guided tours. The farm is used as an experimental and demonstration farm, and produce is sold in the summer, Monday–Saturday, 1–6. The association is involved in an active educational program for children and adults; it also sponsors frequent special events. The nature reserve is open daily, dawn–dusk; the headquarters building and office staffed weekdays, 9–5.

About two miles east of the center of town (take E. Delaware Ave. to Federal City Rd.) is Rosedale Park (609-989-6530), a 450-acre county facility. The lake is stocked with trout, and there are family and group picnic areas (the latter by reservation only; call 609-989-6540). Environmental tours of the park for groups by reservation (609-989-6532). Open daily until dusk.

Pennsauken CAMDEN (US 130, NJ 90, C 543) 33,775

The township of Pennsauken lies on the Delaware River (it is in fact bisected by the approach to the Betsy Ross Bridge) and is bounded on the north by Pennsauken Creek. The area was inhabited by Indians, and this is the only town in Camden County with an Indian name (Pennsauken means "place where tobacco was traded"). It is also the site of the first recorded English settlement in West Jersey: in the 1630s a group of English colonists built a fort, which they named after an Indian chief. The fort was abandoned after four years, but the Griffith Morgan House★ (Griffith Morgan La. off River Rd., C 543, by the old United States Steel plant), built c. 1693, is still standing. This stone house, the oldest house in Camden County, is being restored; the first two floors will eventually be furnished with period pieces, and the top floor will be opened as a museum. Open house is held each year the Saturday before Thanksgiving. Tours by appointment (call Gloria Moczydlowski at 609-665-1000 or 609-662-8579).

The Burrough-Dover House★ (9201 Burrough-Dover La.), an early 18th-century stone house with a late 18th-century addition, serves as headquarters of the Pennsauken Historical Society. The society opens the house several times a year and gives tours by appointment (call 609-662-9175, 609-663-4191, 609-662-0873).

Perth Amboy MIDDLESEX (NJ 35, 440) 38,951

Perth Amboy, situated at the mouth of the Raritan River, was established in 1683 by William Penn and 11 other men, the Proprietors of East New Jersey, who had purchased the East Jersey tract from the estate of Sir George Carteret, the original grantee, in 1682. Their aim was to set up East Jersey's principal town on what was described as "a sweet, wholesome, and delightful place," and the town plan they developed, with its central green, survives more or less intact today. The town was actually settled by a group of Scottish proprietors, but their attempt to name the settlement New Perth, in honor of the earl of Perth, was unsuccessful, and eventually their choice merged with the community's original name, Ambo Point, to form today's Perth Amboy.

The community did indeed serve as the capital of East Jersey from 1686 to 1702 and then as one of the twin capitals of New Jersey; in 1718 it became the first incorporated municipality in the colony. Because of its strategic position at the mouth of the Raritan River, Perth Amboy suffered in the Revolution—it was occupied by the armies of both sides—and in 1790 the capital was moved to Trenton. Three years later the county seat was moved to New Brunswick, and for a while the city stagnated.

In the early 19th century, Perth Amboy became a fashionable resort and began to develop an oyster industry. The arrival of the railroad in the 1830s encouraged increased industrial activity; the town's rich clay deposits led to a flourishing brick, ceramic, and terra-cotta industry. It was also a leading center of copper and silver refining, and at one point had the second largest copper refinery in the world. Perth Amboy suffered the fate of the early industrializers, but it is now part of an 11-city project to clean up and develop the Raritan River and optimistic about its future. The Raritan Copper Works (Elm and Market sts.) are listed in the state register of historic places, but the giant American Smelting and Refining Company plant is gone.

The increased pace of industrialization after the Civil War resulted in a wave of immigration; by the 1930s close to three-quarters of the inhabitants of Perth Amboy were foreign born. Slavs predominated, followed by Danes, Italians, and Poles; today a large portion of the residents are from Puerto Rican, other Hispanic, and Caribbean backgrounds. In 1984, for example, there were more Anguillans living in Perth Amboy than live on the island of Anguilla, and in 1977 the Anguillan Sons and Daughters Benevolent Society (founded in 1921) took over the former union hall of the American Smelting and Refining Company (State St. and Pulaski).

The heterogeneity of Perth Amboy's population is reflected in the town square (intersection of Market and High sts.). In this spacious square the weekly markets were held; from the 1740s to the 1840s, the market house, a large brick shed, stood in the middle of the square. Now the square is a park; the statue of George Washington, by Nils Alling, a local sculptor, was given to the town in 1896 by the local Scandinavian community. Scattered about the park are

plaques commemorating trees planted in honor of George
Washington in 1932 (the town's 250th birthday) by Perth
Amboy's various ethnic associations, including those of
Italians, Poles, Germans, Scandinavians, Hungarians,
Ukrainians, and Greeks.

At 260 High St. are the city hall,★ the oldest public building in continuous use in the United States, and the surveyor
general's office.★ Begun in 1713, the city hall, which is
painted white to hide the scars of numerous fires and alterations, served as the county courthouse until the county seat
moved to New Brunswick; it also housed the state assembly
until 1790. It was in this building that New Jersey became

276   *Perth Amboy*

Raritan Bay

the first state to ratify the Bill of Rights and Thomas Mundy Peterson the first black to vote under the auspices of the 15th Amendment. The surveyor general's office, built in 1860, houses the records of the Board of Proprietors of Eastern New Jersey, the oldest active corporation in the state.

The houses around the square generally date to the 18th and 19th centuries; in the one at 83–85 Market St. (1730), William Dunlap (1766–1839), sometimes called the father of American drama, who was also a painter (he studied with Benjamin West) and a historian of the theater and design, received his early education. The Gothic Revival First Presbyterian Church (1902) was built on the site of an 1802 church; its manse (1887) is at 236 High St.

The Proprietary House★ (149 Kearny Ave.; 201-826-2100) is the country's only remaining official royal governor's house. Built in the 1760s, this imposing brick Georgian mansion originally sat on 11 acres. Occupied first by Chief Justice Frederick Smyth, it was Governor William Franklin's home from 1774 until his arrest for supporting the English cause in 1776. (His father, Benjamin Franklin, visited him here in an unsuccessful attempt to persuade him to change his allegiance.) In 1809 it was converted to a resort hotel, the Brighton, and the third floor and south wing were added. (The wing involved the first use of structural cast iron in the United States.) It has also served as a retirement home for Presbyterian clergymen, a hotel, a private residence, and a rooming house. It was once even rumored that Joseph Bonaparte was going to live in the house (see Bordentown). The property was subdivided in 1904, and the house began a long decline. It is now being restored, with three-quarters of it being converted to commercial uses. It is hoped the remaining quarter will become a museum.

The Kearny Cottage★ (63 Catalpa St.; 201-826-1826) dates from the 1780s and was the home of Elizabeth Lawrence Kearny, the poet Madame Scribblerus and half-sister of Captain James Lawrence of "Don't give up the ship" fame (see Burlington), and her husband, Michael Kearny. Their son, Lawrence Kearny (1789–1868), who was born in the house and lived there all his life, was a naval officer whose name is associated with the U.S. open-door policy in China. Operated as a house museum by the Kearny Cottage Historical Society, the cottage's four rooms contain displays reflecting the nautical background of the owners and the history of Perth Amboy; the colonial garden has plant specimens that go back to the first half of the 19th century. Open Tuesday–Thursday, 2–5; guided tours by appointment.

At the foot of Smith St. is the Perth Amboy ferry slip (201-672-0100). Service between Perth Amboy and Staten Island began in 1684 and continued until 1963. The present structure, a shed★ containing a wooden lift mechanism, was built in 1904 by the Staten Island Railroad and is presently being restored to serve as a maritime museum. Guided tours by appointment.

At the intersection of Rector and Gordon sts. is St. Peter's Episcopal Church, the oldest Episcopal parish in the state (first service 1685, organized 1698). The present Gothic Revival building, on the site of one begun in 1719, dates from 1849, the cemetery from 1722. William Dunlap and Thomas Mundy Peterson are buried here. The rectory (222 Rector St.) is a Tudor Revival building built in 1914.

From Water St. there are fine views of the harbor and many interesting houses, most from the 19th century, but including Perth Amboy's oldest house (228 Water St.) from the early 18th century. At 160 Water St. the striking house (c. 1875), now occupied by the Raritan Yacht Club, has its original double doors. At 222 Water St. is the old rectory of St. Peter's (1815).

Along the waterfront, at the corner of Front and Gordon sts., is the old United States Naval Armory. Built in 1929 this large brick building has recently been converted to commercial space (restaurants, bistros, and the like); scattered throughout the building are artifacts relating to Perth Amboy's nautical past. The armory project is part of

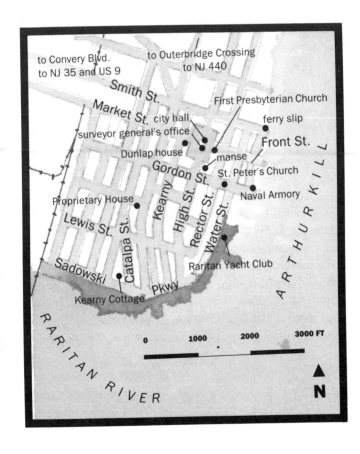

the city's waterfront plan, which includes the new city marina and fishing pier (the longest in Raritan Bay), as well as a 12-foot-wide harborwalk that will run from the old ferry slip to the park abutting Sadowski Parkway to S. 2d St.

At 313 Convery Blvd. (near Smith St.) is the George Inness house, all that remains of Eagleswood, which was a military school and an experimental and artistic colony. The abolitionists Sarah Grimke, Angelina Grimke Weld, and Theodore Weld lived at Eagleswood. In this particular house (built for him in 1864) the painter George Inness lived and worked from about 1864 to 1867. Among the students he taught here was Louis Comfort Tiffany.

Outerbridge Crossing is a cantilevered structure that crosses Arthur Kill to reach Staten Island. Opened in 1928, it was named not for its location but for Eugenius H. Outerbridge, once chairman of the Port Authority of New York and New Jersey. It carries almost 20 million vehicles each year.

There are many other buildings of interest in Perth Amboy. An excellent walking guide has been published by the city and is available from the Middlesex County Cultural and Heritage Commission (201-745-4489).

Pine Beach OCEAN (US 9, C 617) 1,795

Situated on the south bank of the Toms River roughly a mile inland from Barnegat Bay, Pine Beach is the home of Admiral Farragut Academy (Riverside Dr.; 201-349-4406), the country's first naval preparatory school, founded in 1933. In Farragut Hall, the former Pine Beach Hotel, is the Farragut Marine Museum. The museum's collection includes the long glass of David Glasgow Farragut, the navy's first commissioned admiral, remembered for his call, "Damn the torpedoes," in the Civil War. There are memorabilia from other ships and battles, as well as replicas of famous ships, and a large oil painting that, when lit, makes the museum look like a real ship. Open weekdays, 8–4. Weekends and groups by appointment (201-349-4406).

Piscataway

According to one version of Piscataway's history, the community was settled in 1666 by people from the Piscataqua River valley in New Hampshire, which accounts for its name.

In other versions the name derives from various Indian words—the possibilities include "it is getting dark," "place of dark night," and "division of the river." Whichever version is correct, it is apparently undisputed that there was a settlement here on the east bank of the Raritan River in the 17th century, that there was for a time a flourishing shipping trade at the community known as Raritan Landing, and that the competitive advantages of the Delaware and Raritan Canal and the greater depth of the river at New Brunswick put an end to Raritan Landing's days as a shipping center.

Some of the buildings that date from Raritan Landing's more prosperous days do remain, however, among them the Cornelius Low House★ (1225 River Rd.; 201-745-4177, 201-745-4489), also known as Ivy Hall. Built in 1740–41 for Low, a prominent merchant, surveyor, and attorney, the sandstone Georgian manor house now serves as the Middlesex County Museum. Open Wednesday–Sunday, 1–4. (The museum parking lot is on Sutphen Lane on the Rutgers University Busch campus.)

The Metlar House-Peter Bodine House★ (1281 River Rd.; 201-463-8363), also once part of Raritan Landing, was built in 1728. It is now a museum and has a permanent collection of Piscataway memorabilia, as well as rotating exhibits and programs of historical interest. Open Thursday, 12–4, Friday–Sunday, 11–4; guided tours and other hours by appointment.

Rutgers University's Busch campus falls within Piscataway, as do most of Livingston College and the football stadium. The College of Medicine and Dentistry of New Jersey is one of the facilities on the Busch campus.

Stretching along the banks of the Raritan for about two miles, with a view of New Brunswick across the river, is Johnson Park (201-247-2634), one of Middlesex County's most popular parks. Established on land donated by the family of the Johnson and Johnson firm, the park contains a small zoo and animal shelter and a wildflower sanctuary, as well as picnic areas, a trail, lakes, playgrounds, and athletic facilities. The annual Middlesex County horse show takes place here, and there are also dog shows, a fishing derby, and summer concerts. One of the Piscataway area's many prehistoric sites is located in Johnson Park.

Also within the park is East Jersey Old Town (River Rd. and Hoes Lane; 201-463-9077), a 12-acre site on which 17 colonial and revolutionary war buildings have been moved from other central New Jersey locations and arranged as they might have been in a real 18th-century village. The buildings include houses, a school, a barn, a church, and the Indian Queen Tavern (1686), visited by John Adams and others of the founding fathers. Open weekdays, 9:30–2, but it is best to call first. There is a charge for tours.

At the township municipal building (445 Hoes La.; 201-981-0800), art shows are hung in the council chamber in the central part of the building. These shows change monthly; one show each year is generally devoted to work by senior citizens, one to the high school art department, and one to artwork produced in the parks department program. Open weekdays, 8:30–4:30. Closed holidays. The Piscataway libraries also often have art exhibits.

Northwest of the municipal building is Ambrose Dotys Park (Sidney Rd.), a largely undeveloped county park with playing fields and trails.

Pitman GLOUCESTER (NJ 47, C 553) 9,744

Pitman was founded in 1871 as a summer religious camp and named Pitman Grove Camp Meeting in honor of the Reverend Charles Pitman, a powerful camp-meeting preacher. The community was laid out in the shape of a wheel, with an auditorium at the hub, 160 small frame cottages on spokes radiating from the center, and a circular road marking the perimeter. (The Pitman Grove historic area* includes East, West, North, South, Webb, S. Oak, Wesley, Embury, and 1st–12th aves.) The meetings were very popular in the 1880s and 1890s, attracting thousands of visitors—12,000 one day in 1880. Gradually the year-round population began to increase and the cottages were winterized and enlarged; in 1905 the borough of Pitman was incorporated and in 1910 the Episcopalians built a splendid stone church. Pitman's residents today tend to commute to Camden, Philadelphia, and nearby Glassboro State College.

Plainfield

Plainfield was settled in the 1680s by Scottish families from Perth Amboy, who called it Blondyn Plains. After a gristmill was built on the Green Brook in 1760, it became known as Milltown, and in 1800 it received its current name. During the Revolution there was a militia post on the east bank of the Green Brook, and George Washington was in Plainfield often during and after the battle for the Watchungs. In the early 19th century Plainfield was known for the many hatteries operating along the Green Brook. Rail service to Elizabeth began in the 1830s, and after direct service to New York City (including a ferry at Jersey City) was established in 1869, Plainfield developed as one of the first bedroom communities. It was also one of the wealthier railroad suburbs, as can be seen today from the scale of the houses. (Over 100 millionaires are supposed to have lived in the Van Wyck Brooks historic district alone.) Some industry had arrived by the 1880s, but the city, though distinctly urban, is still primarily residential. (In the days of the Jack Benny radio show, Plainfield achieved considerable, probably unwanted, publicity in jokes about Mary Livingston's mother.) Its symphony orchestra, founded in 1919, claims to be the oldest in the state. After a period of urban decline, Plainfield is undergoing a revival, and many of its large late 19th- and early 20th-century houses are being restored or converted to apartments. There are realtors who specialize in publicizing the attractions of Plainfield houses in New York City newspapers.

In the four areas designated historic districts, you will find a large variety of buildings, most from the late 19th and early 20th centuries, which reflect many of the building styles popular over those years. The areas are Crescent⋆ (including Crescent Ave.; 1st, 2d, and 3d places; Park Ave. between Crescent and 9th St.; 9th St. between Park Ave. and Watchung Ave.; Watchung Ave. between 7th and 9th sts.; 7th St. between Watchung Ave., 9th St., and Franklin Place); Hillside Ave.⋆ (Hillside Ave. from Watchung to Martine Ave.); the North Ave. commercial district⋆ (parts of Park, North, and Watchung aves.); and the Van Wyck Brooks area (parts of W. 8th and 9th sts., Arlington, Madison, Central, Stelle, and Field aves.), named for the author who lived in the area for a time.

One of Plainfield's earliest structures is the Friends' Meetinghouse (Watchung Ave. and E. 3d St.), which has

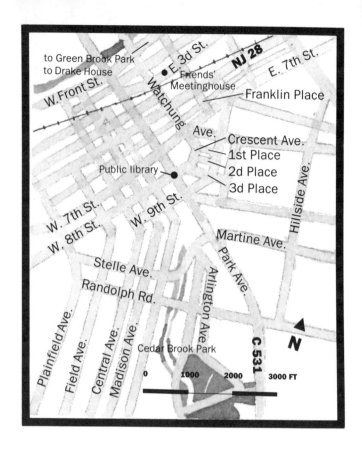

been in continuous use since 1788. This was the first house of worship in Plainfield, and there are Indians buried in the graveyard. The Nathaniel Drake House★ (602 W. Front St.; 201-755-5831) was built in 1746 and served as Washington's headquarters in June 1777. In the 1860s the Drake family sold the house to John Harberger, president of the New York bank that was to become Chase Manhattan. At that time the house was enlarged and altered (the towers were a still later addition). Now operated as a museum, the house has period rooms from the 18th century, from the 1830s, and from the 1870s. Open Saturday, 2–4. Groups by appointment other times. Admission charged.

Among the many eye-catching buildings, note the Masonic building (525 Park Ave.), which now houses stores; the Netherwood railroad station★ (Netherwood and South aves.), 1894; the public library (Park Ave. and 8th St.); the Orville Taylor Waring house★ (900 Park Ave.), 1881; the old Elks building (116 Watchung Ave.); Grace Church (E. 7th St.), 1892; and the 7th Day Baptist Church★ (501 Central Ave.), built in the 1890s.

Cedar Brook Park (Park, Randolph, and Pemberton; 201-756-2220) is an 86-acre county park built on a former garbage dump and swamp. It has a pond where you can fish and skate, playgrounds, and picnic facilities. The Shakespeare garden includes plants mentioned by Shakespeare and common in his day; there is also an iris garden, as well as noteworthy displays of daffodils, peonies, and dogwood. Green Brook Park (West End, Myrtle, and Clinton aves.), 100 acres along a stretch of the river, has picnic facilities, athletic fields, and playgrounds.

Pomona ATLANTIC (Garden State Pkwy exit 44, US 30, C 575) 2,358 (CDP)

Pomona is the home of Stockton State College (College Dr.), opened in 1971 on a forested 1,600-acre tract (this includes the land leased to two hospitals), 400 of which have been set aside as an ecological reserve. The campus is remarkable for its prize-winning architecture; most activities take place in a series of buildings that are linked by an interior street. The Performing Arts Center (609-652-9000) sponsors guest productions in dance, popular and classical music, and theater that are open to the public.

The Atlantic City International Airport is at Pomona. Built by the federal government during World War II, the airport was bought by the Federal Aviation Administration in 1958 as a test center. The FAA now runs a large research-and-development center (5,000 acres, 1,500 employees), concerned with problems of air traffic control, aircraft safety, and communication and navigation, while Atlantic City uses 80 acres for its airport.

Port Monmouth
MONMOUTH **(NJ 36)** [Middletown Township]

Port Monmouth is the site of the first house built on the New Jersey shoreline, the Shoal Harbor Plantation Homestead★ (119 Port Monmouth Rd.; 201-787-1807, 201-291-0559), more often referred to as the Spy House or the Seabrook-Wilson House. Built in 1663 by Thomas Whitlock, the house remained in the hands of his descendants until the early 1900s. It is called the Spy House because, converted to an inn by the time of the Revolution, it served as a clearinghouse for information collected by Americans spying from a nearby hill. Some 39 raids are supposed to have been made possible by information relayed to the house. Now part of a museum complex, Spy House actually consists of three houses joined together, incorporating parts from later in the 17th century and early in the 18th. Also in the complex are a store moved from Lincroft and Port Monmouth's first barbershop. Exhibits include displays devoted to local shipping and fishing, to artifacts of daily life, and to bayshore farming. The museum also sponsors special events, such as the annual reenactment of two revolutionary war engagements, clambakes, and pet shows. Open weekdays, 9:30–3:30; Saturday, 1:30–3:30; Sunday, 2:30–5, but it is advisable to call first.

Princeton MERCER (US 206, NJ 27, C 526, 571, 583) 12,035 (borough) 13,683 (township)

Once known primarily as a university town of quiet, tree-lined streets, Princeton has grown considerably since World War II and is currently in a period of transition that will alter it even more radically. Settled at the end of the 17th century, principally by Quakers, the town was known as Stony Brook until 1724. It grew along the site of an old Indian trail, now Nassau St., which was to prove an important thoroughfare in the Revolution. The town played a significant role in the revolutionary war; many historians consider the battles of Trenton and Princeton as turning points in the struggle for independence. For a brief time in 1783, while the Continental Congress sat in the university's Nassau Hall, Princeton was the capital of the country. Midway between New York and Philadelphia, it prospered in the 19th century as a stagecoach stop.

The university, founded by Presbyterians as the College of New Jersey in 1746 in Elizabeth, moved from there to Newark, and settled in its present location in 1756. Other educational institutions followed, among them the Princeton Theological Seminary, founded in the early 19th century by a group of dissident Presbyterians who felt the university had become too lax. The Institute for Advanced Study was founded over 50 years ago; Abraham Flexner was its first director, Albert Einstein one of its first professors. Also in town are the American Boychoir School and the Westminster Choir College. The Gallup Poll has been a

Princeton institution since 1935, and the Educational Testing Service, although it is actually in Lawrence Township, has a Princeton address.

Corporate research laboratories moving into the area, among them RCA and Cyanamid, changed the character of the town after World War II. More recently, many large corporations have been moving their headquarters or other offices to the so-called Princeton Corridor (US 1 between Trenton and New Brunswick) or other parts of what is now referred to as Greater Princeton, and even those actually located in neighboring communities often list their address as Princeton. The focus of the town is thus increasingly toward the outside. With the resultant increases in population, the town is busier and the buildings in the center are higher, but you can still find prerevolutionary buildings on Nassau St., and it is still lined with trees.

Many famous names have been associated with Princeton. Aaron Burr and Grover Cleveland are both buried in the Princeton cemetery (Witherspoon and Wiggins sts.), as are most Princeton University presidents and Paul Tulane, the founder of Tulane University. At 112 Mercer St. you can see the 1870s house★ (now a national historic landmark) where Einstein lived. T. S. Eliot, a visitor at the Institute for Advanced Study in 1948, wrote much of *The Cocktail Party* at 14 Alexander St. Thomas Mann lived in the house now owned by the Aquinas Institute at the corner of Stockton St. and Library Place; Woodrow Wilson lived at 72 and 82 Library Place and at 25 Cleveland La., Grover Cleveland at 15 Hodge Rd.★ (Cleveland's house, built in the 1850s, is a national historic landmark.) Other literary figures associated with either the university or the town include, of course, F. Scott Fitzgerald and John O'Hara and, more recently, John McPhee and Joyce Carol Oates.

Although a considerable variety of architectural styles is represented on the Princeton University campus, the tone is set by Collegiate Gothic. As you stroll through the arches and courtyards, keep an eye out for gargoyles. (Notice, too, the black squirrels, descendants of specimen squirrels released from a private estate, although they may have been native to the area earlier.) Setting off the Gothic atmosphere is a large collection of 20th-century outdoor sculpture by distinguished artists. The Henry Moore, located in the courtyard formed by Stanhope, West College, Alexander Hall, and Nassau Hall, is a special favorite of children, as the highly polished lower portion will attest. There are also works by Picasso, Lipchitz, and Nevelson. George Segal's

Kent State memorial, rejected by Kent State University, is
in the courtyard below the chapel and Firestone Library.

Nassau Hall,★ built in 1756 but several times remodeled,
is reputed to have been at one time the largest building in

Princeton

the colonies. A national historic landmark, it once housed
the entire college and has also served as barracks, hospital,
and home of the Continental Congress. It is now used for

higher administrative offices and faculty meetings. The Faculty Room contains portraits of past university presidents and a Charles Wilson Peale portrait of George Washington. Note how worn the interior steps are.

Of the fieldstone buildings planned to harmonize with Nassau Hall, Stanhope and West College remain. Stanhope, an early 19th-century building, has a lovely staircase and stairwell and contains public toilets.

Although the stacks of Firestone Library (2 million volumes) are no longer open to the public, the exhibits in the Rare Books room and Graphic Arts gallery are worth a visit. The chapel, considered an outstanding example of Collegiate Gothic, is one of the largest university chapels in the United States. The art museum, housed in McCormick Hall, features changing exhibits; the permanent collection is particularly strong in early Mediterranean, Oriental, and pre-Columbian art. From October to May there are public gallery talks. The recently renovated museum is scheduled to reopen in 1988 (call 609-452-3787 for information).

Chancellor Green Library and Alexander Hall are examples of later 19th-century Ruskinian and Richardsonian architecture. The exuberance of Alexander Hall, which now contains the Richardson concert hall, has won it many ardent devotees.

Prospect House, from 1879 until 1969 the home of the university's presidents and now a faculty club, is one of several examples of John Notman's Italianate buildings to be found in Princeton. Its formal gardens are open to the public, and the splendid trees around the building, like many other trees on the campus, carry identification plaques.

Modern university buildings include Robert Venturi's Thomas Molecular Biology building (Washington Rd.) and the Woodrow Wilson School (Washington Rd.), designed by Minoru Yamasaki; the decorative pool in its courtyard was for a time so popular in the summers that it became a sanitary problem. The mansions on Prospect St. just east of Washington Rd. belong to the eating clubs; these social clubs at which many students eat their meals function as Princeton's alternatives to fraternities (some of the clubs no longer exist, and their buildings have been converted to serve more academic purposes). The university's Orange Key Guide Service, located in Maclean house* (73 Nassau St.; 609-452-6303), until 1879 home of the university's presidents and itself a national historic landmark, offers walking tours of the campus Monday–Saturday, 10, 11, 1:30, 3:30; Sunday, 1:30, 3:30. These last about one hour;

they visit Nassau Hall and the chapel and usually go through the Prospect gardens, the exact itinerary varying with the size of the group.

The town also has its outdoor sculpture, much of it the work of Seward Johnson (see Hamilton Township). Note the man reading the *New York Times* in front of Borough Hall, the man reading a book near the kiosk in Palmer Sq., and the fishermen in Community Park North.

Princeton's historic district* includes 18th–20th-century buildings on Nassau, Mercer, Prospect, William, Stockton, Wiggins, Alexander, and Olden sts.; Springdale and College rds., Lovers La., and Library Place, but older houses remain in almost all areas of central Princeton. Bainbridge House (158 Nassau St.; 609-921-6748) is a prerevolutionary building, the birthplace of William Bainbridge, commander of the frigate *Constitution* (better known as *Old Ironsides*). Run as a house museum by the Princeton Historical Society, Bainbridge features period furnishings and a children's museum. You can pick up a brochure for a self-guided walking tour here; the society also arranges guided tours

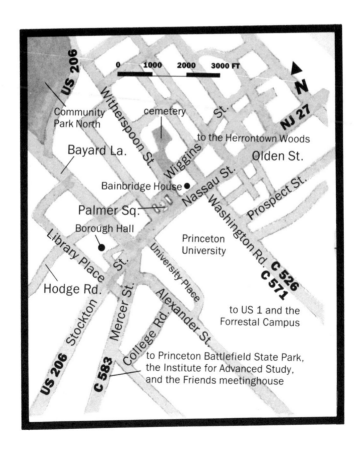

of historic Princeton. Open March–December, Tuesday–Sunday, 12–4.

Morven* (55 Stockton St.), built c. 1754 for Richard Stockton, a signer of the Declaration of Independence, was for many years the governor's mansion. The national historic landmark is now a museum of 18th-and 19th-century American decorative arts run by the New Jersey State Museum (609-292-6300). The Friends meetinghouse (Quakerbridge Rd. and Mercer St.), 1760, is thought to resemble closely the original building (1724), destroyed by fire. Two particularly attractive concentrations of houses from a single period are the row of white frame houses on upper Alexander St. built by Charles Steadman in the 1830s and 1840s and the 18th-century group at the crossroads known as Queenston or Jugtown (Nassau and Harrison sts.).

The Institute for Advanced Study (Olden Ave.; 609-734-8000) is not architecturally distinguished, but the lovely woods behind the main building, which connect to the Charles Rogers wildlife sanctuary, are open to the public. A swaying suspension bridge, according to legend built by visiting scholars, is a favorite of children. Both the institute woods and the Rogers sanctuary are particularly attractive to bird watchers.

Princeton Battlefield State Park* (Mercer St.; 609-737-0623), the site of the Battle of Princeton and a national historic landmark, is about 1½ miles west of the center of town. At the southwest end of the battlefield, its back to the field, is the Thomas P. Clarke House (500 Mercer St.; 609-921-0074), a prerevolutionary farmhouse that has been converted to a museum of 18th-century life. The house is furnished as it would have been in the 1770s; outside there are period gardens, and eventually there will be a working farm. Open Wednesday–Friday, 9–12, 1–5; Saturday, 10–12, 1–5; Sunday, 1–5. Special events are scheduled throughout the year. The columns on the northern side of the field are not related to the battle; they come from a stately home that was torn down in the 20th century.

Across US 1 on the university's Forrestal campus is the Plasma Physics Laboratory (609-683-2750), where scientists, in their search to produce energy by fusion, which unlike fission does not leave radioactive waste products, have already reached temperatures higher than the core of the sun. They expect to be able to produce more energy than that required to produce it by the end of the decade. Tours by appointment.

North of the center of town is the Herrontown Woods Arboretum (Snowden La. and Herrontown Rd.; 609-989-6532). This 142-acre woodlands was donated to the county by Oswald Veblen, a professor at the Institute for Advanced Study (and a nephew of the economist Thorstein Veblen). The arboretum contains a range of habitats that provide a clear illustration of succession; its 3½ miles of trails are well marked. Open daily until dusk. Tours by appointment.

Community Park North (US 206 north of the center) has hiking trails, a fitness course, and a pond. Concerts are given in the amphitheater in the summer. Woodfield Reservation (take Elm Rd. north to the Great Rd. W.) also has trails that go through hilly woods. Access to the Delaware and Raritan Canal Park (see Kingston) is possible at Basin Park (Alexander St.), Washington Rd., and Harrison St.

Rahway UNION (NJ 27, 35) 26,723

Possibly named for the Indian chief Rahwack, Rahway is one of the oldest settlements in New Jersey. The first houses date from the mid-17th century and the first sawmills from the 1680s.

Rahway was a transportation center, first as a stop on the stagecoach line between New York and Philadelphia, then, after the Revolution, as a port, and, after 1835, as a stop on the railroad. In later years the town became an industrial center: Three-in-One oil was developed in Rahway in the late 19th century, and a few years later the Merck company, one of the world's largest producers of prescription drugs, bought land in Rahway (the firm now has 150 buildings on 200 acres). Rahway is also the home of Tofutti, the nation's biggest seller of frozen tofu desserts, and possesses what is reputed to be the nation's first solar-heated city hall (Main St. and E. Milton). Among its best-known native sons are the economist Milton Friedman, the former senator Clifford Case, and the author and scientist Carl Sagan. Abraham Clark, a signer of the Declaration of Independence, is buried in the Presbyterian cemetery (St. Georges Ave. near Westfield Ave.).

The Merchants and Drovers Tavern★ (St. Georges and Westfield aves.; 201-381-0441) dates from the mid-18th century. This frame building, unusually large for a colonial structure (it is said to be the only four-story colonial inn still standing), continued in use as a tavern until 1932. Converted to a house museum, the tavern has been temporarily closed for structural repairs. On the same property is the Terrill Tavern (c. 1763), a much smaller building now at its third location. George Washington was a guest here on one of his trips through the area. Open September–December and March–June, 1st Sunday in the month, 2–5. Donations requested. Group tours by appointment at other times.

At the corner of Central Ave. and Irving St. is the Rahway Theater (1928), built as a vaudeville house and now the home of the Union County Arts Center. The 1,400-seat theater's gold-leaf decor has been restored, and the original Wurlitzer organ is in place.

The Rahway River Parkway (St. Georges Ave. and River Rd.), designed by the Olmsted firm, has places where you can fish, as does Milton Lake Park (W. Lake and Madison aves.), both county facilities.

Ramsey BERGEN (NJ 17, C 507) 12,899

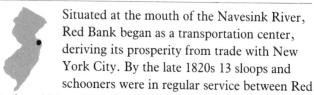

Now primarily a commuters' town, Ramsey was originally settled by the Dutch. In one of their early stone houses (c. 1745) is the Old Stone House Museum★ (538 Island Rd.; 201-327-0028). Three rooms on the main floor are furnished to show how a prerevolutionary Dutch household would have looked. A junior museum with toys and other items from the turn of the century is upstairs. There are also changing exhibits. Open Sunday, mid-May–mid-October, 2–4. Admission fee. Groups by appointment.

Other 18th-century stone houses can be found at 171 Lake St., 538 Island Rd.,★ and 245 Shadyside Rd.★ Part of Darlington Park (see Mahwah) extends into Ramsey.

Red Bank MONMOUTH (NJ 35, C 34, 520) 12,031

Situated at the mouth of the Navesink River, Red Bank began as a transportation center, deriving its prosperity from trade with New York City. By the late 1820s 13 sloops and schooners were in regular service between Red Bank and New York City, taking vegetables, wood, and oysters to New York and coming back with manufactured goods. Regular steamship service began in the 1830s and continued until the 1920s, after which Red Bank's career as a port was over. The once-prized local oysters have also disappeared, casualties of polluted water. One of Red Bank's water-related activities, iceboating, has continued. Farm sled races, presumably the ancestors of iceboat races, were recorded here as early as 1879, and the North Shrewsbury Iceboat and Yacht Company, founded in 1880, is still active and has taken up renovating and racing late 19th-century boats.

Red Bank (the name can be found in a 1734 log and presumably derives from the clay in the river banks) can boast at least two famous native sons: Edmund Wilson, the author and critic, was born here in 1895; Count Basie, the jazz musician, was born here in 1904 and began his career playing piano to accompany films at the Palace Theater.

The town has a distinctly late 19th-century appearance, partly the result of a fire that led to the complete rebuilding of Broad St. in the late 19th century. But red brick and other 19th-century features are found on other streets as well: note, for example, the borough hall* (1892; 51 Monmouth St.), once the Shrewsbury Town Hall; the railroad station* (1878; Bridge Ave. and Monmouth St.); the Navesink Hook & Ladder Company #1 (1872; Mechanic St.); the library (84 Front St.), once the Red Bank Seminary and for a time at the turn of the century the home of bandmaster and composer John Philip Sousa; the lumber company that was once the St. James School (1879; 9 Wall St.); St. James Church (1894; Broad St. at Peters Place).

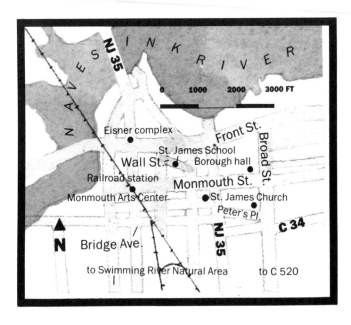

The largest uniform-manufacturing company in the world was started in Red Bank by Sigmund Eisner in 1885. Specializing in military and boy-scout uniforms, the company stopped manufacturing in the late 1940s. Its five buildings on Bridge Ave. and W. Front St. have been converted into a commercial complex with offices, shops, restaurants, and art galleries. The clock tower was added in 1986.

At 99–101 Monmouth St. is the Monmouth Arts Center (201-842-9000). It includes the Count Basie Theater, a 1,500-seat theater built in 1925 for vaudeville and converted to a movie house; the Monmouth Conservatory of Music; the Art Alliance (201-842-9403); art studios; classrooms; and workshops. The theater has recently installed the old Carnegie Hall seats. The center presents concerts and other entertainment year round; the Art Alliance holds ten shows a year in its three gallery spaces. Art Alliance open Tuesday–Saturday, 10–4.

Up the Swimming River a mile or two from Red Bank is the Swimming River Natural Area. There is a wide variety of habitats in these 100 acres: salt and freshwater marshes, wet and dry forests, steep slopes, and expansive stands of wild rice.

Ridgewood BERGEN (Garden State Pkwy exit 166, NJ 17, C 507)   25,208

Because the Dutch Reformed Church in Ridgewood, built in 1735, was situated at a strategic crossroads, it was used steadily for military purposes during the Revolution and fell into disrepair. Although it may have served as George Washington's headquarters for a few days, and had witnessed Aaron Burr's marriage and part of Charles Lee's court martial (Lee's court martial was held in several places to avoid taking army officers away from their wartime duties; see Freehold), the congregation decided to replace it and in 1800 built the Old Paramus Reformed Church* (660 E. Glen Ave.). The bell ordered from London for the 1800 church is still in use.

On the church grounds in an 1873 schoolhouse is the Schoolhouse Museum (650 E. Glen Ave.; 201-652-4584), run by the Paramus Historical & Preservation Society and devoted to local history. Among the exhibits are a Dutch room containing a 1690 Dutch Bible and other items from the Netherlands that the Dutch settlers, preponderant in this area, might have brought with them, a Victorian schoolroom containing old school equipment, an early 18th-century kitchen and a kitchen contemporaneous with the building, and a church exhibit containing items from both the 1735 and 1800 churches. Open April–October, Sunday, 2–4. Other times and tours of the church by appointment.

In the center of Ridgewood in Van Neste Sq. is a World War I memorial column designed by Henry Bacon, the architect of the Lincoln Memorial. There are in Ridgewood several examples of early Dutch stone houses. Note, for example, the David Ackerman house★ (415 E. Saddle River Rd.); most of it was built in the 1720s and 1730s, but the earliest portion may be late 17th century. Other old houses are to be seen on E. Glen, Lincoln, Doremus, N. Maple, and E. Ridgewood aves., Grove and Prospect sts., and E. Saddle River Rd.

Ringoes   HUNTERDON   (US 202, NJ 31, 179,
C 579)   [East Amwell Township]

The log hut that John Ringo built at the intersection of two Indian trails in 1720 was the nucleus around which today's attractive town of Ringoes developed. The hut became not just Ringo's house but a tavern as well, and the tavern prospered after 1769, when it became a stop for the Swift-Sure Stagecoach line. According to one legend Ringo made a fortune, but fearing robbery, buried it and died without revealing its location.

The Amwell Academy (NJ 179, the Old York Rd.), now an inn, was built as a school in 1811 and bought by Dr. C. W. Larison in 1868. Well known as an educator in the 19th century, Larison believed strongly in phonetic spelling and in 1885 published *Geografy: A Text Buk in Fonic Orthografy.* Across from the inn is the Landis house, possibly the oldest house in Hunterdon County. The marquis de Lafayette is supposed to have recuperated from an illness here.

The Black River & Western Railroad (C 579; 201-782-9600), which runs an old-fashioned steam train between Ringoes and Flemington, has its yards and depot in Ringoes. From mid-April through November, there are several round-trips to Flemington on weekends and holidays; in July and August, trips also run Tuesday–Friday afternoons; and on Sunday afternoon, May–October, trains run to Lambertville as well. Fee charged.

Ringwood   PASSAIC (C 511) 12,625

Located near the New York border, the borough of Ringwood developed first as an iron-mining town and then as a summer resort (there are many lakes in the area). It is now a rapidly growing commuter town. (The population has more than tripled over the last 25 years and increased more than 40-fold over the last 50 years.) The Ringwood Manor, Skylands Manor, and Shepherd Lake sections of Ringwood State Park fall within its borders. Both the Ringwood and Skylands manor sections contain over 1,000 acres each, the Shepherd Lake section contains over 500. The Ringwood Manor section can be reached from Sloatsburg Rd. (off C 511); the other two sections are to the east.

Ringwood Manor★ (201-962-7031), a national historic landmark, is a rambling, unfortunately somewhat neglected mansion of 70-odd rooms, situated on spacious grounds. It too owes its existence to the iron industry. The Ringwood Company was active in this area from the 1740s to the early 1930s, and during the American Revolution the ironworks were important suppliers to the Continental troops. At that time the works were run by Robert Erskine, general surveyor to the Continental army and known for the accuracy of the maps he drew for George Washington (a frequent visitor to Ringwood). Although ironmasters first lived on this site in the mid-18th century, the earliest part of the present mansion dates to 1810 when Martin Ryerson was the ironmaster. In the mid-19th century, the works and house were owned by Peter Cooper, a versatile inventor, entrepreneur, and philanthropist, perhaps best known as the founder of Cooper Union in New York City. His daughter and son-in-law, the Abram S. Hewitts, decided to make Ringwood their permanent summer home, and most of the present house was built by them between the 1850s and the 1870s. Among the noteworthy features are the wood-paneled great hall and dining room and the Delft-tile fireplace in the library. The furnishings reflect the occupants' lives over the 200 years from 1810 to 1930 and include many fine pieces. Various mementos of the iron industry lie about the grounds, including links from a chain similar in type to the one stretched across the Hudson during the Revolution as a barrier to British ships. Within this section of the park there are picnic tables, fishing ponds, and hiking trails. The area is also suitable for cross-country skiing. Manor house open May–October, Tuesday–Friday, 10–4; weekends, 10–4:30; and for Victorian Christmas. Park open sunrise to half-hour after sunset. Parking charge Memorial Day weekend–Labor Day weekend.

At the Skylands Manor section of the park (210-962-7031) is New Jersey's first official botanic garden. Originally designed in the 1920s by Clarence McKenzie Lewis, an investment banker who was also a trustee of the New York Botanical Garden, the 300 acres of gardens were neglected for many years and only saved with the help of volunteers. There is almost always something blooming here amid the variety of formal and less formal layouts. The 40-room mansion, also built by Lewis in the 1920s, is rented out by the state for various functions. The gardens are open from sunrise to one-half hour after sunset. There are also hiking trails here, and there is hunting in season.

The Shepherd Lake section (201-962-6526) is north of Skylands Manor and centers around the lake where you can swim, fish, boat, and picnic.

At the southwestern corner of the borough, adjacent to the Norvin Green State Forest (201-962-7031), is the Weis Ecology Center (150 Snake Den Rd.; 201-835-2160). The center building contains displays, and the center sponsors a variety of programs, from mushroom hunts to autumn hawk watches to cross-country skiing instruction. The 2,000 acres of forest contain hiking and nature trails, and, in season, you can hunt, cross-country ski, and sled.

Some three miles west of Ringwood Manor (take Margaret King Ave., which becomes Greenwood Lake Tnpk), along the Wanaque River, are the remains of the 18th- and 19th-century Long Pond Ironworks.* These works, which were run by the same ironmasters who were active at Ringwood and were last operated in the 1880s, take their name from the former name of nearby Greenwood Lake. The site includes remains of the ironworking complex and its surrounding village. Tours start at the Ironworks Store, April–October, 1st Sunday of the month at noon, or by appointment (write the Friends of the Furnace, Box 809, Hewitt 07421). Donation requested. (For more information call Ringwood State Park, 201-962-7031.)

East of Hewitt is the Wanaque Wildlife Management Area, some 2,000 acres just east of Greenwood Lake and including Green Turtle Pond. The area is open for fishing, hiking, and hunting.

River Edge BERGEN (NJ 4,
C 503)   11, 111

River Edge played a crucial part in the Revolution when George Washington, in November 1776, led his army over the Hackensack New Bridge after the surprise attack by the British at Fort Lee. At that spot is the Steuben House★ (1209 Main St. just north of NJ 4; 201-487-1739), a state historic site that houses the museum of the Bergen County Historical Society. The oldest portion of the sandstone house was probably built in 1713, but there had been a gristmill on the site for several years before that. During the Revolution the house was owned by Jan Zabriskie, a leading merchant and a Tory. It was confiscated and offered to Major General Baron von Steuben in gratitude for his work in training the American troops. According to legend, Steuben declined the offer because he didn't want to displace the Zabriskies; it is more likely that the abuse the house had suffered—because of its strategic location at the bridge it was used for various military purposes, including serving as a fort, throughout the Revolution—decreased its attractiveness as a place to live. Steuben rented the house to the Zabriskies who entertained him there and charged the costs of the entertainment to the general's account. Eventually Steuben sold the house to Zabriskie's son for a handsome sum.

The Steuben House has an idyllic setting, known as New Bridge Landing Historic Park, and there is a picnic area on the grounds. Most of the items on display, including, for example, the furniture and pottery, were manufactured or used in the area. An Indian dugout canoe found in Hackensack in the mid-19th century is also to be seen. Various special events take place at the Steuben House, including an annual Christmas exhibit that traces the evolution of the holiday from ancient to modern times. Open Wednesday–Saturday, 10–12, 1–5; Sunday, 2–5. Groups by appointment.

There are other buildings in the park, including the Campbell Christie House,★ a colonial sandstone house being restored by the Bergen County Historical Society. Individual and group tours can be arranged by calling the society at 201-343-9492. The Demarest House (Main St.; 201-262-1354, 201-261-0012) was built by the Huguenot settler David des Marest in 1678. One of the oldest houses in Bergen County, it was moved here from New Milford in the 1950s. Group tours by appointment. A late 19th-century barn and an 1880s iron-truss swing bridge are also in the park. The two houses and the barn are opened for visits during special events at the park.

Riverton BURLINGTON (C 543) 3,068

Situated on the Delaware River and founded in 1851 as a resort by a group of wealthy businessmen from Philadelphia, Riverton has lovely views of the river along Bank Ave. Several of the mansions built by the founders remain, as does the Riverton Yacht Club (Bank Ave. at the foot of Main St.), built in 1880 at the end of an 1869 iron pier. A walk or drive along Bank Ave., Main St. (note the public library), Lippincott St., and Carriage House La. (where many of the Victorian carriage houses have been converted to residences) is a pleasant way to see what kind of a community its founders must have intended.

Rocky Hill SOMERSET (C 518, just east of US 206) 717

This small town (less than a square mile in area) served as George Washington's headquarters in the fall of 1783 while the Continental Congress was meeting in Princeton. Here Washington entertained, among others, Alexander Hamilton, John Witherspoon, Thomas Jefferson, Thomas Paine, and James Madison, and here he wrote the address that has come to be known as "Washington's Farewell to the Troops" (he could not have delivered a farewell to the troops here because there weren't many around). Washington's house, Rockingham* (C 518 c. ½ mile east of the Delaware and Raritan Canal; 609-921-8835), is now a state-run historic house museum. Moved from its original site in the late 1890s and moved again in the 1960s because it was threatened by blasting from the nearby Traprock Industries quarry, the house is furnished with pieces from 1783 or earlier, and includes reconstructed outbuildings and a colonial herb garden. Among the special events offered is a Christmas program. Open Wednesday–Friday, 9–12, 1–6; Saturday, 10–12, 1–6; Sunday, 1–6. Closed

New Year's Day, Thanksgiving, and Christmas. Groups by appointment.

Rocky Hill is a well-preserved and attractive village. Its historic district★ includes 19th- and 20th-century buildings on Washington St. and Montgomery, Crescent, and Princeton aves. The prerevolutionary mill at 200 Washington St., now a potter's studio and gallery, was once owned by John Hart, one of New Jersey's five signers of the Declaration of Independence.

The Millstone River and the Delaware and Raritan Canal★ come through Rocky Hill, and you can walk (or bicycle or horseback ride) along the towpath here (see Kingston). The remains of a well-known terra-cotta plant, which supplied the tiles for the Woolworth Building in New York City, are visible from the towpath. (You can also see examples of the terra-cotta work in the Rocky Hill firehouse, 156 Washington St.)

Roebling BURLINGTON (Delaware River between Bordentown and Burlington just west of US 130) [Florence Township]

Roebling was founded as a company town in 1904, when the Roebling Company, famous for making the wire rope used in suspension bridges, decided to make for itself the steel that went into the rope. The plant was built on the site of a 115-acre peach and potato farm that bordered the Delaware River, and turned out a variety of products, including the cable used in the George Washington Bridge. The town was designed by Charles G. Roebling, the third son of the famous John Roebling, who had invented steel cable, had created the Roebling Company, had built his first cable suspension bridge in Pittsburgh in 1846, and had designed and begun construction of the Brooklyn Bridge. The younger Roebling envisioned a model community for the workers in the new plant. He laid out the town on a rectangular grid, with Main St. a boulevard that expanded into a circle at the intersection with 5th Ave., and provided a park, an auditorium, and a variety of shops. Those higher up in the company lived in the larger houses along Riverside Ave., but the workers' brick rowhouses were solidly built, and the view of the river from the park is lovely. In the 1950s the plant was sold. The town is now part of Florence Township, many of the original structures are gone, and the buildings are privately owned, but the distinctive quality of the community is still apparent. The Roebling historic district* includes 2d–8th, Alden, Norman, and Amboy aves. In the library (Hornberger and 6th aves.), built as a recreation center with bowling lanes, pool tables, and shuffleboard courts, is a display showing the history of Roebling. Open weekdays, 9–12; other times by appointment (call Louis Borbi, 609-499-2415). St. Nicholas Church (Norman Ave.) has a picnic grove at the end of the street where ethnic festivals sponsored by the church are held several times a year.

Roosevelt MONMOUTH (C 571) 835

 Conceived as a utopian community that would be a self-sufficient agricultural and industrial unit, Roosevelt,* founded in the 1930s and known as Jersey Homesteads until the death of President Franklin Delano Roosevelt, was actually owned by the federal government. The early community, a project of the Federal Resettlement Administration, contained a cooperative factory (the Workers Aim Cooperative Factory on N. Valley Rd., dedicated in 1936, now housing studios and a woodworking shop) and a cooperative store. Communal farms were also part of the original conception.

Although 151 of the original structures remain, the farms have been sold, the cooperatives are long since gone (though some residents maintain a food coop), and the government sold the town to the residents in the late 1940s. But underneath the extensive architectural alterations, you can still see the boxlike houses and rational layout of the original Bauhaus-inspired scheme, the work of Alfred Kastner (his assistant was Louis Kahn).

Most of the residents are now commuters, but the town has long been a haven for artists and writers, of whom Ben Shahn is probably the best known. His large mural, depicting incidents and people involved in the history of labor, immigration into the United States, and the founding of Roosevelt, is to be found in the elementary school. In the park with the amphitheater on the west side of C 571 (N. Rochdale Rd.) is a monumental bust of Roosevelt, modeled by Shahn's son Jon.

At the corner of N. Valley Rd. and Homestead La. is

Britton House, one of the farmhouses predating the foundation of Jersey Homesteads. And at the foot of Farm La. is a prize-winning project from the 1980s, Roosevelt Solar Village, a low-income solar housing project for the elderly, modeled on an English village.

To the south and west of Roosevelt, off C 571 (and also accessible from C 524, C 539, and many lesser roads) is the Assunpink Wildlife Management Area, 5,400 acres con-

Roosevelt

taining three lakes, open fields, marsh, lowland forest, upland woods, and hedgerows. Some of the land is leased to
farmers. The area is reputed to be one of the best spots for
bird watching in central New Jersey, with over 250 species
having been seen there. Fishing is possible along most of the
shore of all three lakes, you can hike, and there is limited
hunting. The state is building a major equine center (the
Horse Park at Stone Tavern) in the area, with facilities for
international equestrian events of all kinds.

Roseland ESSEX (I 280, C 527) 5,380

The Joseph C. Minish Center for Environmental Studies (621 Eagle Rock Ave.; 201-228-2210) is a county facility located near the Passaic River in West Essex Park. At the center are a greenhouse, library, educational exhibits, interpretive trails, and picnic facilities. The center offers an extensive (averaging 120 a month) and varied series of programs, ranging from preschool environmental education programs to canoeing and cross-country skiing lessons to guided walks. Open daily, 9–4:30, except holidays.

The Harrison house★ (126 Eagle Rock Ave.), a white clapboard house with an attractive garden, dates to the 1820s and serves as the headquarters for the Roseland Historical Society.

Roselle UNION (NJ 27) 20,641

The first city in the world to be lit by incandescent bulbs (and the first in the United States to be lit by electricity), Roselle was settled in the late 1670s by Abraham Clark, who migrated here from Long Island and was the great-grandfather of the Abraham Clark who signed the Declaration of Independence. It remained basically rural for almost 200 years until John C. Rose, after whom it is named, began buying up farms and developing the area. Today Roselle has an attractive, lived-in look and many interesting buildings, including the Federal-style Cavalier Jouet house (238 E. 2d Ave.) and the Wheatsheaf Tavern (St. Georges Ave.), once a stagecoach stop.

A replica of the Abraham Clark house, which burned in the early years of this century, has been built at 9th Ave. and Chestnut St. The house, not that distinguishable from its neighbors, sits a few hundred feet from the site of the original house on land that once belonged to Clark. The museum wing features a small collection of items primarily related to the history of the Clark family and the history of Roselle, including for example, some early light bulbs. Open by appointment only. (Call Mrs. Olson at the public library, 201-245-5808, to arrange an appointment.)

The First Presbyterian Church (5th Ave. and Chestnut

St.; 201-245-1161) dates from the 1890s, but still uses the original lightolier that made it the first church in the United States to be lit by electricity.

In the southeastern corner of the borough (Thompson and St. Georges aves.) is Warinanco Park, best known for its indoor skating rink (201-241-3263, 201-241-3262). The 210-acre park, one of Union County's many Olmsted-designed parks, was named for a chief of the Lenape Indians. The park has facilities for boating (201-289-1699), fishing, and picnicking, as well as bicycle paths, a fitness trail, tennis courts (201-245-2288), a playground, and athletic fields.

Rutherford BERGEN (NJ 3, 17) 19,068

Once a settlement known as Boiling Springs (there is a Boiling Springs Ave. just over the border in East Rutherford), Rutherford was developed in 1862 on land that had belonged to John Rutherford, a patriot and friend of George Washington. There are still early 18th-century houses to be seen in Rutherford: Fairleigh Dickinson University, for example, owns the Nathaniel Kingsland house (245 Union Ave.), where Washington rested on his journey

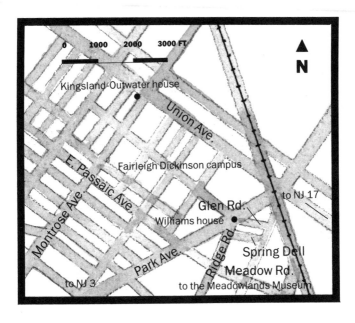

from Newburgh to Princeton; its oldest portion dates from 1670, making it one of the oldest houses in the state. (The adjoining Richard Outwater house dates from 1821.) Washington also visited the Kip Homestead★ (12 Meadow Rd.). Another old Dutch stone house, the Yereance-Berry House,★ contains the Meadowlands Museum (91 Crane Ave.; 201-935-1175), which specializes in area history, but also exhibits fine and decorative arts and crafts. Permanent exhibits include New Jersey minerals, antique toys and dolls, and early kitchens; there are also changing exhibits. Open Monday and Wednesday, 1–4; 1st and 3d Sundays of the month, 2–4. Group tours by appointment.

Rutherford is the birthplace of the poet William Carlos Williams, and until the 1970s his house★ (9 Ridge Rd. at Park Ave.) remained in the hands of his family. One block from his house is the William Carlos Williams Center (Park Ave. between Glen Rd. and Spring Dell; 201-939-6969), built around the Rivoli, a 1922 vaudeville theater that was converted into a movie house but burned in 1977. Claiming to be one of the few arts centers in the United States to be named after a poet, the Williams Center features poetry readings, workshops, and seminars, as well as a music series, theater, and art exhibits. Plans call for converting the Rivoli into an 1,800-seat concert hall.

Fairleigh Dickinson first opened in Rutherford in 1942 as a junior college, and although the main campus is now in Madison, the 15-acre Rutherford campus is still in use. The Castle (E. Passaic and Montrose aves.), the building the college purchased when it first opened, was built as a summer home in the 1880s and was inspired by the French châteaux of Chaumont and Amboise.

Salem SALEM (NJ 45, 49) 6,959

 In 1675 a group of Quakers led by John Fenwick settled on the banks of the Delaware River and named their community Salem, from *shalom*, the Hebrew word for peace. Immigrants from other countries had preceded them—the Swedes and Finns, for example, had established a settlement at Fort Elfsborg (also known as Fort Myggenborgh because of the mosquitos, located near today's Point Elsinboro) in 1643, and there had also been Dutch and Puritans from New Haven in the area—but their communities did not last (Fort Elfsborg was abandoned in 1653), and Salem became the first permanent English settlement in West Jersey.

Salem thrived as a shipping center (it was designated an official port in 1682) until the Revolution, when shipping activity moved to Camden and Philadelphia. The port fell into disuse, but in 1982, some 300 years after its founding, it was officially reopened, and a load of grain was shipped out of the harbor for the first time in 100 years. New facilities are being built, and some three to five ships a month leave the Salem port now with lumber, scrap steel, and frozen meats and fish. Further plans for the waterfront include construction of a 17th-century Swedish village in a wooded wetlands area that will also include nature paths. It is hoped the village will be open in 1988.

Improvident farming practices depleted the soil around Salem, and in the early 1800s many of its citizens headed west, among them Zadock Street, who left in 1802 and founded the towns of Salem, Ohio, and Salem, Indiana. His son Aaron Street was responsible for Salem, Iowa, and Salem, Oregon.

The discovery of marl nearby made it possible to replenish the soil, and agriculture prospered again. Salem, in fact, has a footnote in agricultural history. Robert Gibbon Johnson, a wealthy local landowner, is credited with importing the first tomato plants from South America. On 15 September 1820, he is supposed to have stood on the courthouse steps and eaten a tomato, which most people believed to be poisonous. Tomatoes are now, of course, an important crop in New Jersey, and many of them are grown in Salem County.

Johnson was also one of the founders of the New Jersey Historical Society (1845) and its first vice president. His elegant house (90 Market St.), built in 1806 with additions dating from 1850, now serves as a county building and is one of the many brick buildings that, with the wide streets, help give Salem its distinctly West Jersey look.

At Market St. and Broadway is the old Salem County Courthouse. Portions date from 1735, but the courthouse was almost completely rebuilt in 1817. Extensively remodeled again in 1908, the outside now dates basically from 1817, the inside from 1908. To visit the courthouse, stop in at the Chamber of Commerce, on Market St. Open weekdays 9–12, 1–4.

Next to the Johnson house is the mid-19th century Presbyterian Church, which has a Tiffany window over the pulpit in the sanctuary. Farther along Market St. (north of

Grant) is St. John's Episcopal Church, originally Church of England. The present building dates from 1836. Both churches are open to the public.

At 79–83 Market St., in the Alexander Grant House, part of which dates from 1721, are the headquarters, museum, and library of the Salem County Historical Society (609-935-5004). The museum exhibits antiques that reflect the county's heritage, as well as various special collections, including glass from Wistarburg, the first glassworks in the colonies (1739), Indian relics, and dolls. Behind the Grant House on the historical society's property is the John Jones law office, a tiny octagonal brick building, c. 1735, believed to be the oldest surviving law office in the country. There is also a stone barn built in 1957 that contains some of the larger items owned by the society. Open Tuesday–Friday, 12–4. Admission charged.

On the north side of E. Broadway at Walnut St. is the Salem Friends Meetinghouse. Dating from 1772, it has the longest record of continuous service of any religious building in New Jersey. Built of brick in a Flemish-bond pattern, its walls are 16–18 inches thick, much of its glass may be from Wistarburg, and its fences are made of New Jersey bog iron.

On W. Broadway opposite Oak St. is the Friends burial ground. Here you will find the famous Salem oak, a massive white oak tree believed to be some 500 years old. Under this tree in October 1675 John Fenwick signed a treaty with the Indians. There is concern that the oak may have only 50 years to live and that a severe storm could topple it now.

If possible, walk up and down Market St. and along Broadway (a large section of Market St. and E. Broadway are in the Market St. historic district,* and many buildings have identifying plaques). Many of the houses in the area were derelict or had been vandalized, and the renovation efforts have been heroic. The Greek Revival house at 28 Market St. (c. 1800) is one of those renovated. It stands taller than its neighbors because it was built by a tailor who had his shop in the basement (the basement windows and doorway have been removed). See also the small frame salt-boxes at 18 Market. The First United Methodist Church (Walnut St. opposite Church St.) dates from 1888, the First Baptist Church (130 W. Broadway) from 1846.

About five miles northwest of Salem (north on NJ 49 about 2 miles, left, or west, on Lighthouse Rd., C 632, about 2 miles, left again on Fort Mott Rd., C 630, another mile) is Fort Mott★ State Park (609-935-3218), a 104-acre waterfront park with buildings and concrete gun embattlements dating to the Spanish-American war. Acquired by the state in 1947, the park has a splendid view of the Delaware and facilities for picnicking and fishing. Open year round during daylight hours. On the same spit of land is Finn's Point National Cemetery★ (609-935-3628), where many Confederate soldiers are buried. The lodge dates to the late 19th century, as does the marble monument to the Union dead (the cupola was added in 1936); the Confederate obelisk dates to 1910. Each year before Memorial Day, Civil War buffs hold memorial services at the cemetery, where several German World War II prisoners are also buried. Open daily, 8–5.

About two miles east of the park at the intersection of Lighthouse and Fort Mott rds. is the Finn's Point Rear Range Light★ (609-935-1487), a 115-foot lighthouse with a Greek doorway, built in 1876, a rare surviving example of a wrought-iron lighthouse. The view from the lighthouse, which was decommissioned in 1950, is spectacular. Open

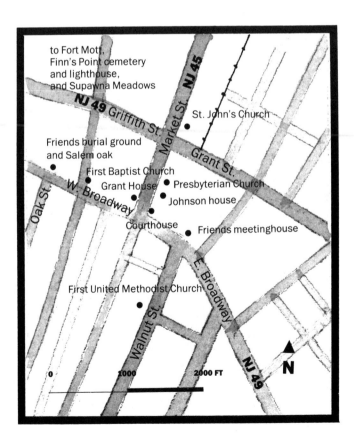

April–October, 3d Sunday of the month, 12–4. Groups by appointment. The lighthouse is part of the Supawna Meadows National Wildlife Refuge, and an interpretive display at the site has information about the light on one side and about the refuge on the other. The refuge, of interest to naturalists because it is less saline than the ocean, is a good spot for glossy ibis, cattle and snowy egrets, red-winged blackbirds, and mute swans.

The roads around Fort Mott traverse salt marshes and wild rice marshes, but it is often difficult to see the marshes because of the tall Phragmites that line the roads. Also in this area is the Killcohook Coordination Area. This is where the army engineers, engaged in a never-ending battle to keep the Delaware River open to navigation, dump the sludge from their dredging. Fifty years of dumping have produced hills that are 30–40 feet high. If you drive around the perimeter of this desolate area, you will pass into the state of Delaware, even though you will still be on the east side of the Delaware River. This is because the original deed for Wilmington included the land within a 12-mile radius of a particular point, and since this was all swamp at the time, no one paid the anomaly much mind.

Scotch Plains UNION (US 22, NJ 28, C 509) 20,774

Scotch Plains was settled in 1684 by Scottish dissenters from Perth Amboy who were soon followed by Quakers. By the 1740s there were more Baptists than Quakers or Scottish dissenters. An agricultural community, Scotch Plains grew slowly (by refusing to let the railroad come through the town, it stayed rural longer), but after World War II it doubled in size and became a commuter town. James Manning, the founder of Brown University, came from Scotch Plains, and Arthur Brisbane, the journalist and editor, was a resident.

Scotch Plains's first substantial building, the Stage House Inn* (Front St. and Park Ave.; 201-322-4224), built c. 1737, and from roughly 1769 to 1829 a stagecoach stop on the Swift-Sure Stagecoach line, is now the cornerstone for Stage House Village, in which various older buildings, some from other sites, have been converted to shops and restaurants. Nearby is the Cannonball Osborn House (1840 Front

St.; 201-899-4137, 201-233-3829), c. 1720, so named because it was hit by a cannonball (fired by a Continental soldier) during the Revolution. Maintained as a museum by the Scotch Plains and Fanwood Historical Society, the house has its original kitchen, complete with a beehive oven. One parlor is furnished with colonial pieces, the other with Victorian ones. Open the 1st Sunday of the month, 2–4. Tours by appointment.

The Ruskinian-Gothic Baptist Church (311 Park Ave.) dates from the 1870s, but the parsonage* (Park Ave. and Grand St.) is almost 100 years older (1786, with a later addition). Built of boulders from the Green Brook, supposedly because the new parson was from Pennsylvania and accustomed to stone, it was the first stone parsonage in the area. The Second Baptist Church (Grand and Union), now the YMCA, dates from c. 1817. Note also the Romanesque All Saints' Episcopal Church (559 Park Ave.), 1882. The Ephraim Tucker farmhouse (Jerusalem Rd. near Plainfield Ave.; 201-322-6700), c. 1740, now serves as the clubhouse for the Scotch Hills Golf Club.

At the corner of Raritan and Terrill rds., on land that was once a camping ground for the Lenape Indians, is the Terry Lou Zoo (201-322-7180), a private zoo founded in 1949. Close to 300 animals live on its seven acres, and the zoo is engaged in a successful breeding program for endangered Siberian tigers. Open weekdays, 10–4; weekends, 10–6.

Across Raritan Rd. from the zoo is the Ash Brook Golf Course and Reservation (see Clark).

Part of the Watchung Reservation falls within Scotch Plains (see Mountainside).

Seaside Park OCEAN (NJ 35) 1,795

The tiny beach community of Seaside Park is nestled between Seaside Heights to the north—with its boardwalk and night life, reputed to have more people per square inch in the summer than any other community—and Island Beach State Park (201-793-0506) to the south—ten miles of one of the last completely unspoiled beaches in New Jersey and one of the last undeveloped barrier islands along the North Atlantic. Owned in the 1920s by Henry Phipps, a partner of Andrew Carnegie, who planned to convert the area into a luxurious seaside resort, Island Beach was purchased by the state and turned into a park in the 1950s. One of the Phipps houses saved by the state now serves as the governor's summer home. Another building houses the visitor center, which contains changing displays related to the island. There is a short, self-guided tour here, and you can pick up trail maps. The lifesaving station★ dates from the 1890s.

Because there are no jetties or groins on Island Beach, the natural forces shaping the beach are unimpeded. Actually, Island Beach is no longer an island, its name dating to the time when it was, from the mid-18th to the early 19th century. This is a beautiful place, and the park, with the ocean on one side and Barnegat Bay on the other, offers visitors a wide variety of activities. Over half the acreage consists of natural areas, but there are recreation areas as well. There is only one road into the park, and when the parking lots are full (in high season as many as 10,000 may visit daily) no more cars are let in. (There is no limit on beach buggies driven by those who are planning to fish.) The park naturalists conduct tours through the northern natural area, and you are free to walk in the wildlife sanctuary to the south. The bay side is generally closed, but tours can be arranged, except in winter. From the third week in June to Labor Day some areas of the beaches are protected by lifeguards, and it is also possible to fish, scuba dive, and surf in designated areas. The bird watching is excellent, and although there are no tables or fireplaces, you are welcome to picnic on the beach; you may build a fire (except in the bathing areas) as long as you keep your fire at least 50 feet east of the dunes. Even at the height of the summer season, you can find empty stretches of beach to walk along if you leave the guarded areas. From mid-October to mid-April you can bring a horse onto the beach (advance reservations are necessary). Parking charges in summer.

Secaucus HUDSON (NJ Tnpk exits 16E, 17, NJ 3) 13,719

Secaucus, which must have one of the worst reputations of any city in the state, was settled in the early 1680s by a few hardy souls willing to cross the damp meadowland to reach high ground. The name comes from an Indian word meaning "where the snake hides," and the Indians are said to have avoided the area. Laurel Hill, the nearly leveled mineral-rich rock formation familiar to those who travel by train, bus, or car to or from New York City, was once known as Snake Hill and is said to have been used by George Washington's troops as a lookout during the Revolution.

Part of Secaucus's bad reputation came from its pig farms—until about 25 years ago, there were some 50 of them—and slaughterhouses. When the New Jersey Turnpike was built, several of the farms were destroyed, and the town forbade the establishment of new ones. One pig farmer, Henry Krajewski, ran for president as an Independent Populist in 1952 and 1960.

Known also as an area of warehouses and freight yards, Secaucus may have suffered from the idea, accepted until fairly recently, that marshland was waste land, good only for pig farms and freight yards. In recent years, however, Secaucus has attracted more than $1 billion worth of industrial, commercial, and residential development. In fact, there is considerable concern now about overbuilding on the marshland. Among the projects are the immense Harmon Cove and Harmon Meadow developments, which contain housing, marinas, office and hotel space, child-care facilities, shops and restaurants, a cinema and a health club, all set in the midst of the marshes.

The new studios of WOR-TV (1 Harmon Plaza; 201-330-8950) are in one of the few buildings in the country built specifically as a television facility. Tours are available by written appointment. Lincoln Towers (County Ave. near Dorigo La.) is a striking, barrier-free housing project for the elderly and handicapped, the last subsidized project to be approved by HUD before funds were cut in 1981. Note also the dramatic municipal building (1203 Paterson Plank Rd.).

Secaucus today is a popular stop for shoppers because of the abundance of factory outlets. What is interesting about these outlets is that they are located among working warehouses, so that to go from one store to another shoppers must negotiate around 18 wheelers, driving down streets with names like Enterprise Ave. and Frozen Food Plaza.

Sergeantsville HUNTERDON (C 523, 604) [Delaware Township]

 First settled around 1700, Sergeantsville (pronounced sir-gents-ville) is named for Charles Sergeant, a revolutionary war soldier. (Before the 1830s it was known as Skunktown.) This tiny village at the intersection of county routes 523 and 604 (the Stockton-Flemington Rd. and the Rose-

mont-Ringoes Rd.) lies in as yet largely undeveloped rolling land characteristic of Hunterdon County. From Sergeantsville came Dr. George Larison, the founder of Hunterdon County's peach industry. He first planted his orchards in the 1850s; by 1890 there were 2 million peach trees in Hunterdon County, yielding some million bushels of peaches a year. An infestation of San José scale in the 1890s resulted in the destruction of most of the trees.

Roughly a mile southwest of the crossroads on the Rosemont-Ringoes Rd. as it crosses the Wickecheoke Creek, is Green Sergeant's Covered Bridge,★ the last of New Jersey's 75 covered bridges. Built in 1872 on the site of one dating to 1750, the bridge was threatened with a modern replacement in the 1950s. Saved by concerned citizens, it was rebuilt on a steel frame, retaining over half of the original trusses and members.

Sergeantsville has applied for designation as a historic district, and there are many 18th- and 19th-century buildings to be seen. The inn was actually built as a private house in

Hunterdon County Farm

the 18th century and greatly enlarged in 1835. The fieldstone and stucco house on the southeast side of C 604 at the
creek dates from around 1740. At the intersection of C 604
and Headquarters Rd. is the mid-18th-century Headquarters Farm, so named because George Washington is believed to have camped here on the way to Trenton. Included
on the property are a stone mansion, a tenant house, slave
quarters, and a four-story gristmill. Well into the 20th
century there was a community here with a store and post
office. Since 1973 Sergeantsville has held a house tour
shortly before Thanksgiving (609-397-8337); it is possible
then to see some of the many remaining 18th- and 19th-
century houses and farms.

Shrewsbury MONMOUTH (NJ 35, C 13A)   2,962

Shrewsbury is one of New Jersey's oldest settlements (the first buildings date to 1664; the township was incorporated in 1667) and over 40 of its buildings are at least 100 years old, but because its historic center is at the intersection of two broad, heavily traveled highways, much of the feeling of the past is obscured by the noise of the traffic. Part of the Monmouth Patent of 1665, Shrewsbury was settled by Quakers, Anglicans, and Scotch Presbyterians, many of whom came to the area by way of Rhode Island and Long Island. The spot put its settlers to mind of Shrewsbury in England, and they named it accordingly. (During World War II Monmouth County's Shrewsbury raised a considerable amount of money to help England's Shrewsbury, and the contact has continued; in the summer of 1985, the vicar of the abbey in Shrewsbury, England, preached in Christ Church in Shrewsbury, New Jersey, while Christ Church's vicar was visiting in Shrewsbury, England.) Sycamore Ave., one of Shrewsbury's two main crossroads (Broad St. is the other), follows the Burlington Trail, an old Indian path that ran from Freehold to the sea; Broad St. was once the Kings Highway; together they define Shrewsbury's historic district.*

At their intersection are two churches, an old house, and an old estate. On the northwest corner is the Allen House* (201-462-1466), built in 1667; at various times it has served as a private residence, a tavern, a tea room, and an antiques shop. Since 1968 it has belonged to the Monmouth County Historical Association, which now operates it as a museum. The furnishings have been gathered and arranged to show what a tavern would have been like in the mid-18th century. From April to November a special exhibit is shown upstairs. Past exhibits have included displays of New Jersey glass, pottery, portraiture, and needlework. Outside is a colonial herb garden. Open April–December, Tuesday, Thursday, Sunday, 1–4; Saturday, 10–4. Admission charged.

At the northeast corner is the Friends Meeting House (1816). The earliest Quaker meetinghouse was built in 1672; it was Shrewsbury's first public building. In 1727 bricks were imported from Holland to build another meetinghouse, and some of those bricks were used again in the present building.

At the southeast corner stands Christ Church, erected in 1769 with funds raised largely by a lottery. (In 1879 President Ulysses S. Grant attended the church's centennial celebration.) Among the curiosities of the church are its crown, its Bible, and the canopied pew for the colonial governor. The crown sits on the ball and weather vane atop the tower (added in 1874); during the Revolution soldiers tried to destroy this symbol of the English monarchy, and the scars from their shots are apparently still to be seen on the ball. The Bible is a Vinegar Bible (a Bible printed at Oxford in 1717, full of typographical errors, including the substitution of "vinegar" for "vineyard" in the first verse of Matthew 20). Tours by appointment (201-741-2220).

On the fourth corner are Borough Hall★ and the Shrewsbury Historical Society (201-530-7974), the former on an estate that can be traced back to the 1600s, the latter in a new building (1982) built for it on the site of the estate's carriage house, which burned. The society runs a library and a small museum. Of particular interest are scale models of Shrewsbury's churches, which means you can see what the interiors of the churches look like even when it is not possible to enter them. There are also memorabilia from the Broadmeadow family (James Broadmeadow began canning tomatoes in a factory on Sycamore St. in 1863). Open Tuesday and Thursday, 1–4; Saturday, 10–4.

The Presbyterian Church (1821) stands east of Christ Church on Sycamore Ave. and replaces an early 18th-century building. On Broad St. near Sycamore is Paddington Farms, a housing development built on the former 86-acre Chalmar horse farm, an early 19th-century estate that once served as a summer retreat for Louis V. Bell. (Bell was a wealthy New Yorker who, contrary to legend, was probably not related to Alexander Graham Bell.) The estate later became the home of David H. Marx, president of the Louis Marx Toy Company, at one time the world's largest toy manufacturer; Dwight Eisenhower visited the estate when Marx owned it. The 22-room Georgian mansion (1910) has been preserved, as has the 19th-century farmhouse.

About one mile south of Shrewsbury on NJ 35 is the main entrance to Fort Monmouth, the headquarters for the army communications and electronics command and the largest employer in Monmouth County (its presence is one reason traffic is so heavy in Shrewsbury). Built during World War I on the 128-acre site of the old Monmouth Park race track, the camp until 1925 was known as Camp Vail, after Alfred Vail, who helped Samuel Morse develop the telegraph (see Morristown). It now has 2,000 military and 7,700 civilian employees. In Kaplan Hall (Building 275) is the Army Communications-Electronic Museum (201-532-2445), a recently renovated museum devoted to the development of communications and electronic equipment within the army and to the history of Fort Monmouth itself. Among its collections are memorabilia from the days when the base served as headquarters for the Carrier Pigeon Service. Some exhibits change periodically, and there are hands-on displays as well. Open weekdays, 12–4. The musuem hopes to expand its hours soon. Also on the base is the Army Chaplain Center and School (Watters Hall, Building 1207, Ave. of Memories; 201-532-4211), which sponsors a museum with artifacts and memorabilia related to the history of the United States's military chaplaincy from colonial times to the present. Open weekdays, 8:30–4:30.

Smithville ATLANTIC (US 9, C 561 Alt)

[Galloway Township]

Begun as a reconstruction of a colonial village, Smithville has become primarily a commercial venture. The Smithville Inn dates to 1790 (it has been altered considerably over the years), and the late 19th-century apothecary* and many of the other buildings are genuinely old, but the emphasis now is on the stores and restaurants, not history.

Somers Point ATLANTIC (Garden
State Pkwy exits 29, 30, US 9, NJ 52, C 559) 10,330

This rapidly growing community is the oldest settlement in today's Atlantic County. Formerly known as Somerset Plantation, it was founded in 1693 by seven men (four of English, two of Dutch, and one of Swedish extraction), most of whom came from Long Island. Once a stagecoach stop, the port of entry for Great Egg Harbor (1791–1913), and the site of the county's first post office

(1806), Somers Point was an active shipbuilding center in the 19th century. By the mid-19th century it was known as a resort. Today it is a popular spot for fishing and boating. It is also the home of the South Jersey Regional Theatre (Bay Ave.; 609-653-0553), the only Equity theater with a full season in southern New Jersey. Because developers must now provide a public-access boardwalk around any new developments or marinas, you can walk along the shore here, despite all the new condominiums.

The Richard Somers Mansion* (Shore Rd. at Somers Pt. Circle; 609-927-2212), built in the 1720s, is Atlantic County's oldest surviving building. Made of brick in a Flemish-bond pattern with an unusual roof (thought to have been built by a shipwright, it looks like an inverted hull), the house was built for Richard Somers, the harbormaster, a descendant of one of the town's original settlers and the grandfather of Somers Point's most illustrious native son, Richard Somers, commander of the *Intrepid*, blown up in Tripoli in 1804. The Somers family continued to live in the house until 1937. Now owned by the state and partially furnished to look much as it would have when the Somers family lived there in the 18th century, the house is due for further restoration (it was partially restored by the Works Progress Administration [WPA] in the late 1930s). Open Wednesday–Friday, 9–12, 1–6; Saturday, 10–12, 1–6; Sunday, 1–6. Closed New Year's Day, Thanksgiving, and Christmas.

Just north of the Somers Mansion is the Atlantic County Historical Society library and museum (907 Shore Rd.; 609-927-5218). The museum contains artifacts dating from precolonial days to the early 20th century, as well as material relating to Richard Somers and to Somers Point's nautical role. Of particular interest are the explorer dolls, a local WPA project. Open Wednesday–Saturday, 10–12, 1–4, and by appointment on the 1st Sunday afternoon or 1st Friday evening of each month (call 609-641-4607). Closed legal holidays.

Somerville SOMERSET (US 22, 202, 206, NJ 28, C 533) 11,973

The seat of rapidly growing Somerset County, Somerville is changing from the center of an agricultural region to a city supporting professional and commercial services. Somerville is the birthplace of the opera singer Frederica von Stade and the home of the Memorial Day Somerville 50-mile bicycle race, the oldest continuously run bicycle race in the country. A bicycle under glass at West End and Mountain aves. is a memorial for two young men who won the race in its first years and died in World War II. The race draws some 40,000 spectators each year.

The white marble Palladian courthouse (Main St. between Grove and Bridge sts.), built in 1908 and superseded by a new courthouse in 1987, is famous as the site of the Halls-Mills murder trial (1922), in which Mrs. Hall and her brothers were acquitted of having murdered her minister husband and one of his married choristers. Around the courthouse and the railroad station, the signs of new downtown growth are obvious.

Two of Somerville's historic buildings are, however, of particular interest. The Old Dutch Parsonage★ (65 Washington Place; 201-725-1015), built in 1751 by the congregation of the First Reformed Dutch Church, is a state-run historic house museum. The country's first Dutch Re-

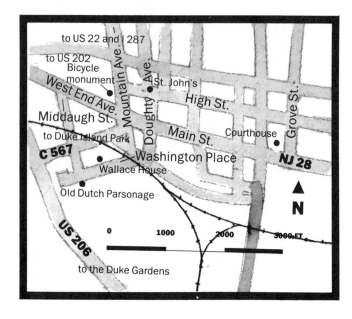

formed Theological Seminary was established here in the 1750s by John Frelinghuysen; eventually it was to become Queens College, which in turn became Rutgers University. The house features special exhibits focusing on local history and the decorative arts. Farther along and across the street is the Wallace House* (38 Washington Place; 201-725-1015), also a state historic house museum. The house, which belonged to John Wallace, a Philadelphia merchant, was used by George Washington as his headquarters in the winter of 1779 while his troops were encamped at Middlebrook. It is furnished to reflect what a house would have looked like at the time of Wallace's ownership. Both houses have special events, including Christmas programs. Both are open Wednesday–Friday, 9–12, 1–5; Saturday, 10–12, 1–5; Sunday, 1–5. Closed New Year's Day, Thanksgiving, and Christmas. Groups by appointment.

Somerville has many attractive buildings. Note the public library (35 West End Ave.) across Mountain Ave. from the bicycle monument and the mid-19th-century Speer Van Arsdale funeral home (10 West End Ave.). In one of the city's handsome older residential districts is St. John's (W. High St. and Doughty Ave.), an 1890s stone church with a stone rectory.

South of town on US 206 (just past the Raritan River), on what is left of the Duke estate, are the Duke Gardens (201-722-3700), 11 display gardens representing various geographical and historical gardening styles. The estate itself was created out of flat farmland by building hills and importing trees. You can get some sense of its former extent by simply following the stone wall, said to be built of stone from Schooley's Mountain, on the western side of 206. Open October–May, daily, 12–4. Admission by reservation only. Fee charged.

West of Somerville (and of the town of Raritan as well) is Duke Island Park (C 567, the Old York Rd.; 201-722-4118), one of the county's first parks. South of the Old York Rd. are about 170 developed acres; north of the road is a 100-acre undeveloped portion. The park includes playgrounds and playing fields and facilities for family and group picnics, fishing, and ice-skating. Concerts are given in the amphitheater in the summer.

Continuing north from Duke Island Park (take Milltown Rd. off C 567, crossing US 202) is North Branch Park (201-526-6118), another county facility with frontage on the river (the park is actually in Branchburg Township). The county fairgrounds are here, as are horse-show rings, with shows generally scheduled the first Sunday of every month (except in the depth of the winter). This is a popular spot for fishing, and there are picnic groves and a softball field.

A bit farther north (adjacent to Station and River rds. in North Branch Station) is the Ralph T. Reeve Cultural Center, 35 acres of county land dedicated to promoting the arts. At present the Printmaking Council of New Jersey is housed here (440 River Rd.; 201-725-2110), but the county hopes to accommodate other visual and performing art forms soon. The Printmaking Council has classes, studios, workshops, a library, and a gallery. The exhibits are open Tuesday–Friday, 10–3; Saturday, 1–4.

More directly north of Somerville (take 202 north c. 1½ miles to Garretson Rd.; turn left) is the Green Knoll golf course (201-722-1300) and tennis center (201-722-1303). Golf course open daily, dawn–dusk; tennis center open weekends, mid-April–May; daily, 8 A.M.–9 P.M., April–October.

South Brunswick

MIDDLESEX **(US 1, 130, C 522)** 17,127

George Segal, the noted sculptor, makes his home in the township of South Brunswick, where the population is expected to triple in the next 20 years. A township with large industrial parks, South Brunswick also has some undeveloped areas, among them the county's Davidson's Mill Pond Park (US 130 and Davidson's Mill Rd.; 201-297-9651), 400 acres with a pond, trails, picnic areas, playing fields, and playgrounds. At Davidson's Mill the county grows food for its zoo animals.

South River **MIDDLESEX** **(C 527, 535)**
14,361

The South River Borough Hall (64–66 Main St.; 201-257-1999) is located in the former Old School Baptist Church, built in 1785. The church's foundation was made from rocks used as ballast by cargo ships, and the walls were of local cedar. The South River Cultural Arts and Heritage Commission sponsors occasional exhibits inside the hall (for information on exhibits call 201-238-1520). Among the stones in the cemetery behind the building is an urn by John Frazee in memory of his wife who died in the 1832 cholera epidemic. Frazee was the first sculptor in the United States to receive patronage from the federal government: in 1831 he was commissioned by Congress to do a bust of John Jay for the Supreme Court chambers. Open weekdays, 9–5.

Springfield UNION (US 22, NJ 124, C 507) 13,955

Located at the head of the Rahway River and named for its springs, Springfield was first settled in the early 18th century by colonists from Hackensack. Only four colonial buildings remain, however, since the British burned the town in 1780 after losing the Battle of Springfield. It was during this battle that the Reverend James Caldwell, minister at Elizabethtown (the fighting parson to the Americans, the high priest of the Revolution to the British), broke into the church, grabbed the Watts hymnals, and took them to the troops, who were running out of wadding for their cannon. "Give 'em Watts, boys, give 'em Watts!" he is supposed to have cried, and just two weeks after his wife had been murdered by the British (see Union), he rallied the troops and helped spur their victory in the last major engagement on New Jersey soil. A monument to the battle is at Washington Ave. and the river.

The Cannonball House* (126 Morris Ave.; 201-376-7523, 201-467-3580, 201-376-1343), one of the buildings that survived the fire, derives its name from the cannonball that lodged in its northwest gable during the battle. General Jonathan Dayton, from the family that founded Dayton, Ohio (James Caldwell was chaplain to his unit), lived here after the war. The house is now a historic house museum run by the Springfield Historical Society. Open the 1st and 3d Sunday of the month, 2–4, or by appointment.

The new First Presbyterian Church (Morris Ave. and Church Mall) was built in 1791. The present parsonage (41 Church Mall) was built in the 1840s on the foundations of the earlier building, which had served as George Washington's headquarters for a time in June 1780.

Spring Lake MONMOUTH (NJ 71,
C 524)   4,215

Developed as a seaside resort for the wealthy in
the 1870s (note the stone gate at the northern
entrance on Ocean Ave.), Spring Lake is
named for a serene lake in the center of town.

A family resort that once had the reputation of
being the gathering place for wealthy Irish, Spring Lake is
increasingly becoming a year-round town. Although many
of its buildings are being converted to other uses (some of
the older houses, for example, have become bed and
breakfasts, and the famous Essex-Sussex beach hotel, where

Spring Lake

the movie *Ragtime* was filmed, has been converted into condominiums), the structures themselves are well preserved and the town has an old-fashioned prosperous look. It is not surprising that croquet tournaments are held in Spring Lake. The park by the lake is attractive, and along Tuttle, Jersey, Mercer, Sussex, Monmouth, Atlantic, and Union aves., among others, you can see some of the buildings from the golden era of the late 19th century. Note also the railroad station and the mourners in front of St. Catharine's. On the second floor of the municipal building is the historical society's museum (5th Ave. and Warren St.; 201-449-0800), devoted to local history. Open June–September, Tuesday, 9–12; 1st Sunday of the month, 2–4; October–May, 1st Sunday of the month, 2–4.

Spring Lake has two miles of ocean beach and a boardwalk as well. For information on beach fees, call 201-449-8920.

Stanhope SUSSEX (US 206, NJ 183, C 601, 602) 3,638

The borough of Stanhope, once an iron town and the site of the country's first anthracite furnace (c. 1841), like the other iron towns in New Jersey, stopped growing when the iron industry shifted westward. It has, however, seen its population double over the last 20 years.

Southwest of Stanhope is another mid-18th-century iron town, Waterloo Village* (west on C 604 off US 206; this is well marked; 201-347-0900). Once known as a deserted village, it has been restored and has been open to the public since 1964. Situated on the Musconetcong River, Waterloo (before 1815 and Napoleon's defeat in Belgium it was known as Andover Forge) lies within Allamuchy Mountain State Park (see Hackettstown). In 1760 it could boast of a gristmill, sawmill, forge, and mansions for the ironmaster and forgeman (the furnace was north of the village). Their owners being loyalists, the ironworks were seized by the revolutionary government, and Andover Forge supplied cannonballs for the revolutionary army. Becoming a port on the Morris Canal when it opened in 1831, the village entered its period of greatest prosperity. A general store was built that year and continued in business for over a century. The railroad also came to Waterloo by the mid-19th century, and over the years various members of the Smith family, important as landholders in Waterloo since late in the 18th century, built mansions for themselves. Competition from the railroads put the canal out of business, and when the iron industry moved west, Waterloo lost its economic raison d'être. As a restored village, it now draws tens of thousands of visitors each year. Some of the buildings are house museums, others are used by working craftsmen. There is an exhibit of Lenape culture (Indians once lived in this area), there are working mills, the canal association has its museum here, the mid-19th-century Methodist Church still holds services, and the locks and inclined planes are being restored. Open April–October, Tuesday–Sunday, 10–6; November and December, 10–5. Admission charge. Last ticket sold at 3. Closed Thanksgiving and Christmas. The Waterloo Festival for the Arts (201-347-4700) takes place on weekends May–October and features a wide variety of music as well as dance.

Just east of Stanhope off 206 is Wild West City (Lacka-wanna Dr., C 607; 201-347-8900), a reproduction of an 1880s frontier town with picnic grounds, a petting zoo, museums, and shops. Open mid-May–mid June and Labor Day–October, weekends, 10–3; mid-June–Labor Day, daily, 10:30–6. Groups by appointment other times. Fee charged. During the winter trails are open for cross-country skiing.

Stockton HUNTERDON (NJ 29, C 523)
643

 Stockton, located on the Delaware River roughly three miles north of Lambertville, started as a ferry town in the early 18th century. Colonel John Reading, believed to be the first settler of Hunterdon County and a major force in laying out the Old York Road, ran the ferry until his death in 1717. Because the main road from New York to Philadelphia ran through Lambertville, attempts to revive the ferry were not successful. A bridge was built early in the 19th century (it lasted until the 1920s and its replacement, the bridge you see today, was built on the piers and abutments of the earlier one).

Stockton was the home of John Deats, who in the mid-18th century invented the Deats plow and corn sheller. His son Hiram set up a factory in 1852 that made threshers, reapers, mowers, and corn shellers. Another Stockton man, Joseph Wilson, was involved in Hunterdon County's famous egg industry; Wilson was the first man to ship day-old chickens.

Stockton may be best known today as the site of Colligan's Stockton Inn, made famous by Lorenz Hart and Richard Rogers's song, which contains the lines "There's a small hotel, with a wishing well." Built around 1710 as a private home, the building may have been converted to a hotel in the 1830s; the wishing well is still there, and the murals were painted during the Depression. The Woolverton Inn, also first intended as a private home, was built in the late 18th century by John Prall, and from 1957 to 1972 was owned by St. John Terrell, producer of the now-defunct Music Circus in Lambertville.

Academy Books and Bindery (C 523 and Wilson Dr.; 609-397-4035) has art shows on the first floor of an 1863 school building (along with the bindery workshop and a bookstore). Special exhibits change four times a year and often feature drawings associated with book illustration. Open daily, 11–6.

The Prallsville industrial district,⋆ the area bounded by Smith's Mills, NJ 29, the Delaware River, and the Wickecheoke Creek, is a complex of buildings that are now part of the Delaware and Raritan Canal State Park (see Kingston). The first mill was built at this beautiful spot in the early 1700s; John Prall, for whom the area was named, bought the property in 1794. The mill area includes a gristmill (1877), which is open to the public, an attached granary (c. 1900), a stone linseed-oil mill (1794), a sawmill, and a stable (which houses the canal commission offices). Eventually, the stone mill will include a gallery (until that happens, you can visit the gallery in the stable, which has an exhibit dealing with the Hunterdon section of the park), and in the gristmill you will be able to see how mills worked. The area is used now for special events like crafts shows and folk concerts and as a meeting space for nonprofit community organizations. Office open weekdays, 8–4. From the mill you can hike or bicycle on the old railroad bed past Bull's Island to Frenchtown.

Stone Harbor CAPE MAY (C 619, 657) 1,187

Situated on a barrier beach island (which it shares with Avalon), Stone Harbor is the only municipality in the United States to run a heronry. Registered as a national natural landscape, the Stone Harbor Bird Sanctuary occupies over 20 acres between 111th and 116th sts. and 2d and 3d aves. The birds are attracted by thickets of cedar, holly, sassafras, and bayberry and feed on the adjacent marshes. They return from their wintering grounds around mid-March and nesting is usually well underway by early April. At the height of the nesting season some 10,000 birds occupy the sanctuary. The flights are most spectacular at dawn as the day feeders leave and the night feeders return home, and again at dusk when the pattern is reversed. At the parking area on the 3d Ave. side, you will find a good view of the birds; coin-operated binoculars are available.

The Wetlands Institute and Museum (Stone Harbor Blvd.; 609-368-1211) occupies 6,000 acres of protected salt marsh interspersed with tidal creeks. At the museum are exhibits of raptors, saltwater aquariums, and wonderful views of the surrounding marsh from the observation tower and lecture room. There are hiking trails through the marsh (a brochure for a self-guided tour is available), including in one area a boardwalk that goes by a tide pool. The institute sponsors many special events and programs, including canoe trips and lectures. Guided group tours by appointment. Open June–September, Tuesday–Saturday, 10–4:30; October–May, Tuesday, Thursday, and Saturday, 10–4:30.

Beach tags, good for Avalon's beaches, too, may be purchased at Borough Hall (95th and 2d Ave.). At 95th and 3d Ave. note St. Mary's by the Sea (1911). The borough information center is at 96th and 2d Ave. For beach information call 609-368-5102.

This is generally a good area for bird watchers, and both Stone Harbor Point (follow 2d or 3d Ave. to the end) and Nummy Island (take 3d Ave. to Ocean Dr. and cross the bridge) are favored spots. Stone Harbor Point is one of the last nesting sites in the state for the least tern and piping plover.

Summit UNION (NJ 24, 124, C 512, 527)
21,071

Known before the Revolution as Turkey Hill, Summit began to change into a suburb when the Morris and Essex Railroad was put through the town in the 1830s. It was popular as a resort in mid-century, and in the 1880s many of the wealthy visitors became permanent residents and commuters.

Summit has long had a reputation as a culturally active town. The Summit Chorale developed from a singing group founded in 1909; the Summit Playhouse for many years occupied the old Summit library (10 New England Ave.), a Romanesque Revival structure from the 1890s. The Summit Art Center (68 Elm St.; 201-273-9121), founded in 1933 and housed in an interesting new building (1973), specializes in contemporary American painting and sculpture. There are two galleries, and new exhibits open every four to six weeks. The center has an extensive program of art classes, and special events, including concerts, are scheduled frequently. Galleries open weekdays, 12-4; weekends, 2–4. Group tours by appointment.

In the northern part of Summit is the Reeves Reed Arboretum (165 Hobart Ave., near NJ 24; 201-273-8787), 12½ acres that were once part of a revolutionary war farm. The arboretum includes a natural hardwood forest, native and imported trees, open fields, lawns, formal gardens, a rose garden, and an herb garden. Trails go through the woods. On the property are several kettles from the Wisconsin glacier; in one large kettle in the front thousands of daffodils are planted, forming a carpet in spring. The Colonial Revival house, which dates from the late 1880s, serves as an office and education center with a discovery room for children. You can pick up a self-guided-tour brochure here. Grounds open daily year round; office open Monday, Tuesday, Thursday, 9–3.

Briant Park (Springfield Ave. and Briant La.; 201-352-8431), has facilities for fishing and ice-skating, a fitness course, and a picnic area. You can also fish and picnic at the Passaic River Park (Passaic Ave.; 201-352-8431), which has a nature trail as well. Part of the Watchung Reservation (see Mountainside) falls at the southern edge of Summit.

High Point State Park

Sussex

Sussex, in the heart of the county's dairy country, used to be known as Deckertown, in honor of Peter Decker, who built a cabin here in the 1730s. About one mile southwest of Sussex on C 565 (head south out of Sussex on Loomis Ave., C 639) is Sussex Airport, site of an annual air show (201-875-9919). Held the last weekend in August, the show features stunt flying, balloon rides, model airplanes, parachute jumping, and the like.

About four miles west of Sussex on NJ 23 is the Elias Van Bunschooten Museum (201-875-3887, 201-875-3330), a late 18th-century house built by the local Dutch Reformed minister. The house, which stayed in the same family until the late 1920s, contains both 18th- and 19th-century furnishings, some dating back to the original owner. Open mid-May–mid-October, Thursday and Saturday, 1–4.

Another four miles north and west on 23 (and picking up C 519) will bring you to the entrance to High Point State

Park (201-875-4800), over 13,000 acres in the Kittatinny Mountains. Given to the state in 1923 by Colonel and Mrs. Anthony R. Kuser, the park encompasses the highest point in New Jersey (1,803 feet above sea level). At this point, accessible by car or foot, is a monument from which there are spectacular views out over New Jersey, New York, and Pennsylvania.

The Kusers had used this area as their summer home: the superintendent now lives in the Gatehouse (1912), and the state is restoring the Lodge, once High Point Inn (1888), but converted by Kuser into his summer mansion.

Within the park is the state's first natural area, the 200-acre cedar swamp known as the John Dryden Kuser Natural Area (in honor of the former senator and noted conservationist), dedicated in 1965. The swamp is an excellent example of a mature bog, with a stand of Atlantic white cedar unusual at 1,500 feet. The bog, accessible on foot, contains a wide variety of plants and animals, including insectivorous plants.

The extensive trail system, which includes a stretch of the Appalachian Trail, offers a wide range of possibilities, from Sunday strolls to strenuous up and down hikes. Many of the trails were developed by the CCC (Civilian Conservation Corps), which also constructed shelters and dams. Lake Marcia is a spring-fed glacial lake. No hunting is allowed in the park, but you can fish, swim, camp, boat, picnic, and cross-country ski. Trails lead directly to Stokes State Forest (see Branchville), and the headquarters of the Raccoon Ridge Bird Observatory are here. The park is open year round, though weather conditions in winter sometimes make it impossible to get in. Admission charged Memorial Day weekend–Labor Day.

Swedesboro GLOUCESTER (C 538, 551, 605) 2,031

Swedish farmers settled along Raccoon Creek in the mid-17th century, and Swedesboro, first known as Raccoon, was for many years the Swedish center of the area. It later became a transportation center for the surrounding agricultural region. Trinity Episcopal Church* (Church and Main sts.), familiarly known as Old Swedes, is the oldest deeded church property in Gloucester County and was the first Lutheran congregation in the state (it became Episcopal in 1786 when the Swedes stopped sending ministers to the colonies). Among its ministers was Peter Kalm, the noted Swedish naturalist whose journal is a mine of information about 18th-century New Jersey. Today's Flemish-bond brick building, which dates from the 1780s, replaced a log-cabin church that burned in the Revolution; the tower and steeple were added in the 1830s. The congregation still uses on occasion a beaten silver communion service dating to 1730. Many revolutionary war heroes are buried in the churchyard, among them Colonel Bodo Otto.

The Hatton house (935 Kings Highway) is a mid-18th-century house that belonged to John Hatton, a customs collector who tried to enforce the Stamp Act. He fled to England during the Revolution and the house was confiscated by the county. The original lion's-head door knocker, a symbol of the British crown, remains on the front door. There are interesting 19th-century buildings in Swedesboro; at the intersection of the Kings Highway and Lake Ave. note the early 20th-century borough hall.

Just north of Raccoon Creek on the Kings Highway is Stratton Hall,★ built in the 1790s. Charles C. Stratton, governor of the state 1845–48, was born in the brick house in 1796 (he died there in 1858). Stratton was the first governor from Gloucester County and the first elected by popular vote rather than by the legislature.

Northwest of Swedesboro (take Locke Ave. out of town to the Swedesboro-Bridgeport Rd. and continue on Oak Grove Rd., C 671) is Adams Methodist Episcopal Church★ (Oak Grove and Stone Meeting House rds.), the oldest Methodist church building in the county. Note how the even stones are in front, the uneven ones in back.

Three miles south of Swedesboro on the Sharptown Rd. (take C 605 to the fork and bear right) at Oliphant's Mill is the Moravian Church,★ built in the 1780s of brick in a Flemish-bond pattern. The church is open for services once each June and September. Tours may be arranged by calling the Gloucester County Historical Society (609-845-4771).

Tenafly BERGEN (US 9W, C 501) 13,552

One of Bergen County's Dutch settlements whose name may be derived from the Dutch words for Garden Valley, Tenafly developed in the 1870s when the railroad reached the town. Service ended in the 1960s, but the sandstone station★ (1872–74; Hillside Ave.) with its Venetian Gothic details, thought by some to have been designed by J. Cleveland Cady, has been converted to a shop. While downtown note also Ye Olde Tenafly Diner (1926; "Stop for . . . a bite, day or nite") and the building that houses the apothecary. The feminist Elizabeth Cady Stanton came from Tenafly, and her house★ (135 Highwood Ave.) is a national historic landmark.

At 23 Bliss Ave. is the S.M.A. Fathers African Art Museum (off Engle St., C 501, at the southern edge of Tenafly; 201-567-0450). Founded in France in the mid-19th century, the S.M.A. (Society of African Missions) Fathers collected and preserved West African artifacts. In addition to its exhibits of pieces in wood, ivory, brass, bronze, and other metals, the museum sponsors crafts, educational, and outreach programs. Open weekdays, 9–5; tours and other hours by appointment.

Greenbrook Sanctuary (US 9W; 201-768-1360), run by the Palisades Nature Association, is a 165-acre nature preserve on top of the Palisades. The sanctuary contains a five-acre pond and adjoining bog, the 250-foot Greenbrook Falls, hemlock ravines with 150–250-year-old trees (many of which may be doomed), and seven miles of self-guided trails. Since 1946 the association has been conducting research and field studies; it offers weekend field trips and programs about flora, fauna, geology, and ecology. Open by appointment only.

Teterboro BERGEN (I 80, NJ 17, 46) 19

One of New Jersey's tiniest municipalities (the population had increased to 22 by 1986, but Tavistock in Camden County is still smaller; see Haddonfield), Teterboro is home to New Jersey's second busiest airport. The airport, owned by the Port Authority of New York and New Jersey and operated by Pan American Airways, is one of the busiest in the country for private craft (in 1984, 285,000 takeoffs and landings were logged). It has been in more or less constant use since 1920, and many of the nation's leading pilots, among them Floyd Bennett, Admiral Richard E. Byrd, Amelia Earhart, and Charles A. Lindbergh, trained at Teterboro. The astronauts Buzz Aldrin and Walter Shirra got their first flying experience at this airport. Gates's Flying

Circus operated out of Teterboro, and Anthony Fokker (who designed the Red Baron's plane) manufactured aircraft here. Most of the borough is taken up by the airport and plants belonging to various companies, among them the Bendix Aerospace Division of Allied Corporation, the borough's largest employer and the owner of all the houses in town (there are seven).

Located in two buildings at the airport is the Aviation Hall of Fame & Museum of New Jersey (201-288-6344), dedicated to "preserving the history of aviation in New Jersey and honoring those who made it." Part of the museum is on the east side of the field in the old control tower (up five steep flights). The tower is in radio contact, so you can look out over the field (and into New York City, six miles away) and listen while the controllers guide planes on and off the field. Here there are also memorabilia from the early days of New Jersey's flying history and Arthur Godfrey's aviation collection, and short films are shown on old-time stunt flyers and the destruction of the *Hindenburg*. On the western side of the field is the educational center, which displays some larger objects, including various historic engines and wooden propellers, as well as a helicopter, uniforms, and a model plane collection. A film on the history of the airport is shown here, and there is a small picnic area. Open daily, April–December, 10–4; January–March the control tower is open daily, 10–4, but the educational center is only open on weekends. The tower can be rented for birthday parties. Admission charged.

Titusville MERCER (NJ 29) [Hopewell Township]

This tiny Delaware River community lies near the spot where George Washington crossed the ice-choked river on 25 December 1776 to begin the famous Battle of Trenton, generally believed to be a turning point in the revolutionary war. Titusville's 19th-century historic district* lies along River Dr. West of the historic district is Washington Crossing State Park (bounded by NJ 29, Church Rd., C 546, and C 579; 609-737-0623). The 850-acre park is a national historic landmark, and its visitor center (off 546; 609-737-9304) concentrates on the events that occurred in the crucial ten days between 24 December 1776 and 3 January

1777. A memorable collection of revolutionary war artifacts is on display at the center, as is a Russell Hoover painting of Washington crossing the Delaware that is more accurate than the much more famous Emanuel Leutze painting; a short film is presented at the center. Also at the park is the restored ferry house, which was Washington's temporary headquarters during the crossing, and each Christmas the crossing is reenacted. The park's nature center has four rooms of exhibits, one showing examples of New Jersey owls, and there is a discovery room for children with hands-on displays. Formerly the site of the state tree nursery (see Jackson Township), the park still maintains some seed orchards and boasts over 80 species of trees and shrubs. The park also includes the George Washington Memorial Arboretum, a 100-acre natural area, picnic areas, a fitness course, and an open-air theater. Park open daily. Admission charge summer weekends and holidays. Visitor center open daily, 9–5, Memorial Day–Labor Day; Wednesday–Sunday, 9–4:30, the rest of the year. Nature center open Labor Day–Memorial Day, Wednesday–Sunday, 10–4. Tours by appointment (609-737-0609).

About three miles north of Titusville on 29 is the Mercer County Wildlife Rehabilitation Center (609-989-6901 weekends, 609-989-6532 weekdays), located on the grounds of the county corrections center, where injured and orphaned wild animals are treated and rehabilitated. Open 24 hours a day, the center in 1985 treated 1,100 birds and ran up a food bill of $65,000.

At the northern boundary of the corrections center is the road leading to the Belle Mountain public ski area (Valley Rd.; 609-397-0043, off season 609-989-6533), a county-run ski area with four slopes, the main one 1,200 feet, a chair lift and tows, a rental shop, and a ski school. Open December–March, weather permitting, 9–5 and 6–10 P.M. An adjacent picnic area, with a small fishing pond, is open daily until dusk.

Farther east on Valley Rd. is the 19-acre Valley Rd. group picnic area (609-989-6540), with playing fields as well as picnic facilities. Open April–October, 10–dusk, by reservation only.

Still farther east (turn left on Woodens La.) is the Howell Living History Farm (609-397-0449), a county park dedicated to farming as it was done c. 1900–10. Weekend programs at this working farm include demonstrations of various aspects of horse-drawn farming, such as haying, sowing, harvesting, and cultivating. There are also demonstrations of blacksmithing, sheep shearing, and maple sugaring, as well as hayrides for children and nature walks. The farm is open to the public Saturday throughout the year (except the second half of December) and on Wednesday–Sunday, mid-May to October, but the schedule is complicated, and it is probably best to call for information. Groups by appointment other times.

Toms River OCEAN (NJ 37, C 571)

7,465

Situated on the northern bank of the river from which it takes its name, Toms River has been a fishing and boat-building community; a yachting center (the Toms River Cup is said to be the "oldest continually raced-for trophy in yachting"); the site during the Revolution of an important saltworks; and, since the county was founded in 1850, the Ocean County seat. The central portion of the courthouse (Hooper Ave.), built in 1850, was planned as a more modest imitation of Hudson County's (the wings date from 1950). Since the mid-1950s Toms River has been the home of the Garden State Philharmonic Symphony Orchestra, a 45-member orchestra founded as a community orchestra in Lakewood over 30 years ago. Although the city may no longer be as financially dependent on water-related activities as it once was, much of its interest for visitors still lies along the river.

The Ocean County Historical Society Museum (26 Hadley Ave.; 201-341-1880), located in a Victorian house, features a variety of displays, including a Victorian kitchen, old dolls and toys, quilts, and Indian artifacts. Open Tuesday and Thursday, 1–3; Saturday, 10–12. Groups by appointment.

The Robert J. Novins Planetarium at Ocean County College (College Dr. off Hooper Ave.; 201-255-4144) has programs for the general public (most are not suitable for children under six). These are usually scheduled for Thursday, Friday, and Saturday evenings at 8 and Saturday and Sunday at 2. Groups by appointment. Admission charged.

Cattus Island Park (Cattus Island Blvd. off C 571 north of the center of town; 201-363-8712) is a 500-acre county park with a variety of habitats, including salt marshes, maple-gum lowland, pine-oak upland forest, a white-cedar swamp, and a mature pitch-pine stand. The park is named for John V. A. Cattus, who, in 1895, built a mansion on Cattus Island as a hunting and fishing lodge. (The mansion was destroyed by an arsonist in the 1970s.) The park has some ten miles of hiking trails, including a boardwalk path through the swamp; open playing fields; and facilities for picnics. At Cattus Island Park is the Cooper Environmental Center (201-270-6960), named for Betty and A. Morton Cooper, who helped preserve this section of the shore. Among the innovations at the center, which draws two-thirds of its energy needs from a passive solar system, is a porous parking lot, which allows water to drain. In the center is a nature display, including live reptiles and fish; the exhibits change from time to time. The center sponsors occasional programs, like weekend nature walks and canoe trips; for information call 201-270-6960 or 201-370-7360. Groups by appointment.

Trenton MERCER (US 1, 206, NJ 29, 31, 33, C 579) 92,124

 Located at the navigable head of the Delaware River, New Jersey's capital was almost the nation's: the Continental Congress, meeting in Trenton in 1784, voted money for the construction of federal buildings in Trenton, but for various reasons, including, apparently, George Washington's opposition, it never came to pass. A thriving community with about 100 houses, several churches, and considerable economic activity at the time of the Revolution, Trenton became a major manufacturing center in the 19th century. The city was known the world over for steel (the Roebling Company that made the cables that support suspension bridges was located here; see Roebling); pottery, both fine (Lenox, the first American company to make china for the White House, was founded in 1889; Greenwood Pottery, the first to make china for restaurant use in the mid-19th century) and sanitary (the oversize bathtub ordered by President William Howard Taft for the White House because he kept getting wedged in the one that was there was made by Motts in Trenton); and rubber goods. Like other industrial cities, Trenton suffered after World

War II, but unlike some, the decline was largely downtown, and many neighborhoods survived almost intact. In addition, extensive construction of various state offices and facilities has injected a considerable amount of money into the city's economy, and today many people relocated into the area because of the corporate boom along US 1 have discovered Trenton as a city with housing bargains. These factors make optimistic statements about Trenton's renaissance seem believable. (In 1985, wages increased more in Trenton than in any other metropolitan area.)

Mahlon Stacy, Trenton's first white settler, in 1679 built a house and gristmill near the falls of the river. In 1714 William Trent, a Philadelphia merchant and later New Jersey's first chief justice, purchased from Stacy's son some 800 acres along the Assunpink Creek, and in 1721 he divided it for sale and established Trent's Town. The town prospered: it became a shipping center for communities up the Delaware, and regular ferry service across the Delaware was inaugurated in 1727, simplifying travel between New York City and Philadelphia. Two important revolutionary war battles were fought in Trenton, the first on 26 December 1776, after George Washington had crossed the Delaware some eight miles upstream (see Titusville). Although the Hessians may not have been in the post-Christmas drunken stupor commonly ascribed to them, the Americans did surprise them and did win the battle, taking close to 1,000 prisoners, and, of greater importance, taking the initiative away from the British. The second battle, on 2 January 1777, was again a victory for the Americans.

Trenton became the state's capital in 1790, and by 1792 the State House was begun. It is today the second oldest state capitol still in use, although very little of the current building dates from the 18th century, and much that does has been remodeled and looks Victorian.

Trenton's importance as a transportation center was encouraged by the work of John Fitch, who had a steam-powered boat running on the Delaware in 1786, 20 years before Fulton. By 1789 there was regular steamship service on the Delaware, but Fitch, who during the Revolution had been expelled from his church for repairing Continental guns on Sunday, did not remain in Trenton. The road along the Delaware behind the State House honors him.

In 1806 the first permanent bridge across the Delaware was built, and today Trenton's most famous bridge—the

The State House

one at Bridge St. with the "Trenton Makes, the World Takes" sign—rests on those original piers and abutments. The sign resulted from a contest sponsored by the Chamber of Commerce in 1910, and the slogan won out over almost 1,500 other entries. The city spends some $7,000–$8,000 a year to light and insure the sign; heavy winds and the vibration from traffic can knock out letters. In 1982 a windmill was built to provide the electricity to light it. The oldest bridge across the Delaware still used for vehicular traffic is the Calhoun St. Bridge*; the current (1884) span was placed on the original (1861) piers and abutments.

Despite all the massive new state buildings, you can still find a little of Trenton's colonial past. William Trent's house* (15 Market St.; 201-989-3027), the oldest in the city (1719) and a national historic landmark, now belongs to the city. Built of bricks brought from England as ballast, this elegant house has been restored to its colonial appearance. It is furnished with an unusual degree of authenticity, for Trent's son had made an exact inventory of Trent's belongings in 1729, and this was followed when the house was converted to a museum. Open Monday–Saturday, 10–4; Sunday, 1–4.

Another 18th-century national historic landmark is the Old Barracks* (Barrack St.; 609-396-1776), built c. 1758. It is the only barracks remaining of the five built in New Jersey to house soldiers fighting in the French and Indian wars. Many of the Hessians captured in the first Battle of Trenton were quartered here, and at various times it also housed British troops, Continental troops, and prisoners of war, and served as a military hospital. After independence, it was sold; considerably altered, it was put to a variety of uses. It has now been restored to its colonial appearance and is set up as a museum, with period rooms (showing, for example, what colonial barracks were like) and gallery space with permanent and changing exhibitions. The collection includes firearms, prints, and mementos of Washington. There are special holiday exhibits. Open Monday–Saturday, 10–5; Sunday, 1–5; groups by appointment. Admission charge.

Close by the Old Barracks is the Old Masonic Lodge (Barrack St. and W. Lafayette), built in 1793 with a mid-19th-century brick addition. In the 1830s the state's first free school opened in this building. The lodge was replaced by a new one in the mid-1860s, but this building was returned to masonic control, restored, and moved to this site c. 1915. Now maintained as a museum, the lodge has restored the ceiling designs in the upstairs room, where you can also see some of the lodge's original furniture. Among

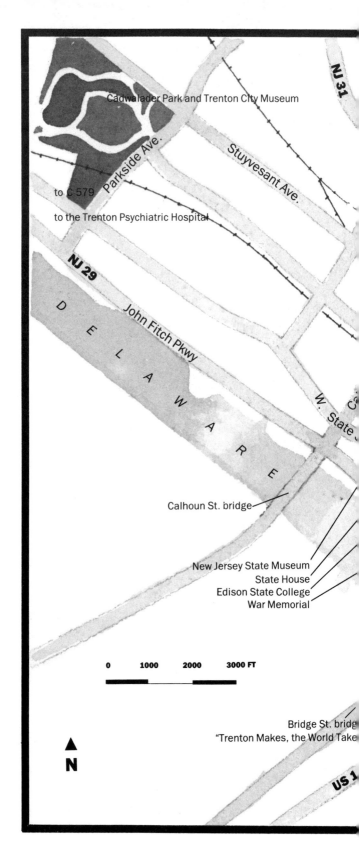

Cadwalader Park and Trenton City Museum

Parkside Ave.

Stuyvesant Ave.

NJ 31

to C 579

to the Trenton Psychiatric Hospital

NJ 29

John Fitch Pkwy

D E L A W A R E

W. State

Calhoun St. bridge

New Jersey State Museum
State House
Edison State College
War Memorial

| 0 | 1000 | 2000 | 3000 FT |

Bridge St. bridg
"Trenton Makes, the World Take

US 1

N

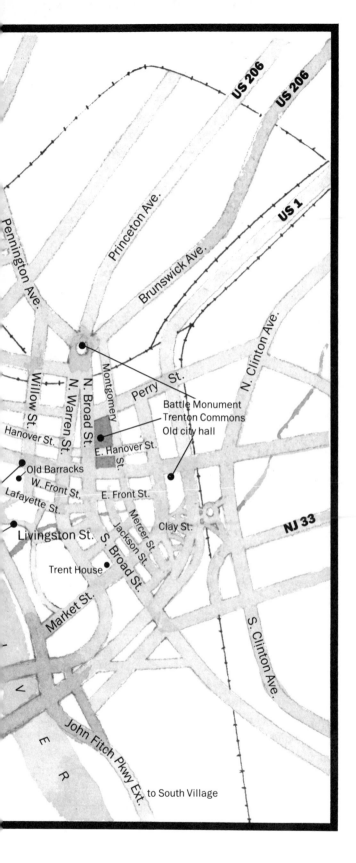

US 206

US 206

US 1

Pennington Ave.

Princeton Ave.

Brunswick Ave.

N. Clinton Ave.

Willow St.

N. Broad St.

N. Warren St.

Montgomery St.

Perry St.

Hanover St.

Battle Monument
Trenton Commons
Old city hall

E. Hanover St.

Old Barracks

W. Front St.

E. Front St.

Lafayette St.

Mercer St.

Jackson St.

Clay St.

NJ 33

Livingston St.

S. Broad St.

Trent House

Market St.

S. Clinton Ave.

V

E

R

John Fitch Pkwy Ext.

to South Village

Trenton **345**

the items on display are the gavel Washington used in Virginia, a Bible printed by Benjamin Franklin, and cannonballs fired in the first Battle of Trenton. Open weekdays, 10–4.

The successful stand against the British in the second Battle of Trenton took place in what is now the Mill Hill historic district★ (E. Front, Mercer, Jackson, Market, Livingston, Clay, and Broad sts. and Greenwood Ave.). After the battle Washington met with his advisers in the Douglass house★ (Front and Montgomery sts., moved from S. Broad), which dates from 1766, and planned the next day's battle at Princeton. Each December the Old Mill Hill Society sponsors a tour.

Marking the spot where the Continental artillery pounded the British garrison is the Battle Monument★ (Broad and Warren sts., Brunswick, Pennington, and Princeton aves.; 609-737-0623). Built in 1891, the tower is over 150 feet high. At its base are copies of bronze plaques done by Thomas Eakins depicting scenes from the battle (the originals are on display in the New Jersey State Museum). An elevator takes you to the observation platform. Open Wednesday–Saturday, 10–5; Sunday, 12–5.

Among the large complex of new state buildings is the New Jersey State Museum (205 W. State St.; 609-292-6300), devoted to both the arts and the sciences. Permanent exhibits in its main building include painting, the decorative arts, natural science, Indian studies, ethnology, and local porcelain. The adjacent 150-seat planetarium (609-292-6333) has shows for the general public (children must be seven to attend). The auditorium is used by the museum for a variety of programs, including films, concerts, lecture-demonstrations, and plays. Open Tuesday–Saturday, 9–4:45; Sunday, 1–5. Groups by appointment (609-292-6347).

The State St. historic district★ includes W. State and Willow. Tours of the State House (125 W. State St.) have been discontinued during its renovation. Other buildings of interest include the Contemporary Victorian Museum (176 W. State St.; 609-392-9727), an Italianate townhouse from the 1840s, owned by the Contemporary Club, with high ceilings, detailed woodwork, etched glass, and a handsome square piano. Open 3d Sunday in the month, 3–5, and by appointment. Edison State College (101 W. State St.; 609-984-1100) occupies the Kelsey building, built in 1911. Kelsey, a local banker and philanthropist, commissioned the building as a memorial to his wife and donated it to the

Trenton School of Industrial Arts. It was modeled on the Palazzo Strozzi in Florence and designed by Cass Gilbert. The Prudence Townsend Kelsey Memorial Room houses Mrs. Kelsey's collection of ceramics. In the 200 block note the seven brick buildings, dating from the 1870s, known as the Pride of Lions because of the reliefs of lions on the façade. Note also the detail on the façade of the Kuser Mansion★ (315 W. State St.), from 1910. By the spring of 1987 George Segal's 23-foot-high sculpture of construction workers among interlocking steel I-beams and other paraphernalia of a building site should be in place in front of the new commerce building (W. State and Warren sts.). Farther east is the old city hall★ (309 E. State), built in 1907.

Trenton's War Memorial (between the State House and the river; 609-393-0871), finished in 1932 and now being restored, is listed in the state register of historic places. It is used for concerts and operas, including a regular series by the New Jersey Symphony Orchestra. Two of Trenton's most famous musical citizens, the tenor Richard Crooks and the composer George Antheil, were classmates at Trenton High School (Antheil's father was superintendent of schools).

West of the state buildings, in Cadwalader Park (Parkside and Stuyvesant aves.), is the Trenton City Museum (609-989-3632). Housed in Ellarslie, a mansion built in the 1840s for Henry McCall, a Philadelphia industrialist, the museum displays on its upper floor artifacts, art objects, and documents either made in Trenton or related to its history. On the first floor are changing exhibits of works by local artists. Open weekdays, 11–3; Sunday, 2–4. The park itself was laid out by the Frederick Law Olmsted firm in the 1890s; among its other attractions is its deer park. It honors Dr. Thomas Cadwalader, a pioneer in smallpox inoculation and the donor of the state's first public library. South of the park is the Berkeley Square historic district★ (Parkside, Riverside, and Overbrook aves. and W. State St.), an area built up c. 1890–1910, and notable for its solid houses with stained-glass windows, chestnut and oak woodwork, marble fireplaces, and the like. West of the park is the Trenton Psychiatric Hospital, founded in the 1840s under the influence of Dorothea Dix, who lived her last years in an apartment at the hospital.

North of the state buildings in the headquarters of the

fire department is the Meredith Havens Fire Museum (244 Perry St.; 609-989-4038). The collection includes equipment and other items related to the history of fire fighting with special emphasis on Trenton's fire departments. The museum also has a collection of Civil War material. Open weekdays, 9–9; other times by appointment.

Many of Trenton's old buildings are being put to other uses. The headquarters of the Mount Carmel Guild (73 N. Clinton) was once the home of the head of Greenwood Pottery. The turn-of-the-century Stokely-Van Camp cannery complex* (Lalor St. at Stokely Ave.) has become part of South Village I and II, a public housing development and senior citizen residence; the Trenton Convalescent Center (off Lalor St.) was once part of the J. L. Mott complex, where sanitary porcelain products were manufactured; a Spanish-looking 1930s cigar factory* (507 Grand St.) has been converted to apartments. The Mercer County administration building (S. Broad St.) was once part of the historic Roebling complex, which is being redeveloped; the U.S. Steel site (between NJ 29 and the river) is being converted to apartments, riverside offices, and a health club.

Although sanitary pottery is no longer as important to the city, the production of art porcelain continues with the activity of the Cybis, Boehm, and Ispanky firms. The Boehm galleries (25 Fairfacts St.; 800-223-0049, 800-257-9410) are open weekdays, 9–4:30. Groups by appointment.

The first Saturday in June Trenton celebrates its past with Heritage Day on the Trenton Commons. Other annual events include the State Street Stroll and the Feast of Lights in September and in the winter the reenactment of the Battle of Trenton.

Tuckerton OCEAN (US 9, C 603) 2,472

 Settled in the late 1690s, Tuckerton was an important port in colonial days. In later times it served as the shopping center for the surrounding region. Today it is the western terminus of the world's first fiber-optic transatlantic cable, which when completed in 1988 will be able to carry some 40,000 simultaneous telephone conversations. Many of Tuckerton's older houses have been restored, and the

Bartlett Mansion, currently being restored by the Tuckerton Historical Society, will eventually be open to the public. West of Tuckerton, just south of US 9, is the Giffordtown Schoolhouse Museum (Wisteria La. and Leetz Blvd.), an 1880s school building, run as a museum by the Tuckerton Historical Society. Its two rooms contain artifacts related to various aspects of local history, including the Tuckerton railroad and the early Quakers. Open 15 June–September, weekends, 2–4. Donations accepted.

South of Tuckerton is the Great Bay Boulevard Wildlife Management Area (Great Bay angles south off US 9 just west of the intersection with Green St.), one of the largest (over 5,000 acres) and least-disturbed stretches of marshland in the state. The area is heavily used by waterfowl and nesting shorebirds and is much favored by bird watchers. It is also favored by those who like fishing, boating, waterskiing, clamming, and crabbing, although the insects can be fierce in summer. Parking and launching ramps are available off Great Bay Blvd.

About five miles northwest of the US 9–Green St. intersection is Bass River State Forest (609-296-1114), over 18,000 acres with facilities for picnicking, swimming, boating, hiking, hunting, and, in winter, ice-skating and fishing. A short nature trail in the Lake Absegami region gives a vivid depiction of the Pine Barrens as it moves through various types of forest to a cedar bog and back. A nature center is usually open in the summer five days a week, including weekends. The center sponsors a variety of programs, including nature and bird walks, generally focusing on the particular nature of the Pine Barrens. Call for the specific schedule. Office open 9–4 in winter, extended hours in summer.

Union UNION (Garden State Pkwy exits 139, 140, US 22, NJ 82) 50,184

Settled in 1667 by several families from Connecticut, Union (known at first as Connecticut Farms) claims to have the tallest watersphere in the world—familiar to many motorists on the Garden State Parkway. Union's Connecticut Farms Presbyterian Church* (Stuyvesant Ave. at Chestnut St.) was the first building in New Jersey to be placed in the national register of historic places. The church was built

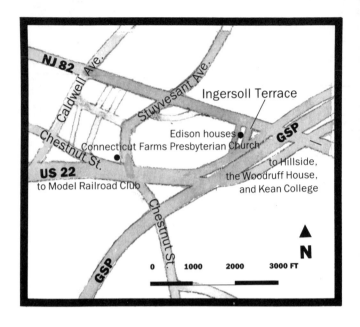

in 1788 to replace the 1730 church burned by the British during the Revolution. The Reverend James Caldwell, the fighting parson (see Springfield), then minister at Elizabethtown, had moved his family here, apparently believing they would be safer. Versions of what happened differ, but his wife was killed by British snipers as she sat in the parsonage in June 1780. A later parsonage, built c. 1783 on the foundations of the earlier one, is now the Union Township Historical Society Museum★ (909 Caldwell Ave.; 201-688-2633). It is decorated to show what life might have been like in a 19th-century parsonage. The carriage house also contains historical artifacts. Open March–May and October–December, Sunday after the 3d Thursday in the month, 2–4. Tours by appointment.

On Morris Ave. just north of North Ave. is Liberty Hall★ (1772), also known as the Livingston-Kean house, a national historic landmark built by William Livingston, New Jersey's first elected and very popular governor (he served until 1790). George and Martha Washington both stayed in Liberty Hall, as did Alexander Hamilton, and Livingston's daughter Sarah married John Jay (before he became the first Supreme Court chief justice) in the house. Liberty Hall remained in the Kean family (John Kean, a member of the Second Continental Congress, married Livingston's niece Susan) until 1986 when plans were announced to develop the property, which includes in addition to Liberty Hall a small smokehouse, a large icehouse, a stable, and a garage with a collection of antique carriages and early motor vehicles. Liberty Hall will be converted into a museum, and the development will also include a 60-acre park with an inn and shops, townhouses on the Elizabeth River, and an office building.

Across Morris Ave. from Liberty Hall is Kean College (201-527-2371), founded in 1855 as Newark State College. In 1958 the college moved onto 120 acres that were also once part of the Kean estate. A complex of French Norman buildings, once part of the Kean family farm and now known as Kean Library, houses the nursing department, and the 1790 James Townley house★ is used by the first-aid squad. Most of the campus buildings, however, are new. Exhibits in the James Howe Gallery, which is located in the striking Vaughn Eames Building, are open to the public Monday–Thursday, 10–2, 5–7; Friday, 10–12. The theater, which serves as the home of the Garden State Chamber Orchestra and the New Jersey Ballet, puts on productions that are open to the public throughout the school year. The college's Holocaust Center is also open to the public Monday and Wednesday, 12–4; Tuesday and Thursday, 8:30–12:30. Guided tours of the campus start Friday at 10. Just east of the campus in Hillside, on the old grounds of the Pingry School, one of the nation's oldest country day schools, is Kean College's east campus (take North Ave., NJ 439).

At Ingersoll Terrace (south off Morris Ave. just west of the Garden State Pkwy) are the Thomas Edison Houses, poured concrete houses made by a process invented by Edison in 1908. Fewer than a dozen of the unusually shaped houses remain, and some have been bricked over.

At the Model Railroad Club (Jefferson Ave. off US 22 just east of the Cedar Lawn Cemetery; 201-964-8808) are two layouts: an HO and an N. The HO is roughly 40′ × 40′ with a heavy-duty main line, a trolley line, and a short line; the club's long-range plans involve increasing it some 100 feet. The smaller N layout runs along one edge of the HO and is roughly 10′ × 30′. Open Saturday, 1–4 (club members are usually working on the trains at this time, although some equipment is running). A Christmas show is usually held on the first three weekends following Thanksgiving, at which time the trains are run as an exhibit. Admission charged.

Also in Hillside is the Woodruff House★ (111–113 Conant St.; 201-352-9270, 201-353-1773), maintained by the Hillside Historical Society as a "museum of three centuries." The central section of the house, which remained in the Woodruff family until 1978, was built in 1790, but there are also an 1890s kitchen and a 1900–1930 store. The museum has restored the store to reflect a general or neighborhood store of the early 20th century. In the central section the furnishings are generally mid-19th century, but the house also contains 18th-century items, and there is a smokehouse in the attic. Future plans include a garden and a barn in which to display farm artifacts and offer demonstrations. Tours by appointment, but the society expects to add regular monthly openings.

Vernon Township SUSSEX
(NJ 94, C 515, 517, 565)   16,302

Vernon Township's location in the mountains of the Highlands has determined the character of its two largest industries: satellite telecommunications (microwave transmission is least disturbed in mountains) and recreational skiing. With the country's highest concentration of microwave transmitters, the residents of this large (68 sq. miles) and rapidly growing township (the population increased almost sevenfold between 1960 and 1980) are concerned about the effects of these transmitters on their health.

Within the township is the Hamburg Mountain Wildlife Management Area (NJ 23, C 517), 3,700 acres of mountainous, heavily forested land. Access to the area is limited, but it is open for hiking, skiing, fishing, and hunting. Within the management area is the Vernon Valley-Great Gorge ski facility (201-827-2000), which is converted to an amusement park in the spring. Call for hours and rates.

South of Vernon Valley and surrounded by the Hamburg Mountain management area is the Silver Lake ski touring center (201-827-7212). Open weekends.

North of the Hamburg Mountain area is the Hidden Valley ski area (201-764-6161). Open weekdays, 9 A.M.–10:30 P.M.; weekends and holidays, 4–10:30.

Vineland CUMBERLAND (NJ 47, 55, C 540, **552, 555)**   53,753

Physically New Jersey's largest city, Vineland is also one of New Jersey's first planned cities. It was founded in 1861 by Charles K. Landis, then only 28, who envisioned businessmen and industrialists living in the center of his city, while artisans with farms and orchards surrounded the core. To prevent speculation he stipulated that anyone who bought land had to build a house and till the soil. Each homeowner also had to plant shade and fruit trees and follow Landis's sanitary codes. Recruiting Italians to come as farmers, he encouraged workmen to buy property, offering them long-term loans to build houses on their own land. Within 20 years the population had reached 6,000.

He had hoped the community would prosper by growing grapes (hence the name), but in the 1880s a blight destroyed the vines. Agriculture did flourish, however, and Vineland is now the dandelion capital of the world (dandelions bring in some $300,000–$400,000 to the town each year). An annual dandelion festival is held in mid-March or April (609-691-3000). It is also a major center for eggplant (New Jersey ties Florida as the leading eggplant producer), and an eggplant festival takes place in August. Once a major egg center, Vineland still has an egg auction, but its declining importance reflects that of the entire New Jersey egg industry. Vineland's produce auction (N. Main Rd.), however, is one of the largest in the country. Most of the produce sold at the 55-year-old auction is for fresh consumption, not for canneries, and most of it is being picked while the auction is going on (sample cases are brought in for the auction). Open daily, late April–September.

Welch's grape juice was a 19th-century Vineland creation. T. B. Welch was a Vineland dentist and staunch Methodist who objected to the use of fermented grape juice in the church. He introduced unfermented juice, and by the time he moved his company from Vineland in the 1890s, it was on the way to becoming a major firm.

Because of the sandy soil, many cities in Cumberland County are centers of glass manufacturing, and this is one of Vineland's primary industries. (John Mason patented his lid for the Mason jar, familiar to home canners, in 1858.) Other local industries include textile manufacturing, food processing, construction, and truck-related operations.

The Vineland Training School (Landis Ave., C 540, between Main and Spring rds.) was founded in 1888 to serve the mentally retarded. The institution was the first in the country to use the Binet intelligence scales; it also drafted the first army IQ tests; its research and therapy programs have won it an international reputation.

You can still see some of the logic of Landis's plan as you drive through town. The streets are straight, the intersections at right angles. The railroad tracks, which run through the center of town (and ran through the center of Landis's property when he bought it), have been integrated into a boulevard. Notice also the rows of brick houses, some with interlaced color at the corners, on Chestnut St., east of the railroad. And for a splendid example of another era, note the white marble building built for the Vineland Trust Company in 1913, with its stained glass, ceramic tiles, brass, and mahogany.

Artifacts on display at the Vineland Historical and Antiquarian Society (108 S. 7th St.; 609-691-1111) can be seen Saturday, 1–4, or by appointment (the office is open for research Tuesday–Saturday, 1–4).

Five miles northwest of Vineland is Parvin State Park (Centerton-Norma Rd., C 540; 609-965-7039). Within its 1,125 acres is a variety of terrain, including woodland, swamps, lakes, and streams, and of species, including those from the Pine Barrens, the Piedmont, and the Inner Coastal Plain. Much of Parvin, which dates from 1933, was developed by the CCC (Civilian Conservation Corps), which had a camp there. The CCC dug mud out of the lakes and replaced it with sand, cleared trails, built roads, built bridges over swamps, and dug a new lake, all without power equipment. They constructed buildings out of bricks salvaged from structures that were being torn down in Philadelphia. Their barracks (now gone) were used during World War II to house German POWs, Japanese from the West Coast, and the Kalmuks exiled from the Soviet Union. The park, open all year, includes 15 miles of hiking trails, a 3-mile blacktop trail for bicycles, a nature center, a 450-acre preservation area, picnic tables, and facilities for boating, swimming, fishing, camping, ice-skating, and cross-country skiing. The protected swimming area is staffed from Memorial Day to Labor Day. Admission charged Memorial Day–Labor Day. Guided hikes by reservation.

The road from Vineland to Parvin passes through Norma, one end of the 19th-century Jewish settlement of Alliance. The other end (turn right on Gershel Ave.) is at Brotmanville (named for a Mr. Brotman, who established a factory here). Very little is left of the settlement, but at the Alliance Cemetery (Gershel Ave. less than a mile from 540) is a brick chapel, which contains artifacts, old documents, and photographs showing what life was like in these settlements in the 1880s. A synagogue is across the street, and an old house or two can be seen. The chapel is open to the public on Sunday for about four weeks before the High Holidays. For information call the Cumberland County Jewish

Federation (609-696-4445). Occasionally a festival is held here to try to raise money to restore what remains of these settlements.

Walpack Township

SUSSEX **(C 615)** 150

 A township with a population density of 6.6 people per square mile, Walpack is located within the Delaware Water Gap National Recreation Area (see below), where you can find some of the state's most spectacular mountain scenery. It is an area that is also rich in history, although how much of the physical evidence of that history will be around for people to look at depends on what the National Park Service decides should be the future of the recreation area.

For now, you can still visit the mid-19th-century Walpack Center historic district★ and explore the remaining old houses along the Old Mine (see Blairstown) and other roads. Southwest of Walpack Center the 19th-century village of Millbrook has been restored; it contains a blacksmith's, a weaver's, and a shoemaker's shop, a store, a church, and a school, and is open for visitors daily, May–October, 9–5.

The Isaac Van Campen Inn (Old Mine Rd., 2 miles north of the intersection with Pompey Rd.) was built in the mid-18th century as a farmhouse. The solid stone structure served as a fortress during times of trouble with the Indians, and because it was frequented by travelers, has come to be known as an inn. John Adams was among its visitors, George Washington mentioned it by name in correspondence, and Count Pulaski used the house as his headquarters for three months during the Revolution. Although much altered over the years, the house retains many of its original features (doors, hinges, stair structure, paneling). Open on limited weekends in the summers and by appointment (717-588-6637). The stretch of the Old Mine Rd. north of Pompey Rd. runs along the river; it is beautiful, but it is not maintained, and to save your car you may prefer to approach from the other direction (take Kuhn Rd. west out of Peters Valley [see Bevans] and turn left on the Old Mine Rd., driving south for about 2½ miles). Near the inn in an old cemetery is the grave of Anna Symmes, mother-in-law of William Henry Harrison (she died in 1777).

About five miles southwest of Walpack Center is the Walpack Wildlife Management Area. It is one of the earliest such areas (begun in 1932) and is located on over 350 acres of woodlands and fields. The Big Flatbrook, which goes through the tract, is one of the state's best-known trout streams, and the area is also open for hiking, bird watching, and hunting. The office is on C 521 at Bevans in the Flatbrook-Roy Wildlife Management Area.

The Delaware Water Gap, where the river has carved out a channel through the Kittatinny Mountains some 1,300 feet deep (the river itself is only 900 feet wide at this point), is a breath-taking site, long an attraction to tourists and painters. In pursuit of its plan to build a huge dam and recreation area at Tocks Island, the federal government came to own some 70,000 acres on both sides of the river, most of it north of the gap. The project was at least temporarily stalled, and the government has converted the area into the Delaware Water Gap National Recreation Area. Although the army engineers destroyed many of the old buildings, they are not all gone, and some of the villages, like Walpack Center and Millbrook (see also Bevans), have been converted to tourist attractions or are being used for environmental education programs. Recreational opportunities in the park abound: you can hike, fish, rock climb, canoe, hunt, and bicycle. In winter, designated sections are open for ice fishing, ice-skating, cross-country skiing (201-496-4458), and snowmobiling. Information and trail maps are available at the information center (off I 80). Center open daily, May–October, 9–5; weekends, November–April, 9–4:30. Interpretive tours for groups by appointment (717-588-6637).

Washington WARREN (NJ 31, 57)   6, 429

For some time the marketing center for a large area, Washington, with its broad main streets, looks larger than it actually is. First a stop on the Morris Canal, then on the railroads, Washington was once a major producer of pianos and organs—for a time, in fact (until the advent of the phonograph), it was known as the organ capital of the world. It has also been a center of hosiery manufacturing; that industry has also faded, and the Pohatcong Mills, for example, have been converted to apartments.

The Doll Castle Doll Museum (37 Belvidere Ave.; 201-689-6513, 201-689-7550) grew out of a private collection. The small museum, on the second floor of a downtown office building, displays dolls of many materials and from many countries, with a few from the 19th century, some from the 1930s and 1950s, many of recent vintage, and many made by doll artists, rather than manufacturers; there is also a small library. Open June–October, Wednesday–Friday, 10–4. Other hours and groups by appointment. Admission charge.

The Goat Works (2½ miles west of town on NJ 57, across from the Warren County Vo-Tech; 201-689-6899), a goat farm and one of the largest farm producers of goat cheese in the United States, is open for tours Monday and Friday, 10–12, or by appointment.

The Miniature Kingdom (1 mile south of town on NJ 31; 201-689-6866) presents buildings and scenes from various countries and periods, ranging from an 8th-century Carolingian gate, the Kremlin, and King Ludwig of Bavaria's castle to a modern Swiss hotel, all on a scale of ½ inch to the foot. Memorial Day–Labor Day, open daily, 10–5; 15 February–Memorial Day and Labor Day–10 January, open Tuesday–Sunday, 10–5. Closed New Year's Day, Thanksgiving, and Christmas. Admission charge; group rates available.

Wayne PASSAIC (US 202, NJ 23, C 502, 504) 46,474

Even when it was incorporated in the 1840s (and named in honor of Mad Anthony Wayne), the township of Wayne did not have a single center, but was made up of a collection of settlements. Now as the population increases (some 25 percent since 1960), the spaces between the communities are shrinking.

Wayne was the home of Albert Payson Terhune (1872–1942), best known for his tales of the collies he raised at Sunnybank. His house was destroyed, but the land (on the Terhune Dr. section of US 202 at the northern end of the township) now forms Terhune Memorial Park (sometimes referred to as Sunnybank Park), with gardens and a picnic ground. Terhune's great-grandfather can be seen in Emanuel Leutze's famous painting of George Washington crossing the Delaware (he's the near bow oarsman). Cecil B. DeMille's childhood home was near Sunnybank Park.

In Preakness Valley Park is the Dey Mansion (199 Totowa Rd.; 201-696-1776). Built c. 1740–50, this beautiful Georgian house was the home of Theunis Dey, a revolutionary patriot, and served as Washington's headquarters in July, October, and November of 1780. Here he heard the news of Rochambeau's arrival and here he came after Benedict Arnold's treachery. The county has restored the house to its 18th-century appearance and furnished it with pieces appropriate to the first three-quarters of the 18th century, some on loan from the Metropolitan Museum in New York City. In the attic is a sort of catch-all museum, open only in the summer. On the grounds near the house are a cottage modeled on the 18th-century Doremus house in Towaco (and built from old stones), reconstructed old-style barns, an herb garden, and a picnic grove. Open Tuesday, Wednesday, and Friday, 1–4; Saturday, 10–noon, 1–4; Sundays and holidays, 10–4. Closed New Year's Day, Thanksgiving, and Christmas. Admission charged. Groups by appointment. Special events are scheduled at the house, including an annual Christmas holiday exhibit. Also in Preakness Park (201-742-6373), one of Passaic County's most heavily used parks, are a golf course, shag field, and tennis courts.

The Wayne Museum (533 Berdan Ave.; 201-694-7192) is in the Van Riper-Hopper house, built in 1776 by descendants of 17th-century Dutch settlers; their descendants were active as farmers until 1920. The house is furnished with period furniture, but also features a few Terhune memorabilia. Special events, including, for example, classes in colonial fireplace cooking, are scheduled at the museum. The view across the grounds to the Point View Reservoir (which serves as a bird sanctuary supervised by the Audubon Society) is lovely, and on the grounds are the early 18th-century Van Duyne house, an archaeological research laboratory, an herb garden, and an orchard. Open Friday– Tuesday, 1–5.

On a wooded hilltop in the northeast corner of the township, with views over the surrounding metropolitan area, is William Paterson State College. (Access to parking lots is from Pompton Rd., C 504.) Most of the buildings on the 250-acre campus are new, but the administrative offices are in Hobart Manor, a neo-Tudor building erected in the 1870s and expanded to 40 rooms in 1915 by John McCollough, a Scottish immigrant who had made a fortune in wool. There are public art exhibits at the Sarah Byrd Askew Library and at the Ben Shahn Center for the Performing Arts (201-595-2110).

Other historic houses in Wayne include the Van Saun house (23 Laauwe Ave.), an 18th-century house that may have been Lafayette's headquarters in 1780; the Demarest house (Fairfield Rd.); and the late 17th-century Schuyler-Colfax house (2343 Paterson-Hamburg Tnpk).

Weehawken HUDSON (I 495, C 505) 13, 168

From about 1799 to 1835 Weehawken, situated on the bluffs overlooking the Hudson, was notorious for its "infamous dueling ground," a grassy shelf some 20 feet above tidewater. The most famous duel to take place there was, of course, that between Alexander Hamilton and Aaron Burr. A monument to Hamilton can be found in Weehawken, but not at the actual site. (An earlier monument on the site was destroyed in the 1820s by citizens outraged by the practice of dueling; the grassy shelf itself was later swallowed by the railroads.) Today's monument is on Hamilton Ave. (off Blvd. East as it makes a right-angle turn). A bust of Hamilton rests atop a stone on which, according to the inscription, "rested the head of Alexander Hamilton." The inscription replaces a bronze plaque, several times stolen; the four holes are sometimes seen as bullet holes. The semicircular stone wall is supposed to have been built by a friend to keep Washington Irving, who used to fall asleep while viewing the Hudson, from falling over the edge.

Just north of the monument, on Blvd. East, is Hamilton Plaza, a popular scenic overlook maintained by the town of Weehawken. Stop here for a spectacular view of Manhattan and the river. Awareness of Weehawken as a viewing spot goes back to the 18th century, and the town was once a resort town, the bluffs occupied by estates, beer gardens, and large, Adirondack-style wooden hotels. Ferry service ran from New York City, and elevators carried the visitors up to the buildings on the cliff.

The New Jersey entrance to the Lincoln Tunnel, the world's only three-tube tunnel, is in Weehawken. The first tube opened in 1937; today's three tubes carry some 40 million vehicles a year between Weehawken and Manhattan.

Many drivers entering and leaving the tunnel are aware of

the Richardsonian gray stone Weehawken Public Library. There are other splendid late 19th-century stone buildings to be seen on the bluffs; for a coherent Victorian neighborhood, walk through the Kingswood section near the Hamilton monument. (Walk along Hamilton and King aves., Bonn Place, Bellevue St., and Kingswood Rd.; much of this area was built by a single developer around 1900.)

The Hackensack Water Company's brick tower★ (4100 Park Ave.), dating from 1883, is all that remains of a large complex where the Tower Plaza Mall now sits. Modeled on the Palazzo Vecchio in Florence, the 175-foot tower formerly held the water company's offices in its base and a 150,000-gallon water tank at its top; it is listed in the navigation guides for river boats and blimps.

A 600-seat restaurant has been built on one of the no-longer-active piers (when the restaurant opened in May 1985 the International Longshoremen's Association picketed on the grounds that it had the right to control the waterfront). Ferry service to New York City was restored in 1986, and various plans are underway to develop the entire waterfront area.

Westfield UNION (NJ 28, C 509) 30,447

Westfield was founded in the 17th century— West Fields meant the western fields of Elizabethtown (now Elizabeth)—and remained primarily a farm community until the railroad came through in the 1860s. The Revolution intruded in 1777 when the British camped in and plundered Westfield and again in the 1780s when James Morgan, an American sentry, killed the Reverend James Caldwell (also known as the fighting parson; see Elizabeth and Springfield). The circumstances of the murder are unclear, but Morgan was tried and condemned in the Presbyterian Church on Mountain Ave. (The church now standing on the site dates from the 1860s.) He was hanged a few blocks from the church on Gallows Hill Rd. The cemetery contains a substantial number of 18th-century tombstones (the date and nature of many of the graves have been color coded by the D.A.R.).

At 614 Mountain Ave. is the Miller-Cory House★ (201-232-1776), a living museum of early American farm life. With the help of an early 19th-century inventory, the house has been decorated to reflect life at the time it was built (c. 1740). On the grounds are a colonial rose garden, kitchen gardens, a utility garden, and the like. Among the crafts demonstrated at the museum are open-hearth cooking, sheep shearing, candle making, and maple sugaring; the museum is also involved in extensive educational programs. Open mid-September–mid-June, Sunday, 2–5 (in January and February the hours are 2–4), except on major holiday weekends. Groups by appointment other times. Admission charged.

The home of the cartoonist Charles Addams, Westfield is a prosperous community with an attractive downtown. Note in particular the Spanish Revival fire headquarters★ (404 North Ave.), and the railroad station, now used by the United Fund.

West Long Branch

MONMOUTH (NJ 71, C 32) 7,380

West Long Branch is the site of Monmouth County College (Cedar and Norwood aves.; 201-571-3475), a 50-year-old institution located on two former estates. Much of its 125 acres retains the formal landscaping of another era. Woodrow Wilson Hall★ (1929), formerly Shadow Lawn, is a 130-room limestone mansion modeled on Versailles. This national historic landmark was built on the site of Woodrow Wilson's summer home, which burned; among the many features of this extraordinary building (Daddy Warbucks's mansion in the movie version of *Annie*) are a three-story great hall and a Venetian stained-glass skylight, believed to be the largest of its kind in the world. The art galleries (in an old barn and an icehouse) feature some ten exhibits during the academic year; when exhibits are in place they are open to the public, weekdays, 1–3 (but call first to make sure there is an exhibit). The Guggenheim Theater, housed in the former carriage house of the Murry Guggenheim estate, features programs of theater and dance. The college also sponsors a classical-music series. Across Cedar Ave. from Shadow Lawn and the theater is the Murry Guggenheim Mansion★ (1903), which contains the school's library.

The public library (95 Poplar Ave.; 201-222-5993) has frequent art exhibits. Open in the summer (Memorial Day–Labor Day), 10–1; winter, Monday, Tuesday, Thursday, 1–5, 6:30–8:30; Wednesday, 10–5, 6:30–8:30; Friday, 1–5; Saturday, 10–1.

West Orange ESSEX (I 280, NJ 10,
C 508, 577) 39,510

Just over 100 years ago, Thomas Alva Edison settled in West Orange, buying a house in Llewellyn Park and setting up his laboratory —an invention factory he called it—on Main St. From 1887 until his death in 1931 Edison developed a steady stream of inventions; his years in West Orange yielded over half the 1,093 patents he received in his lifetime (more than any other individual has received). New ideas or improvements stemming from the West Orange years involved the phonograph, motion pictures, storage batteries, poured concrete, the fluoroscope, and the extraction of rubber from goldenrod (the U.S. Army is today experimenting with deriving latex from other plants). The laboratory itself was an invention, the prototype of today's industrial research lab, where large groups work simultaneously on assigned projects. The laboratory included a physics laboratory, a chemistry laboratory, and a metallurgical laboratory, and since Edison built his own machines to run his experiments, a machine shop and a pattern shop. Although the poured-concrete factory buildings that surrounded the laboratory are gone (at one time T. A. Edison Inc. employed some 6,000 to 7,000 people in manufacturing operations here, in nearby Bloomfield, and in Warren and Sussex counties), most of the laboratory buildings remain and are now a national historic landmark (Main St. between Alden St. and Lakeside Ave.; 201-736-5050, 201-736-0550). Some 40,000 people visit the site each year.

The visitor center (in the former powerhouse) is open Wednesday–Sunday, 9–5, and has on display samples of most of Edison's major inventions. The labs themselves can be seen only by guided tours, which are offered Wednesday–Sunday, 9:30–4:30 (the last tour begins at 3). As late as 1984 one of the tour guides had worked in the labs when Edison was alive, but even without such a direct human link, the physical arrangements of the labs convey a strong sense of what this organization, which was so influential in shaping American life today, was like in its heyday. Groups by appointment (201-736-1515).

Llewellyn Park (1857), where Edison bought his home, was one of the country's earliest planned residential developments and the site of the first large-scale naturalization of crocus, narcissus, and jonquils. The development is now listed in the state register of historic places. When Edison moved there, the houses were all large, as was their acreage

(Edison's house has 22 rooms and was then on 11 acres). Only those who lived there or their authorized visitors could enter Llewellyn Park, and that is still true today. Edison, who apparently did not like fussing about such things, bought Glenmont (Park Way and Glen Ave., less than ½-mile west of Main St.) completely furnished and ready to move into from an executive who had embezzled money to pay for the house. Arrangements to tour the recently renovated building can only be made at the laboratory, and it is assumed that once inside the gates, you will drive only to Glenmont.

Part of the South Mountain Reservation (201-228-2210), a 2,000-acre county park designed by the Olmsted firm, which West Orange shares with South Orange, Maplewood, and Millburn, is at the southwestern edge of West Orange (take Main St. south to Northfield and head west on Northfield). At this end of the park is Turtle Back Zoo (560 Northfield Ave.; 201-731-5800), which has some 750 animals representing 250 species. The zoo is involved in a program to reintroduce endangered species to the wild, including the reintroduction of bald eagles to New Jersey's wilderness, and it also features a petting zoo and a children's zoo and arranges birthday parties for children. A nature-interpretation trail, showing the geological and natural history of the region, begins at Turtle Back. Open Monday–Saturday, 10–5; Sunday, 11–6. Also at this end of the park is the South Mountain Arena (201-731-3828), two ice-skating rinks that together provide 13 time slots open to the public each week.

South Mountain Reservation is on a ridge that protected Washington's army when it was quartered at Morristown in the winter of 1779–80, for from the ridge the soldiers could keep an eye on the British troops on Staten Island. The reservation contains many miles of carriage roads and paths suitable for jogging, walking, hiking, horseback riding, and cross-country skiing. Picnicking and fishing (with a permit) are also possible.

At the northern end of West Orange is another county park, Eagle Rock Reservation (Eagle Rock Ave.; take Prospect, C 577, north out of West Orange), also designed by the Olmsted firm, which West Orange shares with Verona and Montclair. Its overlook is considered one of the state's most spectacular spots for viewing the New York City skyline. Casino in the Park, an early 20th-century Italian Renaissance structure next to the overlook, is being converted into a restaurant. Eagle Rock also has picnic tables and fireplaces, bridle and foot trails, and a wildlife reservation.

The Francis A. Byrne golf course (Pleasant Valley Way and Mount Pleasant Ave.; 201-736-2306) is also a county facility.

West Windsor Township

MERCER (US 1, C 526, 533, 535, 571) 10,500

Like many of New Jersey's townships, West Windsor Township is made up of several small communities that were formerly separated by farmland. Parts of West Windsor were settled in the late 18th century, and the township remained an agricultural community until fairly recently. Over the last 25 years, however, its population more than doubled, and it is expected to reach 15,000 by the next census. The growth in commercial activity has been equally striking; US 1 between New Brunswick and Trenton is seeing a rapid expansion of corporate centers, corporate headquarters, other forms of office space, and shopping malls, and a fair amount of this expansion falls within West Windsor: in 1984, for example, one-third of the nonresidential construction in Mercer County was within West Windsor's borders.

The earliest mill in the area was at Grovers Mill, a community made famous in 1938 by Orson Welles's radio play, *The War of the Worlds*, in which Martians landed on Grovers Mill Pond (Clarksville and Cranbury rds.). The broadcast was so realistic that telephone switchboards all over the country were jammed by frightened callers. The township hopes that the 50th anniversary celebration of the broadcast will raise enough money to restore the pond. Other older communities that retain some coherence and charm include Dutch Neck and Edinburg.

Mercer County Park (access from Hughes Dr. and Edinburg and S. Post rds.; 609-989-6530) occupies 2,500 acres in the southwestern corner of the township. One hundred of these acres are devoted to playing fields, but the park also has a fair-size boating lake (swimming and gasoline motors are not permitted), a five-mile bicycle path, two picnic groves, an ice-skating rink (609-586-8090), and tennis courts. There are unpaved trails, and you are welcome to walk north of the lake and Assunpink Creek, although here you must be careful to respect the private homes and the fields that have been rented to farmers. The brick house on the hill near the marina is the mid-18th-century John Rogers House★ (S. Post Rd.), which the West Windsor Historical Society is restoring. The park is open year round, the lake mid-April–October, the tennis courts mid-March–November, and the ice-skating rink mid-November–mid-March.

Adjacent to the park is Mercer County Community College. Art exhibits can be seen at the library gallery (609-586-4800). Open Monday–Thursday, 8 A.M.–10 P.M.; Friday, 8–5; Saturday, 9–4. There is also an art gallery in the United Jersey Banks headquarters (US 1; 609-987-3200). The changing exhibits here are open weekdays, 9–5.

For a really striking building, drive east on C 571 to the PA Consulting Services, Inc., headquarters (just east of the intersection with C 535; this is actually in East Windsor Township). This architectural tour-de-force has an exposed structure, a roof suspended from cables with the heating and ventilating equipment hung from its center, and translucent walls that glow at night like a lantern.

Whippany MORRIS (NJ 10,
C 511) [Hanover Township]

Whippany is known as a center of paper manufacturing. Among the buildings of interest on Whippany Rd. note particularly Our Lady of Mercy Chapel★ (1853; 100 Whippany Rd.) and the green Queen Anne part of the Crestwood Nursing Home (Whippany Rd. and Eden La.). (There are interesting buildings on NJ 10 as well, but the traffic moves so quickly that it is hard to see them.) In the yard of the old Morristown & Erie Railway depot yard is the Whippany Railway Museum (1 Railroad Plaza, NJ 10). Rolling stock and locomotives are on display, and you can sit at the controls of a steam locomotive. In the former freight house (c. 1904) are toy trains, scale models, and railroad memorabilia. Open April–October, Sunday, 12–4. Donations requested.

About one mile north of the museum (in Parsippany-Troy Hills Township) is Old Troy Park (Reynolds Ave.; 201-829-0474), a 90-acre county facility, with ballfields, picnic sites, and hiking and cross-country ski trails.

The Wildwoods CAPE MAY (NJ 47,

C 621) 4,913 (Wildwood) 4,714 (North Wildwood) 4,149 (Wildwood Crest)

The Wildwoods—Wildwood, North Wildwood, and Wildwood Crest—share some five miles of Atlantic beach. Before they were developed as resorts, these areas were used by mainland farmers to graze their animals, and the problems caused by feral animals continued into the 20th century. Fishermen settled here in the 1870s, about the time the lighthouse was built (see below). Paradoxically known both as family resorts and for their night life, the communities today are basically summer resorts (the population of North Wildwood, for example, goes from about 5,000 in the winter to 66,000 in late spring and summer, and the meters are removed from the municipal parking lot in the fall). In Wildwood there are several amusement piers and some 14,000 hotel and motel rooms. The George Boyer Historical Museum (4400 New Jersey Ave.; 609-522-2444, ext. 35), featuring local history, is open all year, Monday, 1–3; Tuesday–Friday, 10–12, 1–4.

In North Wildwood the Hereford Inlet Lighthouse★ (Central Ave.; 609-522-1407) has been converted to an information center and maritime museum. Built in 1874, the lighthouse continued in use until 1963.

For information on beach fees, in Wildwood and North Wildwood call 609-522-1407, in Wildwood Crest, 609-522-7351. The Wildwood information center is on the boardwalk at Shellinger Ave., the North Wildwood center is in the Hereford lighthouse, and the Wildwood Crest center is at the Wildwood Crest pier.

Winfield UNION (Garden State Pkwy exit 136) 1,785

Union County's smallest municipality in both population and size (0.2 sq. mile), Winfield began as Winfield Park, a community built by the federal government to house shipyard defense workers and their families in 1941. Enclosed within the Garden State Parkway and the Rahway River, Winfield purchased itself from the government after the war and paid off its mortgage in 1984. Somewhat similar to a cooperative apartment, Winfield is a community-owned community. The street names—Gulf Stream, Seafoam, Wavecrest—reflect its nautical origins, and the houses, despite the additions of decks, porches, and extra rooms, still betray their barrackslike origins as defense workers' housing.

Woodbine CAPE MAY (C 550, 557) 2,809

One of South Jersey's 15 path-breaking 19th-century Jewish settlements, Woodbine dates from the 1890s, when several hundred Russian refugees established over 50 30-acre farms here. The Baron De Hirsch Agricultural School, opened in Woodbine in 1894, is said to be the country's first agricultural technical high school. Although little of Woodbine's past remains, you can still see the Woodbine Brotherhood Synagogue★ (612 Washington Ave.), built in 1896.

North of Woodbine on Webster Ave. (C 550) is the largest segment of Belleplain State Forest (609-861-2404), over 11,000 noncontiguous acres of swamp hardwood forest. The CCC (Civilian Conservation Corps) was active here from 1937 to 1941, and in addition to doing a great deal of tree work, the corps built roads, bridges, the shelter at the main picnic area, and the park office, mostly by hand. It also created Lake Nummy, named for the last Indian chief to rule in this part of the state, out of an abandoned cranberry bog. There are lifeguards at the lake in the summer, and two self-guided nature trails nearby. The forest is also open for hikers, campers, and hunters. Trail maps are available from the park warden.

Cape May County

West of Woodbine (and another section of Belleplain) is the Dennis Creek Wildlife Management Area, 5,000 acres of salt marsh open for hiking, boating, bird watching, fishing, crabbing, and hunting. Shingles made from Dennis Creek cedar windfalls (healthy trees knocked over by the wind) are apparently very durable, and shingles from

Dennis Creek cedars were used on the roof of Independence Hall in Philadelphia. Although some people are still mining cedar from the swamps in this area, the industry is no longer as important as it once was. This is also a good place to see raptors (birds of prey) in winter and sometimes otters in spring, but it can be ferociously buggy in summer.

Woodbridge MIDDLESEX (NJ Tnpk
exit 11, I 95, US 1, 9, NJ 27, 35, C 514)   90,074

The oldest original township in the state (settled in 1664, chartered in 1669), Woodbridge remained relatively small until the Garden State Parkway was built in the 1950s. The colony's first gristmill was erected in 1670 by Jonathan Dunham, and his house, built in 1670 from bricks brought from Holland as ballast, is now the rectory of Trinity Church (see below).

Woodbridge was settled largely by New Englanders, most of them from Newbury, Massachusetts (among them Captain John Pike, an ancestor of Zebulon Pike). According to one theory the town was named for the assistant pastor of the Newbury church, one John Woodbridge, but he spent very little time in Woodbridge; others say it was named for a town in Suffolk, England. The settlers built their first sawmill in 1682 and their first tavern in 1683. In 1730, they drank the first cup of tea in the colonies. In 1751, the first permanent printing press and publishing house in New Jersey were established by James Parker (1714–70). Parker, who had served as an apprentice to Benjamin Franklin and William Bradford and was the official printer for New Jersey until his death, in 1758 printed the first magazine in today's meaning of the word: The *New American Magazine* contained articles on current events and history, essays, and short stories. (An earlier periodical, the *Independent Reflector,* printed in 1752, was unsuccessful.) Joseph Bloomfield is the only Woodbridge-born citizen to become governor of New Jersey. Much later, in 1877, at a graduation ceremony at the Union Town school, Thomas Alva Edison demonstrated the telephone. And, later still, in 1929, Woodbridge became the first community in the United States to have a cloverleaf highway intersection (at US 1 and NJ 35).

Although the first Episcopal service in Woodbridge took place in 1698 and the first building dates to 1713, today's

Trinity Church (650 Rahway Ave.) dates to 1860. Contrary to popular belief, Richard Upjohn did not design the building, although he did draw up some plans for it and the church possesses one of his renderings. The church owns many 18th-century artifacts including its royal charter, a silver chalice, and a first edition of the American book of common prayer. The cemetery dates to 1714, although the earliest existing stone is from 1750. The rectory was considerably altered some 300 years after Dunham built it, but you can still see its original Flemish-bond brickwork, and the adz-hewn beams remain.

In Barron Library★ (1877) Woodbridge had one of the first free public libraries in the state. This small but wonderfully detailed Romanesque Revival stone structure, designed by J. Cleveland Cady, who designed the old Metropolitan Opera House and the American Museum of Natural History in New York City, now houses the Barron Arts Center (582 Rahway Ave.; 201-634-0413). The building has a massive clock tower, ornamented cornices, a Delft-tile fireplace, and an elaborately foliated foyer. The center's exhibits range from the fine arts to local history to theater design and change roughly once a month. The center also presents monthly concerts and poetry readings. Open weekdays, 11–4. Groups by appointment. Other hours can be arranged, and the center is sometimes open on weekends, so it is best to call.

The Parker Press building (Rahway Ave.; 201-634-9397, 201-634-0413) is a reconstruction of Parker's shop,

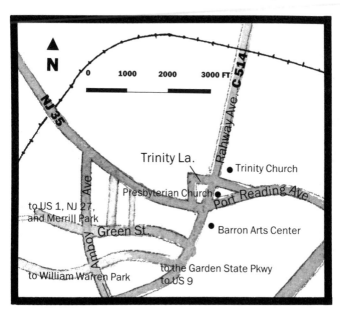

which was burned by the British in 1777. Inside are two presses, one late 18th century and the other early 19th, which will eventually be restored to working condition, and some type. Guided tours by appointment.

Although there is little left of Woodbridge's very early history, you will still feel a sense of community in the center of town, and Woodbridge has several times been designated an all-American or typical American city. Other buildings you might want to look at are the tavern George Washington slept in (in terrible condition on St. George's Ave. behind the 7–11); the Presbyterian Church (600 Rahway Ave.), known locally as the White Church, remodeled and covered with white brick so that you would be hard pressed to guess its age (it was built in 1803); the main library (George Frederick Plaza; 201-634-4450), which has changing exhibits in its lobby; the Board of Education administration building (School St.), an 1876 school. The Middlesex County Cultural and Heritage Commission (201-745-4489) has published a walking-tour guide for Woodbridge.

West on Green St. into Iselin will take you to Merrill Park (Middlesex-Essex Tnpk; 201-381-3555), 182 acres that include walking and nature trails, playing fields, tennis courts, fishing and picnic areas, and a small zoo that features farm animals. There are free concerts in the summer and ice-skating in the winter.

South of the center of town (take NJ 35) is William Warren Park (Florida Grove Rd.; 201-636-5423), a county park that also offers concerts in the summer. Much of this 120-acre park, which has athletic fields, picnic groves, and woods with foot trails, is built on reclaimed clay pits. In the 19th century clay mining and brick manufacturing were Woodbridge's principal industries; the clay from these pits was used to make fire bricks.

Woodbury GLOUCESTER (NJ 45, C 533, 534, 551) 10,353

Founded in 1683 by Henry Wood, a Quaker from Bury in England, Woodbury has been the seat of Gloucester County since 1785. Located near the confluence of the Delaware River and Woodbury Creek (originally called Pescozacka-sing, a Lenape word possibly meaning "place of black burrs"), it was once something of a manufacturing center, with lively traffic in patent medicines, glass, and other products. Today's residents tend to work in county offices, the hospital, at the nearby Mobil facility, and in Philadelphia and Camden. Broad St., the major north-south thoroughfare and once part of the old Kings Highway from Burlington to Cape May, is, as so often happens in South Jersey, appropriately named. There is an interesting mix of buildings in Woodbury, many preserved in their original 18th- and 19th-century form, others adapted, often gracefully, to contemporary uses.

Among the early buildings is the Friends Meeting House★ (120 N. Broad St.), the west side of which dates from 1715 and the east from 1785. The building was used as a barracks and hospital for British troops after the nearby battle of Red Bank in 1777 (see National Park). Unlike what happened in many other Quaker communities during the Hicksite-Orthodox split, in Woodbury the two groups continued to use the same meetinghouse, simply dividing it with movable partitions. From 1827 to 1927 they shared the building, and in 1954 the two groups rejoined. Another Quaker building from the 18th century now forms the easternmost part of the city hall (33 Delaware); this is the Deptford Free School building, dating from 1744 (the second story was added in 1820).

In 1793, the country's first airborne trip ended in Wood-

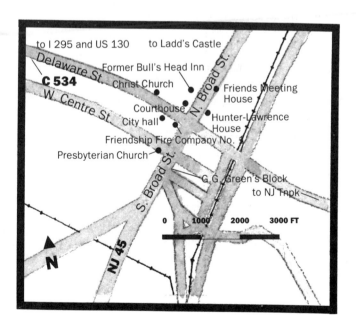

bury, when Jean-Pierre Blanchard, who had taken off in Philadelphia, landed his hot air balloon in a farmer's field a few miles northwest of town (near Clements Bridge off NJ 42 where the RCA plant is). In that same year the Gloucester County Abolition Society was formed, one of the first in the nation.

The county courthouse (Delaware and Broad sts.) is a splendid stone building, completed in 1887. Its white-columned neighbor dates from 1926, as does the Masonic Temple across the street.

At 58 N. Broad St. is the Hunter-Lawrence House★ (c. 1765; 609-845-4771). The Hunter refers to Reverend Andrew Hunter, a chaplain in the revolutionary army and a participant in the Greenwich tea party (see Greenwich), who was head of the town's distinguished Woodbury Academy (founded 1791); the Lawrence to John Lawrence, older brother of James Lawrence, the naval hero (see Burlington), who lived with his brother while attending the Woodbury Academy. The house is maintained as a museum by the Gloucester County Historical Society, which bought it in 1924. The society's collections include period furniture, guns, toys, and other artifacts. Among the society's holdings are a mahogany desk and bookcase that had belonged to Elizabeth Haddon (see Haddonfield) and an audience chair (#425) that was in Ford's Theater the night Lincoln was shot. The society has reconstructed in its basement the fireplace from Hugg's Tavern near Gloucester where Betsy Griscom, known as the designer of the American flag, and John Ross were married. A copy of their license hangs over the mantel (the original is in the society's library). Built into the library is one wall from the Cooper house, used by Cornwallis as his headquarters (bayonet marks made by British soldiers trying to force a door are still visible). Open Wednesday and Friday, 1–4; also, from September to May, the last Sunday in the month, 2–5. Groups by appointment.

Opposite the meetinghouse (111 N. Broad St.) is the former Bull's Head Inn, possibly built c. 1720 (the earliest records date to 1737), supposedly from bricks left over from the construction of the meetinghouse. This building has functioned continuously as a tavern and restaurant for over 250 years.

At the corner of S. Broad and W. Centre sts. is the Presbyterian Church (1833). The congregation was founded in

1721, and this building replaces an earlier one, supposedly abandoned because it had been used by British troops in 1777 and was thought to be haunted. This odd-shaped building does not look its age. In 1906 the church was connected to its stone chapel (1895) and the entire structure was faced in stone. Then in 1965 the stone was removed, new bricks were used, and the front was extended. At that time a cupola was built to house the church's 12th-century bell, cast in Bordeaux and brought to Woodbury in the late 18th century from Santo Domingo, when the French Revolution caused upheaval on the islands.

Next door to the city hall is the Friendship Fire Company No. 1, founded in 1799, though its present building is 100 years older (1891). The Goodwill Fire Company (N. Broad), with its round window and cupola, was built in 1889. Other buildings of interest include the post office (1928), the First Baptist Church (1857), and the Kemble Methodist Church (1888), all on Broad St. Also on Broad St. between Centre and Hopkins sts. are the remains of the splendid red brick G. G. Green's Block (1880). Green was perhaps Woodbury's most successful entrepreneur, making a fortune from patent medicines and associated businesses. His former factory (Green St.) is now used by other companies. On the north side of Delaware is Christ Church Episcopal Church (1856), with two hitching posts still in place.

About one mile north of town (take NJ 45 north to Colonial Ave. and turn left, or west) is Ladd's Castle (1337 Lafayette Ave.), also known as Candor Hall. Built in 1688 by John Ladd, who is said to have surveyed Philadelphia for William Penn and to have been thrown out of the Society of Friends for marrying non-Quaker couples, it is now a private home.

Woodstown SALEM (US 40, NJ 45)

3,250

A Quaker settlement dating back to the early 1700s, Woodstown retains many of its old buildings, and a string of 18th-century structures can be found along Main and Marlton sts. Among them is the Joseph Shinn house* (68 N. Main St.); its central section was built in 1742, and its southern section may have been a 17th-century Indian trad-

ing post moved from another location. The Woodstown
Friends meetinghouse is also on N. Main, as is the Samuel
Dickeson house (42 N. Main), the home of the Pilesgrove-
Woodstown Historical Society. The society's museum,
which concentrates on genealogy and items of local history,
is open Wednesday, 1–4.

Roughly two miles west of Woodstown, just west of
Sharptown (a stop on the Underground Railroad) is the
Cowtown Rodeo (US 40; 609-769-3207, 609-769-3200),
which has been in existence since the mid-1950s. An outgrowth of the local livestock auctions, the rodeo is run by a
family that has lived within a few miles of Sharptown for 11
generations. It is sanctioned by the Professional Cowboys
Association and draws riders from all over the country.
Open Memorial Day–Labor Day, Saturday, 7:30 P.M.
Admission charged. The auctions, which take place on
Tuesdays at noon, and which are accompanied by a giant
flea market, are also open to the public, as is the year-round
farmers' market, Saturday, 8–4.

Wyckoff **BERGEN** **(NJ 208, C 502)** 15,500

Bergen County's James A. McFaul Wildlife
Center (Crescent Ave. south of C 502; 201-
891-5571) is in Wyckoff. This 81-acre wildlife
sanctuary has outdoor displays of native mam-
mals and birds in shelters, a woodland trail (a
trail guide is available), massed plantings (early spring bulbs
and wildflowers in March and April, azaleas, rhododen-
drons, and other flowering shrubs April to June), and an
herb garden. Inside the exhibit hall are live native animals,
natural history displays (including a demonstration beehive
with a glass viewing panel), an observatory overlooking the
pond, and a changing art exhibit. The center sponsors nature education programs for schools and other groups. The
building is open weekdays, 9–4:45, weekends, 9–5:15, and
holidays (except Christmas and New Year's Day), 1–5:15.
The park is open until sunset. Groups by appointment.

Wyckoff was originally a Dutch settlement, and some of
the early Dutch stone houses remain (try Wyckoff and
Franklin aves.). One of these, the Van Voorhees-Quacken-
bush-Zabriskie House (421 Franklin Ave.; 201-891-0057),

is now a living museum. Started in 1730 (the larger section dates from 1824), the house was occupied almost entirely by direct descendants of the original builder until 1973 when it was given to the township. Its furnishings, which reflect the Dutch colonial heritage, are period pieces collected by the last inhabitant. Open Friday, 9–3, and for a variety of special occasions throughout the year. Note also the Wyckoff Reformed Church (E. Wyckoff Ave.), which dates from 1806.

THE NEW JERSEY TURNPIKE TOUR

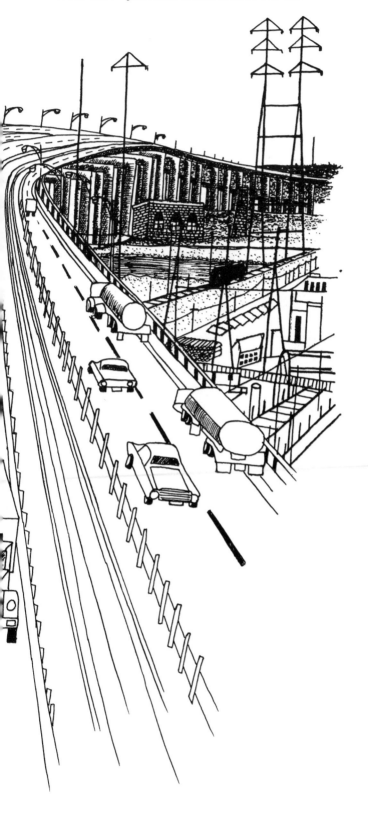

Opened in November 1951, the New Jersey Turnpike is the most heavily traveled toll road in the United States, and one of the safest. On the average day over half a million vehicles pass along some of its 141½ miles. Traditionally, the heaviest single day is the Wednesday before Thanksgiving, but traffic records began falling in the mid-1980s. In the fall of 1986 the record for a single day stood at 641,000.

The turnpike's 1,200-foot acceleration and deceleration lanes, median double guardrail (currently being replaced with material that can withstand the heavier trucks now allowed on the roadways), and full shoulder lanes on all bridges help contribute to its safety record. (Such features also contribute to its cost—the eight-mile Newark Bay-Hudson County extension, opened in 1956, remains the most expensive stretch of toll road in the United States.) Other safety features include computerized traffic control: electronic detectors that monitor traffic have been placed under the most heavily used section and fog sensors in the area most prone to foggy conditions; these relay information to the administration building in New Brunswick. Some of the decisions such information might provoke can be handled electronically: the message signs and the speed limit signs, for example, can be controlled from New Brunswick.

All 141½ miles are limited-access highway, ranging in width from 4 to 12 lanes (the turnpike authority refers to the 12-lane portions as the dual-dual). They consist of a 117½-mile mainline; the Hudson County extension and a Pennsylvania Turnpike extension, which together total 14 miles; and a westerly alignment that adds 10 miles. Tolls—each tolltaker handles an average of 1,800 transactions a day—provide the turnpike's principal source of revenue (it uses no municipal, state, or federal tax funds), and the cards themselves provide a good deal of information and even a small amount of income (the used cards are sold to a recycler).

Contrary to received opinion, the turnpike is not just an efficient means of connecting Philadelphia and New York City: in fact, almost 90 percent of the vehicles on the turnpike at least begin or end their trip within the state (over half do both). Even so, for many people the turnpike has created a negative impression of the state as a whole. Presumably, this is because those entering from the north at the Lincoln Tunnel immediately pass into an industrial area, which most people find unattractive and which at times does smell (usually of mercaptan, a harmless byproduct of various chemical processes). For many years, though, pig farms were numerous at the northern end, and they smelled all the time. And many people remember when the landfills, still visible, smoldered, producing, with the pig farms, a pungent combination. There are no more pig farms and the landfills no longer smolder (they are, in fact, being converted to parks and artworks), but the unfortunate reputation lingers on. The southern end has its industrial stretches too, but land is cheaper at that end, and more of it has been used for plantings that screen the factories. And it is only at the northern end that the turnpike actually travels *through* an oil refinery.

The turnpike authority is currently engaged in widening the roadway and hopes that the plan, which has not been without controversy, will make the road able to handle traffic easily to the year 2050. Some sections may become dual-duals, others may end up with 14 lanes, and some of the toll plazas are to be expanded. The authority is also engaged in a beautification program, with a goal of planting 3 million trees. Progress toward the goal has not been dramatic: finding a reasonable location to plant trees is not all that easy, roadside conditions are not ideal for a young tree, maintenance men mowing the grass sometimes decapitate the young trees, and in some areas planting has been postponed because of the construction plans. The state is trying to encourage the turnpike's neighbors to plant trees along the borders of their property (unfortunately often their back yards), and even to do a little landscaping. To prevent the theft of evergreen trees during the holiday season, the turnpike authority coats likely victims with a compound that releases a disagreeable odor when it hits room temperature, an odor that lasts well beyond the Christmas season.

This tour is meant for those who are going to be using the turnpike anyway and assumes that if you know what you are looking at as you speed by, you will find it more interesting. The tour may not convince the doubters that the turnpike is attractive, but it may make the time pass more quickly. To help you identify sites, the turnpike authority's mileage markers are used (they are the numbers on the small green stakes along the edges of the roadway). They start in the south and increase as you go north, so if you are traveling south, you will have to begin at the end of the tour. Each entry begins with a mileage number. The letter following that number tells you which side of the road is being talked about: N means the right side when you are traveling north (toward New York City), S the right side when you are traveling south (toward Philadelphia). Mainline mileage is given without a prefix; the western alignment is prefixed by a W, the Hudson extension by an H. Thus, W 115 S tells you to look to the right when you are traveling south on the western alignment (away from the George Washington Bridge), to the left when you are traveling north on that stretch.

Unfortunately, the mileage indicators cannot tell you exactly when to look. The particular mileage marker at which you see something depends on how fast you are traveling, which part of the dual-dual you are in (the all-car or the car, truck, and bus section), how much traffic there is, which lane you are using, and what kind of vehicle you are traveling in. If traffic is heavy, you may be able to see very little to your left, particularly if you are in the right half of the dual-dual. This tour, unlike other entries in this guide, recognizes that you cannot stop the car and turn around to get a second look, or park it and get out for a closer one. Most of the items described in the tour, however, are large enough that you will not miss them if you don't look at precisely the right moment unless you are traveling way over the speed limit.

The entries come thicker and faster for the northern, more industrial parts of the tour; the southern stretch is more like other high-speed roads—in fact, people even complain to the turnpike authority that the southern stretch is boring. Although southern New Jersey is developing rapidly, large areas are still rural, and, as mentioned before, it is often harder to see what borders the highway in the south because of the screening (this is true for farms and stables, not just the industrial parts). Because many of the trees are deciduous, the southern stretch is particularly attractive in the fall (and you can see more in the winter). The tour starts near Deepwater in Salem County.

In the first 20 miles you will find many farms that raise Holsteins, vegetables, and grain, yet much of the state's chemical industry is along the Delaware River just north of the Delaware Memorial Bridge.

1 N,S—Interchange 1 to the Delaware Memorial Bridge. The highway here crosses Game Creek. The concrete guard rails often prevent you from seeing the many rivers crossed by the turnpike. You may notice Game Creek again at 3 S.

2–4 N,S—There are farms and stables on both sides of the highway here, though most of them are obscured by trees. At 3 N,S the road crosses Penny Run.

5 N,S—John Fenwick (N) and Clara Barton (S) service areas. All the turnpike's service areas are named for individuals with ties to the state, generally with ties that are geographically close to the service area. Barton and Fenwick are both associated with southern New Jersey (for Fenwick see Salem; for Barton Bordentown).

7 N,S—The road crosses Oldman's Creek, which divides Salem and Gloucester counties. There are farms visible for the next two miles.

11 N,S—The road crosses Narraticon Run. Lake Narraticon (S) and the old community of Swedesboro (S) are nearby; you can see a church steeple in Swedesboro.

12 N,S—Interchange 2. One of the turnpike's least busy interchanges, 2 is the one you should take to visit Swedesboro or to get to US 322, which goes west to the Commodore Barry Bridge over the Delaware and east to Glassboro. The road crosses Raccoon Creek, which flows along the northern edge of Swedesboro, itself first known as Raccoon.

13–18 N,S—You can see one of the turnpike's maintenance yards (N), and the road crosses Still Run, Edwards Run, and Mantua creeks. Mantua Creek is particularly lovely.

19–21 N,S—The turnpike passes through Woodbury Heights, crossing Woodbury Creek.

23–25 N,S—The turnpike crosses first a tributary of and then Big Timber Creek itself, the boundary between Gloucester and Camden counties. Walt Whitman used to spend his summers near here (see Laurel Springs). In Camden County it also crosses Beaver Branch and goes through Runnemede and Bellmawr.

26 N,S—Interchange 3. This is where you get off for Woodbury, South Camden, and NJ 168. The road continues through Barrington and Lawnside.

27 N—The next few miles are an industrial area; at this point a large fiberglass plant is visible.

29 N,S—The highway crosses the Lindenwold high-speed line.

29 N—The Hussman Corporation's water tower is clearly visible. This company, which began manufacturing supermarket equipment at this spot in the late 1950s, represented the first major industry in the area.

29 S—In this mile are a Ryder truck-rental maintenance depot and the Melitta Filter company which makes coffeemakers and filters.

30 S—The Walt Whitman Service Area: Whitman lived his last years in Camden. The mushroom-shaped Cherry Hill water tower is 133 feet tall and holds 2 million gallons of water.

33 N,S—The road crosses Pennsauken Creek, which divides Camden and Burlington counties, and goes through an area of small industrial establishments and housing developments.

34 N,S—Interchange 4. This exit takes you to Camden and to NJ 73 (to the Tacony-Palmira Bridge, a drawbridge notorious for its effect on rush-hour traffic). On both sides of the turnpike there are hotels serving the Camden area.

35 N—The tanks of the Colonial Pipeline Company are visible.

35 S—The large industrial buildings here include an RCA facility (see 38 S and Camden).

38 S—What appears to be a landlocked ship belongs to RCA's Missile and Surface Radar division; since 1977 the "cruiser in the cornfield" has been the center for land-based testing and training for the U.S. Navy's Aegis combat weapons system. Seen from a little closer, the cruiser looks less like a warship and more like what it is: a 122-foot superstructure, bristling with radar antennas, perched on the roof of a three-story building. The RCA radio tower is also visible. Some 3,500 of the 4,500 employees at this RCA plant work on the Aegis system, designed to protect ships from missile threats. In the fall a "Beat Army" banner often hangs from the superstructure. I 295 can be seen running parallel to the turnpike.

39 N,S—The turnpike crosses Parkers Creek; those heading north will find the James Fenimore Cooper Service Area. Cooper was born in Burlington.

41 N,S—The turnpike crosses Rancocas Creek. A family of herons lives right next to the turnpike (N). A boardwalk goes into this nature area, but if you want to walk here, approach it from off the turnpike. For Rancocas State Park, see Mount Holly.

43 N,S—The road crosses Mill Creek. This is an area of large dairy farms—one you pass has over 300 Holsteins.

44 N,S—Interchange 5: use this exit for Burlington and Mount Holly.

47–49 N, S—Farms, stables, fields, and woods continue. The road crosses Assiscunk Creek.

51 N,S—Interchange 6 takes you to the Pennsylvania Turnpike spur. Trees screen the highway for most of the spur's six miles; in some cases the woods are reclaimed pastures.

53 N,S—Interchange 7, for Bordentown, Trenton, and US 206. The highway is close to the Old York Rd., which crosses it. The road goes over Blacks Creek.

56 N,S—The highway crosses Crosswicks Creek, which divides Burlington from Mercer County and flows into the Delaware at Bordentown.

56 S—The road skirts the New Jersey Youth Correctional Institution.

58 N,S—Here are the Woodrow Wilson (N) and Richard Stockton (S) service areas. Both these men are associated with Princeton. Farms are still visible on both sides of the highway.

60 N,S—Interchange 7A: here you can get to I 195, taking you north to Trenton and Hamilton Township and south to the shore.

61–63 N,S—There are farms on both sides of the road, and the highway crosses Assunpink Creek and goes through a portion of the Assunpink Wildlife Management Area (see Roosevelt).

66 N,S—Cedar Brook is crossed.

66 S—A sign lets you know that the Peddie School golf course lies beyond the woods (see Hightstown).

67 N,S—Interchange 8, taking you to Hightstown, Freehold, and NJ 33. Between here and Interchange 8A are many chemical companies. The highway crosses Rocky Brook.

67 S—At the turnpike authority's large maintenance depot here, you can sometimes see the green roadway signs being worked on. The road passes Local 827 of the AFL-CIO International Brotherhood of Electrical Workers' building.

68 N,S—The highway crosses the Millstone River, which divides Mercer from Middlesex County.

69 N,S—The highway crosses a tributary of the Millstone River and Conrail tracks. IBM has offices to the west. Over the next ten miles much of the land adjoining the turnpike is owned by housing developments.

70 N,S—Cranbury Brook is on both sides of the highway.

70 S—The Jamesway Distribution Center abuts the highway here.

71 N—Carter Wallace, a large manufacturer of pharmaceuticals, diagnostic kits, and over-the-counter products, has a facility here.

71 S—The Molly Pitcher Service Area. Molly Pitcher is associated with the Battle of Monmouth (see Freehold).

72 N—A General Foods technical center. Among other projects it looks into packaged convenience foods.

73 N,S—Interchange 8A takes you to Jamesburg and Cranbury.

73 N—The turnpike's neighbors here are Forsgate Country Club and Rossmoor (see Jamesburg).

73 S—This is a growing industrial area. Among the firms in this mile are Aeroquip, Kar Products, and Couristan Carpets.

74 N,S—The highway crosses the former Jamesburg branch of the Pennsylvania Railroad.

74 S—A large BASF facility manufactures a Styrofoam product; Frasse-Basset and Arnok also have plants.

76 S—The vividly blue pond belongs to Local 825 of the International Union of Operating Engineers (AFL-CIO), which operates a training school here. Each year over 1,000 carefully screened applicants (including many who have already spent years in the construction industry) come to this school to learn to operate over a dozen kinds of equipment: bulldozers, front-end loaders, pans, graders, combination backhoes, cranes. The center works with the Occupational Safety and Health Administration (OSHA) and the state's Department of Environmental Protection, offering, for example, a course in hazardous waste removal. The center serves all of New Jersey and part of New York State.

77 N,S—The turnpike crosses Ireland Brook. Middlesex County is developing a park along the brook.

78 N—The Joyce Kilmer Service Area. Kilmer was born in New Brunswick.

78 S—Much of the land in this mile belongs to the Tamarack County Golf Club.

80 N,S—Crossing the road here is a turnpike service road. The Continental Can Corporation (part of the Continental Group) has a facility to the east.

81 N,S—The turnpike crosses the Saw Mill Brook and the (freight only) Raritan River Railroad.

83 N, S—Interchange 9 for New Brunswick, NJ 18, and the shore. The highway crosses Lawrence Brook.

83 S—The tall green office building (Tower Center) is the tallest in central New Jersey. Eventually the complex will contain two 16-story towers with a 360-room hotel and parking for 4,200 cars. The turnpike's administration building can be seen above the road.

84 N,S—In this mile the highway crosses the Raritan River and the old Lehigh Valley railroad tracks.

84 N—The origins of the ferryboat in the Raritan River are obscure, but its owners (one of whom was once mayor of New Brunswick) apparently hope to convert it to a restaurant or nightclub. Public Service Electricity and Gas Company has a generating station here. Groups can make an appointment to visit Public Service facilities by calling 201-430-5862 between 8:30 and 4.

84 S—Raritan Center is one of the largest industrial parks in the East. Over 10,000 people work on its 2,350 acres, once part of the Raritan Arsenal, an army supply depot. Middlesex Community College and Thomas A. Edison Park (see Edison) are also on the site. At this point the river is deep enough to accommodate medium-size ocean-going ships.

85 N—An Emerson air-conditioning facility occupies the large building. This is an area of warehouses (among them W. H. Smith and Mazda), industrial parks, and garden apartments. The United States Army Reserve's 78th Division armory is visible.

86–87 N,S—The road crosses Bridge-Mill Brook and the old Bonhamptown branch of the Pennsylvania Railroad and passes through an area of warehouses and garden apartments. American Can has a plant to the west.

87 N—An empty air-conditioning facility, this one the former Fedders Corporation headquarters with almost 1 million square feet of office and warehouse space.

88 N,S—Interchange 10, taking you to I 287, Metuchen, and Perth Amboy. The highway goes under I 287 and crosses Conrail's Perth Amboy branch.

89 N—A fire tower is visible here atop the hill.

89 S—There are Tudor condominiums and a municipal playground on this side.

90 N,S—The road going over the turnpike is the Garden State Parkway, and Interchange 11 will take you to that parkway, as well as to Woodbridge and the Amboys. With 24 toll booths, this is the largest single interchange on the turnpike. Between this exit and Interchange 12 you will notice many more oil-storage terminals.

90 S—The New Jersey National Guard and a racquet club are visible here.

91 N—The clay pits here once provided the material used to produce millions of bricks; Middlesex County has reclaimed much of this land as part of William Warren Park (see Woodbridge). The turnpike authority stores salt at the maintenance facility. In 1985, not a particularly snowy winter, it used 19,000 tons of salt. The igloos you see from time to time along the turnpike are used for storing salt. The building with the cupola is St. Joseph's Convent, in Woodbridge, the American headquarters for an order of nuns founded in Poland (most of the sisters are Polish). The house was built in 1856 by a brick magnate as a wedding present for his daughter; it was later used as an orphanage. The house has beautiful woodwork and other fine details, and there are hopes that eventually it can be opened for tours.

91 S—The Hess Oil office building, over ten stories high, was the first high-rise building in Woodbridge. Its luxurious interior has solid teak walls and Italian and Vermont marble floors.

92 N—The Grover Cleveland Service Area is named for the only president of the United States to serve two nonconsecutive terms (see Caldwell). The road crosses the Woodbridge River.

92 S—The Thomas Edison Service Area (see Edison and West Orange).

93 N—You can see the Hess storage tanks and refinery. The red-and-white stacks in the distance belong to the Chevron refinery on the Arthur Kill. There's a good view of the New York City skyline.

94 S—The Colonial Pipeline Company stores heating oil and liquid petroleum products here.

95 N,S—Interchange 12 to Carteret and Rahway is one of the least busy interchanges on the turnpike.

95 N—There are garden apartments here and small companies, including International Wholesalers, which reproduces antiques.

95 S—Several businesses here, among them White Castle, Maybelline, Di-Gel, Wilson Jones, Plough, Inc., and the Bagcraft Corp.; Public Service also owns land in this area.

96 N,S—The highway crosses the Rahway River, which divides Middlesex from Union County.

96 N—Conrail tracks are to the side of the road.

96 S—There are over 50 tanks in the Citgo tank farm; they contain jet fuel, gas, and heating oil. During the gasoline shortages in the 1970s, most of the oil companies along the turnpike painted out their identification signs. Joseph Medwick Memorial Park, a recently renovated Middlesex County Park honoring a member of the Baseball Hall of Fame who grew up in Carteret, is along the river.

97 N—The Allied Chemical plant here dates from World War I. The company's first plant, it was one of the state's first chemical factories. Now part of GAF, it makes a wide range of products, at one time including fluorocarbons.

98 N—Public Service Electric and Gas Company's Linden generating station, with its three steam turbines and six gas turbines has half the capacity of the generators at Boulder Dam. In 1974 a natural-gas plant was added to the site; it is turned on during periods of peak demand in the winter. The plant has an arrangement with the Bayway plant (see 98–99 N,S) to send over its surplus steam in exchange for fuel and water to run the generators.

98–99 N,S—Here the turnpike cuts right through the 1,500-acre Exxon Bayway refinery, the world's largest catalytic cracking plant and the country's third largest refinery (after Baytown, Texas, and Baton Rouge, Louisiana). Bayway, constructed on swampland between 1907 and 1909, is considered the birthplace of the country's petrochemical industry. When it opened, the plant's employees outnumbered the residents of Linden, and the principal product was kerosene. The automobile changed all that. Today high-octane gasoline, heating oil, and jet fuel are manufactured at Bayway and distributed throughout the Northeast. The plant, which employs some 1,200 people (Linden's population has in the meantime grown to 38,000), is the world's largest producer of synthetic lubricants for turbine engines. Crude oil is unloaded on the east side of the turnpike from lighters that have come up the Arthur Kill and transferred to the refinery on the west side of the turnpike. The tanks you see hold various byproducts of the refining process, including adhesives, antifreeze, cosmetics, and resins. What people think of as the characteristic odor of the turnpike comes mainly from this area and is caused by mercaptan, also a (harmless) byproduct of the refineries (and of the 100 or so chemical plants in the area). The gases are cleaned before they are discharged, and on cool days the discharges look like fluffy white plumes. The flames you see at the top of the 200-foot-high stacks are nonpolluting gases being burned off. This whole scene can be spectacular at night. Exxon, incidentally, is taking part in the turnpike's beautification program, but don't expect it to mask the refinery. The interchange is 13, taking you to I 278, Elizabeth, and the Elizabeth seaport.

99 N—The Goethals Bridge over the Arthur Kill to Staten Island provides a direct connection between the turnpike and the Staten Island Expressway. Opened in 1928, this cantilevered structure has a center span of over 650 feet. Its four lanes carry some 10 million eastbound cars a year. The road crosses the Elizabeth River. You can sometimes see ships on the Arthur Kill.

100 N,S—The highway passes through the eastern part of Elizabeth, the state's fourth largest city (see Elizabeth).

100 N—More good views of the New York City skyline come in this mile. The Conrail tracks once belonged to the Central Railroad Co., and you can still see the Elizabeth Gas Company's production plant. Several interesting buildings are visible. The black triangular steeple belongs to Greystone Presbyterian Church, built in 1893 from stones blasted from the bottom of New York's East River. The gold Byzantine dome belongs to St. Peter and St. Paul's Greek Catholic Church, built in 1919. The church with the green copper roof and the clock tower is St. Adalbert's Roman Catholic Church, built in 1905. Its congregation, once largely Polish, is now becoming Hispanic. The twin Gothic spires belong to St. Patrick's. Built in 1887, apparently by Irish Catholics weary of walking to Newark, St. Patrick's is modeled on various French cathedrals and is so big it's hard to heat.

100 S—For part of this mile the houses are extremely close to the turnpike. From the street it is clear that the highway has sliced right through a neighborhood, and the elevated roadway casts a shadow over the remaining houses.

101 N,S—Interchange 13A is a relatively new connection to Newark Airport, Elizabeth, and Elizabeth seaport.

101 N—The William F. Halsey Service Area. Admiral Halsey, commander of U.S. naval forces in the Pacific during World War II, was born in Elizabeth. Note the igloos in the turnpike maintenance yard.

102–103 S—This is Newark Airport, the metropolitan area's only airport until just before World War II, when LaGuardia Airport opened. Legend has it that Fiorello LaGuardia, at the time mayor of New York City, refused to get off a plane when it arrived at Newark Airport, saying he had bought a ticket to New York and this was not New York, and thus was born LaGuardia Airport. As it happens, the future LaGuardia Airport was by then already under construction and reporters had been tipped off in advance. This very busy airport belongs to the city of Newark and is run by the Port Authority of New York and New Jersey. (For more information on Newark Airport, see Newark.) The dividing line between Union and Essex counties runs through the airport and into the Elizabeth Channel.

103 N,S—Here you can see four modes of transportation cheek by jowl. Starting from the east you have Ports Elizabeth and Newark, Conrail yards, the turnpike, and Newark Airport. The two ports make up one of the world's largest facilities for container shipping, Port Elizabeth having been built in 1958 specifically as a container port. (Port Newark dates to 1915.) Liquor, bananas, and cars are the three major imports, by weight—in 1984, for example, over 360,000 new cars passed through the two ports, and this is also where most imported beef enters the country. Iron-and-steel scrap makes up a large part of the exports, but the imbalance in exports and imports is reflected in the piles of empty containers to be seen along the turnpike.

103 N—Shipping lines, among them the United Arab Shipping Line, the Barber Line, and the Polish Orian Line, and associated industries (a Sea-Land lot, for example, and warehouses) dominate this mile; the most obvious landmarks are the Sea-Land warehouse and the giant Maersk cranes.

104 N,S—Interchange 14, taking you to I 78, US 1 and 9, Newark Airport, and the Hudson County extension. (For the Hudson County extension, see H 1–8 at the end of the tour.) This interchange was newly landscaped in 1985.

104 N—A deepwater inlet and the Port Authority's Port Newark administration building are here.

104 S—You can see guidance lights for aircraft right along the highway.

At this point the highway begins to split, the eastern branch going to the Lincoln Tunnel and the western to the George Washington Bridge.

105 N,S—This is an area of container storage, auto wreckers, small plants, trucking companies, and warehouses.

105 N—The Passaic Valley Sewer Commission has a pumping station here.

105 S—An Englehard facility occupies much of this mile.

106 N,S—Interchange 15E to Newark, Jersey City, and US 1 and 9. The plantings you see at this interchange (50 oak trees) are part of the governor's beautification program. This mile contains more warehouses, chemical companies, container storage, car dumps, and a good view of the Newark skyline.

106 N—The Newark police have a car pound and pistol range here.

106 S—In this mile there's an example of an endangered species—a drive-in theater; unfortunately, it endangers the species that pass by.

107 N,S—The Pulaski Skyway crosses the turnpike. Built in the 1920s, it was named for the Polish general who fought with the Continental army. Soaring 145 feet over the Passaic and Hackensack rivers, when it was built it cut the travel time between New Jersey's two biggest cities, Newark and Jersey City, from 25 to 5 minutes. It now carries US 1 and 9 over the Passaic River. The turnpike crosses the Passaic River.

108 N,S—The road crosses the Hackensack River.

108 N—On the site of a closed landfill, a work of art entitled *Sky Mound* is being created. The latest environmental principles are being followed in closing the dump, and the completed *Sky Mound* is expected to create spectacular visual effects, from the mound itself, from the turnpike, from a railroad car, from an airplane. For example, at sunrise and sunset, light will reflect to the center of the mound and radiate down the side of the hill in eight distinct rays.

108 S—At this point you can cross over to Exit 15W.

109 N—This is the Public Service Electric and Gas Company's Essex generating station (for tours see 84 N). AM radio towers are visible here (see W 111–114 N, S).

109 S—An Essex County garbage dump is in this mile, and a fallen AM tower can still be seen in the marsh.

110 S—The dark rock, usually decorated with graffiti, is Laurel Hill (formerly Snake Hill), a volcanic mass that has been leased from the County of Hudson to mine its rock. (Contrary to rumor, the entire hill will not be mined away; the turnpike is structurally dependent on it.) A lookout point for Continental soldiers during the Revolution, it has also been the site of a poorhouse, insane asylum, sanitarium, and communicable disease hospital. In the late 19th century, it served as the inspiration for the Prudential Insurance Company's Rock of Gibraltar advertising slogan: an advertising executive on his way home from a meeting with the Prudential company struck on the idea as his train passed the hill. Cedar trees once grew in the Hackensack Meadowlands, but salt water entered the area, killing them off.

111 S—The Alexander Hamilton Service Area. Hamilton met his future wife in New Jersey (see Morristown), he was responsible for founding the city of Paterson (see Paterson), and he met his death in New Jersey (see Weehawken).

112 N,S—Here are Interchanges 16E to the Lincoln Tunnel, Secaucus, and NJ 3, and 18E to the George Washington Bridge, I 80, I 95, and US 46.

112 S—Interchange 17 is a limited-access interchange. If you are coming from the north you can exit here and head for the Lincoln Tunnel. You can also enter at 17, but only if you want to head north. In this mile are a state motor vehicle inspection station, a Public Service transformer, Meadowview Hospital, a UPS facility, and an industrial park.

113 N—A large Meadowlands Development project is here.

114–115 N—Among the many warehouses here are ones belonging to Caldor, K-Mart, Fashion Industries, and Variety Knit.

115 N—The silo belongs to a trucking company. There are many companies here, among them Tetley Inc. and Holiday Fair.

115 S—Note the Phragmites, a tall aggressive reed grass that is relatively tolerant of pollution. Phragmites have taken over large portions of New Jersey's wetlands, but, unfortunately, they are not as nourishing for birds and animals as some of the vegetation they have driven out. Four AM radio towers, arranged in a rectangle, can be seen, as can the bridge from the turnpike's western alignment, which looks particularly graceful.

116 N,S—The Vince Lombardi Service Area. Early in his career Lombardi coached at an Englewood high school. Mrs. Lombardi donated the trophies on display inside. Wildlife preserves border this service area (created by the turnpike to compensate for areas destroyed in construction).

117 N,S—The western alignment joins the main branch and the turnpike ends shortly thereafter.

117 S—This is Public Service's Bergen generating plant; for tours see 84 N.

The western alignment was built in 1966. It took almost a year to dredge and fill the Hackensack Meadowlands so that the road could be built. The turnpike authority has pioneered in engineering methods for building on swamps. Fog sensors have been placed along the western alignment, where foggy conditions often make travel hazardous.

W 107 N,S—The turnpike goes under the Pulaski Skyway (see 107 N,S) and crosses the Passaic River.

W 107 N—Note the vertical draw railroad bridge. In the next few miles there are several drawbridges.

W 107 S—Here you can cross over to Exit 15E.

W 108 N,S—Interchange 15W to Newark, the Oranges, and I 280 was landscaped in 1985.

W 108 S—A sanitary landfill is visible here, as is the environmental and visitor center of the Richard W. DeKorte State Park (see Lyndhurst), named after a state assemblyman. Eventually the landfill will become part of the park, and gas from bacteriological decomposition will heat indoor facilities. At the park you will be able to ski, hike, camp, boat, and play tennis, softball, and football. In the meantime, the center, which concentrates on environmental concerns, is open and well worth a visit.

W 109 N,S—The highway crosses the main Amtrak line.

W 109 S—In this mile there's a good view of the Newark skyline and a landfill mesa.

W 111–114 N,S—In this stretch you will see a good many radio transmitters. Salt marsh provides an efficient medium for AM radio waves, which is why so many of New York City's AM stations have their towers here. Visible are those of WMCA (3 towers in a line), WABC (single tower), WOR (3 towers in a triangle), WNEW (4 towers in a box, one higher), and WINS (4 short towers in a line).

W 111 N—Harmon Cove, Harmon Plaza, the Meadowlands Hilton, and the Tiger Racquet Club are along this stretch. This is a Hartz Mountain development (the company used to be known for its pet products; it is now also a major real estate developer). Included in this 800-acre development, which began in the late 1960s, are townhouses, condominiums, research facilities, offices, warehouses, retail stores, a hospital, hotels, movie theaters, marinas, and industrial space.

W 112 N,S—Interchange 16W takes you to Secaucus, Rutherford, the New Jersey Sports Complex, and NJ 3.

W 112 S—This is the New Jersey Sports Complex. The Brendan Byrne Arena is the building closest to the highway, but the complex also includes a race track and a stadium (see East Rutherford).

W 113 N,S—Interchange 18W to the George Washington Bridge, I 80, I 95, and US 46. The highway also crosses Cedar Creek.

W 114 N,S—The road crosses Moonachie Creek. Note the poplars.

W 115 N,S—Another entrance to the Vince Lombardi Service Area (see 116 N,S). The road crosses the Hackensack River.

W 117 S—Public Service's Bergen station is here (for tours see 84 N). The turnpike's western alignment joins the mainline, and the turnpike ends in Ridgefield Park.

Even when the Hudson County extension is not actually going north or south, the suffix N means what is to the right as you are driving toward New York City, the suffix S what is to the right as you are driving toward Philadelphia.

H 1–2 N,S—The turnpike crosses Newark Bay.

H 1 N—There are usually an impressive number of new cars unloaded on the dock here, awaiting shipment elsewhere. Oil tanks are also visible.

H 1 S—At the Newark Industrial Center you can see the Toys-R-Us warehouse.

H 2 N—A city park is along the water.

H 3 N,S—Interchange 14A to Bayonne.

H 3 N—The tracks belong to Conrail's Greenville yards. From here on there are often good views of the New York City skyline.

H 3 S—According to one story, in one of Jersey City's dirtier election campaigns, someone jammed the elevators in this public housing project to keep its residents from voting.

H 4 N—At Caven Point there is a United States Army Reserve Center. Pittston Petroleum storage tanks are visible.

H 4 S—Auto wreckers are prevalent in this section.

H 5 N,S—Interchange 14B, one of the turnpike's least busy exits, takes you to Jersey City, Interchange 14C about ½-mile north of 14B, to the Holland Tunnel.

H 5 N—Liberty State Park (see Jersey City) and the Statue of Liberty are visible now. The Morris Canal basin is at the northern end of the park.

H 6–8 N,S—As the road goes through Jersey City, you may see the Colgate Palmolive factory (N) and various municipal parks and other facilities. The building with the stepped side next to the three tall buildings at 7 S is the Pollak Hospital for Chest Diseases. The very large yellow-and-white building with classical elements on the hill at 7 S is Dickinson High School.

INDEX

The index is divided into the following categories:

Art exhibition spaces

Cultural and perform-
ing arts centers

Historic house
museums

To the users of this book:

No matter how careful one tries to be, errors are bound to creep into a guidebook of this kind. If you do come across mistakes, I hope you will send them to me at 40 Pine Street, Princeton 08542. I would also welcome suggestions for additions and other improvements for possible future editions. Thank you.

Barbara Westergaard